AUG 30 1982

AF859280

102

Legal Research and

Law Library Management

LEGAL RESEARCH
AND
LAW LIBRARY MANAGEMENT

Julius J. Marke
New York University School of Law

Richard Sloane
University of Pennsylvania School of Law

101572

LAW JOURNAL SEMINARS-PRESS
233 Broadway
New York, New York 10279

KLEBERG, DYER, REDFORD & WEIL
LIBRARY

Copyright © 1982 Law Journal Seminars-Press
New York, New York

Library of Congress Cataloging in Publication Data

Marke, Julius J.
Legal research and law library management.

Bibliography: p.
Includes index.
1. Legal research—United States. 2. Law libraries—United States. I. Sloane, Richard, 1916- . II. Title.
KF240.M24 340'.072073 81-19297
AACR2

Foreword

This book collects fifty of the author's articles on wide-ranging phases of legal research and law library management. Its table of contents shows their scope. But the real value of this book is in the insights that it gives and the solutions that it proposes to the mutual problems of lawyers and librarians.

It impels one to step back from the daily pressures of practice and reflect on what it means to be a lawyer and what is the real dignity of our profession. It is then that one recalls so many of the highlights that a lawyer owes to the knowledge and help of librarians. They place the entire sweep of history before lawyers: the Magna Carta, the development of parliaments and courts, the writings of Pollock and Denning in England and Holmes and Cardozo and Gilmore in America. In various other ways librarians help us to become familiar with the best in legal literature. In doing so, they help us to draw inspiration from the great lawyers who have gone before us. On looking back over decades of practice, many of the really memorable moments are ones shared, enjoyed with librarians and sparked by them.

I applaud the publishers for bringing these updated writings together. I read many of them in their original form when they were published as columns in the *New York Law Journal.*

As a user of law libraries for more than fifty years, I found them refreshing, imaginative and realistic. The two authors together have also worked for fifty years in the law libraries of private firms and law schools—but from the research, management and teaching side. They discuss private law library planning and design, book selection, methods of research and service to lawyers.

I have been fortunate to receive superior and imaginative service from the able John Marsh and his colleagues in the law library of my firm. I believe that both the legal and library professions will learn to their benefit from this book—as I have—what goes on behind the scenes in the quest for excellence in legal research and library management. And other readers will share my gratitude to our scholarly brethren who guide us so well.

I should like to add a specific example of the contribution of legal literature which I treasure because in the end it is largely through the literature of the law, made easily available by skilled librarians, that the quality of the profession is transmitted to every new generation of lawyers, which is how it is maintained as a noble profession. That was never better stated than in the speech of the great New York lawyer, Joseph H. Choate, President of the New York Bar, a beloved American Ambassador to England just before World War I, who said to the Chicago Bar Association in 1898:

> "Let us magnify our calling. Let us be true to those great occasions, and respond with all our might to those great demands, so that when our work is done, of us at least it may be said that we transmitted our profession to our successors, as great, as useful, and as spotless as it came to our hands."

These remarks were appropriately read at his Memorial Service in 1917 by his great friend, Elihu Root.

On the front of the St. Louis Public Library is the statement: "Only through books can civilization become cumulative." Much the same could be said of the law and it is such librarians as the authors who help to make it come true.

Whitney North Seymour

October 19, 1981

Introduction

This manual collects in a single volume basic practical guidance on legal research and law library management—both private and institutional. At the same time it points up the contributions that librarians make in raising the professional sights of lawyers. It must be stressed that librarians are almost always teachers and many are skilled lawyers as well.

The book draws on the combined experience of the writers as librarians, as lawyers and as library consultants to law firms, corporate legal departments, law schools, courts, bar associations and government agencies during the past quarter century. It is based on their *New York Law Journal* articles written between 1972 and 1981. Each chapter has been carefully updated to reflect the latest research methods and technological advances.

It is organized in three main divisions:

I. An introductory overview in which it discusses basic legal research methods and describes the tools needed to facilitate the work of lawyers.

II. Phases of legal research that range from an explanation of the English sources of American law, an analysis of federal and state legislative history and of administrative law research problems to a discussion of research on particular subjects, for example, environmental law, transnational matters and inter-disciplinary studies and a review of non-legal research resources.

III. Library management, including book selection, publishing practices and law office library planning, design and management. It discusses the role of librarians. It makes clear the pitfalls and problems of law library construction, the skills needed and particularly the care required in preparation for moving a library and the contributions of a consultant in these various phases of library design and management. Finally, it offers a realistic program for coordinating, indexing and retrieving lawyer work products—the memoranda of law, opinion letters, forms and precedents that represent the distillation of a lawyer's best written efforts. They are frequently lost to use. This book shows how to preserve them.

Table of Contents

PART ONE

Legal Research Overview

CHAPTER 1

THE RESEARCH LAWYER

The purpose of this and succeeding chapters is to sharpen the research skills of lawyers and librarians. It attempts to do so in three ways:

(1) It evaluates the available research tools.
(2) It shows where those publications can be found.
(3) It explains their use.

To the practicing lawyer, legal research starts and ends with the problems that clients bring them. It exists to solve and, if possible, to anticipate those problems.

Fact-Finding Work

The first discovery that every young lawyer makes is that the solution of legal problems requires a knowledge of facts which are not found in law books alone. Law school may show him how to analyze facts. It will not tell him how to find them. Nor will it predict that the mixture of legal facts and non-legal facts he must acquire in his work is astonishingly lop-sided—in favor of non-legal facts.

The second discovery he makes is that fact-finding is an elusive and time-consuming process.

It is no wonder that the gulf constantly widens between each lawyer and the books he uses. The day-to-day demands on a lawyer's skills are many. He must be a persuasive negotiator and advocate, a skilled draftsman and a sophisticated businessman. He must also be able to extract answers from a growing maze of legal and non-legal literature. Few lawyers can do all these things well.

Moreover, the best litigating or negotiating lawyers are not necessarily the best researchers. When such lawyers work under pressure to complete a task in a limited number of days or hours, they are at a psychological disadvantage—sometimes approaching panic—that the trained researcher does not suffer.

The solution is the research lawyer—a new specialist. He would take part in the discussion of every novel problem that enters his office. He would not be responsible for solving it. But he would collect the basic literature and bring to his colleagues the skill in its use that the solution of the problem requires.

Moreover, he would make it his business to know which problems had been researched in the office before, who had done the work and what were the solutions.

Almost any issue of *The New York Times* will illustrate the fact-finding work that lawyers perform. Here are three examples from the *Times* for Sunday, Feb. 13, 1972.

(1) A page-one story traces some of the steps taken by lawyers for Time, Inc., McGraw-Hill and Hughes Tool Company to determine whether or not Clifford Irving's manuscript is a hoax.

(2) A report of the findings of the National Commission on Marijuana and Drug Abuse appears on the same page. Its recommendation to eliminate all criminal penalties for the private use and possession of marijuana is based on numerous statistical studies—made by lawyers and others—and will be used by lawyers in discussing sentences and by legislators in revising drug laws.

(3) A front-page story in the business section on the same day is captioned, "How Big is Too Big?" It discusses a Justice Department and several private antitrust suits against IBM. Implicit in the story is the massive amount of economic research on the computer industry that lawyers for all the parties are presently conducting.

Not all legal business is so newsworthy that it captures headlines in the *Times.* But the point is clear: Lawyers cannot survive without facts.

What then should the research specialist in a law office know and what should he do? To begin with, he should be so familiar with clients' activities that he has a firm grasp of their present and potential problems. Client matters fall basically into two distinct classes, the familiar and the unfamiliar or:

(1) Those that the office takes care of regularly and can plan for in advance, such as lease renewals, loan agreements, union negotiations, and the like; and

(2) Those that are unique and arise from new kinds of personal or business ventures that require sophisticated legal advice or are the result of stumbling blocks in old matters and may lead to litigation.

The research specialist must be equipped to handle both types of problems, quickly and effectively. To accomplish this the office must meet two minimum standards. First, it must have on its premises or be able to find nearby, all the legal and non-legal publications needed to handle both the routine and the unpredictable problems. Second, he must be able to use and to train others in the use of those publications.

The Office Library

The office library may already contain the very publications needed to solve those problems. It should reflect the profile of the firm's practice. The drawing of such a profile is the first step in determining the library's adequacy. The profile can be constructed from interviews with partners and associates, a review of office and opponents' briefs, office memoranda and other lawyer work products and, in some instances, an analysis of lawyers' diaries and detailed bills to clients.

This is the raw material from which one can determine what the associates and partners do all day and all year—and what their research requirements are.

Next, an inventory of the library and of all the other intellectual resources in the office should be compiled. A plan for doing this is set forth in the article, "Law Office Needs: Books-Equipment-

People" (24 The Business Lawyer 511 [January, 1969]) and need not be repeated here.

Profile and Inventory

Finally, the profile and the inventory should be compared. Can the library resources solve part, most or virtually none of the legal problems that arise? Is the library underequipped with looseleaf services? Has it retained hundreds of rarely used books? Are there treatises to buy but their existence is not known to anyone in the library? The comparison may answer these and a host of other questions about one's practice.

One may find as a byproduct of the profile that every lawyer in the office is doing some research but that one lawyer is better at it than all the others. The research specialist may already be on the scene. He simply needs to be recognized.

Whatever else the comparison shows, it will tell what proportion of one's efforts go into gathering facts. By applying a system to legal research and to fact-gathering generally, the amount of effort can be reduced and the result improved.

CHAPTER 2

LEGAL RESEARCH: MASTERING A MAJOR TOOL OF LAW PRACTICE

The things they never taught at school:
The administrative rule, the statutory tool,
The superseded code and obvious abode
Of the elusive, unobtrusive wellsprings of the law.

Tho I ran my school review
And wrote a prescient note or two,
They make me look the sap without a simple map
Of all the sources and resources of the law.

The rule against perpetuity, no match to my ingenuity;
And yet for lack of that bloody research knack,
They make me out the fool
And hint I'd best go back to any other school of the law.

Many second-year law students (summer interns) and graduates will soon enter the practice of law. How they fare depends on many factors, one of which has been largely ignored by both law schools and practitioners—the effective use of legal-research tools. In an attempt to fill this void in the training of their associates, one of New York's oldest firms will have a law professor-librarian in its library during a portion of the summer. His function will be a dual one: (1) to help sharpen the research abilities of new associates, and (2) to brief that firm's reference librarians in legal and nonlegal research methods.

What is the irreducible minimum in knowledge of research methods that a beginning practitioner should possess? The ability to find the applicable law is basic to every lawyer. But more is required than the mere locating of the statutes and court rules, the administrative decisions, regulations and legal commentaries. Implicit in locating these sources is the mastery of using them to advantage in marshalling legal facts and applying them to a particular legal problem. Considered in turn below are (1) Statutes, (2) Court Rules, (3) Court Decisions, (4) Administrative Regulations, (5) Looseleaf Services, (6) Legal Commentaries and (7) Computer Services.

In each case the instruction should center about a single legal problem, be it one involving food regulation, insider trading or creditors' rights.

Statutes

A review of statutes must cover the two forms in which they appear: session laws and codes, both annotated and unannotated. It must trace the process by which laws are made, covering for federal law the range of bills, transcripts of hearings, committee prints, reports and debates that comprise legislative histories and, for state and local law, a similar but smaller collection of papers.

The survey should stress the existing statutory indexes and tables that help a lawyer determine not only what the law is today but what it was at any earlier time.

It should examine published legislative histories and study the services that purport to cover pending legislation, federal, state and local.

The *CIS (Congressional Information Service)* has enormously simplified the work of identifying and locating Congressional hearings, reports and committee prints through its monthly annual and multi-year (1970–1974 and 1975–1978) cumulative summaries and indexes. Similarly, the detailed annual index to the *Monthly Catalog of United States Government Publications* is a valuable reference source as is the 1900–1971 *Cumulative Subject Index* to that Catalog. From time to time the Senate Library publishes a list of its collection of transcripts of hearings. The latest two show additions during the periods 1971 to 1974 and 1975–1976.

Finally, the survey should include a review of commentaries on particular laws such as those published, for example, at the beginning of various new titles in McKinney's *Consolidated Laws of New York*, in law reviews, local bar journals and annual surveys of American and state laws.

Court Rules

Few libraries make the effort to collect their court rules in a single place and arrange them by jurisdiction. As a consequence lawyers frequently have to scramble to find them at the moment a brief is being drafted or a court paper filed.

In federal law, it is a simple matter to pinpoint the United States Supreme Court Rules and Circuit Courts of Appeals Rules for each of the federal circuits. They appear in the rules volumes of the *Supreme Court Digest* and in Title 28 *USCA*, where they are updated through annual pocket supplements. In addition, the West Publishing Company conscientiously publishes many rule changes in the advance sheets. But these are usually thrown out when the bound volumes arrive. It is therefore unwise to rely completely on any of these sources for the most current rules.

The CCH Supreme Court service does provide the current rules of that court. The two-volume local court rules portion of the *Federal Rules Service* (Callaghan & Company) is the only compiled source of federal district court rules. It also contains the rules of the Circuit Courts of Appeals. Some of these Courts issue Appendices to their rules relating, for example, to student appearances or implementing various plans. The *Federal Rules Service* edition, which is looseleaf, curiously omits Appendices A and C for the First Circuit though it carefully shows their existence in the table of contents. On the other hand it includes all the Appendices for the Second Circuit but fails to identify them in the introductory table. A minor flaw. The *USCA* edition of the same rules appears to be complete.

Familiarity with sources for the Federal Rules of Evidence, Appellate Procedure and Bankruptcy Rules is also important. Nor can the rules of special federal courts be overlooked.

State court rules are frequently presented in single volume compilations. In New York, the *Civil Practice Annual*, the successor to *Clevenger's Civil Practice Manual*, is widely used, as is the paperback *New York CPLR Redbook.* Both are Bender publications. As New York lawyers know, the Civil Practice Law and Rules have been incorporated in the *Consolidated Laws of New York* as Book 7B of *McKinney's* and contain Dean Joseph M. McLaughlin's masterly *"Practice Commentaries."* What is not commonly known is that there is an official repository of New York court rules covering all courts in the state. They appear in Title 22 of the State of New York looseleaf *Official Compilation of Codes, Rules and Regulations.*

Court Decisions

Using the various West digests, it goes without saying that a beginning lawyer should be able to find any reported case through either the plaintiff's or defendant's name, or by topic, key phrase or West "Key Number." How one goes about it, however, will determine whether the search takes a few seconds or the better part of an hour. The ability to choose cases that are actually in point from among all cases found is an art that distinguishes the keen researcher from the indifferent one.

Federal Law Digests

Most federal case law is digested in three related West Digests: (1) *Federal Digest*, from the beginning to 1939 (the red set), (2) *Modern Federal Practice Digest* from 1939 to 1961 (the green set) which despite its name covers both substantive and procedural law and (3) *West's Federal Digest Practice* 2nd, from 1961 to date (the blue set) which is simply a repository for all the pocket and cumulative supplements to the green set. There are also separate digests for Supreme Court reports and combined decennial digests with two- or three-month supplements that cover both state and federal law. The Callahan *Federal Rules Service Digest* analyzes the cases set out in that publisher's *Federal Rules Service.* The latter is a collection of federal procedural decisions arranged within each volume in rule number order. The cases in *F.R.D.* appear approximately in chronological order.

State Law Digests

In addition to the "Decennials," there are current digests for all states except Utah and Nevada and all regions except the "Southwest" and "Northeast." The latter was discontinued in 1971. *Abbott's New York Digest* is almost identical to the federal digests in structure. It too comprises three separate noncumulative sets: (1) *Abbott's Digest* (the blue set to 1929), *Abbott's Digest 2nd* (the red set, 1929 to 1961) and *West's New York Digest 2nd* (the bright blue set, 1962 to date).

Clark's Digest is the key to cases appearing in the *New York Law Journal* and contains both a case name and topical index. It also lists *New York Law Journal* columns. It is issued monthly and is cumulated annually.

Administrative Regulations

The body of federal establishment law is voluminous and often difficult to pin down. The regulatory record of a single food definition dispute resulted in 24,000 pages of hearing transcripts and some 75,000 pages of documents.[1] In this matter, a proposed FDA order became effective only after twelve years of agency hearings and conferences, industry objections and court appeals up to the United States Supreme Court.

Federal regulatory law comprises presidential proclamations and executive orders, cabinet department and independent agency regulations and numerous series of agency rulings, opinions and decisions. The Federal Trade Commission Decisions and ICC Reports alone run to several hundred volumes. Equally useful may be the modest nine-volume run of Opinions of the Solicitor of the Post Office.

Rulings and decisions aside, the basic federal regulations and their finding aids appear in three groups of publications:

1. The Code of Federal Regulations
2. The Federal Register and
3. The United States Government Manual.

---

[1] Corn Products Co. v. FDA, 427 F. 2d 511 (3d Cir.), *cert. denied sub. nom.* Derby Foods, Inc. v. FDA, 400 U.S. 957 (1970).

The Code of Federal Regulations. This annual work in fifty titles is comparable in arrangement to the USCA. About one-fourth of the titles are revised every three months in regular sequence. Its combined master index and finding aid volume is the chief key to its use. In addition, a few titles are separately indexed in greater detail, among them, Title 3 (The President), Title 11 (Highways) and Title 37 (Patents, Trademarks and Copyrights).

A 790-page codification of presidential proclamations and executive orders that covers the period from 1961 to 1977 was issued in 1979. It too is arranged in fifty chapters roughly paralleling the fifty titles of CFR. Its outstanding feature is its disposition table that enables the user to trace changes in these documents since 1961.

The acid test of this guide is its treatment of alien property controls and blocked accounts that originated with Executive Order 8389 (April 10, 1940). Lawyers who have struggled for some forty years to keep up with its subsequent history will appreciate the information that appears on page 392 of this volume. Similar data are also collected in the authority note to 31 CFR Part 520 (Foreign Funds Control Regulation). The full texts of the later executive orders are reported in a note following 50 USC Appendix Section 6.

The Federal Register. Current and proposed regulations, agency notices, proclamation and executive orders appear in this newspaper that is issued weekdays Monday through Friday. Each issue contains a finding aid feature and index which are cumulated monthly, quarterly and yearly. These daily issues provide an array of elusive and unevenly indexed matter that in 1980 ran to 87,012 pages.

Probably the most useful of the finding features is the List of CFR Sections Affected that is cumulated daily throughout each month, quarterly and annually. It gives the user assurance that a particular regulation has or has not been amended during the period of its coverage.

Teaching the use of these tools has been simplified through tabular aids. But the indexing of both *CFR* and the *Federal Register* needs constant refinement. Until recently the indexing of both publications frustrated every sensible teaching approach except "hit or miss." The *Cervase* case is a modest triumph in the cause of indexing reform.[2]

The United States Government Manual. This massive directory and handbook describes the functions of the various federal departments and agencies, giving for each its statutory authority, a roster of its principal officials and a list of its leading publications. Equally important, it sets out in bold face type the telephone number of an official in Washington, D.C. who can answer regulatory questions.

State and Local Regulation

Most states have codified their rules and regulations, arranging them by agency and publishing them in multi-volume sets that run to as many as thirty or more volumes. The New York *Code*, referred to above for its collection of court rules, is one of the most elaborate of these.

Most states also publish manuals that are usually called "blue books." In New York it is the *New York Legislative Manual*. It is similar in format to the *United States Government Manual*. Its unofficial counterpart is the *New York Red Book*.

City regulations are infrequently codified and are best obtained in most localities from the agency concerned. In the City of New York, for example, the *Rules and Regulations of New York City Agencies* was last issued in two volumes in 1967 and has been out of date for some thirteen years. One might consult the New York City Charter and Code to learn if any statute requires the issuance of regulations. But that code is a collection of ordinances and not rules.

---

[2] Cervase v. Office of the Federal Register, 580 F. 2d 1166 (3d Cir. 1978). Cervase's attempt to require the Office of the Federal Register to publish an analytical index to the CFR was originally rebuffed by the U.S. District Court of New Jersey. But the United States Court of Appeals reversed and plaintiff Cervase agreed to a dismissal following the publication of a more detailed CFR index in July 1979 and on the government's promise to institute other indexing improvements.

A Singular Service

The Municipal Reference Library is a singular institution whose staff members have, for nearly half a century, provided lawyers with information that the agencies concerned were often unable to find. A member of its staff has been updating on cards that same 1967 code of City of New York rules. Anyone calling Mrs. Shirley Paris (212-566-4284) can immediately obtain information on current rule changes and discover that the term "service" in civil service is still very much alive at the Municipal Reference Library in New York.

Lawyers who deal with any New York City agency should also become familiar with the annual "little green book," the *Official Directory of the City of New York.* It is packed with information and is similar in format to the federal and state manuals referred to above.

Looseleaf Services

Looseleaf services give practitioners more information more quickly than any other form of publication. Their use is rarely stressed in the law schools. Indeed many graduates will have handled only the Supreme Court volume of *Law Week* by the time they start to practice.

The ways in which the looseleaf services bring together a mass of current information on each of twenty or thirty major legal subjects can be taught to small groups in about two hours. The resulting time saved can be incalculable. It comes as a surprise to most lawyers to learn that in securities law, for example, the *CCH Federal Securities Law Reporter* collects in a single set of books the existing statutes, regulations, proposed regulations, rulings, releases, numerous annotations and the full text of current court and SEC decisions. Typical of most CCH services are their indexing and updating features that are, in general, superior to those of the *CFR* and *Federal Register*.

The Bureau of National Affairs services, which are noted for their editorial content in such fields as taxation, labor, environmental law, corporations and criminal procedure, offer unique compilations of legal materials.

A third publisher, Prentice Hall, Inc., issues the only current service that includes the full text of all state corporation laws, together with "doing business" information, news of legislative developments and tables showing corporate tax rates.

Legal Commentaries

Not merely *where*, but *what* is the law, is the objective of legal research. The writings of legal specialists range in value from definitive and incontrovertible to near useless. They appear in encyclopedias, ALR annotations, law reviews, and practitioners' journals, in treatises and in the *Restatements*.

Good judgment and experience will determine which to consult in a particular situation. The spine markings on the books rarely proclaim their contents or the fact that one article or one chapter may be worth a week of research. Each is separately indexed or cataloged. The beginner should learn first simply how to locate what exists. The ability to discriminate among various writings will come quickly enough. This again is an art to be learned—and is one not always perfected in law school.

The professor in residence or the research lawyer in a law firm library should explain to the summer lawyers and to the firm's librarians the chief features and format of the existing catalogs, bibliographies and indexes. He should stress the importance of the best examples of current legal literature and draw up criteria for evaluating them.

In addition he should outline the research resources of the city in which the firm is located. For example, in the City of New York, which is still the publishing center of the country, lawyers should become familiar with the services offered by the publishing houses, trade newspapers, public and private libraries (law and business in particular), the specialized book stores, the trade associations, proxy solicitors, underwriting houses, consulates, foundations and government agencies. The services of any of these institutions may become indispensable in the solution of some future legal problem.

Computer Services

After their first year in school, most law students are given virtually unlimited use of the "Lexis" or "Westlaw" terminals. A large minority of students do take advantage of these remarkable systems.

Once in practice lawyers should be encouraged to use computers, not only as case-finders, but as the source of commercial, financial and corporate news. Many offices subscribe to computer services that supply these additional kinds of information either through "Lexis" and its companion "Nexis" on a single terminal, or through a separate terminal. In addition "Lexis" has an arrangement for the use of "Autocite" and both "Lexis" and "Westlaw" are linked to Shepard's *Citations.*

In numerous offices around the country, the reference librarians themselves perform these computer services for lawyers.

The first orientation session that a firm holds should stress what is available in the office library: what the book collection contains and, most important, which services the various members of the library staff perform. A concise statement of the library rules will go far both in overcoming the missing book problem and in maintaining high library staff morale.

PART TWO

Phases of Legal Research

A: CASE LAW

CHAPTER 3

HOW TO FIND ENGLISH LAW

The occasion for an American lawyer to refer to English law occurs often enough to warrant some guidance on how to use English legal materials.

Why Be Interested in English Law?

First, English cases are frequently cited by our courts as persuasive authority. In *Palsgraf v. Long Island Railroad Co.* (248 N.Y. 339, 162 N.E. 99, 1938), for example, Justice Cardozo, in the opinion of the court, not only cited as relevant authority English decisions but also English legal treatises and Law Review articles.

Second, English decisions interpreting English commercial statutes which have formed the basis of American statutes such as the law of sales or civil procedure, have similarly influenced the reasoning of American judges.

Third, English decisions prior to 1776 are considered as primary authority in the U.S., as the basis of American case law is to found in the common law of England. In this context, American states have some sort of "reception" statute or constitutional provision, relating to the legal effect of English decisions. The New York State constitution, Article 1, Section 14, limits the reception of English Common law in New York to "such parts of the common law, and of the acts of the legislature of the Colony of New York, as together did form the law of the said colony, on the 19th day of April, 1775."

They are construed, however, as binding by the courts only to the extent that they are not in conflict with American public policy and law. They are also subject to such alterations as the legislature makes concerning them.

Fourth, then again, lawyers representing American clients involved in commercial transactions with English firms, or otherwise personally affected by English law, often need to refer to English legal authority to determine their rights and obligations under English law.

Location of English Legal Materials in New York City

All law school libraries, in order to meet the standards of the American Bar Association and the Association of American Law Schools, maintain basic collections of English law, as do the libraries of the Association of the Bar of the City of New York, the New York County Lawyers' Association, the Law Institute and some court libraries.

How and Where to Start Your Research

The sources of English law are to be found in Acts of Parliament, reported cases of English court decisions, and administrative regulations known as Statutory Instruments. Except for the fact that England has no written constitution, and hence Parliamentary Acts are not subject to review of their validity by the courts, research in English law bears a marked resemblance to research in American law. The English system of legal publishing is closely similar to the American system, consisting as it does of classified statutory compilations, court reports, digests, encyclopedias, treatises, law review articles and something similar to Shepards. As a result, the methods of research are also similar and the researcher can use the fact method or descriptive word index, the topic method and the case method in locating legal authority.

Sequence of Use of Material

Having analyzed the factual and legal aspects of the problem and having decided on the words and topics descriptive of its salient points, reading an orderly presentation of principles in a treatise, textbook, article in an encyclopedia or law review article is a good beginning for comprehension of general principles and leading cases pertaining to a specific legal problem.

Treatises and Texts. An excellent source for locating English treatises and texts on specific subjects is *Law Books in Print*, edited by J. Myron Jacobstein and Meira Pimsleur and published by Glanville Press in 1976. It is a four volume set, kept current by quarterly and annual cumulations of *Law Books Published.* Volume 3 offers a subject arrangement of these texts. The researcher need only refer to the topics reflected in the problem and note the titles listed thereunder. For example, by checking the topic *Estate and Gift Taxes—Great Britain,* most English textbooks in print on that subject will be brought out with list price and bibliographical information.

The English counterpart to *Law Books in Print* is *A Legal Bibliography of the British Commonwealth of Nations* in seven volumes published by Sweet and Maxwell, London. It is kept current by cumulative bound volumes published intermittently. Volumes 1 and 2 are on English law; the others cover all other nations presently, or formerly, a part of the British Commonwealth. Books are listed alphabetically by author and arranged by subject.

Legal Periodical Articles. Articles in legal periodicals are good sources for learning about current developments in English law and identifying emerging English legal principles.

Although the *Index to Legal Periodicals* is an American publication, published monthly and in annual and triennial cumulations by the H.W. Wilson Co., New York, it not only indexes by subject articles published in American legal periodicals, but also those published in Canada, Great Britain, Australia and New Zealand. Case notes or discussions of recent cases are listed by the names of the case discussed at the end of the subject under the subheading "Cases."

A separate section entitled "Table of Cases" lists cases alphabetically by plaintiffs' names. Another section entitled "Book Review Index" lists reviews under the name of the author or under the title of the work if the author is unknown. It should also be noted that a number of American legal periodicals feature articles on English legal subjects. The Winter 1971 issue of the *Vanderbilt Journal of Transnational Law*, for example, offers an article on "Securities regulation in the United Kingdom, a comparison with U.S. Practices."

There are a number of specialized and general legal periodicals published in England of value to American lawyers researching English law. To list a few, British Tax Review, Cambridge Law Journal, Conveyancer and Property lawyer, Criminal Law Review, Journal of Business Law, Law Quarterly Review, Modern Law Review, Public Law and the Solicitors' Journal.

Legal Encyclopedias. The English counterpart to *Corpus Juris Secundum* and *American Jurisprudence, 2d* is *Halsbury's Laws of England.* Presently in its fourth edition (about forty volumes have been published to date; the 3d ed. consists of forty-two volumes), it is a complete restatement of the whole law of England according to its editor. *Halsbury's Laws* differs from its American counterparts in that it focuses considerably more attention on statute law and each volume contains a "Table of Statutes cited," which enables the researcher to go directly to textual comment on the statute. *Halsbury's Laws* differs also from American legal encyclopedias in that it has a cumulative "Table of Cases cited," which permits the researcher to refer to editorial comment on a given case (decision law). *Halsbury's Laws* is similar to American encyclopedias in that it has the analytical (topic) approach such as "Larceny." It also has the Fact Approach such as "Stealing," which can be found in its General Index. As stated above, it has unlike American encyclopedias, the Table of Cases approach to finding applicable decisional law. (See its Consolidated Table of Cases for the entire set.)

Added Feature

Another added feature is the cross-reference from one's case to the topic and paragraph in *English and Empire Digest* (see Post under *Search Books*), where that case, like cases, and later cases in point may be found. To find a discussion of a specific statute, the Table of Statutes in the respective volume or the cumulative *Table of Statutes* for the entire set refers to the applicable page. Incidentally, if a case is found in the *English and Empire Digest* it can be located back in *Halsbury's Laws'* Table of Cases or through direct citations to *Halsbury's Laws* in the *English and Empire Digest.*

Each volume of *Halsbury's Laws* is divided into numbered paragraphs, with numbering consecutive throughout the volume rather than by topic and number as in American encyclopedias. The cumulative single volumes issued annually to supplement the set are keyed to these numbers.

Statutes and Statutory Instruments

The Acts of Parliament from 1235 onwards, to the extent that they were in force in 1948, are to be found in a collection of official volumes entitled *Statutes Revised* (3d ed. in 32 volumes), arranged in chronological, not classified order. There are extensive notes and each volume has its own subject and chronological index. The Acts of the years after 1948 will be found in the official *Annual Volumes of the Public General Acts and Measures,* each of which also contains an index, alphabetical and chronological lists of the year's *Acts and Measures* and a table showing their effect on those of earlier years.

As England is consolidating many of its Acts, *The Statutes Revised* quickly became outdated. Then again as there is no cumulative supplement, it is awkward to use.

Revised Edition

In 1972 a new official revised edition of the Statutes was started entitled, *Statutes in Force.* When completed around 1981 it will supersede the *Statutes Revised.* It is being published in loose-leaf volumes with each act in a separate pamphlet. It will be kept current by replacement pamphlets when an act is either repealed or considerably amended.

There are a number of works of reference, published by authority and unofficially, which will help the researcher ascertain (1) whether there are any statutes which cover a specific subject or topic, and if so, where to find the relevant provisions, and (2) whether such provisions are still in force and whether they have been amended.

To find a citation to statute law on a particular subject, the subject can be looked up in the *Index to the Statutes in Force*, an annual publication in which all the public general statute law in force at the end of the previous year is collected under subject headings. This *Index* will give the citation to the Act and the section where the subject is treated.

To determine whether a specific section of an Act has been repealed or amended, use the *Chronological Table of the Statutes*. Published annually, and cumulative, this reference work lists all the general Acts made since 1235, showing which are still in force and which have been repealed and giving details of all amendments of those still in force.

Compilation of Statutes

Although not really comparable to the United States Code Annotated or United States Code Service, *Halsbury's Statutes of England* (3d ed. 40 vol.), serves a similar purpose. Actually it is an encyclopedic compilation of English statutes in force, arranged by title or topic so that all acts on the same subject are brought together under a specific title such as "Husband and Wife," etc. At times, the American lawyer will have to exercise some ingenuity in locating the characteristic English titles, e.g., "Maintenance of Illegitimate Children and Their Legitimation." Each of these main titles begins with a Table of Contents corresponding to the analysis in the conventional American case digest, e.g., *West's N.Y. Digest* 3d, or encyclopedia such as *Corpus Juris Secundum*. Then comes the chronological table of all statutes included under that title. Following that is an essay note explaining the subject matter of the title and then the texts of the various acts printed verbatim are set forth. Following the text of each section of an act are notes in small type which "Shepardize" the act by referring to both subsequent legislative and judicial (decisional) action therein. *Halsbury's Statutes* also contain cross-references to *Halsbury's Laws* where textual treatment is available. In essence therefore, it serves not only as a statutory compilation of the statutes of England and Northern Ireland in force arranged chronologically under topical headings, but also as an encyclopedia, a statutory "digest" and a citator.

Kept Up To Date

Halsbury's Statutes is kept current by annual continuation volumes and a cumulative supplement. Paragraph key numbering, the special feature used in *Halsbury's Laws* and the *English and Empire Digest* is also used in *Halsbury's Statutes.* A number is given to each statute paragraph and used in the later cumulative supplements to update information on the subject of the paragraph number. In a way it is a substitute for Shepardizing a statute. Each volume has a table of statutes which are in part or full printed therein as well as a table of cases interpreting such statutes and its own subject index.

To locate earlier or historic English statutes refer to the *Statutes of the Realm* (published 1810–22 in nine folio volumes). It covers the period from 1225 to 1713 and is considered the most comprehensive and accurate edition of the statutes for the period covered. See also *Pickering's Statutes at Large* covering the period from Magna Charta to 1869. This is a popular edition published in various series under different titles.

How to Cite English Statutes

English statutes before 1962, according to *A Uniform System of Citation* (13th ed., 1981), are cited by name, regnal year, chapter, section and schedule (if any) e.g., Supreme Court of Judicature Act of 1915, 15 & 16 George 5, c. 49 Sect. 226, sched. 6. If the name is omitted or does not include the date, indicate the year parenthetically at the end of the citation (Hypnotism Act, 15 & 16 Geo. 6 & 1 Eliz. 2, c. 49, Sect. 117, at 938 [1952]). For statutes after 1962, omit the regnal year: Airports Authority Act 1965, c. 16.

Statutory Instruments

These consist of Orders in Council and certain orders, rules, regulations, etc., made by Ministers, all known as *Statutory Instruments* ("S.I.") and previously as *Statutory Rules and Orders* ("S.R. & O"). In 1948, the government published the *Statutory Rules and Orders and Statutory Instruments Revised* as the official English administrative code. This is kept current by the *Annual Volumes of Statutory Instruments.* The government also publishes an *Index to Government Orders* which leads the researcher to orders, rules, regulations, schemes, etc., on a given subject which are in force.

The English lawyer usually depends on *Halsbury's Statutory Instruments* to locate administrative regulations. Arranged by subject and published as a companion to *Halsbury's Statutes of England*, it is kept current by replacement volumes and loose-leaf cumulative supplements. It is similar in format to the *Code of Federal Regulations* in this country.

English Court System and English Law Reports

Introductory Comments

A casual comparison of English Law Reports with American Law Reports would suggest how similar they are. They both have titles, prefatory statements, headnotes, facts, opinions and identification of the author of the opinion. They both appear in numbered sequences and reflect the decisional law of a specific court or court system. But there are significant differences which must be noted by the American lawyer.

English law reports are at best only quasi-official. They are not published by the courts nor by the government. Throughout the ages, the opinions of English judges have been given orally in open court, usually immediately after both sides rested. Briefs are not submitted by counsel to the sitting judges for consideration in arriving at a decision. Up until 1865, law reporting in England was dependent upon the initiative of private persons or societies. Some were quite poor, others could be much better and some were superb.

In all, there are at least 300 different sets of reports published prior to 1865 which can be cited in English courts. From 1537 to 1765, there were more than 100 named reporters alone who published one or more volumes each of the opinions of English judges, encouraged to do so by the lack of official reporting. These reports created difficulties for the English lawyer.

As there was no official control over these reporters, their law reports merely reflected their own version of what they considered to be important. Some were in the form of personal notes of a judge or practitioner, never intended to be published. Actually, some of them were stolen or plagiarized–often after the "reporter's" death and published unrevised. When a case was considered sufficiently significant, it would be reported by several reporters, all with their own version of it. The case of *Clerk v. Day*, for example, was reported by "Croke," by "Owen," by "Moore" and also in "Rolle's Abridgment," yet Lord Raymond is supposed to have asserted that it was not accurately reported in any of them, even as to the name of the parties!

Lord Holt said of the fourth volume of Modern Reports: "See the inconveniences of these scrambling reports; they will make us appear to posterity for a parcel of blockheads." Lord Mansfield refused to allow practitioners to cite in his court, "Barnardiston, Banbury, and Atkyns." Barnardiston, on occasion, would fall asleep during a court proceeding and wags would scribble all kinds of comments in his notebook which he subsequently published apparently without checking their authenticity.

Of course, this situation was not true of all court reporting prior to 1865. "Lord Coke's Reports" (1572–1616) are excellent and were known as "The Reports." Along with "Plowden," they are considered as the classical repositories of the old common law. "Plowden" was the first private reporter and covered the period from Edward III (1327–1377) to Elizabeth (1550–1580). "Coke" and "Plowden" believed in complete reporting. They thus reported the pleadings, the points at issue, arguments of counsel and grounds of the judgment. Each reporter also commented on the cases offering a textual analysis of the decisional law of the period.

Modern law reporting in England really begins with "Burrow's Reports" (1757–1771), which covers Lord Mansfield's earlier years on the King's Bench as its Chief Justice. Burrow was the first reporter to provide the facts and issues of the case in the form of a prefatory system. He also reported the arguments of counsel, as well as the opinions of the judges and the judgment of the court. Lord Mansfield is supposed to have taken a personal interest in these reports, actually revising them before publication. Whatever the reason, "Burrow's Reports" are known for their accuracy and clarity.

To suggest how the many other law reports prior to 1865 could at times improperly reflect what took place in a court, note "Campbell's Nisi Prius Reports" (1807–1816). Campbell, later Lord Chancellor himself, reported Lord Ellenborough's cases. He maintained a drawer in his desk marked "Bad Law." When he disagreed with a ruling of Lord Ellenborough, he would refuse to report it and instead put it into the drawer. He later commented that he derived great satisfaction to hear Lord Eldon conclude, "How uniformly correct was Lord Ellenborough in his decisions." The editorial license he had exercised with reference to the "bad cases" he believed was a primary factor in this achievement. When Campbell's home was later destroyed by fire, all these "bad cases" went up in flames too, and as a result a number of them have never been reported to this day. As one observer has noted, not only was Campbell a good reporter, "but he only reported good cases. That discrimination is denied to reporters today."

The systematic reporting of cases in effect today in England dates from 1865. Actually, it is a system of cooperative reporting in which participating barristers report cases decided in the Superior Courts to the Incorporated Council of Law Reporting. They are then published by the Counsel as the *"Law Reports"* in distinct series for each of the courts. As these law reports are reviewed for accuracy by the judges rendering them and approved by them prior to publication in the *"Law Reports"* they are considered in this sense as quasi official for court citation.

English law reporting is different from American law reporting in other ways. For example, the English reports reflect the fact that English judges deliver their opinions separately and hence there is no opinion of the court or majority opinion, as is characteristic of American Reporting. Therefore, when three judges hear an appellate argument and their opinions appear in the Report of the case, it may be necessary to count heads to determine which of the three opinions reflect the prevailing judgment, which could be dissenting and which could be concurring. Each of the judges speaks for himself in this context rather than for the court.

English reporting is also highly selective, much more so than in the United States. Only those cases are published in the *"Law Reports"* which are deemed to be significant and of permanent value. As a result, it is important to learn about the bibliography of English Reports in order to locate a case which may not have been published in the *"Law Reports"* after 1865. Prior to 1865, another situation prevails, involving selectivity as well. An understanding of the English Court system as it has changed over the years is helpful here.

English Court System–Prior to 1873 and 1875

Prior to 1873, the following were the courts of original jurisdiction:

(1) Court of King's Bench or Queen's Bench. The K.B. or Q.B. can be traced back to the thirteenth century and was the most important of the common-law courts. It had jurisdiction over pleas of the crown (criminal cases) and actions in which damages were sought for injury to person or use of force. Its jurisdiction was later extended to cover all actions between private persons. It could also issue extraordinary writs such as mandamus and quo warranto.

(2) The Court of Common Bench or Common Pleas is referred to as far back as the twelfth century as having jurisdiction over pleas between private persons.

(3) The Court of the Exchequer originated out of the Treasury function of collecting and enforcement of taxes. Its jurisdiction was similar to that of the Common Pleas except that only the Common Pleas had jurisdiction over actions pertaining to realty.

(4) The Perogative Courts of Canterbury and York were ecclesiastical courts with jurisdiction over the probate of wills, administration of estates and all matrimonial causes. In 1857, the Court of Probate and the Court for Divorce and Matrimonial Causes assumed jurisdiction over these matters.

(5) The Court of Chancery is known to have been functioning during the reign of Richard II (1377 to 1399) with jurisdiction over equity cases.

(6) The Court of Admiralty can trace its origins back to the fourteenth century with jurisdiction over maritime affairs.

Appellate Courts

A system of appeals from these common law courts to the King's Bench and other courts evolved in the early periods.

Prior to 1873, three courts of intermediate appeal were established:

(1) The Exchequer Chamber (1830), which heard appeals from the common law courts (Court of King's Bench, Court of Common Pleas and Court of the Exchequer).

(2) The Court of Appeal in Chancery (1851), which heard appeals in equity cases.

(3) The Full Court in Matrimonial Causes, which heard appeals from the Court of Divorce and Matrimonial Causes.

The final court of appeals was the House of Lords to which an appeal lay from the three intermediate courts of appeal and also from the Scotch and Irish Courts.

Appeals from the Admiralty and Ecclesiastical Courts and from the Colonial Courts were heard by the Judicial Committee of the Privy Council.

English Court System— Effect of the Judicature Acts of 1873 and 1875

The Judicature Acts of 1873 and 1875 and subsequent amendments established the modern system of English courts.

All courts of original jurisdiction and intermediate appeal were replaced by the Supreme Court of Judicature which was divided into two parts:

(1) The High Court of Justice (subdivided into (a) The King's or Queen's Bench Division, (b) The Common Pleas Division, (c) The Exchequer Division, (d) The Chancery Division, and

(e) The Probate, Divorce and Admiralty Division). The jurisdiction of these courts was equivalent to that of the old courts similarly named. They were given the added jurisdiction of applying equitable rules. In 1880, the Common Pleas and Exchequer Divisions were consolidated with the Queen's Bench Division.

(2) The Court of Appeal (Appeals from the Divisional Courts are now taken to the Court of Appeal. Appeals from the Court of Appeal are taken to the House of Lords).

Thus the system of English courts exercising civil jurisdiction up to 1970 was as follows:

(1) House of Lords—consisting of the Judicial Committee of the Privy Council. Lord Chancellor presides when he attends, and nine Lords of Appeal in Ordinary.

(2) Supreme Court of Judicature—Appeal by Leave of Court of Court of Appeal or by Appeal Committee of the House of Lords.

(A) Court of Appeal. Master of the Rolls and eight Lords Justice of Appeal; Justices sit in three divisions; Appeal from High Court to Court of Appeal as of right on Law and fact.

(B) High Court of Justice.

(i) Chancery Division. Chancery Division actually an anomaly, because Law and Equity cases have been merged; cases standing in equity, e.g. reformations of contract, constructive trusts; Lord Chancellor (does not sit) and six Puisne Judges.

(ii) Queen's Bench Division. Lord Chief Justice and about twenty-seven or more Puisne Judges; also, jurisdiction over Criminal libel, sedition and treason.

(iii) Probate, Divorce and Admiralty Division. President and nine or more Puisne Judges.

The head of the English judicial system is the Lord Chancellor. He is appointed by the reigning monarch upon recommendation of the Prime Minister. His position is political in that he is a member of the Cabinet of the party in power in Parliament, and presides as Speaker in the House of Lords. When the government is overthrown, the victorious party appoints the new Lord Chancellor. As England's highest judicial officer, he is presiding Judge of the House of Lords and also a member of the Judicial Committee of the Privy Council. He is also the President of the Chancery Division and President of the Court of Appeal. He recommends appointments for vacancies in the membership of the High Court Divisions. All the County Courts of England are also under his supervision and the judges of these courts are appointed and can be removed by him.

The Lord Chief Justice is next to the Lord Chancellor in importance. He presides over the Queens Bench Division.

The Administration of Justice Act of 1970 established a new Family Division of the High Court and abolished the Probate, Divorce and Admiralty Division.

On the Criminal side up to 1966, the hierarchy of the English Court System was as follows:

(1) House of Lords

(2) Court of Criminal Appeal. (Lord Chief Justice presides when present with three or more Puisne judges).

(3) Central Criminal Court (London) (Old Bailey) and Assizes. (Murder, treason, arson, rape).

(4) Quarter Sessions. (Burglary, larceny).

(5) Petty Sessions. (Magistrates Court).

The Court of Criminal Appeal Act of 1966 abolished the Court of Criminal Appeal and transferred its jurisdiction to the Court of Appeal which now has a civil and criminal division.

The Court Act of 1971 abolished all courts of assize and quarter sessions and transferred their jurisdiction to a new Crown Court. The Crown Court was made part of the High Court of Justice and established as a Superior Court of Record with jurisdiction throughout England and Wales. When the Crown Court sits in the City of London, it is still known as the Central Criminal Court. All appellate jurisdiction heretofore conferred on any court of Quarter Sessions is transferred by the Act to the Crown Court. There is now a right of appeal to the Crown Court from a Magistrates Court, and from the Crown Court to the Court of Appeal.

At a result of these changes the English Court Structure today is as follows:

(1) House of Lords. (civil and criminal appeals).

(2) Court of Appeal. (Civil and Criminal Division; civil and criminal appeals).

(3) High Court.

(a) Queen's Bench Division. (including the Admiralty Court and the Commercial Court. Jurisdiction in admiralty and page matters assigned from the Probate, Divorce and Admiralty Division).

(b) Chancery Division. (Contentious probate business transferred from the Probate, Divorce and Admiralty Division in addition to equitable jurisdiction).

(c) Family Division. (Noncontentious probate business continues to be assigned here. Also matrimonial causes and dissolution of marriage, adoptions, wards and guardians).

(d) Crown Court. (Unlimited criminal jurisdiction and limited criminal and civil original and appellate jurisdiction, transferred from Quarter sessions).

(4) County Courts. (First instance civil jurisdictions to a limited amount).

(5) Magistrates Courts. (Limited first instance criminal jurisdiction and miscellaneous petty civil jurisdiction).

English Law Reports–Prior to 1865

The lack of official law reporting prior to 1865 led to many duplicating and often inaccurate reporting of cases.

As a result, the English lawyer, in general, cites cases prior to 1865 to *English Reports–Full Reprint* (1378–1865). This is a set of 176 volumes, offering complete verbatim reprints of reported cases from the earliest times to 1865, considered by the editors to be the best version of the case found in the several original duplicating reports.

Court Groupings

About 300 or more different series of law reports through 1865 and about 100,000 cases with parallel citations to reports of the case in other series are thus reported. Reporters are grouped by court covered, with original paging preserved by insertion of page numbers in brackets (star-paged to the original). A chart lists the original reports by name alphabetically giving volume numbers in Reprint series. The set also features a two-volume alphabetical list of cases reprinted therein.

The cases are collected by courts in separate volumes as follows:

Case Collection

Volumes 1-11—House of Lords (1694-1865).

Volumes 11-20—Privy Council (Ind. Indian Appeals) (1809-65).

Volumes 21-47—Chancery (incl. collateral Reports) (1557-1865).

Volumes 48-55—Rolls Court (1829-1865).

Volumes 56-71—Vice-Chancellor's Court (1815-1865).

Volumes 72-122—King's Bench (1378-1865).

Volumes 123-144—Common Pleas (1486-1865).

Volumes 145-160—Exchequer (1220-1865).

Volumes 161-167—Ecclesiastical (1752-1857), Admiralty (1776-1840), Probate & Divorce (1858-1865).

Volumes 168-169—Crown Cases (1743-1865).

Volumes 170-176—Nisi Prius (1688-1867).

Cases published in the *English Reprints* are cited as follows: *Jones v. Smith*, 145 Eng. Rep. 631 (Ex. 1723).

There is another reprint of English Reports entitled the *Revised Reports*. Edited by an esteemed English legal scholar, Sir Frederick Pollock, it republished from 1891 to 1917 in 149 volumes, those cases of the English courts of common law and equity, decided between 1785 and 1866, which were believed to be still of practical utility. The *Revised Reports* not only duplicates cases published in the *English Reports—Full Reprint*, but also reprints many collateral (unauthorized) report series not represented in the *Reprint* set. The *Revised Reports* are used only if the case does not appear in the *English Reports—Full Reprint.*

English Law Reports—After 1865

From 1865 on, the English lawyer uses the quasi-official *Law Reports*. When a case is published in the *Law Reports*, the courts require that it be cited to the *Law Reports*. If the case does not appear in the *Law Reports*, then he must cite to *Weekly Law Reports*. If the case appears in neither of these reporters, then a general unauthorized report can be cited such as *All England Law Reports, Law Journal Reports, Law Times Reports* or *Times Law Reports*. In the event the case is not reported in any of the above, then the *Weekly Notes* or a special unauthorized report, such as the *Solicitors' Journal* can be cited.

When the *Law Reports* were first issued by the *Incorporated Council of Law Reporting*, a separate series was established for each of the courts, including the House of Lords and the Judicial Committee of the Privy Council. There were eleven units or series. *A Uniform System of Citation* (11th ed., 1967) gives examples of how to cite them on pages 57–58.

Reduction Made

The Reorganization of the courts under the Judicature Acts of 1873 and 1875 resulted in the number of the series being reduced to six: (1) appeal cases; (2) chancery; (3) Q.B. or K.B.; (4) Exchequer Div.; (5) Common Please Division; (6) Probate Division.

Citation Form: *Jones v. Smith* (1972) A.C. 350. If year of decision differs from the volume year, it is parenthetically indicated at end of citation, e.g., *Jones v. Smith* (1927) A.C. 350 (1971).

In 1881, the Common Pleas Division and Exchequer Division of the High Court of Justice were consolidated with the Queens Bench Division and the number of the series was reduced to four.

Law Reports include Appeals Cases (A.C.), Chancery Division (Ch.), Queen's or King's Bench Division (Q.B. or K.B.) and Probate, Divorce and Admiralty Division (P).

Then the Administration of Justice Act of 1970 established a new Family Division of the High Court and abolished the Probate, Divorce and Admiralty Division. Hence, the Law Reports now consist of Appeal Cases (A.C.), Chancery Division (Ch.), Queens or Kings Bench Division (Q.B. or K.B.) and Family Division (F).

Monthly Parts

The *Law Reports* are published in monthly parts, with annual indexes and tables. Each volume contains a "table of cases judicially noticed" and of "statutes judicially considered" by cases printed therein.

The *Law Reports*, it should be noticed, are selective reporters. Their purpose is to report "every reportable case of general interest." The editor is the final arbiter. The cases published in the *Law Reports* "consist of new points of law and are therefore cases of permanent interest to the legal profession." The *Law Reports* are cited by the court or division. Up to 1975, e.g., *Jones v. Smith* (L.R. 10 Q.B. 400) indicates that this case can be found in the *Law Reports*, volume 10, of the Queens Bench Reports, page 400.

1st Consolidation

After 1875, when the first consolidation took place, cases were cited by the division.

E.g., *Jones v. Smith* (L.R. 15 Q.B.D. 300) indicates that the case can be found in *Law Reports*, volume 15, of the Queens Bench Division, page 300.

In 1891, a new style of citation was established; the year being added to the citation. E.g. *Jones v. Smith* (1962) 2 Q.B. 600, indicates that this case can be found in the *Law Reports*, volume 2 of the Queens Bench Division for the year 1962, page 600.

Generally, only one volume of reports is published annually for the appeal cases and the Family Division (as well as the old Probate, Divorce and Admiralty Division). The Queens Bench or Kings Bench Division usually publish two volumes a year as does the Chancery Division.

House Decisions Only

It should also be noted that the cases reported in the appeal cases are those decided by the House of Lords only and not those decided by the Court of Appeal. Decisions of the Court of Appeal are published in the series of the *Law Reports* for the court from which they were originally appealed. There is no separate series for the Court of Appeal. Therefore, a case appealed from the Queens Bench to the Court of Appeal is reported in Q.B. reports.

As indicated above, not all cases decided by the House of Lords, Court of Appeal, Chancery Division, Queens Bench Division and Family Division (formerly Probate, Divorce and Admiralty) are published in the *Law Reports*. When a case is considered for publication by the editor of the Incorporated Council of Law Reporting, it is first published in the *Weekly Law Reports* (1953 to date). The *Weekly Law Reports* is similar to an Advance Sheet to the *Law Reports* series. Published weekly, it prints every decision likely to appear in any general series of reports. It is issued in two parts. Part I publishes cases which will not be subsequently reported in the *Law Reports* and are "starred" as such.

They are reported by barristers, but are not revised by the judges involved in their authorship. Part II, publishes those reports which will later appear in the *Law Reports*, without arguments of counsel. After these reports are revised by the judges, they are subsequently republished in the *Law Reports* series along with arguments of counsel. Each issue of the *Weekly Law Reports* has a cumulative table of cases for the volume and an index of the subject matter digesting cases therein. These indexes cumulate annually.

The *Weekly Law Reports* superseded the *Weekly Notes* (1860–1952) which printed reports of cases decided in all courts covered by the *Law Reports*. Many of these reports were subsequently reported in the *Law Reports*, others marked by an asterisk were not.

Thus, the *Weekly Law Reports* selectively reports cases decided by the House of Lords, the Court of Appeal, the Chancery, Q.B. and Family Divisions of the High Court of Justice. From these cases are selected those for publication in the *Law Reports.*

Other References

The Council of Law Reporting has published a *Consolidated Index*, based on the *Law Reports*, the *Weekly Law Reports* and the *Restrictive Practices Reports* which incorporates references for all series of reports including *All England Law Reports, Criminal Appeal Reports, Lloyd's Law Reports* and other special reports, e.g., *Tax cases*.

A Table of Subject Matter covers all cases reported in the *Law Reports*, the *Weekly Law Reports* and includes references to most cases appearing exclusively in the specialist reports.

It also features indexes for cases, statutes, statutory instruments, etc.

Weekly Updating

There is a basic *Consolidated Index* (1951–1960) and a supplement (1961–1970). These are brought up to date weekly in the *Weekly Law Reports*, supplemented by periodic "pink books" and by "red books" in which the Index from Jan. 1, 1971, will be consolidated anew at the end of each year.

A *Consolidated Index* for the period 1971 to 1979 has recently been published. This *Index*, used with the two volumes of the Law Reports Index covering the years 1951 to 1970, provides references to any reported case since 1950, arranged by title or subject matter with cross references, when necessary.

The *Index* also contains tables of cases, statutes, statutory instruments and overseas enactments judicially considered. Thus, if in any reports covered by this *Index*, a judge has said anything which might be argued to affect the weight or effect of any previous decision or the meaning of any enactment, a reference will be found in the appropriate table to the previous decision or enactment. The Table of Cases Judicially considered is not limited to decisions mentioned in the headnote of the reports.

In addition to the cases reported in the *Law Reports*, the *Weekly Law Reports*, the *Industrial Cases Reports* and the *Restrictive Practices Reports*, the *Index* includes cases reported in: *All England Law Reports, Lloyd's Law Reports, Tax Cases* and *Tax Case Leaflets, Local Government Reports, Knight's Industrial Reports, Criminal Appeal Reports* and *Road Traffic Reports*.

The *Law Reports* caused the demise of many sets of reports, although some of the well-established reports continued in competition with the *Law Reports*. They were:

Law Journal Reports (1822–1949); *Law Times Reports* (1843–1858); *Law Times Reports New Series* (1859–1947); *Times Law Reports* (1884–1952), absorbed by the *Weekly Law Reports* in 1953.

The All England Law Reports, Annotated (1936–date) appears weekly and reports cases decided in the House of Lords, the Privy Council, the Divisional Courts and the Courts of Special Jurisdiction. The *All England Law Reports* reports more than twice as many cases as the *Law Reports*, approximately 800 annually as compared to about 300 in the *Law Reports*. Cross-references are noted from the cases reported to appropriate sections of *Halsbury's Laws of England, Halsbury's Statutes of England* for legislation and to the *English and Empire Digest* for other cases in point. As arguments of counsel are not published, the case reports are shorter than those in the *Law Reports.*

Cumulative Table

Each weekly issue contains a cumulative table of cases for the year to date and a table which "notes up" or shepardizes cases and statutes referred to in the decisions.

An annual Index and Notes-*Up* cumulate these tables, covering all reported cases and statutes from 1936 to date.

The *All England Law Reports Reprint* (1558–1935) 36v. is reprinting, working backwards from 1935, selected "living cases." A "living case" is one which has been referred to twice or more in the *All England Law Reports* since 1936, as well as a number of other cases less frequently referred to but of use to practising attorneys. The cases reprinted for the period from 1843 to 1935 have been selected from the *Law Times Reports* and are revised and annotated. An *Index* to *All England Law Reports Reprint*, for the period from 1558 to 1935 lists these cases by subject and alphabetically.

Obviously, there is a need for those additional publications featuring law reports as the *Weekly Law Reports* and the *Law Reports* are so selective in the cases they report. Reference to the *All England Law Reports* and the *Law Journal Reports*, the *Law Times Report*, and the *Times Law Reports*, for the period they covered, may locate a report of most cases decided in a superior court. Although these reports are not official nor revised by the judges before publication, still they are considered as "accredited" by the courts for citation if the report of the case is signed by a reputable barrister.

In addition to the above, there are a number of specialized reports, such as *Butterworth's Compensation Cases, Lloyd's List Reports* (Admiralty and Insurance Cases) (1919–date) *Cox's Criminal Cases* (1843–1941), *Criminal Appeal Reports* (1908–date), as well as others in bankruptcy, copyright, patents and other subjects. Brief reports of selected cases are also published in the *Solicitors' Journal* (1975–date).

Digests

What the West American Digest system attempts to do for American case law, the English and Empire Digest seeks to do for English case law. Its subtitle reads "A complete digest of every English case . . . with additional cases from the courts of Scotland, Ireland, the Empire of India and the dominions beyond the seas." Publication of the set began in 1919 and finished in 1932. It was kept up to date by annual cumulative supplements. By 1950 there were so many accumulated supplements that it became awkward to use as a set. In 1950, the publishers began to issue replacement volumes for the fifty-six original volumes of the set. The original volumes with red bands were replaced with volumes with blue bands at the rate of four volumes a year.

As these replacement volumes required revision themselves, after a period of time, due to the great number of new cases, they too are being slowly replaced by volumes with green bands on their spine. They are referred to as "22 Digest (Reissue)." Thus, the Green Band volume is an up to date and comprehensively revised version of the Blue Band volume it replaces. Some of the reissue volumes are Husband and Wife (v. 27), Evidence (v. 22), Income Tax (v. 28), Landlord and Tenant (v. 31), Custom and Usage (v. 17) and Intoxicating Liquor (v. 30).

Chronological Grouping

The English and Empire Digest classifies all the cases digested under 164 main topics and many sub-topics; arranged alphabetically following the arrangement of titles adopted for *Halsbury's Laws of England*. Cases digested under a topic are generally grouped in chronological order and assigned case numbers. Actually, each paragraph digest indicates the holding of the case digested rather than giving a point in the case such as is brought out in the American Digest System. As a case is digested in only one place under the assigned case number and as all digest paragraphs are numbered consecutively for each separate topic, every case is separately identified by its number. In other words, the number is not a classification number covering all cases of similar import as in the West American Digest System.

Every case digested is cited to all the reports of the case. Following the digest is an "annotation" which refers to other cases which have commented on, or construed the digested case. This is very much like Shepardizing the case and is called "noting up."

The annual cumulative supplements and the reissue volumes keep this information current by referring to the serial numbers originally assigned to the case. References are also given to relevant parts of *Halsbury's Laws of England* and *Halsbury's Statutes of England* where the case involved and like cases, as well as statutes, are discussed. Reference to dominion or colonial cases in point are also given.

The *English and Empire Digest* may be searched for citations through the topic analysis for each topic, the Fact Index and its Table of Cases. Every volume contains its own Table of Cases and Index and there is a Consolidated Table of Cases and Comprehensive Index covering the whole work.

Mews Digest of English Case Law. 2d ed. (1924) consists of twenty-four volumes with ten-year cumulative and annual supplements since 1946. It is a digest of selected older English cases and all recent cases, arranged topically. Volume 23 features an Index of Cases Judicially noticed, which serves as a citator and a Table of Statutes Judicially considered. These are kept up to date in annual supplements. A Table of Cases is given in volume 24.

Current Law

Subtitled "all the law from every source," issued monthly and cumulated into annual volumes, *Current Law* digests cases, statutes and administrative regulations and cases continuing them under approximately 200 Main Topics alphabetically arranged. There is a separate Scottish edition. Articles in legal and related journals are noted under their proper headings in the monthly parts and a list of new books appears inside the back cover. A classified list of books and articles published during the year appears at the back of Year Book. The subject index to the monthly parts is cumulative. The case citator in the monthly parts is cumulative too. It gives the researcher, all decided cases of the year and all cases judicially considered. The Case Citator issued with the Year Book is cumulative back to 1948.

It gives full contemporaneous references to all cases reported from 1948 to date and all cases (of whatever date) judicially considered or overruled by statute since 1948. The Statute Citator, which appears in the parts of Current Law Statutes issued during the year shows (1) all Acts passed during the year, (2) all acts (of whatever date) amended or repealed during the year, (3) all rules, orders and regulations made under statutory owers and (4) all cases construing statutes. The Statute Citator which is issued with the Year Book gives everything mentioned above cumulated from 1948 to date. Paragraph members are assigned to each case digest for easy identification.

CHAPTER 4

LAW REPORTING IN NEW YORK

Lawyers all over the country turn to New York for precedents. Many have a New York library in addition to a library representing law from their own states. The recent announcement of the New York State Reporter of Decisions awarding the contract for publication of New York official reports to the Lenz-Reicker Publishing Co. and the changes in contents and style of the *New York Supplement* bring to mind that law reporting in New York over the years reflects not only the changing judicial system of the state but also the evolving development of the common law. An understanding of this background can be helpful to the lawyer concerned with New York decisional authority.

Kent's Lament

Attorneys practicing in the early nineteenth century in New York faced almost insuperable barriers in finding case law. We are indebted to Chancellor James Kent's revealing comments on law reporting of his day to appreciate the extent of the problems involved.

> "In 1814, I was appointed Chancellor," he wrote in his memoirs, "The office I took with considerable reluctance. It had no charms. The person who left it was stupid, and it is a curious fact that for nine years I was in that office there was not a single decision, opinion, or dictum of either of my two predecessors (Ch. Livingston and Ch. Lansing), for 1774 to 1814, cited to me or ever suggested. I took the court as if it had been a new institution and never before known in the U.S. I had

nothing to guide me, and was left at liberty to assume all such English Chancery powers and jurisdiction as I thought applicable under our Constitution. This gave me a grand scope, and I was checked only by the revision of the Senate, or Court of Errors... The result appears in the seven volumes of Johnson's Chancery Reports" (1814–1823).

It should be noted in this context that English common law received early recognition in New York. One obvious reason, of course, for this development was that as a colony New York was under royal authority practically from its inception and the officials of the government applied common law principles to legal matters whenever necessary. As a result, New York became a leader in adapting common law principles to the American juristic scene. Its judges, as Reinisch noted, "became the authoritative expounders of the American form of Common Law."

But on the other hand, as Reinisch explains, "many of the original American ideas in jurisprudence, such as the reform of the law of real property and the law of pleading, which we find in germ in the early history of the other colonies, were carried to completion and given their lasting form in the state of New York, whose jurists had profited from a longer training in a regular system of jurisprudence."

17th Century Courts

In the latter part of the seventeenth century the New York courts of justice were as follows: (1) A court of Chancery, composed of the governor and council, which was the Supreme Court of Appeals; (2) the courts of Oyer and Terminer held annually in each county; (3) the Court of the Mayor and Alderman in New York City; (4) the courts of session (justices of the peace); (5) court commissioners for petty cases; (6) a Court of Adjudicature, a special court established to hear land cases. The laws in force were the *Duke of York's Laws* promulgated in 1665, the acts of the general assembly, and the Common Law as received from England.

In essence, the reception of Common Law in New York was similar in effect to what was expressed by Mr. Justice Story in *Van Ness v. Pacard*, 27 U.S. (2 Pet.) 137, 144, 7 L.Ed. 374 (1829).

"The Common Law of England is not to be taken in all respects to be that of America. Our ancestors brought with them its general principles and claimed it as their birth-right but they brought with them and adopted only that portion which was applicable to their situation."

The New York lawyer after the Revolution, seeking law in the books had little to resort to. Even in England, down to the time of the Commonwealth, there were only about fifteen volumes of reports, other than the *Year Books*, English lawyers could use as authority. Most important of these fifteen were *Plowden* which covered reported cases from Edward III to Elizabeth (1350–1580) and *Lord Coke's Reports* which covered the reigns of Elizabeth and James.

Valuable Commentaries

Of particular value to lawyers was Coke's commentaries on these cases, often approaching a treatise on the point at issue. The others were *Dyer, Keilway, Benlow, Dolison, Davies, Hobart, & Bellevue*. According to Warren, these few reports together with a small number of authoritative reports published in the reign of Charles II, *Croke, Leonard, Yelverton, Rolle, W. Jones, Vaughan,* and *Sanders*, were practically the only reports known in the American colonies and substantially the only ones with any authority as law in England. For the 18th Century, *Lord Raymond's Reports*, covering Lord Mansfield's decisions, were also considered authoritative.

Thus, when Kent became Chancellor of New York in 1814, he had few English reports he could use as authority, and there was an even greater scarcity of New York reports. The principles of Equity developed in England were so vague that Selden spoke of it as "Roguish Equity."

In his Table Talk (1686) Selden wrote: "Equity in law is the same that the spirit is in Religion, what everyone pleases to make it. Sometimes they go according to Conscience, sometimes according to Law, sometimes according to the Rule of Court... Equity is a Roguish thing: for the Conscience of him that is Chancellor, and as that is larger or narrower, so is Equity 'Tis all one as if they should make the standard for the measure we call a Foot, to be the Chancellor's Foot; what an uncertain Measure would be this; One Chancellor has a long Foot, another a short Foot, a third an indifferent Foot: Tis the same thing in the Chancellor's Conscience.'"

As Equity was administered according to the "Conscience" of the Chancellor, there was little reason to publish the Chancellor's decisions. About all the reports Kent could depend on for precedents in Chancery were *Peere Williams* (1695–1735), *Atkyns, Vesey, Sr.* and *Ambler* (included the decisions of Lord Hardwicke, 1736–1756) and *Cox* and *Vesey, Jr.* (decisions of Earl Camden and of Lord Thurlow).

Few Volumes Available

Warren has concluded that as late as 1776 hardly more than 150 volumes of reports were in existence and probably not more than one-half of these could be found in the colonies. Only about thirty were used to any extent by lawyers in America. Except for *Blackstone's Commentaries*, there were not even American reprints of Coke or any standard English legal text, or for that matter, of any English law reports.

The first reports in New York were published by *Coleman* in 1801. *Coleman's Cases* contain reports of practice cases decided in the Supreme Court of New York from 1794 to 1800. The first official reports of New York decisions published by state authority was *Caines' Reports*. They contain cases decided in the Supreme Court from May 1803 to November 1805. They were also known later as the *New York Term Reports*. Caines was the first official New York court reporter. Prior to Caines there were no regular reports of the Supreme Court, although cases decided prior to Caines were collected later and published in *Johnson's Cases* (3 vols. 1799–1803). *Johnson's Reports* (1806–1823, 20 vols.) are noted for containing the decisions of James Kent when he sat in the Supreme Court of the State of New York. These reports also contain reports of cases in the *Court of Errors of New York.*

Filing System Introduced

The system of filing written opinions was introduced in New York by Kent. In his *Memoirs*, he wrote:

> "When I came to the Bench (1798), there were no reports or state precedents. The opinions from the Bench were delivered *ore tenus*. We had no law of our own and nobody knew what it was. I first introduced a thorough examination of cases and written opinions. In January 1799, the second case reported in I, Johnson's Cases of *Ludlow v. Dale*, is a sample of the earliest. The judges, when we met, all assumed that foreign sentences were only good *prima facie*. I presented and read my written opinion that they were, and they all gave up to me, and so I read it in court as it stands."

In this context, another interesting comment of Kent in his *Memoirs* deserves quoting:

> "I gradually acquired preponderating influence with my brethren, and the volumes in *Johnson*, after I became Chief Justice in 1804, show it. The first practice was for each judge to give his portion of opinions, when we all agreed, but that gradually fell off, and for the last two or three years before I left the Bench, I gave the most of them. I remember that in eighth Johnson all the opinions for one term are 'per curiam.' The fact is, I wrote them all and proposed that course to avoid exciting jealousy, and many a per curiam opinion was so inserted for that reason."

Court of Errors

The New York judicial system, early in the nineteenth century, closely resembled that of England. The highest court of the state was actually the upper house of the state legislature, such as the highest court in England was the House of Lords. The first Constitution of New York, adopted in 1777, provided for "The Court for the Trial of Impeachments and Correction of Errors" which became known as the "Court of Errors." In 1784, an act of the Legislature established this Court and it remained in existence until 1846 when it was abolished by the Constitution then adopted, and its powers transferred to the Court of Appeals created thereby. The Court of Errors consisted of the President of the Senate, the Senators, the Chancellors and the judges of the Supreme Court. The Chancellor and the judges were allowed to explain their decisions made below, but were not permitted to vote. By writ of error, the Court had jurisdiction to review the judgments of the Supreme Court, and on appeal decrees and decretal orders of the Court of Chancery.

As a court of last resort, this "senatorial court," consisting primarily of laymen, was resented by the Bar and the judiciary. Chancellor Kent noted bitterly in a letter to William Johnson, the official reporter after Caines, "I am discouraged and heartbroken. The judges have prevailed on the Court of Errors to reverse all my best decisions. They have reversed *Frost v. Beekman*, the *Methodist Episcopal Church v. Jacques, Anderson v. Boyd*, and others. After such devastation what courage ought I have to study and write elaborate opinions? I have never felt more disgusted with the judges in all my life, and I expressed myself to Judge Platt in a way to mortify and offend him. According to my present feelings and sentiments, I will never consent to publish another opinion, and I have taken and removed out of sight and out of my office into another room my three volumes of Chancery Reports. They were too fearful when standing before my eyes."

Despite this resentment, the Court of Errors' decisions were final, and were subject only to appeal to the Supreme Court of the United States. They still control today, unless they have been overruled by the Court of Appeals. After 1846, the Senate retained that part of its judicial power pertaining to impeachments. Today, together with the judges of the Court of Appeals, it constitutes the Court for the Trial of Impeachments.

The decisions of the Court of Errors can be found with the decisions of the Supreme Court in *Caines' Cases* (1796–1805, 2 vols.), *Caines' Reports* (1803–1805), *Johnson's Cases* (1796–1803, 3 vols.). *Johnson's Reports* (1806–1823, 20 vols.), *Cowen's Reports* (1823–1829, 9 vols.), *Wendell's Reports* (1828–1841, 20 vols.), *Hill's Reports* (1841–1844, 7 vols.), and *Denio's Reports* (1845–1848, 5 vols.).

Law and Equity

Similarly, as in England, Law and Equity were separately adjudicated in New York. As in England, the Court of Chancery had jurisdiction in matters involving equitable principles. At first, the governors of the colony exercised what was called an equity jurisprudence and attempted to give equitable relief. By the late 17th century, however, confusion existed in New York as to the role of equity to law. Contemporary records disclose that an appeal to equity was allowed even after a suit at law.

By 1727, a Court of Chancery was established, for there is a record of the Assembly objecting to its creation without its consent. The New York Constitution of 1777 recognized the Court of Chancery as an existing court with equitable jurisdiction, and the Court of Chancery then continued to exercise its jurisdiction until it was abolished by the 1846 Constitution. The 1846 Constitution merged equity and law by transferring the jurisdiction of the Chancery Court to the Supreme Court. Prior thereto the Constitution of 1822 authorized the eight circuit judges of the State to act as Vice Chancellor in their circuits.

In 1831, the volume of business was so great in the First Circuit, which encompassed New York City, that a separate Vice Chancellorship was created and the equitable jurisdiction of the circuit judge was transferred to a Vice Chancellor. In 1839 an assistant Vice Chancellor was created in addition for New York City, and for Rochester in the Eighth Circuit. Appeals were allowed to the *Chancellor* from decrees of the Vice Chancellor and thence to the *Court of Errors*. The reports of decisions of the Chancellor can be found in *Johnson's Chancery Reports* (1814–1823, 7 vols.), *Hopkins' Chancery Reports* (1823–1826, 1 vol.), *Paige's Chancery Reports* (1826–1845), 11 vols.) and *Barbour's Chancery* (1845–1848, 3 vols.).

The reports of decisions of the Vice Chancellors and the Assistant Vice Chancellors appeared in *Edwards' Chancery Reports* (1831–1850, 4 vols.), *Clarke's Chancery Reports* (1839–1841, 1 vol.), *Hoffman's Chancery Reports* (1839–1840, 1 vol.), and *Sandford's Chancery Reports* (1843–1847, 4 vols.).

State Court History

When James Kent became Chief Justice of the Supreme Court of the State of New York in 1804, that court could trace its history back to an act of The Provincial Assembly in 1691. The New York Constitution adopted in 1777 provided for its continuance and for the appointment and tenure of its judges. At that time, the court was composed of a chief justice and four associate justices, called "puisne" justices. These judges had to hold circuit courts throughout the state and courts of Oyer and Terminer for more serious crimes, in addition to sitting *en banc* as an appellate court.

The 1821 New York Constitution reduced the number of justices to three, a Chief Justice and two associate justices, and provided for separate circuit judges to sit in eight new judicial districts. These circuit judges not only took over the functions of the Supreme Court justices in the circuits but also were authorized to try causes in equity as vice chancellors. Appeal from their decisions at law could be taken to the Supreme Court *en banc*. Their jurisdiction was similar to the present Appellate Division of the Supreme Court. This was the organization of the Supreme Court until it was changed by the Constitution of 1846.

After 1846 the state was redivided into eight judicial districts for which there was one Supreme Court having general jurisdiction in law and equity. In 1870, the Supreme Court was reorganized again, with the State being divided into four departments as the Appellate Divisions of the Supreme Court a number of courts that had been functioning independently such as the Superior Court of the City of New York, the Court of Common Pleas for the City & Country of New York, the Superior Court of Buffalo, the City Court of Brooklyn, and the Circuit Court and Courts of Oyer and Terminer, and vested all their jurisdiction in the Supreme Court.

As indicated above, the first official reporter for the Supreme Court was Caines. (*Caines' Reports*, 1803–1805, 3 vols.). *He was followed in a regular series by Johnson* (*Johnson's Reports*, 1806–1823, 20 vols.), Cowen (*Cowen's Reports*, 1823–1829, 9 vols.), Wendell (*Wendell's Reports*, 1828–1841, 26 vols.), Hill (*Hill's Reports*, 1841–1844, 7 vols.), and Denio (*Denio's Reports*, 1845–1848, 5 vols.).

When the Supreme Court was reorganized under the 1846 Constitution, decisions of the courts in the districts were unofficially reported in *Barbour's Supreme Court Reports* (1847–1877, 67 vols.) *Lansing's Reports* (1869–1873, 7 vols.) *were published concurrently with Barbour's Reports*. Lansing was an official reporter but selective in his reporting, and *Barbour* should be used to locate Supreme Court cases not reported in *Lansing's Reports*. Lansing was continued by *Hun's Supreme Court Reports* (1874–1895, 92 vols.). *Barbour* was followed by *Thompson and Cook's Supreme Court Reports* (1874–1875, 6 vols.). Beginning with the organization of the Appellate Division of the Supreme Court in 1895, its decisions have been reported as the *Appellate Division Reports*.

The New York Constitution of 1846 and implementing legislation (Judiciary Act of 1847), N.Y.Law 1847, c. 280 and the Code of Procedure, N.Y.Laws 1848, c. 379 (Field Code) considerably changed the organization and jurisdiction of the courts of the state. As indicated in Part I of this article, the 1846 Constitution abolished the Court of Errors and the Court of Chancery, substituting in place thereof, a new Court of Appeals. The Supreme Court of New York was reorganized and its jurisdiction changed along with a number of other courts, such as the New York City Superior Court, County Courts, the Surrogate Courts and the Courts of Session held by a county judge and two Justices of the Peace.

Begun in 1847

Law Reporting in New York thereafter reflected these changes. By authority of N.Y.Laws 1847, c. 277 and N.Y.Laws 1848, c. 224 (under the N.Y.Constitution 1846, Art. VI, Section 22), the publication of the *New York Reports* to cover the cases decided by the New York Court of Appeals was commenced in 1847. The reporter for this series was designated the State Reporter, but rather than being appointed by the court, he was appointed by the Governor and Lieutenant Governor for three year terms. The *New York Reports* became the first of a continuing official series of state-wide reports. The citation form for the *New York Reports* at first was: 1–4 N.Y. (Comst.), 5–10 N.Y. (Seld.), 11–14 N.Y.

(Kern). From volume 15 on, all the reports were brought into one series and are now cited *N. Y.*

Unofficially, the decisions and opinions of the Court of Appeals have also been reported in *North Eastern Reporter*, also a continuing publication, beginning with 99 N.Y. 1 (1885), together with the opinions of the Courts of last resort of four other states (Mass., Ohio, Illinois and Indiana). Then again in 1888, the *New York Supplement* began publishing decisions of New York Courts. Commencing with volume 183 N.Y.Supplement, all the new opinions of the Court of Appeals are included.

As indicated above, the New York City Superior Court was changed considerably by the 1846 Constitution and ensuing legislation. The Superior Court had initially been created by statute in 1828 to relieve the Supreme Court and Court of Common Pleas of the great number of cases pending before them. Its jurisdiction was similar to that of the Supreme Court, and it also heard appeals from the judgments of the Marine Court. Later, however, this appellate jurisdiction was transferred to the Court of Common Pleas. The Superior Court then consisted of a chief Justice and two associates who were all appointed by the Governor. Its decisions were reviewable on writ of error by the Supreme Court.

Changed by Charter

The 1846 Constitution radically changed all this. The number of Justices was increased to six and they were to be elected by citizens residing in New York City. Its jurisdiction was limited to New York City residents, corporations doing business in New York City, and matters in litigation which were local in nature. The Court was divided into Special Terms and General Terms. The Special Terms tried issues of fact and issues of law were appealable to three of the Justices sitting in General Terms. In turn, these were appealable to the Court of Appeals. The Constitution of 1894 abolished the Superior Court and its jurisdiction was transferred to the Supreme Court.

Hall's Superior Court Reports covered the decisions of the Superior Court from 1828 to the end of 1829. Thereafter, from 1829 to 1847, no other reports were published for this court. In 1847, *Sandford's Superior Court Reports* (five volumes, also cited as 3–7 N.Y.Superior Court) published the Court's decisions until 1852. A number of the Superior Court decisions especially those pertaining to practice, can be found in other reporters of the day. *Duer's Superior Court Reports* continued reporting Superior Court decisions from 1852 to 1857 in six volumes. In turn, *Duer* was continued by *Bosworth's Superior Court Reports* in ten volumes for the period until 1863.

Robertson's Superior Court Reports in seven volumes covered the period 1863 to 1868, and in turn, *Sweeny's Superior Court Reports* in two volumes continued reporting decisions of this court by its official reporter from 1869 to 1872. The official reporter's reports of Superior Court cases were continued from 1871 to 1892 in twenty-nine volumes in *Jones and Spencer's Superior Court Reports*. These volumes are also cited as 33 to 61 N.Y.Superior Court cases.

"Worshipful Court"

The New York City Court of Common Pleas was originally known in 1653 as "The Worshipful Court of the Schout, Burgomaster and Scheppens." With the English conquest, this court's name was changed to the Mayor's Court in 1665. It was not until 1821 that the name of the Mayor's Court was changed to the Court of Common Pleas. Until 1847, New York City aldermen sat on this court, and it has been noted that the first judge of the court was John E. Irving, a brother of Washington Irving.

The New York City Court of Common Pleas was organized in special and general terms similar to the manner in which the Supreme Court transacted its business. Until 1810, three judges sat in the court, and thereafter six judges. After the adoption of the 1846 Constitution, this court had equitable as well as law jurisdiction and unlimited jurisdiction over New York City whether by process or subject matter.

Special Term decisions were appealable to the General Term en banc and thereafter were reviewable by the Court of Appeals. The Court of Common Pleas also reviewed judgments of the Marine Court (general jurisdiction up to $500, also cases involving assault and battery, false imprisonment and libel and slander) and its judgments were final in these appeals. The 1894 Constitution abolished the Court of Common Pleas and its jurisdiction was transferred to the Supreme Court.

Common Pleas Reports

The reports of the Court of Common Pleas were published under official authority from 1850 to 1856 by *E.D. Smith's Common Pleas Reports* in four volumes. The first volume contains a history of the Court and the judicial organization of the State. E.D. Smith was appointed by the Court as its official reporter. *Hilton's Common Pleas Reports* continued the official reportory of the Court's decisions in two volumes, from 1885 to 1860. In turn, these were followed by *Daly's Common Pleas Reports* in sixteen volumes of selected cases decided by the Court from 1859 to 1891. Practically all of these reported cases are unavailable elsewhere.

Occasionally, a number of contemporary legal periodicals which published reports of cases decided in the New York Courts, are cited. The *New York Daily Transcript* covered the period from 1859 to 1872. This periodical was continued by the *Daily Register* which became the official law journal of the City and County of New York for the period 1872 to 1889. Its successor, the *New York Law Journal* has continued to this date serving that purpose.

Some practice and procedure reports, unofficially reported, also appeared in the period from 1860 to 1890, which duplicated many of the officially reported cases.

Many changes in the New York Court system took place by reason of the Judiciary amendment of 1869 to the N.Y. State Constitution, such as the creation of the present Court of Appeals and the beginnings of the Appellate Division of the Supreme Court can be traced to it as well, the present state judicial system, however, took on much of its present form with the adoption of the Constitution of 1894. With the Court of Appeals already established, one of the most important provisions of the 1894 Constitution created the Appellate Division of the Supreme Court of New York as of Jan. 1, 1896. To it was transferred the jurisdiction exercised by the Supreme Court at its General Terms, and by the General Terms of the Court of Common Pleas, the Superior Court of the City of New York and Buffalo and the City Court of Brooklyn. Now there is an Appellate Division of the Supreme Court in each of the four judicial departments of the State.

Judges to Justices

The judges of the abolished courts were made Supreme Court justices and all actions and proceedings in those courts were transferred to the Supreme Court. An Appellate Term of the Supreme Court was also established to hear appeals from the lower New York City courts, a function previously exercised by the General Terms of the courts abolished by the 1894 Constitution. About fifteen years later, a similar Appellate Term was established in the second department.

Until 1962, twenty-one different types of courts existed under the New York State Court System. Based on the 1961 Constitutional Amendment (Article VI, the Judiciary article of the N.Y. State Constitution, twenty-two acts implementing the Reorganization Amendment were approved by the Governor on April 24, 1962, effective Sept. 1, 1962. About the same time, a new Civil Practice Law and Rules was passed effective Sept. 1, 1963, which revised practice and procedure in the new court.

The following Courts now exist in New York.

- Court of Appeals.
- Appellate Division of the Supreme Court (*Four Departments: Cases are appealed* from: Supreme Court 1st Dist. to Appellate Division, 1st Dept.; Supreme Court, 2nd, 9th, 10th, 11th Dists. to Appellate Division, 2nd Dept.; Supreme Court, 3rd, 4th, 6th Dists. to Appellate Division, 3rd Dept.; Supreme Court, 5th, 7th, 8th Dists. to Appellate Division, 4th Dept.).
- Appellate Term of the Supreme Court (First and Second Departments).
- Supreme Court (eleven districts).
- Court of Claims.
- County Courts (fifty-seven counties).
- Surrogates Courts (sixty-two counties).
- New York City Court of Criminal Jurisdiction.

- New York City Court of Civil Jurisdiction.
- Family Court of the State of New York (fifty-seven counties and N.Y.C.).
- District Courts of Nassau and Suffolk Counties.
- Town Courts.
- Villages and City Justice Courts.
- Local Inferior Courts.
- Court for the Trial of Impeachments.
- Court on the Judiciary.
- Peacemaker Courts (certain Indian Reservations).

State Reporter's Job

Today all the opinions and decisions of the Court of Appeals and the Appellate Division of the Supreme Court of New York are officially edited by the State Reporter and published in accordance with the state's Judiciary Law. As indicated above, the Court of Appeals' cases have been officially and continuously reported in the *New York Reports* since 1847. The cases of the Appellate Division have been officially and continuously reported in the *Appellate Division Reports* since 1896. The reports of cases of courts of lesser jurisdiction, as well as those of the appellate term, have been officially and continuously reported in the *Miscellaneous Reports* since 1892.

Unofficially, the *New York Supplement*, which began in 1888, and has been published continuously since then, has reported cases decided by all the courts of the state. In essence, therefore, all the cases that can be found in the official reports of the state are also available through the *New York Supplement since 1888. Beginning with volume 42 of the N. Y. Supplement*, it contains the *New York State Reporter* from volume 75 and beginning with volume 183 of the *New York Supplement*, it reports all the cases decided by the Court of Appeals. By reason of a peculiar history, the *New York Supplement* also contains reports of cases decided by lower New York State Courts which were not published in the *Miscellaneous Reports*.

The *Miscellaneous Reports* were a response to a felt need around 1892 for better reporting of decisions of "Courts of first instance" and local appellate courts. Pursuant to N.Y.Laws 1892, c. 598, an official reporter of *Miscellaneous Reports* was authorized. The *Miscellaneous* Reporter was directed to publish every opinion "involving a question of law concurred in by a majority of the court in the general terms" of the Superior Courts of New York City and Buffalo, of the Brooklyn City Court and of the New York City Court of Common Pleas, the City Court of the City of New York, along with such other opinions of the Lower "Courts of Record" as he deemed in the public interest to publish. An observer has noted that "this provision must have been troublesome in view of the price-fixing section setting a maximum price (then) of $2.50 per volume of not less than 500 pages." Thus the *Miscellaneous Reports* became a compilation of selected law reports.

Awkward Situations

Up until the late 1950's, the editorial policy of the State Reporter to cite only to the official *New York Reports* and never to the *New York Supplement* created some awkward situations in connection with the *Miscellaneous Reports*, not only for the State Reporter but for the New York Bar as well. As indicated above, the *Miscellaneous Reports*, by law, is a selective reporter of lower N.Y. Court Cases. The *New York Supplement*, however, published a number of opinions which it deemed warranted publication but which were not selected by the State Reporter for publication in the *Miscellaneous Reports*. As a result, when a judge writing an opinion subsequent in time to the publication of a case only in the *New York Supplement* and not in the *Miscellaneous Reports*, cited that case as authority, the State Reporter was confronted with the problem of identifying that case without citing where it appeared in the *New York Supplement*. The only effective solution available to the State Reporter under the circumstances, which nevertheless created unnecessary difficulties, was to publish that earlier case in a current *Miscellaneous Reports* volume and then to cite to the *Miscellaneous Reports* volume and page number, even though a number of years could have elapsed since the date of that decision.

Davis v. Young, for example, decided by the Appellate Term 1st Department on May 24, 1910, and published in 123 N.Y.S.

363 (1910) was not published in the *Miscellaneous Reports* until 1958 in 9 Misc.2d 209. The *Seagram Distillers Corp. v. Seyopp Corp.,* decided by the N.Y. Supreme Court on Jan. 13, 1938, was first published by the official reporter in 1958, twenty years later in 8 Misc.2d 778 (1958) although it had been published in 2 N.Y.S.2d 550 in March 1938. Similarly, *Fitzsimmons v. N.Y.S. Athletic Comm.*, a 1914 case, reported in 146 N.Y.S. 117 (1914) and affirmed in 162 App.Div. 904, 147 N.Y.S. 111, and cited and quoted extensively in a 1959 Court of Appeals Case (*Rosenweig v. State of New York*, 5 N.Y.2d 404, 185 N.Y.S.2d 521, 158 N.E.2d 229), was first published forty-five years later in the *Miscellaneous Reports* in 15 Misc.2d 831 (1959). A great number of other lower court opinions have thus been published later in time in the *Miscellaneous Reports*—at least three cases, eighteen years later, seven cases, sixteen years later, eleven cases, thirteen years later, fifteen cases, ten years later, thirty-two cases, five years later and forty-six cases, two years later. Since the late 1950's, the editorial board of the *New York Supplement* has been constrained to limit its coverage of reporting to cases selected by the official State Reporter for publication in the official reports.

Accurate Service

Over the years, the official New York reports have provided the Bar with court decisions and opinions accurately edited and within a reasonable period of time. In essence, however, they are merely reports of New York State Court decisions. The *New York Supplement*, however, in addition to reporting these same court decisions promptly and accurately also offers many other features which are becoming of increasing value in legal research. In fact, the *New York Supplement* has not only given a "new look" to its advance sheet pamphlets, but as a result of a survey its editorial board has taken of New York lawyers, it now provides not only all the cases to be found in the official reports but also a valuable legal reference and resource service.

In addition to making readily accessible all federal and state cases in print through its topic and key number system, it is also providing developments of interest to New York lawyers. Under a section entitled "In This Issue," a summary of all cases reported by New York Courts is alphabetically arranged for quick reference. Another regular feature of the *New York Supplement* is an index and brief description of law review articles on New York law of interest to specialists in the field. Also featured is a section which reprints commentaries and special articles of practical value to New York lawyers. In recent issues, for example, there were articles published on *The New York Taxpayer and His Accounting Procedures, The Individual Assignment System in the Southern District of New York*, and *The Strict Liability Cause of Action in New York.*

Legislative News

Now that the official reporter has discontinued the publication of current New York State enactments, the *New York Supplement* is featuring a column entitled "Albany News Letter" which provides state legislative news on a regular basis while the Legislature is in session, so that the New York lawyer can be apprised of statutory changes as they occur.

It appears that the editors of the *New York Supplement* are making a serious effort to improve it, and it is becoming more than a reporting service of New York Cases. In a sense, it is becoming a "law weekly," retaining those features which have been characteristic of West reporters such as Key Number Digests, Words & Phrases, Judicial Highlights, American Bar Association Standards for Criminal Justice and Court Requirements. Other new features, for example, recently announced for advance sheet pamphlets, should also be welcomed by the New York lawyer. They will include opinions of the Attorney General, formal and informal, opinions of the Comptroller, Judicial Decisions of the Commissioner of Education and formal opinions of Counsel and opinions of Counsel for the State Board of Equalization and Assessment.

Obviously, the *New York Supplement* will play a valuable role as a research tool for the New York Bar if it continues to develop this "law weekly" concept.

B: STATUTES

CHAPTER 5

FEDERAL LEGISLATIVE HISTORY

I

"We do not inquire what the legislature meant: we ask only what the statute means." Justice Holmes[1]

Those words, uttered toward the close of the last century, recite the central fact about the construction of statutes. But like other Delphic oracles, Holmes leaves something to the imagination.

What legislative history can contribute to the meaning of statutes is the subject of this chapter: what legislative history is, where it is published and how to find it.

Anatomy of History

Legislative history consists of all the documents pertaining to a bill that were put before the legislators prior to a vote. These documents include the successive versions of a bill or amendments to it and the numbered House and Senate reports on the bill. Sometimes, but not invariably, courts will turn to additional records as legitimate legislative history. These include presidential messages, transcripts of hearings, floor debates, unnumbered committee prints and other more extrinsic papers discussed below.

Justice Douglas, speaking for the majority of the United States Supreme Court, observed:

"In construing laws we have been extremely wary of testimony before committee hearings and of debates on the floor of Congress

[1] "The Theory of Legal Interpretation," 12 Harv. L. Rev. 417 (1899).

save for precise analyses of statutory phrases by the sponsors of the proposed laws."[2]

Indeed few Congressmen ever see transcripts of hearings before a vote is taken. In many cases the transcripts are neither printed nor distributed before the vote. Nor do Congressmen have time to read the hundreds of thousands of pages of committee testimony that cross their desks in a single session.

Unreliable Source

The daily issues of the *Congressional Record* are an unreliable source of the words spoken on the floor because each Congressman has the privilege of revising his remarks. Moreover, attendance at Congressional sessions is imperfect and sometimes not everyone listens.

One of William Gropper's paintings of the United States Senate in the 1930's showed four members on the floor. One senator was conducting a filibuster. One was poring over the sports results in his newspaper. A third was counting his fingers. The fourth senator appeared to be in a catatonic trance. There were ninety-two empty seats. Unfair "invective"? Probably. Yet Gropper's painting is a reminder that the Committee system and the federal agencies have taken over most of the work of congressional bill drafting. It is chiefly the reports of committees that the courts turn to for the interpretation of statutes.

Committee Reports

Committee reports attempt to explain the meaning of terms used in a statute. They help to amplify its language and purpose with the express aim of avoiding future litigation.

In a discussion of various amendments to labor statutes that by *implication* might have afforded a jury trial to anyone charged with

---

[2] S.G.E. Contractors, Inc., v. U.S., 92 Sup. Ct. 1411, 1418 (1972). That the courts have sometimes been less than wary of hearings and debates in the interpretation of statutes can be illustrated from opinions in almost every volume of United States Reports issued in this century.

contempt of court, the Supreme court rejected that notion and quoted with approval the testimony of a counsel to the committee that was holding joint hearings on the revision of the Judicial and Criminal Codes, " '. . . a mere change in wording will not effect a change in meaning unless a clear intent to change the meaning is evidenced. To find out the intent, I think the courts would go to the report of the committee on the bills. . .' "

The Court added:

"In this case . . . the House and Senate Reports caution repeatedly against reading substantive changes into the revision. . ."[3]

The Supreme Court has even turned to a Congressional report written a year *after* the law was enacted to help establish the meaning of a no-strike provision in the National Labor Relations Act:

"Although a 1948 committee report is no part of the legislative history of a statute enacted in 1947, we note that the Joint Committee on Labor-Management Relations, made up of members of the congress which passed the Taft-Hartley Act, in its final report reached the same conclusion we do."[4]

It is only when the language of a statute is unclear and the Congressional reports on a bill do not establish its meaning that the courts typically resort to additional extrinsic aids. Such aids include statements of administrators of federal agencies, interpretations of similar language in other statutes and sometimes even the comments of experts. Naturally, if a floor amendment is adopted after a report is written, the courts will then give weight to floor arguments *on that point.*

Finding Tools

The chief finding tools for congressional reports and other documents of legislative history are six in number.

1. Slip Copies of Public Laws. A list of all numbered reports and the dates of *Congressional Record* issues in which floor debates appear are appended to each slip law.

---

[3] Muniz v. Hoffman. 96 Sup. Ct. Rep. 2178, 2188–9 (1975).
[4] Labor Board v. Lion Oil Co., 352 U.S. 282, 291 (1957).

2. Congressional Record Index. A history of bills and resolutions appears in the back of each *Congressional Record* index volume. It traces the history of each measure from its date of introduction to its signing by the President. During a current Congress the indexes are published in noncumulative paperback form. It may therefore be necessary to consult as many as fifteen or twenty separate indexes in order to locate the documents that comprise a legislative history of a particular recent statute. A year or more may elapse after the close of a session of Congress before the permanent annual index is published.

3. Statutes at Large. The same information that is set forth at the end of each slip law has also been published in tabular form as an appendix to the public law volume of *Statutes at Large* for every year since 1963. This feature is titled, "Guide to Legislative History of Bills Enacted into Public Law."

4. CCH Congressional Index. This index to Congressional action provides a status table of all current and public measures. It is published weekly and is cumulated frequently during each session of Congress.

5. U.S. Code Congressional and Administrative News. This work—a West Publishing Company product—contains the full text of at least one Congressional report and a list of all the other numbered reports on virtually every public law. It began publication in 1941 on a selective basis, but gradually expanded its coverage. It is issued biweekly during Congressional sessions. Its indexes are cumulated with each successive issue and there are annual bound cumulations of the contents of all the biweekly issues. Probably more law offices subscribe to this service than to all the other finding tools combined.

6. C.I.S. (Congressional Information Service) publishes an exhaustive guide to Congressional action. Its various status tables provide detailed information about transcripts of hearings, committee reports and committee prints. Studies on a particular bill made by staff members for the use of Congressional committees are frequently published as unnumbered committee prints. The *C.I.S.* service gives a thumbnail summary of the contents of each of these documents and includes digests of the testimony of witnesses at Congressional hearings as well. It is published monthly. It is cumulated annually and at five-year intervals.

Packaged Histories

It is not always necessary to use finding tools for a search of legislative history because numerous histories have been compiled and issued both by private publishers and by the Government Printing Office.[5]

One of the most comprehensive of the private publications is the *"Legislative History of the Securities Act of 1933 and the Securities Exchange Act of 1934"*, compiled by J.S. Ellenberger and Ellen P. Mahar, and published in eleven volumes by Fred B. Rothman & Company in 1973.

The Environmental Protection Agency prepared a legislative history of federal environmental statutes in some thirty paperback volumes and ten supplements in 1974. It includes legislative histories of statutes on environmental protection generally and of laws relating to air, noise, radiation, water and pesticides.

A fairly comprehensive list of legislative histories in the District of Columbia is the *"Union List of Legislative Histories: 47th Congress, 1883 - 93rd Congress, 1974,"* compiled by the Legislative History Committee of the Law Librarians' Society of Washington, D.C., 4th edition 1975. The publisher: Fred B. Rothman & Co.

The large law libraries in New York and in other major cities compile numerous legislative histories each year. Information about the holdings of the various firm and corporate legal department libraries in each city is disseminated through an informal library network. Members of local chapters of the American Association of Law Libraries form the nucleus of those local networks. In New York the chapter is LLAGNY (the Law Library Association of Greater New York).

---

[5] A sampling of some useful legislative histories published by the Government Printing Office includes:

A Legislative History of the Clean Air Amendments of 1970, 1974. 2 Vols.

Legislative History of H.R. 8000. . . . the Interest Equalization Tax Act. 1966. 1257 pp.

Legislative History of H.R. 8363. . . . the Revenue Act of 1964. 4 Vols. (4404 pp.)

Legislative History of the Internal Revenue Code of 1954. . . . 1967, 1374 pp.

A Legislative History of the Water Pollution Control Act Amendments of 1972. 1973. 2 Vols.

II

"Only when legislative history is doubtful do you go to the statute."[6] Is this quip or canon or gentle criticism? The United States courts, unlike their English counterparts, are said to rely so heavily on extrinsic aids in the interpretation of statutes that they fail to see the plain English words in the laws. This chapter reviews examples of statutory construction ranging from the most "permissive" to the most "restrictive": those cases that turned on statements found in some extrinsic documents and those that rejected their use altogether.

The lawyers who urged expanded reliance on extrinsic aids argue that many statutes are incomprehensible without them. They complain acidly that our schools no longer teach students to read or write and that our bill drafters are graduates of those schools. Hence the dilemma of our judges—some of whom studied before the same masters.

Legislative Reports

Congressional reports are said to rank first in any hierarchy of extrinsic aids. Their use, however, does not preclude reference to other forms of legislative history.

"Congressional reports are indeed entitled to greater weight than less formal indicia of congressional intent such as floor debates."[7]

It is axiomatic that committee reports are accorded greater weight than floor debates whenever they appear to conflict. In such a situation, Justice Harlan made this comment when he upheld the right of the Secretary of Agriculture under the Agricultural Marketing Agreement Act of 1937, 7 USC Sect. 601 to require milk distributors to pay higher prices to "nearby" farmers than to distant ones:

"A committee report represents the considered and collective understanding of those Congressmen involved in drafting and study-

---

[6]Frankfurter, *Some Reflections on the Reading of Statutes,* at 26. New York, Association of the Bar of the City of New York, 1947.

[7]Int. T. & T. Corp. v. General T. & E. Corp., 518 F. 2d 913, 921 (9th Cir. 1975), citing U.S. v. Auto Workers, 352 U.S. 567, 585 (1957).

ing proposed legislation. Floor debates reflect at best the understanding of individual Congressmen. It would take extensive and thoughtful debate to detract from the plain thrust of a Committee report in this instance."[8]

Again, in a dispute over the division of authority between local public housing agencies and the Department of Housing and Urban Development (HUD), the Eighth Circuit relied heavily on a Senate report[9] in holding that Section 1 of the United States Housing Act, 42 USCA Section 1401, gave ultimate power to HUD:

"In taking into account the above legislative history we adhere to the general principle that committee reports represent the most persuasive indicia of congressional intent."[10]

It is a basic principle of English law on the other hand that statutory construction may be based on three factors only: (1) the meaning of the words in the statute as they are used in context, (2) matters generally known to well-informed people about which judicial notice may be taken and (3) the basic reasons for the enactment as outlined in Heydon's case (infra) decided in 1584. Lord Denning summed up when he said:

"In this country we do not refer to the legislative history of an enactment as they do in the United States of America. We do not look at the explanatory memoranda which preface the Bills before Parliament. We do not have recourse to the pages of Hansard."[11]

Viscountess Rhondda was denied a seat in the House of Lords at least in part because an interpretation of the words "Public Functions" favorable to her in the Sex Disqualification Act, 1919, could only be found in "extrinsic aids" and not in the Act itself.

It is consistently the English practice to ignore the discussions of Members of Parliament about proposed legislation in construing the meaning of statutes.

Viscount Haldane observed:

"I do not think, sitting as we do with the obligation to administer the principles of the law, that we have the least right to look at

---

[8] Zuber v. Allen, 396 U.S. 168, 186 (1969).

[9] S. Rept. 41, 86th Cong. 1st Session 36 (1959).

[10] Housing Auth. of City of Omaha, Neb. v. United States, 486 F. 2d 1, 7 (8th Cir. 1972).

[11] Escoigne Properties Ltd. v. Inland Revenue Commissioners, [1958] A.C. 549, 566.

what happened while the Bill was being discussed in Committee and before the Act was passed. Decisions of the highest authority show that the interpretation of an Act of Parliament must be collected from the words in which the Sovereign has made into law the words agreed upon by both Houses. The history of previous changes made or discussed cannot be taken to have been known or to have been in view when the Royal assent was given . . . In *Millar v. Taylor,* the principle of construction was laid down by Willes J. as long ago as in 1769 in words which have never, so far as I know, been seriously challenged: "The sense and meaning of an Act of Parliament must be collected from what it says when passed into a law; and not from the history of changes it underwent in the house where it took its rise. That history is not known to the other house or to the sovereign."[12]

The Companies' Act, 1900 strips a company of the power to "apply any of its shares or capital money,"[13] to the payment of a brokerage fee for finding capital. In interpreting this quoted language, Lord Halsbury observed:

"My lords, I have more than once had occasion to say that in construing a statute I believe the worst person to construe it is the person who is responsible for its drafting. He is very much disposed to confuse what he intended to do with the effect of the language which in fact has been employed. At the time he drafted the statute, at all events, he may have been under the impression that he had given full effect to what was intended, but he may be mistaken in construing it afterwards just because what was in his mind was what was intended, though, perhaps, it was not done."[14]

In this case, Lord Halsbury had himself drafted the statute under review and he added, "For that reason I abstain from giving any judgment in this case myself."[15]

Congressional Hearings

The paring of uneconomic routes under the Rail Passenger Act of 1970 (Amtrak Act), 45 USCA Sect. 501 et seq. was the subject

[12] Viscountess Rhondda's claim [1922] 2 A.C. 339, 383–384.

[13] Hilder v. Dexter, [1902] A.C. 474, 480.

[14] Id. at 477.

[15] Id.

of attack in a suit brought by a group of passengers who were left without rail service. At issue in that case was the right of those private persons–the "abandoned" passengers–to sue inasmuch as Section 307(a) of that Act lists as potential plaintiffs only the Attorney General of the United States and railroad employees in matters involving a labor agreement. Justice Powell, writing for the U.S. Supreme Court, relied on congressional hearings when he rejected the argument that Section 307(a) did not "preclude other private causes of action . . ."[16] The hearings showed that the Secretary of Transportation opposed permitting other private persons to invoke Section 307(a) and the bill was presumably rewritten in conformity to his views.

> "Sanctions are normally imposed by the government. Consequently, I would be opposed to permitting 'any person' to seek enforcement of section 307. I would have no objection, however, if the section were revised to permit employee representatives, as well as employees adversely affected, to seek equitable relief."[17]

In this case the Court took the silence of the committee members to mean their agreement with the Secretary's views–in this instance expressed in a letter to the committee and incorporated into the hearing transcript. His statement was not even delivered to the committee in person.

As a result the committee was unable to question him about his views. The Court concluded:

> ". . . Although the transcript of the House Committee hearings does not indicate that any committee member voiced explicit affirmative agreement with this interpretation, it is surely most unlikely that the members of the Committee would have stood mute if they had disagreed with it . . .
>
> "The members of the committee had before them a specific proposal that would have altered the interpretation that was being placed on Section 307(a), and would have explicitly permitted suit to enforce the Act's provisions by 'any person adversely affected or aggrieved.' The committee's deliberate failure to

---

[16] National R. Passenger Corp. v. Nat. Ass'n. of R. Passengers, 414 U.S. 453, 457 (1974).

[17] Supplemental Hearings on H.R. 17849 and S. 3706 before the Subcomm. on Transportation and Aeronatics of the House Comm. on Interstate and Foreign Commerce, 91st Cong. 2d Sess. at 85 (1970).

adopt that proposal, after learning of the Secretary's views, cannot but give weight to the conclusion that the committee agreed with the Secretary's interpretation of the meaning and effect of the existing language, as well as with his opposition to the proposed change."[18]

The issue of whether the Federal Power Commission or a state agency was to regulate "wholesale" electric power rates was decided almost entirely on the basis of testimony of witnesses before House and Senate Committees.[19] Justice Jackson concurred but complained that the Court was reaching its conclusion by "psychoanalysis of Congress" rather than by analysis of the statute.[20] He argued:

"When we decide from legislative history, including statements of witnesses at hearings, what Congress probably had in mind, we must put ourselves in the place of a majority of Congressmen and act according to the impression we think this history should have made on them. Never having been a Congressman, I am handicapped in that weird endeavor. That process seems to me not interpretation of a statute but creation of a statute."[21]

Floor Debates

Wrongful use of force or violence constitutes "Extortion" under the Hobbs Act.[22] But such acts are not "wrongful" if committed during a legitimate strike. Such is the effect of a Supreme Court decision that relied heavily and quoted extensively from the floor debates on a predecessor bill.[23] At one point, Mr. Hobbs attempted to still the fears of Mr. Marcantonio that strikers or union officials might be punished under the proposed bill by saying:

"... This bill does not cover strikes or any question relating to strikes."[24]

---

[18] National R. Passenger Corp. (supra) at 460–461.

[19] U.S. v. Public Utilities Com'n. 345 U.S. 295, 302, 305–306, 308–309, 313–314 (1953).

[20] Id. at 319.

[21] Id.

[22] 18 U.S.C.A. § 1951(b)(2).

[23] U.S. v. Enmons, 410 U.S. 396, 401–6, 408 (1973).

[24] Id. at 405.

Speaking of Congressman Hobbs, the Court argued:

> "Surely an interpretation placed by the sponsor of a bill on the very language subsequently enacted by Congress cannot be dismissed out of hand . . . , simply because the interpretation was given two years later."[25]

The four-justice dissent made much of the fact that the debates were inapplicable, having been held in a "differently constituted House"[26] two years earlier. But it did not object to the use of debates altogether in the construction of statutes.

Hence the dismissal of the indictment against Emmons and his co-defendants was affirmed chiefly on the basis of words spoken on the House floor in connection with a different bill than the one enacted and in an earlier Congress.

The meaning of the words, "contracts or agreements prescribing minimum prices for resale," became crucial in an action to enjoin alleged unlawful price cutting of liquor. The opinion of the Court rested in part on the use of floor debates.[27]

Justice Jackson objected to this in a concurring opinion:

"Resort to legislative history is only justified where the face of the Act is inescapably ambiguous, and then I think we should not go beyond committee reports, which presumably are well considered and carefully prepared. I cannot deny that I have sometimes offended against that rule. But to select casual statements from floor debates, not always distinguished for candor or accuracy, as a basis for making up our minds what law Congress intended to enact is to substitute ourselves for the Congress in one of its important functions . . . It is the business of Congress to sum up its own debates in its legislation."[28]

The defense urged that reference to the debates in the House of Commons would clear up any doubt as to the meaning of a provision in the Education Act, 1902, that required privately operated schools to pay for the cost of religious instruction. The court refused to make such reference:

> ". . . we have only to deal with the construction of the Act as printed and published. That is the final word of the Legislature

---

[25] Id.

[26] Id at 414.

[27] Schwegmann Bros. v. Calvert Corp. 341 U.S. 384, 393, 394 (1951).

[28] Id. at 395–396.

as a whole, and the antecedent debates and subsequent statements of opinion or belief are not admissible. But they would be quite untrustworthy in any case. *In the case of an Act dealing with a controversial subject ambiguous phrases are often used designedly, each side hoping to have thereby expressed its own view,* and *the belief of each that it has succeeded is more often due to the wish than to any effort of reason* . . . The court must, of course, in construing an Act of Parliament, as in construing a deed or will, do its best to put itself in the position of the authors of the words to be interpreted at the time when such words were written or otherwise became effectual; but this will no more justify us in admitting, as evidence on the construction of an Act, speeches in either House or subsequent statements in the public papers, or elsewhere, of the effect of the Act than it would justify us in admitting on the construction of a will the advice given to the testator by his solicitor before, or the statements of himself or his expectant legatees of the effect of his will, after he had made it."[29] (Emphasis added)

Bills in Congress

Justice Holmes refused to accept the text of an early version of a bill as evidence of the meaning of a Federal statute that fixed the prices of coal, pointing out, "It is a delicate business to base speculations about the purposes or construction of a statute upon the vicissitudes of its passage."[30]

Yet a dissenting state court judge made an eloquent case for the opposite principle.[31] He argued that reliance should be and frequently has been placed on successive versions of a bill in order to resolve ambiguities in a statute that emerged from the various drafts of the bill. The issue in that case was over standing to sue and time to perfect an appeal under the Washington Shorelines Management Act. The dissent cited a Holmes opinion, written only a year earlier

[29] Rex v. West Riding of Yorkshire County Council [1906] 2 K.B.D. 676, 716.

[30] Pine Hill Co. v. U.S., 259 U.S. 191, 196 (1922).

[31] Hama Hama Co. v. Shorelines Hearings Board, 536 P. 2d 157, 165 (Wash. 1975).

than *Pine Hill,* and numerous other authorities. "Justice Holmes once observed, '[A] page of history is worth a volume of logic,' *New York Trust Co. v. Eisner,* 256 U.S. 345, 349 (1921). That history is obtainable by using the familiar, established and approved technique of noting pertinent changes in successive drafts of House Bill 584 (42nd 1971) [State of Washington]."

Legislative Studies

The United States courts have given great weight to the recommendations of Federal legislative committees and commissions, whether those bodies were composed of members of Congress or of other persons. To illustrate, the report issued by Theodore Roosevelt's Commission on Naturalization[32] was cited in support of the view that the Immigration Act of 1906, Section 15, providing the only means of conducting denaturalization proceedings.[33]

In England legislative background studies simply have no place in the construction of statutes except as they are a source of information about the "mischief or defect"[34] which the Act of Parliament was intended to remedy. A tax case turned on the meaning of the words "Any part of his income," in the Finance Act, 1920. The taxpayer attempted to use in his argument explanations set forth in a report of a Royal Commission on the 1920 Act. The attempt failed:

> "It is clear that the language of a Minister of the Crown in proposing in Parliament a measure which eventually becomes law is inadmissible and the Report of Commissioners is even more removed from value as evidence of intention, because it does not follow that their recommendations were accepted."[35]

Views of Administrators

American courts tend to give some weight to the opinions of administrative agency officials in interpreting the ambiguous pro-

---

[32] H.R. Doc. No. 46, 59th Cong., 1st Session (1905).

[33] Bindczyck v. Finucane 342 U.S. 76, 81 (1951).

[34] Heydon's Case [1854] 3 CO. Rep. 7A: 76 Eng. Rep. 637, 638.

[35] Assam Railways and Trading Co. v. Inland Revenue Comm., [1935] A.C. 445, 458.

visions of statutes. Justice Jackson's opinion in an action brought under the Fair Labor Standards Act gives support to this view:

> "We consider that the rulings, interpretations and opinions of the Administrator under this Act, while not controlling upon the courts by reason of their authority, do constitute a body of experience and informed judgment to which courts and litigants may properly resort for guidance. The weight of such a judgment in a particular case will depend upon the thoroughness evident in its consideration, the validity of its reasoning, its consistency with earlier and later pronouncements, and all those factors which gave it power to persuade, if lacking power to control."[36]

The English courts are consistent in dealing with this kind of problem. They generally bar from consideration administrative agency regulations and statements of agency officials. So held the Chancery Division with respect to "Practice Notes" issued by a planning board that interpreted the term "Development" in the Town and Country Planning Act, 1947. The court in this case denied to a land developer a "development" payment that he sued for under the Act:

> "They [the 'Practice Notes'] have no force of law in any way, but are of interest as being the view which has been taken by the board and which counsel for the council has quite properly used as part of the argument."[37]

Having made this obeisance to established principle, the court nonetheless devoted almost its entire argument to a discussion of board regulations and statements of board officials. One senses here that the court was unwilling to admit the force of agency evidence, but appreciated the confirmation that such evidence provided.

III

Ouija boards and crystal globes apart, there is apparently no limit to the kinds of extrinsic aids that American courts will employ in the interpretation of statutes. The judges trace a path through the world of dictionaries, encyclopedias, treatises, law

---

[36] Skidmore v. Swift & Co. 323 U.S. 134, 140 (1944).

[37] London C.C. v. Central Land Board, [1958] 1 All England Reports, 806, 810.

review articles, and even letters, personal affidavits and newspaper stories, as they attempt to extract the meaning of America's laws.

Courts may have stretched "legislative history" to its bursting point. But in doing so, they have brought together an enviable reference library. Its contents are set forth below.

Dictionaries

One may be astonished but not surprised by the number of judges who keep *Webster's New International Dictionary,* third edition or second edition, on their shelves. The courts cite these two works more frequently than they cite any other single dictionary. Noah Webster, we should remember, was quick to correct his wife when she cried, "I am surprised!", on discovering her husband's secretary sitting in his lap. "No," he told her, "*I* am surprised. *You* are astonished."

Is it possible that the office manager of a distinguished Wall Street law firm forbade the purchase in 1961 of the new *Webster,* third edition, because it contained so many crude, ugly, and dirty words?

This edition has been cited for its definition of "affect" in interpreting a provision of a federal drug act,[38] in construing the Bankruptcy Act to prevent the appointment of a new trustee,[39] in ascertaining the meaning of "accrual basis" in a tax case[40] and for a hundred other purposes. We are told that "the word 'desegregate' does not appear in *Webster's* second edition in 1950. But *Webster's New Collegiate Dictionary* (a Merriam-Webster) [does] define desegregation . . .[41] " "This fine little dictionary once helped persuade the court in a union election dispute of the correct meaning of 'runoff.'[42] " A relatively new work *Random House Dictionary*

---

[38] U.S. v. Caldwell, 463 F. 2d 590, 593 (3d Cir. 1972).

[39] In re Eloise Curtis, Inc., 261 F. Supp. 325 (S.D.N.Y. 1966).

[40] Philip Bros. Intercontinent Corp. v. U.S., 66-1 U.S.T.C. ¶ 9421.

[41] U.S. v. Jefferson County Board of Education, 372 F. 2d 836, 838 (5th Cir. 1966).

[42] Wirtz v. Hod Carriers Local 125, 50 CCH Lab. Cas. Par. 19,141 (N.D. Ohio 1964).

(1966) was helpful in determining for the Pennsylvania Supreme Court the meaning of "immediate family" under that state's laws.[43]

Oxford Dictionary Best

But for true scholarship and range of meaning, nothing equals the *Oxford English Dictionary* in twelve volumes and three supplements which settled another question of statutory interpretation in Pennsylvania, namely, the meaning of "transactions" when used in connection with public bodies.[44] The same court cited *Black, Bouvier, Words and Phrases, Webster's* third edition and finally *Funk and Wagnalls Standard Dictionary* in a single case. Thus the court disposed of a teacher dismissal matter under the School code of 1949 that failed to define "incompetency" with sufficient clarity.[45] *Funk and Wagnalls* has also been recognized in a Federal Court in interpreting the term "consent" under an antitrust statute.[46]

The *American College Dictionary* (which competes with the *Webster Collegiate Dictionary*) helped unscramble a chiropractor's New York tax problem by defining "therapy" under the New York Tax Law.[47]

Webster's New World Dictionary, College edition, (1955)[48] was called into play to construe a licensing provision in the Administrative Code of the City of New York[49] that covered "cabarets," but not necessarily concerts in cabarets. The same court objected to the Police Department use of *Funk and Wagnalls* and went on to assert, "All available aids to statutory construction are to be explored in determining the meaning of a statute (citing Sutherland, *Statutory Construction*, 3d ed.). Legislative history is not to be

---

[43] Bertera's Hopewell Foodland v. Masters, 428 Pa. 20 (1967).

[44] Wiley v. Woods, 393 Pa. 341 (1958).

[45] Philadelphia Board of Education v. Bellan, 368 Pa. 82 (1956).

[46] Commonwealth Edison v. Allis Chalmers, 211 F. Supp. 712 (N.D. Ill. 1962).

[47] Chiropractic Ass'n of N.Y. v. Hilleboe, 31 Misc. 2d 554 (Sup. Ct., Albany Cty. 1961).

[48] 9 Enc. Americana 88 (1968).

[49] People v. Ziegler, 29 Misc. 2d 429 (City Magistrates Ct., Borough of Man. 1961).

ignored, even if the words be clear."[50] How unlike the classic—and the English—view of statutory construction!

At one time no library was complete without the celebrated *Century Dictionary and Encyclopedia* 1899 in ten volumes which was used to define "description" in the expression "descriptions of illicit sex" under the then current New York obscenity statute.[51] Finally, New York's Fourth Department, puzzled over the M'Naughten Rule and the distinction between "know" and "appreciate", resorted to *Webster's New Twentieth Century Unabridged Dictionary*—could this be a supermarket loss leader?—and then to *Roget's Thesaurus.* This latter work led the court to assert that " 'know' and 'appreciate' are synonymous."[52]

Technical Dictionaries

Not unexpectedly, the courts turn to technical dictionaries to explain a technical provision in a statute. Thus, the United States Supreme Court quoted Kohler, *A Dictionary for Accountants* (1952) 371, where it defines "salvage value" as "actual or prospective selling price, as second-hand material or as junk or scrap, or fixed assets retired . . ."[53] Similarly it refers to *Dorland's Illustrated Medical Dictionary,* 24th edition (1965) 478–479, 547 and 1689 to analyze terms related to the quickening process as they are used in an abortion statute,[54] and to the United States Department of Labor *Dictionary of Occupational Titles,* third edition (1965) in a labor dispute.[55]

Despite the basic English rule that extrinsic aids are always impermissible, references to dictionaries occasionally appear in the English reports. For example, Lord Macnaghten referred in a dissent to Dr. Samuel Johnson's great work, *A Dictionary of the English Language,* (17-75) to show that limestone quarries should be

---

[50] Id. at 434.

[51] People v. Bookcase, Inc., 14 N.Y. 2d 409, 420 (1964).

[52] People v. Buthy, 38 A.D. 2d 10. 17 (4th Dept. 1971).

[53] Massey Motors, Inc. v. 364 U.S. 92 (1960).

[54] Roe v. Wade, 410 U.S. 113 (1973).

[55] Corning Glass Works v. Brennan, 417 U.S. 188 (1974).

interpreted to mean "mines" for purposes of the Railway Clauses Consolidation Act, 1845.[56]

Foreign-Language Construction

Bilingual problems of statutory construction require special rules. Puerto Rican statutes that are based on American state laws are construed according to their meaning in the English language version, while those laws that originate in Puerto Rico or in other civil law countries are interpreted according to the Spanish meaning. This basic rule has been codified.[57]

The issue in a case under The Civil Code of Puerto Rico turned on whether the word "forthwith" used in connection with the mailing of pleadings means, as the court explained, "*before, after or simultaneously with* as plaintiff contends; or whether it means only *immediately after* as defendant contends."[58] Since this requirement originated locally, the definition of the Spanish term "inmediatemente" applied. *Webster* defines "forthwith" as "immediately, without delay." But the court pointed out, "The Spanish is perhaps more exact. A synonym of "inmediatemente" is "luego" and this word in turn is defined as "Depues de este tiempo o momento. 'Despues' denotes posterioridad de tiempo, lougar or situacion," citing *Diccionario De La Lengua Espanola,* 19th edition (1970). Accordingly, the defendant prevailed.

In a reverse situation under the Code of Civil Procedure, which derives from the California statute, the Supreme Court of Puerto Rico cited an English language source to determine the meaning of "irreparable" in an application for an injunction.[59]

Treatises and Textbooks

A broad range of book titles can be mined from the extrinsic aids that American courts have cited. What for example, can a statute mean by "conduct unbecoming an officer and a gentleman?"

---

[56] Midland Railway Co. v. Robinson, [1890] 15 App. Cas. 19, 31.

[57] Title 32 Laws of Puerto Rico, §§ 3521, 3522.

[58] Gibbs v. Paley, 345 F. Supp. 270, 272 (D.P.R. 1973).

[59] Loiza Sugar Co. v. Hernaiz, 32 P.R.R. 829, 832 (1924).

In trying to solve a statutory intent problem that arose during the Viet Nam war, the United States Supreme Court noted that, "the Court of Military Appeals has repeatedly turned to *Winthrop's Military Law and Precedents,* an 1886 treatise, for an answer."[60]

Thompson on Real Property was cited by the same court in a dissenting opinion to establish the meaning of "encumbrance" under separate Oklahoma, Arizona and New Mexico acts.[61] Early this year, Jennings and March, *Securities Regulation,* third edition, was referred to by that court when it passed on the meaning of "manipulative devices" in the Securities Exchange Act of 1934.[62]

Cited again and again by the courts for its ability to "speak" clearly when the legislators apparently failed to do so is *Davis on Administrative Law,* 1957. In a Fifth Circuit Case, Davis reinforced the court's view that state law governs pension and welfare trust matters.[63] In a California Supreme Court case, this work helped to establish that the statute under scrutiny did require "findings on all material issues."[64] Another California court cited *Davis* on the right of legislatures to delegate their powers.[65]

"The term 'Special Community' had its origin in legislative attempts to enlarge upon the constitutional definition of separate property."[66] The Texas Supreme Court here relied on Cooley's *Constitutional Limitations* to solve its problem. But it cited in addition law review articles published in *Texas Law Review* and *Baylor Law Review* and a commentary on the Community Property Law of Texas published in Vernon's *Annotated Texas Statutes.*[67]

One Landmark Case

A record may have been set when the Fifth Circuit cited some 100 nonlegislative extrinsic aids in interpreting the provisions of

---

[60] Parker v. Levy, 417 U.S. 733, 777 (1974).

[61] Alamo Land & Cattle Co. v. Arizona, 424 U.S. 295 (1976).

[62] Ernst & Ernst v. Hochfelder, 425 U.S. 185 (1976).

[63] Connell v. U.S. Steel Corp., 516 F. 2d 401 (5th Cir. 1975).

[64] Calif. Motor Transport Co. v. Public Util. Comm., 59 Cal. 2d 270 (1963).

[65] Moss v. Gibbs, 370 S.W. 2d 452 (Texas 1963).

[66] Simi Valley Recreation and Park Dist. v. Local Agency Comm. of Ventura Cty., 51 Cal. App. 3d 648 (1975).

[67] Id. at 661.

the Civil Rights Act of 1964.[68] These included a 1965–66 *Survey of School Desegregation* of the United States Commission on Civil Rights; law review articles emanating from Michigan, Harvard, Columbia, and Utah; a note in the *Federal Bar Journal;* a *Southern Education Report;* a statement made by Senator Everett Dirksen at a press conference; a *New York Times* report of a Presidential statement made at a signing ceremony; an open letter from John W. Gardner, Secretary of HEW, to members of Congress and state governors; a joint report issued by the American Friends Service Committee and the NAACP Legal Defense and Educational Fund; and finally two popular books.[69]

In special situations, even the morning mail and the columns of daily newspapers have been used as sources for statutory interpretation.

The Rhode Island Supreme Court concluded in a condemnation proceeding that a recent amendment to that state's practice act did not change the plaintiff's rights. The court pointed out, "Attached to the bill . . . was an explanatory letter from Justice Louis W. Cappelli, then presiding Justice of the Superior Court, in which he stated: *'There are no changes in any matters of substantive law in this bill.'* While such explanatory notes are not conclusive of legislative intent they can be of assistance to this court in construing a statute."[70] (Emphasis added)

The Supreme Court of California commented at length and apparently gave some weight to a sworn declaration by the author of a bill, which declaration he drafted for purposes of that case in which he said that "it was my intent that the requirement of an environmental impact report extend to . . . a private undertaking."[71] The same court quoted from a declaration of another assemblyman which urged the opposite view and from a letter written by the Assembly's legislative consultant which appeared to go both ways.

The court pointed out, however, that the fact that two legislators reported contradictory legislative intent on the same measure

---

68 See N. 4 *supra.*

69 Id. at 846, 849, 850, 853, 887 and 904.

70 Isserlis v. Director of Public Works, 300 A. 2d 273, 275 (R.I. 1973).

71 Friends of Mammoth v. Bd. of Supervisors of Momo County 502 P. 2d 1049 at 1055, 8 Calif. 3rd 247, 104 Calif. Rptr. 761 (1972).

"fortifies judicial reticence to rely on statements made by individual members of the legislature as an expression of the intent of the entire body."[72] Can one assume that absent such "fortification" the California court was ready to accept the sworn declaration at face value or above?

A voting rights provision in the Louisiana Constitution was apparently interpreted on the basis of contemporary newspaper articles, including those in the *New Orleans Times-Picaune.* Explaining that the drafting committee had met in secrecy and that no minutes were kept, the court quoted its earlier comment on the use of newspaper reports.

> "Going to the next best records, newspapers, we find in the record of this case a mass of contemporary newspaper articles, filed by the plaintiffs and by amicus curiae, bearing on the legislative history of Act 2 . . . Affidavits from the authors of the articles attest their accuracy. In all instances they are part of the official records. Their reliability is evidenced by their substantial agreement."[73]

The Division of Consumer Affairs of New Jersey, the successor to the Bureau of Securities, was overruled in its attempt to require state registration of securities under the New Jersey Uniform Securities Law, where the securities had been registered under the Securities Act of 1933. In holding that the registration requirement covered intrastate offerings only, the court quoted *Loss on Securities Regulation* and a number of other "Blue Sky Law" authorities. Had it stopped at that point, there would be no story.

But then it presented evidence from and apparently gave weight to affidavits from industry representatives who had helped get the bill revised along lines that they recommended.

> "The most important of these materials are an affidavit of William J. Ivey, a partner in the law firm of Sullivan & Cromwell, which represented the Investment Bankers Association, and an

[72] Id. at 1056.

[73] U.S. v. State of Louisiana, 225 F. Supp. 353 (E.D. La. 1963).

affidavit of Arthur J. Sills, then Attorney General of New Jersey. The latter affidavit is essentially corroborative of the former. Mr. Ivey's statement, considered together with various memoranda which he and his associates prepared at the time the law was drafted reveals . . ."[74]

Whatever they reveal, the court devoted a key portion of its opinion to this "evidence" of legislative intent. Then it sidestepped any possible criticism for having done so by offering this—customary—caveat:

"Our conclusion as to the meaning and true intent of the statute is reached without reference to any extrinsic materials."[75]

Conclusion

It is true as shown in the footnotes that American courts exclude almost no form of extrinsic aid in the interpretation of statutes. The application of a strict *parol evidence rule* in the construction of statutes would do wonders for reducing the bulk of court opinions, for saving our eyes and preserving the forests. Could it be error to exclude ouija boards as proper extrinsic aids when so much else is admitted?

---

[74] Data Access Systems, Inc. v. State Bd. of Securities, 305 A. 2d 427, 431 (N.J. 1973).

[75] Id. at 432.

CHAPTER 6

STATE LEGISLATIVE HISTORY

Any lawyer who has attempted to ascertain the legislative history of a statute enacted in New York, or the legislative intent with reference thereto, will acknowledge that it is not a simple process. The reason is quite obvious to the initiated. Either the documentation or the extrinsic finding aids are incomplete or actually lacking in many important areas. Still, the documentation does exist to some extent.

Although this article is keyed to the legislative process in New York, still many states have similar documentation and rules of statutory construction, especially when Uniform state laws are involved, which can be used for determining legislative intent in those states, and it will be our purpose to provide a guide to the sources which lawyers can profitably use in this context.

The Legislative Process

The New York State Legislature consists of a Senate and an Assembly, which convenes annually on the first Wednesday after the first Monday in January, and remains in session until it has concluded its business. Extraordinary sessions of the Legislature can be called by the Governor to consider specific legislation he recommends. All legislation, except for certain budgetary proposals submitted by the Governor, must originate in the Senate or the Assembly.

Constitutionally, no law other than the Governor's Budget Bills may be enacted except by a bill introduced either by an Assemblyman or Senator. Bills may be introduced by an individual legislator, by a number of legislators sponsoring the same bill, by order of either House, or on recommendation of a Standing Committee.

When a bill is introduced, it is given an *introductory number* in sequence as submitted. The only one who can make a motion concerning the bill is the *primary introducer.* An amended bill is reprinted and a letter is added to the *introductory number* to indicate that it has been amended. A bill repealing an existing statute either in part or in full is printed with the word "repealed" thereon and with an explanatory note of how it affects the existing statute.

When a bill is amended in the opposite chamber, it is given a *Print Number,* usually beginning with 20,000 or 30,000. A bill introduced in the first year of the legislature and not acted upon, survives as reintroduced automatically for the second year.

Bill numbers may be reserved as of a specific date with the bill to be submitted later. This permits the *primary introducer* to avoid the effect of the Legislature "Going to Rules," which limits and controls the number of bill introductions late in the session.

Legislative proposals affecting the conduct and business of the Legislature are introduced by *concurrent resolutions, joint resolutions* and *Senate* or *Assembly resolutions.* These resolutions are treated as bills, which when passed are certified and transmitted to the Secretary of State.

Bill Passage

Upon introduction, a bill is referred to a Standing Committee. A bill voted out of Committee is placed on the calendar of the Chamber concerned and is given a *third reading.* At this stage it can be subject to debate and a vote. If approved it is sent to the other chamber where it undergoes a similar process. Important bills, are usually given a public hearing before being acted upon by a Committee. If there is a companion bill (also called a "uni" bill), in the opposite Chamber, the original bill is substituted for the bill before that chamber with the position given to it in the first chamber. If there is no companion bill, an identical bill is introduced in the opposite chamber. When a bill is passed by both houses, it is then sent to the Governor for action.

Governor's Role

A bill passed by both houses and sent to the Governor while the legislature is in session becomes law automatically if he fails to take any action thereon within ten days. This is known as a Ten-Day Bill. During this ten-day period, the bill may be recalled by the Legislature. Bills sent to the Governor during the last ten days of the session must be acted upon by him within thirty days. These are known as thirty-day bills, which are considered vetoed if the Governor fails to act on them. Bills vetoed within the ten-day period must be accompanied by a veto message from the Governor. The Legislature may override a veto by a two-thirds vote. A bill approved by the Governor is given a chapter number in order of approval, 12. (N.Y. Laws 1979, c. 12); (N.Y. Laws 1979, c. 13).

Documentation for the Legislative Process

Bills

The original bills with all later substitutions and the form in which they were finally enacted into law, provide a partial means for determining legislative intent. Senate and assembly bills introduced in the Legislature from 1830 to date, whether enacted into law or not, are available in the *Legislative Reference Library of the New York State Library* in Albany on microfilm.

A copy of any bill currently introduced in either the Senate or Assembly can be obtained by writing to the Senate Superintendent of Documents, State Capitol, Albany, N.Y., 12247. It helps to provide the number of the bill or its title.

Subscribers to the *New York Legislative Service* can obtain copies of printed bills for the last two sessions of the legislature from it on request. The New York Public Library has copies of New York bills from 1830 to 1976 on microfilm. Bills for 1977 and 1978 will be available around Jan. 1, 1980.

How to Trace a Bill.

A toll-free phone call to 1-800-342-9860 will connect the caller to the Journal Clerk's Office of the Senate, where a clerk works at a computer that contains "up-to-the second information" on whether a bill is in committee, is on the Senate or Assembly floor, has been passed, or has been signed into law. The data covers Senate and Assembly bills.

The official Journals of the Senate and Assembly, give the record of the introduction of bills and resolutions, noting the number and brief title of each. They carry the record through the various stages from introduction to final passage, including roll-call votes and sometimes changes in wording. They also provide a subject index of bills and resolutions, a subject index of the laws of the specific year reported, bills vetoed by the Governor and proposed amendments to the Constitution.

Unofficially, the *New York Legislative Record and Index* published by the Legislative Index Co., 100 South Swan Street, Albany, New York, and the *New York Legislative Service* (299 Broadway, New York, N.Y., 10007) are helpful in tracing the course of a bill from introduction to enactment or otherwise.

Published Since 1902. The *New York Legislative Record and Index* has been published from 1902 to date. It provides a complete history of each bill introduced in the Senate and Assembly, as well as a cumulative record of all legislation in weekly reports which are cumulated annually. Thus, it presents summaries of all bills in order of introductory numbers, with detailed record of action, printed number tables, subject index of resolutions, bills and laws, bills vetoed by governor, standing committees of Senate and Assembly, public hearings, etc.

If the bill number is known, reference to the sections entitled *Senate or Assembly Introductory Record* under the bill number will reveal the name of the introducer, a summary of the bill, the Committee to which referred, a history of the action taken to date of issue and the bill number of each identical bill, if any. For a bill amended in its own House, the bill number will be given plus a letter of the alphabet for each amendment. A bill amended in the opposite house will be reported with the print number assigned by that house. If only the subject matter of the bill is known, consult the *Subject Index of Bills,* which will indicate the number of the bill. Once this bill number is known, simply turn to the *Introductory Record* for the information described above. The *Subject Index of Laws* reports the chapter number and bill number of all new measures enacted into law, as well as the bill numbers vetoed by the Governor. If only the name of the introducer of a bill is known, consult the *Individual Record,* Senate or Assembly sections, which give the bill number and short title of every bill introduced by each member. Following the summary of the bill in the *Introductory Record,* the history of the action is given. At the end of this history can be found the chapter number of a bill enacted into law and the number of the Governor's memorandum.

Weekly Service. The *New York Legislative Service* (1946 to date) provides a weekly reporting and research service on activities of the New York State Legislature when it is in session. It lists bill introductions, weekly action, Committee and Commission hearings, and other legislative activities. It also provides available background information in the form of bill memoranda and legislative reports. It features sections entitled "Bulletin Page," "Action and Index" and "Reports" which are periodically cumulated. In addition to an Index by Statute and Index by Subject, it lists legislators and their committee assignments, and under *Bulletin Page* highlights significant proposals and important pieces of legislation to watch. Its Index and action section lists bill numbers, describes the bill, and indicates its status. A *Reports* section is subdivided into fourteen parts. Each bill introduced will be cited by its bill number, introducer, committee of referral, statute and sections to be amended along with a brief description of the bill. It also publishes a companion reference tool entitled the *New York Legislative Annual* (see post), which is a compendium of introductory memorandum on bills enacted into law during the year.

Legislative Debates, Committee Hearings and Reports.

When a statute is ambiguous, or when the interpretation to be attached to a statute is doubtful, the courts look to legislative debates and Legislative Committee Reports, as well as other sources for enlightenment. As Judge Collins stated in *Woollcott v. Shubert,* 217 N.Y. 212, 221, 111 N.E. 829, 831 (1916), "We are at liberty to study the debates in seeking and determining the evil against which it was aimed as a remedy. In case they clearly and definitely describe an unworthy or mischievous condition necessitating in the legislative mind, the statute, they furnish the court, laboring to discover the intent of the legislature, with legitimate and trustworthy aid." It has also been stressed, however, that such debates should be cautiously used, for often they merely reflect the opinion or opinions of one or several other legislators, rather than the corporate intent of the both chambers of the Legislature.

Unfortunately, there are no printed records of the debates in the Assembly and the Senate on specific legislation, nor of hearings before their standing committees. One of the reasons for this disgraceful condition is that there is no constitutional provision requiring that the Legislature print a verbatim record of its proceedings. The printed *Journals* of the Senate and the Assembly carry only formal matters such as records of votes on a question and bill tracing as indicated under *Journals,* supra.

Recommendation by Root. Elihu Root, addressing the Constitutional Convention of 1915 strongly recommended that the daily debates of the Legislature be published. "This measure is designed to make the reasons for action on the part of the Legislature matters of public record . . .", he argued. "As it is now, no one knows what the Legislature is doing, or why it is done except as the quite limited news articles of the public press are spread throughout the states. I see no reason sir, why this great state . . . should permit its Legislature to do its business in such a way that there is no means of knowing the reasons for its action." Although the Convention responded by incorporating such a provision in the proposed constitution, that constitution, however was defeated in November, 1915.

It is sometimes possible, however, to obtain a transcript of the debates from the official stenographer of the Senate or of the Assembly upon the payment of a fee.

Section 19 of the N.Y. Legislative Law provides that "the official stenographers of each house shall attend at every session of the body for which they are elected and take stenographic notes of the debates of such body and in the Committee of the whole thereof."

The practice in the past has been that these stenographic notes were not transcribed nor issued except in response to requests by individual legislators as prescribed in the rules of the Assembly and the Senate.

Proceedings on Microfilm. As I understand the situation at present with reference to availability of Legislative Debates, those proceedings in the Senate have been microfilmed, back to 1960, and in the Assembly, back to 1974. A copy of any Senate debate for the current year can be obtained from the Senate Communications Office, Room 416, State Capitol, Albany, N.Y., 12247 for a charge of ten cents per page. It is important to indicate the date and nature of the debates. Debates for past years can be obtained from the Senate Superintendent of Documents, State Capitol, Albany, New York, 12247. There is a charge of 25 cents per page because the debates for that period have to be reproduced from microfilm. Debates in the Assembly can be obtained from the Public Information Officer of the Assembly whose office is in Room 148 in the State Capitol and whose telephone number is (518) 472-6630.

Standing Committees of the Senate and Assembly. Schedules of their forthcoming public hearings can be obtained by writing to the Senate Communications Office and the Public Information Officer of the Assembly. A calendar is also published as the New York State Legislative Senate–Assembly Hearing Calendar, emanating out of the State Capitol.

The Joint rules of the Senate and Assembly provide that whenever a public hearing on a bill or resolution is had before a standing Committee of either the Senate or Assembly, or before a special joint legislative Committee or Commission and stenographic notes of the minutes thereof are taken and transcribed, two copies are to be delivered to the Legislative Library, for reference.

Few Transcripts. As most of the legislative activity takes place in these committees, it is indeed a sad commentary on the legislative process that so few transcripts are made of these hearings or reports published for public review and study. The reason for this situation lies in the fact, that unless mandated specifically by law, such as Temporary State Commissions and Joint Legislative Committees which are directed to make studies, hold public hearings and make reports and recommendations on proposed legislation, the chairpersons of these Committees have absolute control over whether copies of the hearings and reports are to be published in print and deposited in the Legislative Reference Library of the New York State Library as a matter of permanent record for public use. If the chairperson so decrees, it is possible to examine transcripts of public hearings and published reports on proposed legislation before standing and joint legislative committees, commissions and similar bodies, but only if they were deposited in the Legislative Reference Library of the New York State Library. The collection of the Legislative Library located in the state capitol should also be checked for transcripts of hearings and printed reprints of these committees, etc., for I have been given to understand that its holdings are more extensive.

Thus, the lawyer, practising elsewhere than in Albany, necessarily must waste precious time traveling to the state capitol to inspect these records, often not too certain that the record is sufficiently complete to warrant the trouble. In this context, an effort should be made to inspect the files of the chairperson of the Committee, which could be more comprehensive or complete than the library's collection.

Other Primary Sources of Legislative History and Intent

Notes, Comments and Reports of Committees or Commissions which have worked on and recommended certain specific legislation usually are given persuasive weight by the courts, especially when the statute reflects the language proposed. Commissions which frequently append notes to recommended legislation are the Law Revision Commission, the Judicial Council and the Executive Committee of the Surrogates of the State of New York. In this context, it should be noted that these reports and notes are often appended to a bill at the time of its passage. Such notes and reports are considered to be "indicative of its scope and purpose."

Similarly of import as an aid to the construction of a statute are memoranda submitted to the Legislature and to the Governor supporting and arguing for his approval or veto of a bill approved by the Legislature.

Also of value in arriving at a more sophisticated understanding of the legislative history involved are reports of various state departments, institutions and special commissions presented to the Legislature, as well as the views of bar association Committees on state legislation.

Following are sources which should prove of some value in the search for legislative intent.

Governor's Bill Jackets

The *bill jacket* is an envelope containing a copy of the bill, memoranda to the Governor and a variety of other data presented for his review by institutions and persons on whether he should approve or veto a bill passed by both houses of the Legislature. These are usually solicited by the Governor's Counsel's Office, which collects them as well as unsolicited reports and letters from State Departments, legislators (including the sponsoring legislator's introductory memorandum), standing or joint legislative committees, bar associations, lobbyists and persons submitted with the purpose of persuading the Governor to take a specific action on the proposed legislation.

When a bill is approved by the Governor, all these documents are placed in an envelope and arranged according to year and chapter number. Veto jackets are similarly prepared but identified by bill introduction number. Veto jackets should provide insight and understanding of problems and issues confronted and resolved in subsequent legislation of a similar import.

Bill jackets for each legislative bill enacted into law for 1905, and for the period 1921 to 1958 are available in hard copy and microfilm at the New York State Legislative Reference Library in Albany, and in New York City at the Economics and Public Policy Division of the New York Public Library (42nd St. and Fifth Ave.). The New York Public Library Collection of Bill Jackets is available on microfilm only.

For the period 1959 to 1974 microfiche copies are available at the New York State Legislative Reference Library. This permits fiche-to-fiche copy.

For the period 1975 to 1977, *bill jackets* can be consulted at the State Archives (on 11th floor of Cultural Education Center, Albany). Photocopies at 10 cents a page can be ordered from the State Archives. The project of "microfiching" these bill jackets will be undertaken at some future time when funding permits.

The New York Public Library is having difficulty in obtaining the funding for the purchase of the 1959 to 1974 collection of bill jackets on microfiche. Hence, the New York City lawyer must travel to Albany to consult those files. Plans are afoot to make microfiche collections of the bill jackets available around the state. Considering the excessive cost involved, this remains to be seen.

Bill jackets for Governor Carey's period in office can be obtained by contacting Rosemary Hannan in the Governor's Counsel's Office at the State Capitol.

The assistant librarian of the Legislative Reference Library, Robert A. Carter, notes "that bill jackets vary in quality and, in rare instances, do not exist at all. Occasionally, jackets will contain a copy of the bill with no accompanying memorandum."

New York (State) Legislative Annual

Published annually by the New York Legislative Service, Inc., 299 Broadway, New York, N.Y., 10007, a non-profit membership corporation, from 1947 to the present, it compiles primary source material on New York State legislation such as pertinent memoranda prepared by the agencies or individuals initiating or recommending particular legislation, as well as the Governor's approval messages and Governor's veto messages.

New York (State) Legislative Documents (1830 to date)

The various departmental annual reports may contain recommendations and comments on legislation initiated by or affecting them. Other publications of these departments may also give pertinent legislative information. These departmental reports, as well as the messages of the Governor, reports of state institution, special commissions and joint legislative committees presented to the Legislature are bound together in a multi-volumed set at the close of each session of the Legislature and are commonly referred to as the Collected Legislative Documents series.

Joint Legislative Committees are created by concurrent resolutions for the purpose of investigating vital issues of public concern. They conduct hearings and report their findings to the legislature, recommending new legislative measures or amendments to existing laws. It has been estimated that "approximately one-half of legislation in New York originates in studies undertaken by joint legislative committees and by temporary statutory commissions." The

Reports of the Joint Legislative Committees are published as Legislative Documents. Transcripts of Hearings, however, are available only when their chair persons have deposited them in the Legislative Reference Library and the Legislative Library.

Legislative Documents generally can be found in the larger public and bar association libraries of the state, as well as in the Law Libraries of a number of Law Schools in the State.

The State Senate has published a *Cumulative Index to Joint Legislative Committees and Selected Temporary State Commissions* and *Alphabetical Lists of Chairmen and Vice-Chairmen,* 1900–1950 (with a 1951–1965 Supplement and 1965 to 1975 Supplement). The N.Y. State Library, Gift and Exchange Section, publishes a monthly *Checklist of Official Publications of the State of New York* (1947 to the present) which lists studies, reports, and public hearings of legislative committees and commissions. It also has published a *Dictionary Catalog of Official Publications of the State of New York catalogued by the New York State Library from Dec. 18, 1973 to Sept. 24, 1976,* which is helpful in identifying apposite documents, for the period concerned, of relevance in legislative history research.

McKinney's Session Law News of New York (1951–date), published by West, St. Paul, Minnesota, contains "authentic text of the laws together with other valuable legislative and executive materials," such as legislative memoranda, Governor's Memoranda and messages and Judiciary Memoranda; the *New York Consolidated Law Service,* published by the Lawyers Cooperative, Rochester, N.Y., offers a similar service.

The New York State Law Revision Commission.

The New York State Law Revision Commission published its forty-fourth Annual Report to the Legislature on Jan. 1, 1978 (Leg. Doc. (1978) No. 65). The Law Revision Commission was created by Chapter 597 of the laws of 1934, which enacted Article 4-A of the Legislative Law. The Commission is charged to examine the common law and statutes of the state and current judicial decisions for the purpose of discovering defects and anachronisms in the law and recommending needed reforms. It also recommends such changes in the law as may be necessary to modify or eliminate antiquated and inequitable rules of law and to bring the law of New York, civil and criminal, into harmony with modern conditions. A number of studies undertaken by the Commission have been made at the direction of the legislature. Studies have also been made in response to requests by the Governor and by other officers of the State government. Some studies have involved problems suggested by bar associations and other organizations and by public officers, judges, lawyers and laymen.

When the Law Revision Commission selects a problem for study, it also drafts bills to carry out its formal recommendation. These bills are introduced in the Legislature through the ex officio members of the Commission who provide copies of the Recommendations to each member of the Legislature. Copies of these Recommendations are also distributed to bar associations throughout the state and to other agencies and persons concerned with or requesting them.

Copies of the reports are contained in the Legislative Reference Library in Albany. Unfortunately, due to budget restrictions, the research studies considered by the Commission in making its Recommendations have not been printed since 1970 and hence, since then, are not generally available. Copies of these studies as unpublished and unedited material are provided to members of the Legislature who request them. A limited number of copies is also distributed to bar association committee members who prepare reports on the bills recommended by the Commission.

Reports of the Commission can be found in the *Legislative Documents Series.* They are also published in *McKinney's Session Law News of New York* from 1971 to date along with the Commission's Memoranda and Recommendations. Reports by the Commission on bills not officially considered by it are found in the Governors Bill Jackets.

A *Cumulative Topical Index to the New York State Law Revision Commission,* for the period 1952 to 1977 was published in *McKinney's Session Law News of New York* as A-187 in its 1979 volume. This index supplements its *Index to Reports, Recommendations and Studies, 1935–1951,* in sets of bound yearly Commission Reports. Of the three main types of indices found in the 1951 volume, (topical, statutory and table of cases) the 1952–1977 Index only updates the topical. The Commission, however, is planning to complete and publish an update of the other two. Actually, the topical index is the most useful one for researchers in legislative history.

New York (State) Judicial Conference Report

The Judicial Conference was established in 1956. It replaced the Judicial Council (1934–1955), which was created to make a continuous survey and study of the organization, jurisdiction, practice, procedure and administration of the courts, to publish judicial statistics and to recommend remedial legislation to improve the efficiency of the courts. The Judicial Conference functions are broader in scope than those of the Judicial Council as it also administers and supervises the courts of the state. A number of Judicial Conference recommendations for remedial legislation and on the Civil Practice Law and Rules, have been enacted into law. Its reports appear in *Legislative Documents Series,* as well as in *McKinney's Session Law News of New York* and the *New York Consolidated Laws Service.* The *Seventeenth Annual Report of the Judicial Conference* was submitted to the Legislature on Jan. 25, 1979.

New York (State) Governor

The *Public Papers of the Governors,* consisting of his memoranda on approved bills and those vetoed, messages of the Governor to the Legislature on proposed legislation, reports of special commissions and committees appointed by the Governor, are available in this set from 1869–1972, 1877 to date. Usually they appear two years late. For the more current documents of the Governor refer to the *Legislative Documents Series.* Messages from the Governors, comprising executive communication to the Legislature and other papers relating to legislation from the organization of the first Colonial Assembly in 1683 to and including the year 1906, refer to C. 2 Lincoln's edition of 1909 in eleven volumes.

Miscellaneous Sources of Information on Legislative Histories

The Committee on State Legislation of The Association of the Bar of the City of New York carefully studies, analyzes and recommends approving or disapproving bills introduced in the Legislature on State Legislation of The Association of the Bar of the City of New York has published these studies from 1914 to date. A similar service is rendered by the New York County Lawyers' Association and appears in its *Bar Bulletin* from 1943 to date. Beginning in 1938, the June issues of the New York State Bar Association *Bulletin* summarize and analyze state legislation proposed for the year.

Notes or comments on legislation occasionally appear in the law reviews published by law schools in New York State. The *Index to Legal Periodicals* (H.W. Wilson Co., Bronx, N.Y.) indexes these periodicals by subject and author. When a case on appeal involves the interpretation of a statute, the briefs on appeal could be helpful in identifying legislative intent. The *Records and Briefs of the New York Court of Appeals* are available on microfiche in a number of bar and law school libraries. Bar Association Libraries throughout the state maintain sets of records and briefs for the Appellate Courts as well.

It is also possible that a state law may have been modeled after or suggested by a Uniform or Model Act. Uniform state laws and Model State laws are drafted by the National Conference of Commissioners on Uniform State Laws and promulgated with the endorsement of the American Bar Association. The commissioners, appointed by the Governors of their respective states attempt to promote uniformity in state laws on all subjects where uniformity is deemed desirable and practical. Practically every state has adopted one or more of the Uniform and Model Acts, or a part thereof. Thousands of judicial decisions have construed the almost 1,000 adopting state laws of these acts. An example, of course, is the Uniform Commercial Code. Since courts in states adopting a uniform law give some weight to decisions of courts in other states construing similar provisions, these decisional annotations could prove of some value as a research source. The West Publishing Company publishes the *Uniform Laws Annotated, Master Edition,* a multi-volume set, updated by annual pocket part supplementation, which contains every uniform law adopted by at least one state, along with notes of the Commissioners on these laws. The text of each act is set forth and is annotated, section by section, with references to historical notes, general statutory notes by state and notes of court decisions of every state construing parts of the uniform law. The annual *Handbook of the National Conference on Commissioners on Uniform State Laws* provides current information and analyses on proposed laws and recent adoptions. Previous editions of these Handbooks can thus offer similar commentary and analyses on promulgated uniform laws from the period of time when they were under consideration by the Commissioners.

Bibliography on Legislative History Research in New York

Breuer, *Legislative Intent and Extrinsic Aids to Statutory Interpretation in New York.* 51 *Law Library Journal* 2 (1958).

Dana, *Background Materials for Statutory Interpretation in New York,* 14 *Record of The Bar Association of the City of N.Y.* 80 (1959).

McKinney's Consolidated Laws of New York. Book I–*Statutes* (1971). (Not a chapter of New York Consolidated Laws–actually a treatise on statutory construction and interpretation. Note specifically sections on *Legislative Intent as Primary Consideration* and *Extrinsic Aids to Interpretation*).

Source Material Relating to Legislation in the State of New York and Annotated Bibliography of Legislative History and Legislative Intent., by Ernest A. Breuer, 1957. Revised by Robert A. Carter, April 1977. Albany, N.Y., Legislative Reference Library, 1977, 14 p.

CHAPTER 7

CODIFICATION IN THE STATES

Codification is defined in *Black's Law Dictionary,* as a process of collecting and arranging the laws of a state into a complete system of positive law, scientifically ordered and promulgated by legislative authority. This process has been particularly significant in New York, for New York not only was the leader in the movement towards codification, but also closely associated it with legal reform.

Codification should be distinguished from statutory revision and consolidation. There is a periodic need to revise the unwieldy accumulations of statutes in a specific jurisdiction with the purpose of repealing and republishing only statutes in force. This is known as statutory revision. Of greater importance and much more difficult to accomplish properly is the process of consolidation which brings together all the statutes in force on specific subjects and consolidates them into a logical classified arrangement. Codification, however, goes beyond both of these processes for the end product of codification, i.e. the "Code" reflects not only revision and consolidation, but also a scientific, systematic arrangement of the law of the state as expressed in case law, as well as statutory law. Codifications usually also reflect some of the innovative jurisprudential concepts which attempt to remedy the defects in the existing law.

The late Chief Justice of New Jersey, Arthur T. Vanderbilt, believed that some of the finest legislative work involving consolidation and revision was done shortly after the American Revolution in New York and some of the other original states of the Union by able jurists who sought to adapt the needs of those states to the laws of England and of their own colonial legislation.

New York was particularly fortunate during the colonial period and continuing into the nineteenth century in that it attracted and encouraged distinguished jurists to improve the administration of justice by revising and consolidating its laws.

Basically the law of New York was derived from English law. When the Dutch surrendered New Amsterdam to the English in 1664, its laws were in short order supplanted by a code of law known as the *Duke of York's Laws* (1665). The *Duke's Laws* was the first comprehensive code of the colony and although it in turn was subsequently replaced by English common law and statutory law, it is considered as the foundation of the legal and judicial institutions of New York. It was largely compiled from the laws which were generally in force in other English colonies at the time.

During the colonial period, the laws of New York were revised in 1683; then collected and published in 1710 and finally the colonial laws in force in New York in 1762 were "collected, revised and published under the authority of the General Assembly" by William Smith, Jr., and William Livingston. Another official revision was completed in 1774 by Peter Van Schaack.

The first New York Constitution was adopted and published on April 22, 1777. Interestingly, although it was never submitted to the people for approval, it remained in force with minor changes until 1846. John Jay, afterwards the first Chief Justice of the U.S., framed and drafted most of this Constitution, and although hastily prepared, it was highly praised and "generally regarded as the most excellent of all the American constitutions".

The New York Constitution of 1777 declared that "such parts of the common law of England and of Great Britain and of the acts of the Colonial Legislature as together formed the law of the colony at the breaking out of the Revolution in 1775 constituted the law of the State, subject to alteration by the Legislature."

In 1786, the Legislature decided that a revision of the laws of New York was necessary. Samual Jones and Richard Varick were appointed to "collect, revise and digest" all the New York colonial and state laws enacted. As a result, the "Jones and Varick" Laws of the State 1778–1789, the first official revision of New York statutory law was published. A second revision was privately prepared by Thomas Greenleaf as a commercial venture covering the period from 1778 to 1797, nine years later than the Jones and Varick edition. The Greenleaf Revision was accomplished with such accuracy that the courts took judicial notice of its contents.

The next official revision of the laws of the state occurred in 1801 when the legislature appointed James Kent and Jacob Radcliff to review the Jones and Varick revision and the 383 general laws enacted thereafter and "to collect and reduce into proper form, under certain titles, all the public acts of the Legislature of this State". Published in 1802 in two volumes, Kent and Radcliff merely omitted the laws or parts of laws repealed, arranging the laws chronologically in the first volume and by subject in the second volume. The revisers, however, did restate those laws which had been modified by subsequent legislation.

The next revision of the laws of New York which was published in two volumes in 1813 was a more ambitious project. By an act of the Legislature, William P. Van Ness and John Woodward were directed to rearrange systematically under proper heads, with such marginal notes as appeared to be of value to the public, the Kent and Radcliff Revision and the additional 2051 new laws that had been enacted in the ten year interval. The marginal notes, prepared by John V.N. Yates are of historical value even to this day, for they refer to various English and colonial acts with similar provisions and offer a concise history of the statutes to which they refer.

It should be noted in this context that these "revisions", in the main, were merely re-enactments in a consolidated form of the laws in force, with some amendments recommended by the revisers or added by the Legislature. They were drawn in separate acts and little effort was made to arrange them systematically.

It was not until the Revised Statutes of 1828 was enacted into law that we have the first semblance of a code of written law in its true sense. The 1821 Constitution provided for the appointment of Commissioners to revise the laws. In 1824, Erastus Root, James Kent and Benjamin F. Butler were appointed to this post. Butler remained, but Kent and Root resigned. Henry Wheaton and John Duer took their places and later John L. Spencer was appointed in Wheaton's place. Butler had been a law student under Martin Van Buren and later became his law partner. In 1835 he founded the Law School of New York University and became "Principal" of its faculty. In his distinguished legal career, he succeeded Roger B. Taney as attorney-general of the United States when Taney was appointed Chief Justice and also served as secretary of war in President Jackson's cabinet.

As finally constituted, the Commission made its report on March 14, 1826, recommending a bill for legislative enactment which Charles Warren described as "containing a radical and sweeping reformation of the law in many of its features—a bill which may properly be termed the first modern American Code." It has also been noted that this Revision was "the first legal attempt to create and establish for any commonwealth governed by the English Common Law and by Legislative statutes, after the manner of the English Parliament, of a body of written law, systematically arranged, based on the principles of law as a science, regulating the exercise of public and private rights establishing domestic, property and contract relations, and covering the administration of every department of the Government, without touching the integrity of the unwritten law, or transcending the proper bounds of legislative control . . ."

This Revision has also been characterized as the first of Common Law reform acts for it introduced a number of amendments, especially in the field of property which triggered the movement to reform the common law system of actions and property law in the U.S. and even in England. In fact, it became, according to Warren, "the foundation and model for most of the revised and collected statutes adopted in other states in later years, especially for the Revised Statutes of Massachusetts of 1836."

In essence, the *Revised Statutes,* as enacted at special sessions of the legislature in 1828 and published in three volumes in 1829 entirely reconstructed the law of Real Property in New York.

Charles P. Daly, writing in the *Common Law* (1896), aptly noted:

> "It struck at the vital part of the huge fabric that the English real property lawyers and judges had been building for three centuries, until the whole toppled and fell. Even Chancellor Kent, himself a reformer, stood aghast at the extent of the demolition. They remodelled the law of descent, simplified the creation and division of estates . . . remodelled real actions, abolishing fictitious suits, changed the whole law of perpetuities and limitations and

wills . . . reconstructed the entire law of executor and administrator, simplified uses and trusts."

In essence, *The Revised Statutes of 1828,* not only set the pattern for legal reform in New York, but also triggered the movement to reform the common law systems of actions and property law throughout the country and England as well. Subsequently and up to 1896, *The Revised Statutes* was revised nine times. It remained, however, for David Dudley Field, "The American Justinian" inspired by the work of Jeremy Bentham and Edward Livingston, to really institute the movement for legal reform through the process of codification.

The movement in New York for legal reform by means of codification of the law was due to a number of intermingling factors which Warren states as "first, the old, underlying antagonism of the American public towards the common law, as being of English origin; second, the ever-active jealousy, entertained by laymen in a democracy, towards lawyers, as a privileged class and monopoly, and the consequent desire to make the law a layman's law; third, the increase in the number of law reports deemed even then, to be 'vast and unwieldy'; fourth, the success of the Code Napoleon; fifth, the influence of Jeremy Bentham".

In essence, therefore, agitation for Codification in New York around 1830 was a popular movement, partly a revolt against the procedural technicalities characteristic of English common law pleading and practice and partly an attack against the privileged Bench and Bar of the state.

Actually, the technicalities of common law pleading and practice created the basic underlying cause for reform through revision and codification of the procedural law of the state. Cases were lost in the courts, not on the merits but rather on defective pleading.

As the *American Jurist* complained in 1833:

"Take the whole number of reported decisions, both in England and America on the subject of contracts, and we venture to affirm that a majority, yes, a large majority, have gone off on questions of form. This is a stupendous evil. No wonder that the law suffers under the imputation of uncertainty, and of a tendency to encourage quibbling and chicanery. The suitor who is turned out of court on a point of form, when he knows that he has right on his side, has good reason to consider himself oppressed . . . No wonder if with such impressions he imbibes a hatred both of the law and its ministers".

Despite this popular contempt for the technicalities of the law and the persistent demand for change, still the New York bar resisted all such efforts. The common lawyer of the day was proud of his skills in special pleading. He generally agreed with Mr. Justice Story that: "Special pleading contains the quintessence of the law; and no man ever mastered it who has not by that means made a profound lawyer".

Then David Dudley Field launched the movement for codification in New York which significantly brought about a radical reform in the field of remedial law not only in New York but in the nation and in England as well.

The name of David Dudley Field, the "American Justinian," looms large in the movement for legal reform and codification in New York and many other states. Although he later achieved prominence at the American Bar for more than sixty years, he is best known for his public agitation to codify the whole body of New York law, both substantive and adjective; an effort from which he never desisted until his death in 1894 at the age of eighty-nine.

Field believed that "the only men who make any lasting impression in the world are fighters." This became his credo, and as a result there was probably no other lawyer in nineteenth century public life who had as many influential enemies.

Field, according to a contemporary account, was a "man of iron, cold, stern, severe." Another added: "Tall, erect, stalwart, alert and decided in movement, courteous and graceful in bearing, he impressed the observer at once as a man of marked gifts and force. Those who knew him intimately saw a man of strong feelings and passions, an imperious nature quipped with great intellectual power and restrained by intuitive appreciation of the amenities of social life."

Supreme Court Arguments

Field argued before the U.S. Supreme Court many of the leading constitutional cases that arose after the Civil War. In *Ex Parte Milligan,* 71 U.S. 2 (1866), he argued against the suspension of the writ of habeas corpus in territory not under martial law or in the theater of war. In *Cummings v. Missouri,* 71 U.S. 277 (1867), the Supreme Court accepted his argument that it was unconstitutional for a lawyer or clergyman to be deprived of the right to practice his profession because he refused to take the Test oath to the effect that he had not fought for the Confederacy or been sympathetic with it. He also appeared in *Ex Parte McArdle,* 74 U.S. 506 (1869) arguing the unconstitutionality of military government of a southern state. He also argued before the Supreme Court in *U.S. v. Cruikshank,* 92 U.S. 542 (1876) involving validity of the *Enforcement Act* and state rights.

His skill and learning as a lawyer were of the highest repute. In the *Hayes-Tilden* conflict, he served with distinction as counsel for Tilden against William M. Evarts before the Electoral Commission of 1876, which decided the matter. After his death, fifty volumes of "Cases and Points" containing his briefs and records and dozens of scrapbooks of newspaper clippings and other materials concerning his cases were given to the New York State historian.

Interest in Procedural Reform

From his youth, however, Field was interested in procedural reform. While reading law to become a lawyer, he became aware of the way in which the administration of justice was adversely affected and even frustrated by the highly technical pleading and procedural system New York State had inherited from English Common Law. Foremost in his antagonism to that system was his realization of how impractical and inconvenient were the results arising from rights which under certain conditions would be considered legal and on other occasions equitable. These rights often conflicted with each other to the extent that some cases had to be tried twice with accompanying delays and additional costs. Field was also aware of how the technical forms of common law actions and artificial rules, in which form was legally more significant than substance, could deprive a litigant of the remedies he was entitled to on the merits.

Field was also greatly influenced by the writings of Jeremy Bentham on the need for codification of the law. He was also familiar with Sir Samuel Romilly's efforts to reform the bankruptcy and criminal law of England. William Sampson's paper delivered in 1823 before the New York Historical Society on the *History and Nature of the Common Law* in which he discussed the importance of codification and Edward Livingston's *Penal Code* which had been drafted in 1824 were also fresh in his memory. Livingston prepared this code for the state of Louisiana at the request of its legislature. Although not adopted, it was admired for its humane and excellent provisions as well as its practicability. Also known to him was the new, simple system of procedure, free of technical requirements, that had been recommended by Justice William Story's New England Commission to the Massachusetts authorities in 1833.

Field started his long and singularly effective involvement in legal reform and codification only eleven years after he was admitted to practice law by addressing a letter in 1839 to Gulian C. Verplanck on the need to reform the judicial system of New York. Verplanck was a leading New York lawyer and author of an intriguing *Essay on Doctrine of Contracts; being an Inquiry How Contracts are Affected in Law and Morals by Concealment, Error or Inadequate Price* (N.Y. 1825).

Field believed that the substantive law of the state, derived from the English common law, was so disorganized and unmanageable that it had to be reduced to form and system by codification.

He asserted that "by casting aside known rules which are burdensome or unsuitable to present circumstances, avoiding repetition, rejecting anomolous or ill considered cases, reconciling repugnances, molding into distinct propositions and classifying according to scientific method," the common law of the state could be harmonized into a system reflecting the broad topics of the law, and they in turn, could then be enacted into a comprehensive code. By this process the average person and even the members of the bar would be able to attain a more perfect understanding of their rights and duties under the law. As a result "all law [would be] reduced to a statute so that a man might carry in his hand all that the state ordained for the regulation of human conduct."

Field stated he could achieve his purpose by the enactment of five codes. On the adjective side by a *Code of Civil Procedure* and a *Code of Criminal Procedure* which would reflect therein all the procedural law in those areas the judiciary and the bar would have to know; and on the substantive side by a *Political Code* setting forth the duties and obligations of public officers, a *Penal Code* specifying crimes and their punishment and a *Civil Code* delineating personal relationships, property rights and obligations of the public.

This process of codification, Field argued, would allow for the Legislature expeditiously to reform those areas of the law requiring it. It also would permit lawyers to ascertain applicable principles of law without need to waste time in endless research for case law in the numerous reporters and analyzing and synthesizing the rules derived from them. Moreover, "it would bring justice within the reach of all, diffusing among the people in simple, untechnical language a more general and accurate knowledge of their rights and obligations than they could otherwise obtain."

Field then began his program to influence public opinion on the need for procedural reform. He spoke to bar groups and citizens' committees and wrote public letters to legislators and to newspapers. He voluntarily appeared before a Committee of the New York State Legislature, presenting his recommendations for reform in such detail that in 1841 he was able to arrange for three bills he had drafted to be introduced in the Legislature. One bill provided for simpler and speedier administration of justice in civil cases in Courts of Common Law; a second bill was for Courts of Equity and a third was for simplifying indictments. Although no action was taken on these bills, they became the prototypes of the many bills introduced thereafter in the Legislature.

Landmark Year of 1846

The year 1846 is a landmark in New York State legal history. In a sense reflecting the American reaction to the unrest in England and Europe for more democracy and reform in government, a sweeping new constitution for the State of New York was adopted by the New York Constitutional Convention of 1846 and was subsequently approved by the people to take effect on Jan. 1, 1847.

During this time, Field pressed his programs for reform so aggressively that his influence can be seen in the report of the Judiciary Committee of the Constitutional Convention recommending a *General Code* and a single court having general jurisdiction in both law and equity. It also authorized the legislature to appoint "Commissioners to revise, reform, simplify and abridge the rules of practice, pleadings, forms and proceedings of the Courts of Record." As to the *General Code,* the Constitution of 1846 also provided that the Legislature should appoint a commission "to reduce into a written and systematic code the whole body of the law of the State or so much and such parts thereof as to the said commissioners shall seem practicable and expedient."

Thus, the Legislature was authorized to appoint two commissions, one to draft a *Code of Civil Procedure* for the New York courts and another to draft a *Civil Code* of the substantive law of the State.

Presentation of Memorial

Field and fifty leading lawyers of the New York bar then presented a memorial to the Legislature, written by Field, seeking the appointment of the commissioners as directed by the 1846 Constitution. Field noted therein:

"The undersigned members of the bar are persuaded that a radical reform of legal procedure in all its departments is demanded by the interests of justice and by the voice of the people; that a uniform course of proceeding in all cases legal and equitable is entirely practicable and less expedient; and that a radical reform should aim at such uniformity, and at the abolition of all unseless forms and proceedings."

As a result, in April 1847, the Legislature appointed Nicholas Hill, David Graham and Arphaxed Loomis as members of the commission charging it "to provide for abolition of the present forms
mission charging it "to provide for abolition of the present forms
of action and pleadings in cases at common law; for a uniform course of proceedings in all cases whether of legal or equitable cognizance, and for the abandonment of all Latin and other foreign tongues so far as the same shall by them be deemed practicable and any forms and proceedings not necessary to ascertain and preserve the rights of the parties."

Radical and Contentious?

Field, even at that early date, was considered so radical and contentious that he was deliberately overlooked for appointment to the Commission. Hill, however, resigned, and the Legislature was persuaded subsequently to appoint Field in his place. He immediately assumed the leadership in the Commission in drafting a Code and by Feb. 29, 1848, the Commission reported out a *Code of Civil Procedure.* It consisted of fifteen chapters and nearly 400 annotated sections "to simplify and abridge the practice and pleadings of the Courts of this State . . ." It was then considered by the Legislature; amended in approximately eighty of the 391 sections and passed on April 12, 1848 (N.Y. Laws, 1848, ch. 371). Despite the fact that this new Code made startling and radically sweeping changes in the old law not only in theory, but in its practical effect as well, still the Legislature decreed that it become effective on July 1, 1848, a mere two months thereafter.

It should be recognized, as Hepburn notes in *Code Pleading* that "Most of the lawyers and many of the general public were hostile to so radical a change. The task imposed was indeed unparalleled in the history of English or American jurisprudence. A great and venerable system, deeply rooted in the past of a conservative profession and overshadowing the land, was to be supplanted in a day. The prejudices of thousands of practitioners must be disregarded and the habits of their daily lives reversed. The active opposition of many able men recognized as professionally learned in the law must be overborne . . ." In the face of such obstacles, the three commissioners were asked to design and construct a new system which they could recommend as capable of doing all the work of the old, and doing it better."

Strong Opposition

No wonder Hill resigned as commissioner. As a matter of fact, opposition to the Code was so pressing that Hepburn believed that "less expedition might have imperiled the whole enterprise. Opposition to the measure was bitter and intense, among both lawyer and laymen."

The *Code of Civil Procedure* provided for the abolition of the separate jurisdiction of Courts of Law and Equity and merged them into one court, the Supreme Court, with general jurisdiction in both law and in equity. All previous forms of action were abolished and in place thereof, pleadings were to be plain, concise statements of facts. Thus, instead of facts being stated in the declaration as required at Common Law, according to their legal effect only and not on the evidence relied on by plaintiff and also conform to a specific boilerplate form, facts under the *Field Code* could be pleaded without formality. As a result, Field contended the system was made simpler and rights could be determined on the merits rather than on purely formal grounds. The *Field Code* also allowed equitable defenses and counterclaims to be interposed in all actions at law. Other jurisdictional powers formerly exercised only by the Chancery Courts, such as compelling parties to testify and to produce books and papers were transferred jurisdictionally to the Courts of Law.

In essence, the effect of the *Code of Civil Procedure* was to abolish all common law forms of action and of pleading. All matters, legal and equitable arising out of the same transaction whether affecting the plaintiff or defendant could be litigated in one action. Implied as well was the underlying principle that when the equitable doctrine conflicted with the legal rule, the equitable doctrine would prevail.

'Far Reaching Results'

Roscoe Pound regarded Fields' *Code of Civil Procedure* as an outstanding achievement. "No treatise on the theory of legislation and no polemical tracts on law reform have led to such far reaching results", he wrote. "It stands toward procedure in the world of common law where Beccaria's *Treatise on Laws and Punishment* stood toward the nineteenth century criminal law. It showed the way."

Hepburn adds: "If the legislation thus begun had gone no further, the result would still have been among the great events in the history of modern law. But the really significant thing is that the enactment of the New York Code opened, as it were, the floodgates of reformatory legislation and determined the course of its progress."

Between 1848 and 1853, Missouri, California, Iowa, Kentucky, Minnesota, Indiana and Ohio adopted the Field Code and the civil procedure of Mississippi, Massachusetts and Alabama was reformed along the lines of the Field Code. Even the procedure of the English Courts of Law and Equity was simplified by it. By 1873, the Field Code of 1848 had been enacted in practically all of its major provisions by sixteen other states: Oregon, Washington, Nebraska, Wisconsin, Kansas, Nevada, Dakota, Arizona, Montana, Idaho, North Carolina, Wyoming, Arkansas, South Carolina, Florida and Utah. Federal procedure was also affected by the Code and the English Judicature Acts of 1873 were also influenced by the Field Code.

Opposition in New York

Opposition to the Field Code in New York, however, ran rampant. The law reporter for the State of New York critically observed that it was "undoubtedly the greatest innovation upon the common law which was ever effected by a single statute. In one section it struck out of existence all of that law which was inconsistent with the doctrines of equity, and in another obliterated the whole of the two systems of pleading at law and in equity, replacing both by a single and homogeneous body of rules. So radical a change amazed and for a while confounded the entire legal profession. They were unprepared for it and unwilling to believe even that it had been accomplished . . ."

John Austin, a leading jurisprudential figure at the time, independently questioned the feasibility of codification. "Are there men, competent to the difficult task of successful codification and of the production of a code which on the whole would more than compensate the evil that would necessarily attend the change question? For whoever has considered the difficulty of making a good statute will not think lightly of that of making a good code. To conceive distinctly the general purpose of a statute, to conceive distinctly the subordinate provisions through which its general purpose must be accomplished and to express that general purpose and those of subordinate provisions in perfectly adequate and not ambiguous language is a business of extreme delicacy and of extreme difficulty . . . and what is commonly called the technical part of legislation is incomparably more difficult than what may be styled the ethical, it being far easier to conceive justly what would be useful law than so to construct that same law than it may not fail to accomplish the design of the law giver."

The confusion of judges and lawyers on the construction and application of the Code was so great, that the law reports for the period reflect an inordinate number of cases on procedure. Judges, in some parts of the State, actually ignored the Code deliberately, in effect repealing the provisions by judicial fiat.

In addition to being confused, the judges also tried to frustrate the purpose of the Code by construing its provisions so strictly as to make them inoperative. Millar, in his *The Old Regime and the New in Civil Procedure* tells the story of the judge in a New York county who soon after the effective date of the Code held a hearing on a demurrer to a complaint based on the objection that the plaintiff had failed to state a cause of action. The issue turned on the meaning of the complaint's allegations. The Code section involved provided that a litigant was to set forth the facts in his complaint "in ordinary and concise language, without repetition and in such a manner as to enable a person of common understanding to know what is intended."

'Demurrer Overruled'

After reading the complaint and listening to arguments of counsel, the judge handed the complaint to his bailiff. "John", he said, "read over this complaint." The bailiff read it without comment. "John", continued the judge, "do you understand it?" "Yes, your honor", he replied. "Very well", concluded the judge, "I don't understand it, but John does. The demurrer will be overruled."

Because *Field's Code* was in an atmosphere of hostility, the manner in which it was amended by the Legislature and construed by the courts not only perpetuated some of the difficulties of the old common law pleading, but unfortunately also developed technical difficulties of its own.

The original *Field Code* was so well constructed that it required only 391 sections to abolish the distinction between actions at law and suits in equity and substitute instead one form of action, abolish the old common law forms of action, such as trespass, covenant debt, etc., substitute fact pleading for issue pleading and allow liberal joinder of parties and causes of action. The very next legislature, however, reflecting the insistent demands of the bar for its revision, began the process of emasculating its effect. It reenacted the code with a great number of amendments and supplements in 1849 (N.Y. Laws 1849, Ch. 438) enlarging its to 473 sections.

Part of Code

The *Field Code* of 1848 adopted by the Legislature was only a part of the complete *Code of Civil Procedure* submitted by its drafter. In 1850, Field proposed adoption of a complete *Code of Civil Procedure,* consisting of 1885 sections. This draft not only revised the 1849 Amended Code but also fully provided for "Special Actions" and "Special Proceedings" which were then governed by other New York statutes. Even more importantly, it provided for the rules of evidence to be embodied in the Code as well. The new *Field Code,* however, was rejected completely by the Legislature and subsequently again in 1853 when Field proposed it in a revised and condensed form. It is interesting to note in this context that the most scathing criticism of the revised *Field Code* by the bar was addressed to the part relating to evidence—yet the need for a code of evidence is considered today one of the most important requirements in improving practice in the Courts of New York.

The *Field Code* of 1849 was amended in 1851 (N.Y. Laws 1851, ch. 479) and again in 1852 (N.Y. Laws 1852, ch. 392). Thereafter it was continually amended and made so complex that, by 1870, the Legislature authorized the appointment of a Revision Commission and charged it "to revise, simplify, arrange and consolidate all statutes of the State of New York general and permanent in their nature, in force at the final report of the Commissioners." By then the original *Field Code* had been changed 551 times—the number of amendments actually exceeding the total number of sections when first enacted. The complexities usually arose from the legislative purpose when amending the Code, to frame the same section in a manner considered more satisfactory by the bench and bar.

No Close Analysis

The Chairman of the Commission, Montgomery Throop, although charged to revise "all statutes of general import" decided instead to concentrate on the *Code of Procedure* alone. The efforts of the Commissioners were less than distinguished. They failed to closely analyze the problems involved, their arrangement of the statutes was not logical and the phraseology quite complex. They were, of course, familiar with Fields revised work but merely rearranged and redrafted some parts of his code; expanding the number of sections to 3400 sections, although most of the subjects covered by Field were not included in their Code. On June 2, 1876, the *Code of Remedial Justice* became law, pursuant to the Commissioner's draft of "an Act Relating to Courts, Officers of Justice and Civil Proceedings" (N.Y. Laws 1876 Chs. 448, 449), but only after the Legislature agreed to amend it to meet the bitter criticism addressed to its "monstrous-over-detail." In 1877, two acts amended the *Code of Procedure* and changed its name to the *Code of Civil Procedure* (N.Y. Laws 1877, Chs. 416; 422). On May 6, 1880, the remaining revision by the Commissioners was enacted into law (N.Y. Laws 1880, Ch. 178). Before then the Code of *Procedure* of 1848 and its many amendments had been repealed.

Thus the *Code of Civil Procedure,* known thereafter as the *Throop Code* came into effect. From then on the system of civil procedure in New York was called Code Pleading. The *Throop Code* with amendments, additions and repeals remained in force until 1920. In many respects the *Throop Code* caused disastrous results. One critic of the Code, William B. Hornblower noted that it sought to regulate every action of a judge from the time he entered the court house except to prescribe the exact peg upon which to hang his hat. The *Throop Code* not only included a number of substantive laws, but also erred in trying to prescribe exact rules for every detail of procedure and every act of a court or judge. It was "built up under a microscope."

The Last Battle

The last battle on the *Civil Code* took place in 1887 before the Senate Judiciary Committee, with Field's nemesis, James C. Carter leading the opposition. Carter represented the Association of the Bar of the City of New York, and he was indeed a worthy opponent for Field, carrying on the conflict with the same dedication and energy as Field brought to it. Carter published a monograph entitled "The Proposed Codification of our Common Law" which elaborated with great erudition on every conceivable objection to Codification that could be argued. He found the *Civil Code* "grossly defective" and feverishly concluded that codification of common law rules could never be properly accomplished, and certainly Field and his fellow counselors, who were actively engaged in the practice of law, could never produce the ideal result.

Carter was joined by the celebrated jurist Sir Frederick Pollock who described the Field Code as a "mischievous failure", and many leaders of the New York Bar. Carter wrote a number of tracts on the subject which were all subsequently compiled in his well known work, "Law, Its Origin, Growth and Function (1907)". Field characteristically responded to Carter in "A Short Response to a Long Discourse"—An Answer to James C. Carter's Proposed Codification of our common law" (1884). Robert Ludlow Fowler, a Field Supporter, also joined the fray in his article "Codification in the State of New York" (1884).

Pound Disenchanted

Roscoe Pound, many years later, indicated his disenchantment with Field's *Civil Code* considering it rather ill-drawn. He noted, for example, that the part entitled, "Maxims of Jurisprudence" was an imitation of the Title of Justinian's Digest, "On Divers Maxims of the Old Law," and did not include all the common-law maxims that had proven useful to lawyers, and included some of doubtful value. He thought that the maxim "no one should suffer for the act of another" could be "positively mischievous". And how would you construe the following maxim? "Where one of two innocent persons must suffer by the act of a third, he by whose negligence it happened must be the sufferer."

The struggle finally ended with Field's defeat. The Legislature rejected the *Civil Code* in 1885 and the following year, as well. Carter prevailed in New York, but it should be noted here that four states, beginning with California, adopted all of the Field Codes. Justice Stephen J. Field, of the U.S. Supreme Court and David Dudley Field's brother, was highly influential in arranging for California to adopt all five of Field's Codes (The *Codes of Civil and Criminal Procedure,* the *Political, Civil* and *Penal Codes.*)

In this context, Dean Pound cautions that the *Civil Code* accomplished little in the four jurisdictions that adopted it. The courts, especially in California, often ignore the *Civil Code* and are more influenced by the common law. When the *Civil Code* is cited by a court, it usually is done to express the common law rule it reflects.

Partly Successful

Field's efforts bore more success with two of his other codes. The *Code of Criminal Procedure,* containing 963 sections, was enacted into law on June 1, 1881. This enactment along with the *Code of Civil Procedure,* completely codified the adjective law of the state, with the exception of the law of evidence. The same legislature enacted the *Penal Code* (727 section) on July 26, 1881, and it went into effect on May 1, 1882. The *Political Code* suffered the same effect as the *Civil Code.* It failed passage in the Legislature in 1860. In addition to California, Montana adopted the *Penal Code.* Georgia, North Dakota, South Dakota and Montana, in addition to California, adopted both the *Civil* and *Political Codes.*

Charles E. Clark has noted that the adoption of the Field Codes by California was an important development in the western states, for they were highly influenced by California legislation and they adopted their law in this manner from the Field Codes. Thus, they accepted the substantive codes rejected in New York and were never affected by the later New York revision of Field's 1848 Code of Civil Procedure.

C: ADMINISTRATIVE LAW

CHAPTER 8

THE C.F.R. INDEX

Federal agency regulations fill in the details of permissible conduct that the federal statutes paint with a broad brush. The Federal Food, Drug and Cosmetic Act provides for the establishment of minimum food standards.[1] But it is the Food and Drug Administration[2] and the Department of Agriculture,[3] for example, that together spell out the particulars of those standards. This column discusses the indexing of federal regulations, points out some shortcomings and proposes some improvements.

The three basic sources of information about federal regulations are: *U.S. Government Manual,* the *Federal Register,* and the *Code of Federal Regulations.* The *Manual* provides a bird's eye view of the federal establishment. It outlines its organization and functions and lists the principal personnel and the statutory authority of each agency. The *Federal Register* is the daily chronicle of federal regulations and proposed regulations. The *Code* is a subject cumulation of regulations in force. It is published in some fifty titles, most but not all of which match in subject matter the fifty titles of the U.S. Code. Critics of the C.F.R. and the *Federal Register* complain—not unfairly—that it takes so inordinately long to locate the appropriate rule on any subject that the rule may change before the search is completed.

The C.F.R. Index

The Index to the *Code of Federal Regulations,* which is revised annually, is the chief key to the rules and regulations of the entire

---

[1] 21 U.S.C.A. § 601 et seq.
[2] 21 C.F.R.
[3] 7 C.F.R.

federal establishment. The index attempts to cover some 112,000 pages of codified rules of all the Cabinet departments, their offices and bureaus, and each of the independent agencies.

The January 1, 1981 edition of this Index is published on some 569 pages of a single booklet, where it shares space with other finding aids discussed below. It consists of a list of agencies, activities, products and processes, federal statutes and other finding terms including cross-references, combined in one alphabet. Those terms that the indexers apparently deem important are set in easy-to-read bold face type. Each main term is followed by subheadings, set in a smaller face, that relate to the main term. Lawyers point out that there are too few main headings and many of them are poor choices.

There may be a good reason, for example, why such terms as "Spices", "Sleeping bags", "Swine", and "Vinegar" are given bold face treatment. But there is no main heading under such terms as Unfair Competition, Misrepresentation, False Advertising, Vitamins or Saccharine? All are regulated by federal agencies.

To illustrate, the current master index to C.F.R. contains 26 headings and subheadings, only one of which refers to a specific substance, namely "volatile fruit flavor concentrates." Omitted are the thousands of other substances that are subject to regulation.

After exhausting a dozen or more likely indexing leads in the search for "saccharine," one will find a reference to its regulation (but not the term itself) in the "P's" under the subheading, "Permitted in food on interim basis or in contact with food pending additional study, 21 C.F.R. 180." Then on turning to the appropriate C.F.R. volume of Title 21, one finds the "saccharine" rule itself at subpart 180.37.

There ought to be a single well-publicized government compendium in which all regulated substances are indexed in a single alphabet. The CCH Food, Drug, Cosmetic Law Reporter attempts to do what the C.F.R. index so far has failed to accomplish.

A Revolutionary Development

It took barely five minutes of a "Lexis" search to locate the FDA Commissioner's Final Decision on "Aspartame," a sweetener substitute for "saccharine" (Federal Register for July 24, 1981 at pages 38283–38308). A diligent search through the *Federal Register* had failed to locate it.

Paucity of Index Items

Detailed indexing of regulatory matter is essential if one is to find rules. Yet, the publishers of C.F.R. provide barely half a page of indexing for every 100 pages of regulations. By contrast, the U.S. Code provides thirty-three pages of index headings for every 100 pages of statutes or sixty-six times the indexing depth afforded for C.F.R. The paucity of indexing in the 112,000-page C.F.R. helps to explain the difficulty that lawyers have in findings a particular regulation in this unwieldy and complex code of rules.

The publishers of C.F.R. have attempted to overcome the inadequacies of its index by providing a Table of Titles, Chapters, and Parts and a section of Finding Aids.[4] These features all appear in the index volume and serve as a topical outline to the work of the various agencies. They are similar to but much less detailed than the topical outlines found in a typical West Publishing Company digest. By using these tables it is possible to learn, for example, that regulations relating to food additives are set forth in Parts 170–189 of Title 21 C.F.R. By turning to the appropriate C.F.R. volume, one learns that those Parts are themselves divided into some 4,000 subparts with omissions for expansion but that there is a detailed list of subparts printed at the opening of each Part. So even without an index one might eventually reach the regulation of Saccharine at 21 C.F.R. 180.37.

The section of "Finding Aids" also contains a series of tables the most useful of which is its "parallel table of statutory authorities and rules" (pp. 573–658). It cites "equivalent" rules in C.F.R. for each title and section of U.S.C., presenting both in easy-to-follow parallel columns. But it guides the user only to a full "part," never to a subpart. So for complicated regulations like Parts 170–189 with their 4,000 subparts printed on 380 pages, the parallel table needs refinement. It may zero in on a continent or a country or even a city. But lawyers need to find streets and particular numbers on a street. This it does not attempt.

A second finding aid shows where in C.F.R. or the *Federal Register* executive orders, proclamations and related documents that

---

[4]This combined volume of C.F.R. is titled "C.F.R. Index and Finding Aids," revised as of January 1, 1981.

are still in force have been published or cited. It was last cumulated in a separate 1976 "Finding Aids" volume.

As a last resort information not found in C.F.R. may sometimes be obtained by dialing a Washington, D.C., telephone number provided for that purpose in the *U.S. Government Manual* under each federal agency. Not merely as a test but because the practice is a household scourge, this writer telephoned for information about the regulation of loud commercials by the Federal Communications Commission. An information clerk reported immediately that there is indeed a publication entitled, "Statement of Policy Concerning Loud Commercials," dated July 12, 1965, and that a copy would be mailed that day.

Asked if a Commission lawyer could tell me where the policy statement is published and whether one might find reference to it in C.F.R., the clerk gave three citations of the statement and pointed out that policy statements do not appear in C.F.R. itself.[5] As an indexer the FCC spokesman was letter perfect.

Proposed Improvements

Even if the C.F.R. index cannot follow the example set by the indexing of U.S.C., it should at least observe the basic precepts for indexing set forth by the U.S.A. Standards Institute. "The essential functions of an index are to identify or relate specific items in a (code) . . . , correlate the language of the user with that of the index; and indicate relationships between items."[6]

Another improvement would be the publication of a separate index at the end of each title of C.F.R. The user would then have to examine only a few hundred related headings instead of several thousand unrelated ones. This is done for each title of U.S. Code Annotated. Moreover, as recently as twenty years ago, it was also done for each title of C.F.R. See for example, the Food and Drug Administration regulations (21 C.F.R. 1955 edition). Why was this practice virtually abandoned? Only a few titles include separate indexes and partial ones at that.[7]

---

[5] 30 Fed. Reg. 8694 (Aug. 24, 1965); 1 F.C.C. 2d (1965); 5 R.R. 2d 1621.

[6] U.S.A. Standard Institute. U.S.A. Basic Criteria for Indexes. Washington, D.C., The Institute, 1968.

[7] See C.F.R. Index and Finding Aids, 1981 revision, at 571.

Nearly a hundred years ago Sir Henry Thring and a committee of other English legal scholars expressed these ideas in their draft of "Instruction for Indexing the Statute Law":

"The object of an index is to indicate the place in a book or collection of books in which particular information is to be found.... A complete knowledge of the whole law is required before [the indexer] begins to make the index, for until he can look down on the entire field of law before him, he cannot possibly judge of the proper arrangement of the headings, or of the relative importance of the various provisions."[8]

How far short of this mark is the C.F.R. index? One might as soon expect a motor scooter to haul a 112-car freight train up a steep grade as to count on the power of this index to "carry" in its sketchy columns the 112,000 pages of the *Code of Federal Regulations.* However, now that the publishers acknowledge its shortcomings and plan to act (*Federal Register* for April 24, and April 26, 1974) hope and possibly even help is at hand.

---

[8]The Law Magazine & Review, Fourth Series, 491, 493–512 (August 1877).

CHAPTER 9

FEDERAL REGISTER INDEX

Littera scripta manet: What is written endures. This maxim appears on the front cover of each issue of the *Federal Register.* But the chief key to what has been written is a slender monthly and yearly index. Unless one knows how to use this index, it is virtually impossible to find the rules of the federal establishment.

The two most useful facts about the index are these, as stated by the publisher: "Entries are carried primarily under the names of issuing agencies. Significant subjects are also carried."

Question of Size

The *Federal Register* is the daily newspaper of the Executive branch of the federal government, serving as the medium for its rules and public notices. It was begun in 1936, it is published daily Monday through Friday and now runs to some half-million pages of regulatory documents. They are indexed in forty-five separate noncumulative annual indexes and in individual monthly indexes during the current year. Of course, a large proportion of the documents that have permanent interest are collected in the *Code of Federal Regulations.*

It is the *Federal Register* issues and their indexes for the last twelve to twenty-four months that lawyers have to consult most frequently. The *Federal Register* is tied directly to the *Code.*

Five Kinds of Documents

On a typical day, for example, Dec. 28, 1973, which was the date of the year's final issue, any of five kinds of federal documents is likely to be published in the *Federal Register.*

(1) Executive orders, proclamations and reorganization plans; (2) a recodification and updating of particular rules; (3) new regulations or amendments to old regulations; (4) proposed regulations and (5) notices.

Presidential Documents

The index collects executive orders, proclamations and reorganization plans under the term "Presidential Documents." Also grouped under that heading are some of the President's memoranda to various officials and occasional letters, such as the one impounding appropriated funds, dated Jan. 22, 1973. For those who may forget these facts, the indexers provide cross-references directing the researcher from the terms "Executive Orders" and "Proclamations" to "Presidential Documents." In addition, the broad subjects covered by these documents are listed separately in the annual index though not always in the monthly indexes.

How does this work out in fact? An executive order relating to the Interest Equalization Tax was published in the *Register* for Dec. 28. It is listed in both the 1973 annual and December, 1973, monthly indexes as a subheading under "Presidential Documents." It can also be found under the two topics, "Interest Equalization Tax" and "Taxes" in the annual index. But the specific term "Interest Equalization" does not appear in the monthly index. Most of the other executive orders for the year are listed in both the annual and monthly indexes under one or more catch phrases to indicate the subjects covered and, of course, all are listed under "Presidential Documents."

All eighty-four of the year's proclamations received similar broad coverage. Thus there are subject and "Presidential Document" references to both the purely ceremonial proclamations such as "Johnny Horizon '76 Clean Up America Month" and those having substantive legal force such as the one to restrict the quantity of meat imports (Proc. 4183) and the three to limit the importation of nonfat dry milk (Proc. 4177, 4216 and 4230).

Rule Recodification

A great convenience to users of the *Register* is the occasional republication and codification of a host of amendments made to a particular regulation over a period of years. This enables a lawyer to examine in one place what he would otherwise have to seek out in several. Such was the purpose of including the new codification of Part 214.2 "Nonimmigrant Clauses–Special Requirements for Admission, Extension and Maintenance of Status" of Title 8 "Aliens and Nationality" in our typical issue (Dec. 28, 1974). Again the index lists this valuable document in both the annual and December, 1973, indexes under the agency responsible for the work covered by the rule, the Immigration and Naturalization Service. There is no separate subject heading in either index, but there is a cross-reference to the agency under the term "Aliens."

Major Omission

The fact that this document is a recodification is nowhere revealed in the Index. In the single year 1973, one would search through pages 8591, 14962, 17198, 18361, 24891 and 26354 in order to piece together the successive amendments to this rule (Part 214.2 of the immigration rules). Finally, when he reached page 35425, he would learn that his work had been unnecessary. The regulation had been recodified with all the minor changes incorporated in a single document.

This is infuriating to the lawyer-user and unfair to the diligent draftsmen at the Immigration Service who troubled to prepare the "secret" recodification. This kind of well-kept secret should be shared with all readers of the *Federal Register.* One way to avoid missing a recodification is to work backwards toward the latest edition of CFR, checking the most recent entry list.

New Regulations

A federal regulation becomes effective on the day and hour that it is filed with the *Register*–not on the day it is published–unless a later effective date is stated in the rule itself.

On our typical day, Dec. 28, 1973, new rules or amendments to old rules were issued by the Federal Aviation Administration on aircraft emission standards, the Federal Trade Commission on labeling full-size baby cribs and by a host of other agencies covering numerous matters.

Subject Approach

How easily can one find these regulations through the December index? To locate the new FAA rule, for example, one is more likely to use a subject than an agency approach. Only a specialist would be likely to know whether the rule emanated from the Environmental Protection Agency, from the Civil Aeronautics Board, the FAA or some other agency. Such a matter might even be the subject of an executive order or a presidential proclamation.

These are the results, using the following three most likely subject headings: (1) "Aircraft Emission," (2) "Air Pollution" and (3) "Pollution." The term closest to "Aircraft Emission" used as a heading in the December index is "Aircraft and Air Carriers" which is followed by a subheading, "Pollution from." It is a cross-reference that tells the readers to, "see Environmental Protection Agency." The first subheading under "Environmental Protection Agency" is "Air Pollution" and the next line tells the reader, "see also Aircraft and Engines."

Having left "Aircraft," one tries "Engines." But there is no heading for "Engines." Undaunted, one should return to "Environmental Protection Agency" where there are references to some eighty-five different regulatory documents published in the *Federal Reegister* during December. Skipping over those relating to "Ambient Air Quality" and "Clean Air Act" contracts, the patient reader will find a subheading, "Aircraft and Engines." Sure enough a rule relating to emission standards is listed at that point. But unfortunately it is a Dec. 18 rule of the EPA and the one required is a December 28 rule. A later heading "Fuels and Additives–EPA," is another false lead.

The term "Air Pollution" directs the reader to "Pollution" which contains five subheadings: (a) "Air–see Environmental Protection Agency," a false step already taken; (b) "Federal Facilities," a reference to an executive order which is another false step; and (c), (d) and (e) "Noise" (see FAA), "Oil" and "Water," none of which covers the subject under search.

Agency Approach

The subject approach having failed, what about the three agencies? It has already been determined that the document sought is not an EPA rule. A quick search under the column of Civil Aeronautics Board headings in the December index shows that the CAB is not likely to publish such an article. What about the Federal Aviation Administration? There are references to 111 regulatory documents most of which can be eliminated quickly, e.g., "Air Carrier," "Air Taxi," "Airmen and Certificate Procedures." Finally, there appears "Emission Standards–Aircraft smoke and fuel venting" on page 35437. The search, at last, is ended. Even so, it is interesting to note that on the following page of the index–still under the FAA main heading–are two further references. One reads "Pollution–Air–see Emission Standards above." The other index heading under "Smoke . . ." directs the reader to the same page 35437.

This laborious search illustrates what the *Federal Register* indexes announced at the outset. "Entries are carried primarily under the name of the issuing agencies." Their statement that "significant subjects are also carried", at least in the case of this monthly index, is a snare. As was discovered, the air pollution rules issued by the EPA merited a subject heading: but a confirming rule of the FAA did not. However, the annual index corrected some of these omissions, making it possible to locate this rule by subject, but only after a delay of several months.

Proposed Regulations

The indexing of proposed rules is no more nor less thorough than the indexing of final rules. It is often a hit or miss matter whether one will in a particular case find an appropriate subject heading or not. In our typical issue on December 28, a mere *proposed* rule of the FAA on noise pollution (page 35879) happens to be listed in the December index–through cross-references–under the two terms "Noise" and "Pollution." Why the *final* rule of the FAA on "Air Pollution" is indexed under neither "Air" nor "Pollution" remains a mystery.

The more important question of when, if ever, a proposed rule becomes effective can be answered only by reference to the same index and its subsequent issues, or through numerical tables.

Notices

Almost half of the December 28, 1973, issue of the *Federal Register* is devoted to "Notices." According to a legend that appears in each day's issue, they include typically, "Notices of hearings and investigations, committee meetings, agency decisions and rulings, delegations of authority, filings of petitions and applications, and agency statements of organization and functions."

Three notices that actually appeared that day contained (1) a Department of the Interior "Geothermal lease form" in full text, (2) a Federal Power Commission opinion relating to Alabama Power Company and (3) certificates issued by the Department of Labor authorizing the employment of full-time students in several hundred named establishments at less than the applicable minimum wage.

The December index properly refers to each of these notices under the appropriate agency names, although in two cases the cross-references direct the reader to a sub-agency for his information. There is no provision for using subject headings in this *monthly* index to notices.

However, the *annual* index for 1973 lists the subjects "Geothermal Resources" which refers the reader to Land Management Bureau of the Department of the Interior and "Students" which refers him by a series of steps to the Wage and Hour Division of the Department of Labor.

One can conclude then that searching under an agency name—if it is known—is the best method to use when searching the monthly indexes of the *Federal Register* and that the annual index provides some limited subject coverage. Beginning in 1980, each month's index is cumulated for the year to date. The annual index has no greater subject coverage than the monthly issues on which it is built.

The *Federal Register* provides certain finding aids to supplement the index. First of all the last issue of a month contains a list of all agencies that published regulations during the month. Second, each day's issue contains a cumulative list of the month to date of Code of Regulation parts that are affected by documents issued during the month. That monthly table is cumulated at various times during the year and a final annual table is issued soon after the end of each year. Third, the monthly and annual indexes contain a parallel table of inclusive *Federal Register* pages and dates. This eliminates the task of searching through stacks of unbound issues for a particular page.

Summary

The criticism of the C.F.R. that its index is disproportionately thin for its size applies with equal force to the *Federal Register* index. In December, 1973, for example, a thirty-five page index was the *Federal Register's* only key to some 2324 pages of regulatory matter. For the entire year 1973 its 187-page index attempted to cover regulatory documents that ran to almost 36,000 pages. That is about half a page of index headings for 100 pages of regulations. As pointed out in the discussion of the C.F.R. index, the editors of the United States Code provide 112 times greater indexing depth for it than is afforded by C.F.R. The USC index is similarly 112 times more detailed than is the 1973 *Federal Register Index.* By 1980, the Federal Register ran to 87,012 pages, but its index increased to only 255 pages.

As federal regulations become increasingly complex it is essential that access to them be made simpler—not more difficult. Otherwise it will become a false notion that the *Federal Register* provides notice at all.

CHAPTER 10

THE SEARCH FOR FEDERAL ADMINISTRATIVE REGULATIONS

Is the Office of the Federal Register under a statutory duty to prepare and publish an analytical subject index to the *Code of Federal Regulations?* If so, has the office breached this duty by preparing only a 164-page table of contents to the entire 120-volume Code? By failing to provide an analytical subject index to the Code has the public at large been injured by making it almost impossible for them to know which Federal regulations apply to them?

These questions addressed to the United States Court of Appeals by a lawyer appearing *pro se* in *Cervase v. Office of Federal Register,* 580, F. 2d 1166 (3d Cir. 1978) curiously reflect how lawyers are being confounded by the search process involved in locating applicable rules and regulations promulgated by the Administrative branch of the Federal government.

The Issue

In essence, the issue raised by the *Cervase* case is whether the failure of the Office of the Federal Register and its director to prepare and publish an analytical subject index to the *Code of Federal Regulations (C.F.R.)* creates a situation in which the public at large is being subjected to "secret law."

In ancient times, law was a well-kept secret, revealed and made known only to a selected few. In Rome, for example, the pontifices, who as members of the highest priestly organization entitled the Pontifical College, served as an advisory council of the King, later of the Pontifex Maximus, looked upon the law as one of its secrets.

The need and demand for definite written law was expressed in Rome eventually in the Twelve Tables (C.450 B.C.). Romans, however, were still subjected to circumvention of the law by emperors, such as Caligula, who, we are told, arranged for his laws to be written in small characters and placed high on pillars so as "the more effectively to ensnare the people."

In our day, Justice Douglas holding for the Supreme Court of the U.S. that a municipal ordinance making it an offense for a person convicted of a crime punishable in California as a felony to remain in the city for more than five days without registering with the Chief of Police, when applied to a person who has no actual knowledge of his duty to register, and there is no showing made of the probability of such knowledge, is a violation of the Due Process Clause of the Fourteenth Amendment. He added, "Were it otherwise the evil would be as great as it is when the law is written in print too fine to read or in a language foreign to the community," *Lambert v. California,* 355 U.S. 225, 230 (1957).

The Frustrating Search Process

Although it is manifestly not the purpose of our lawmakers today to deny the public ready access to, and retrieval of, applicable law in force, still the labyrinth of the law which they have created by reason of the huge mass of statutes and administrative rules and regulations they have enacted and promulgated, aside from the multitude of cases decided by judges construing them, have accomplished a similar result to the extent that the uninitiated, and even the expert at times, becomes frustrated and even misled by the search process required to identify them. Professor Fuller wisely suggests in this context that "it is generally more important that a man have a clear warning of his legal duties than that he should know precisely what unpleasantness will attend a breach . . ." (Fuller, *The Morality of Law,* 93 (Rev. ed. 1969).

It is in the "jungle" of administrative law, due to its overwhelming mass of source materials and ineffective subject indexing, that the problems of law in the books come to the fore. Problems referred to by the late Chief Justice of New Jersey as "bulk, inaccessibility, inferior craftsmanship, and an adverse attitude on the part of the bar that exist with respect to legislation; the only difference is that these conditions exist in much higher degree with respect to administrative law" (Vanderbilt, *Men and Measures in the Law,* 29 (1949).

Research in Federal administrative law is especially difficult if only by reason of its pure bulk. Commenting on the 1974 statistics, Professor Bernard Schwartz noted in his casebook on *Administrative Law,* (1977), that the C.F.R. "had grown to 127 volumes, containing 65,249 pages. The C.F.R. contained over 50 million words–seventy times as many as in the Bible and sixty times as many as a complete Shakespeare" (*Id* at 247–248). In addition to the thousands and thousands of pages of administrative rules annually published, the researcher is usually also confounded by a process, characteristic of administrative regulation, of jurisdictional powers being shifted from one agency to another, as well as the many births and deaths of regulatory agencies. This awkward situation is even more aggravated by the comparative ease with which administrative rules and regulations can be promulgated, amended and revoked.

The Way It Was

Prior to the *National Industrial Recovery Act,* 48 Stat. 200 (1933), lawyers referred to the typed regulations kept in an agency's files and which were considered to be generally applicable to the public at large merely by being signed, distributed in press releases and filed in the agency's files. Many times, the only method considered reliable, was for the attorney to seek out a regulation by referring to the agency's files, hoping to identify or locate the regulation by a trial and error search.

At the time, the United States was about the only important nation in the world without some form of an official publication similar to the *Diarios* or gazettes published by countries of Europe and South America in which would appear the daily orders, proclamations, administrative rulings and decisions of the various branches and agencies of those governments. Characteristic of the confusion existing then in this context, was a statement which appeared in the *Report of the Special Committee on Administrative Law of the*

American Bar Association (1934) with reference to the manner in which Executive orders were filed in the Department of State:

"Some orders are retained or buried in the files of the government departments, some are confidential and are not published, and the practice as to printing and publication of orders is not uniform. Some orders are made known and available rather promptly after their approval. The publication of others may be delayed a month or more with consequent confusion in numbering. The comparatively large number of recent orders which incorporate provisions purporting to impose annual penalties by way of fine and imprisonment for violations is without numerical precedent in the history of the government" (Id. at 214).

Need for Publication

The urgent need for an official publication, analogous to the Statutes at Large and the United States Code, in which all rules and regulations in force would be systematically and uniformly published was stressed by legal commentators such as Professor Erwin Griswold of Harvard Law School (Griswold, *Government in Ignorance of the Law—A Plea for Better Publication in Executive Legislation,* 48 Harv.L.Rev. 198 (1934)). "Moreover," he added, "with the help of indices and tabulations . . . one could readily determine whether a particular rule or regulation was still in force, and if not, the extent to which it had been changed or modified or superseded."

Then came the "Hot Oil Case" (*Panama Refining Co. v. Ryan,* 293 U.S. 388 (1935)). Title I, Section 9(c) of the *National Industrial Recovery Act,* approved on June 16, 1933 (48 Stat. 195) authorized the President "to prohibit the transportation in interstate and foreign commerce of petroleum and the products thereof, produced or withdrawn from storage by any state law or valid regulation or order prescribed thereunder, by any board, commission, officer, or other duly authorized agency of a state." President Franklin D. Roosevelt issued an executive order on July 1, 1933, activating the prohibition and then by order of July 14, 1933, he authorized the Secretary of the Interior to exercise all of the powers vested in him by Section 9(c), including the promulgation of "such rules and regulations as he may deem necessary." These regulations were issued forthwith by the Secretary. Subsequently, on Aug. 19, 1933, the President issued an executive order approving a "Code of Fair Competition for the Petroleum Industry." On Aug. 28, 1933, another executive order was issued designating the Secretary of the Interior as the Administrator, and the Department of the Interior, as the Federal agency, to exercise all the powers vested in the President by Section 9(c), as implemented by the Code. Thus, there were two sets of executive orders, both conferring powers and duties upon the Secretary of the Interior.

Article III, Section 4, of the Code of Fair Competition, allocated the amount of oil allowed to be produced or withdrawn from storage by the various properties within each state. Paragraph two of Section 4, provided, that any production or withdrawal by a company "in excess of any such quota assigned to [it] shall be deemed an unfair trade practice and in violation of the Code." In the course of modifying the Code, paragraph two was eliminated on Sept. 13, 1933. It was restored to the Code, on Sept. 25, 1934, slightly more than a year later. In the interim, however, an action was instituted in the U.S. District Court for the Eastern District of Texas by the Panama Refining Co. attacking the constitutional validity of the N.I.R.A., certain regulations of the Secretary of the Interior, and of the Petroleum Code. On Feb. 12, 1934, the Court granted permanent injunctions prohibiting Federal officials from enforcing the regulations (5 Fed. Supp. 639).

Decrees Reversed

On appeal to the Fifty Circuit Court of Appeals, these decrees were reversed and the bills dismissed. (71 F. 2d 1, 8 (1934). On appeal to the U.S. Supreme Court, a most unusual situation arose. After ruling that the Executive Orders of July 11, 1933 and of July 14, 1933 and the Regulations made thereunder were "without constitutional authority," Chief Justice Hughes, to the embarrassment of all concerned, noted that no ruling could be made on the constitutionality of the Petroleum Code, because the regulations on which the case was assumedly based had been revoked without the knowledge of the parties or their attorneys.

"The controversy with respect to the provision of Section 4 of Article III of the Petroleum Code was initiated and proceeded in the courts below upon a false assumption," he announced. "That assumption was that this section still contained the paragraph (eliminated by the Executive Order of Sept. 13, 1933) by which production in excess of assigned quotas was made an unfair practice and a violation of the Code. Whatever the cause of the failure to give appropriate public notice of the change in the section, with the result that the persons affected, the prosecuting authorities, and the courts, were alike ignorant of the alteration, the fact is that the attack in this respect was upon a provision which did not exist . . . When this suit was brought, and when it was heard, there was no cause of action for the injunction sought with respect to the provision of Section 4 of Article III of the Code; as to that there was no basis for real controversy . . . For this reason we express no opinion as to the interpretation or validity of the provision of the Petroleum Code."

The 'Hot Oil Case'

According to contemporary newspaper accounts, when the "Hot Oil Case" was argued in the Supreme Court in December, 1934, and the question arose as to whether the provision of Section 4 of Article III of the Code was still in effect, or had been amended, superseded or revoked, some of the Supreme Court Justices expressed astonishment on being told by counsel that there was no central repository or official publication of all administrative orders and regulations; that some of them were not widely distributed, and that they were not always easily accessible even to persons directly affected by them.

Their remarks were widely quoted in the press, along with the Chief Justice's reasons for failing to review the constitutionality of the Code section. Public indignation became so intense, that less than two months thereafter, on March 1, 1935, a bill was introduced in the House "to provide for the custody of Federal proclamations, orders, regulations, notices and other documents, and for the prompt and uniform printing and distribution thereof" (H.R. 6323), which was approved shortly thereafter as the *Federal*

Register Act, July 26, 1935, ch. 417, 49 Stat. 500, 44 USC Sections 1501–1511. The Act provides for the publication of a *Federal Register* and that no document required to be published in the *Federal Register* "shall be valid as against any person who has not had actual knowledge thereof until the duplicate orginals or certified copies of the document shall have been filed with the Division and a copy made available for public inspection." The act also prescribes what the content of the *Federal Register* shall be. It does not, for example, contain news items or comments, treaties, conventions and other international agreements.

Initial Plans for Register

The original plans for the *Federal Register* called for publication of bound volumes similar to the Congressional Record. The first issue of the *Federal Register* was dated March 14, 1936. It then appeared five days a week, Tuesday through Saturday, except for legal holidays. It is presently published daily, Monday through Friday, except for legal holidays. The first three volumes covering the period from March 12, 1936 through June 3, 1938 were published according to schedule. With the publication of the third volume, however, the practice of issuing a bound volume was discontinued, and since then libraries have had to bind their daily copies for permanent use.

Pursuant to the *Federal Register Act,* the documents in force at the time of the passage of the act in 1935 were later to be collected and compiled into a *Code of Federal Regulations (C.F.R.),* to which would be added annual supplements containing the documents first published in the *Federal Register.* A later amendment (50 Stat. 304) extended until June 1, 1938 the period in which the documents were to be included in the *C.F.R.*

Since March 14, 1936, the *Federal Register* has published the following classes of documents as required by 49 Stat. 501 (1935), 44 USC Section 305(a) (1976):

"(1) All Presidential proclamations and Executive orders, except such as have no general applicability and legal effect;. . .

"(2) such documents or classes of documents as the President shall determine from time to time have general applicability and legal effect; and

"(3) such documents or classes of documents as may be required so to be published by Act of the Congress: *Provided,* that for the purposes for this Act every document or order which shall prescribe a penalty shall be deemed to have general applicability and legal effect."

'Document' Defined

Title I of the C.F.R. defines a "document" as including "any Presidential proclamation, or Executive order, and any rule, regulations, order, certificate, code of fair competition, license, notice, or similar instrument issued, prescribed, or promulgated by an agency" (Sec. 1.1). A "document having general applicability and legal effect" is defined as "any document issued under proper authority prescribing a penalty or course of conduct, conferring a right, privilege, authority or immunity, or imposing an obligation, and relevant or applicable to the general public, members of a class, or persons in a locality, as distinguished from named individuals or organizations." (Sec. 1.1.)

Section 7 of the Federal Register Act of 1935 provides that regulations of general applicability are not binding on any person, except one who has actual knowledge thereof, unless and until they are published in the Federal Register. That section also provides that such publication creates a rebuttable presumption as to the validity of the regulation and the accuracy of its text as published.

The *Code of Federal Regulation* is a codification of the general and permanent rules published in the *Federal Register* by the executive departments and agencies of the Federal government. The Code is divided into fifty titles which represent broad areas subject to Federal regulation. Each title is divided into chapters which usually bear the name of the issuing agency. Each chapter is further subdivided into parts covering specific regulatory areas and parts are subdivided into sections and paragraphs. The basic unit of the C.F.R. is the section.

The C.F.R. is *prima facie* evidence of the text of the original documents (44 USC 1510). The contents of the *Federal Register,* however, are required to be judicially noticed (44 USC 1507).

The CFR was authorized by Section II of the Federal Register Act. When first conceived, it was thought that the CFR would comprise a single volume, but as finally completed it consisted of fifteen volumes in seventeen books. It contained the rules and regulations in force and effect as of June 1, 1938 as well as the statutes which created and gave authority to the agency. It was supplemented annually with a cumulative supplement on June 1, 1943. (9 vols.) and subsequent annual supplements.

Recodification Completed

By Executive Order 9930 of Feb. 4, 1948 (13 F.R. 519), a recodification of the CFR as of Jan. 1, 1949 was accomplished. Issued in individual volumes, similar to the United States Code with space for annual supplements in pocket parts, superseding volumes replaced older ones which contained bulky pocket parts. This second edition superseded the first and a process of perpetual revision of the second edition rather than new editions was adopted.

Today, each volume of the Code is revised at least once each calendar year, and issued on a quarterly basis approximately as follows:

Title 1 through Title 16 as of Jan. 1.

Title 17 through Title 27 as of April 1.

Title 28 through Title 41 as of July 1.

Title 42 through Title 50 as of Oct. 1.

The administrative committee of the *Federal Register* is charged with the statutory responsibility for publishing the *Federal Register* and the *Code of Federal Regulations.* In addition, other regulations provide for the indexing of the *Federal Register* and for the annual publishing of a subject index to the *Code of Federal Regulations.* In his brief to the district court, Cervase observed that the 1938 codification consisted of fourteen volumes, with a general index of 513 pages. The current codification has grown to more than 120 volumes covering fifty titles, "while what passes for an index has actually shrunk to 164 pages." Actually, as of 1978 it is 234 pages.

Lower Court Reversed

Holding that a summary disposition of the *Cervase* complaint by the District Court was improper, the U.S. Court of Appeals reversed the dismissal and remanded the case for further proceedings. In doing so, the court ruled that the administrative committee of the *Federal Register* has a mandatory duty to prepare and publish an analytical subject index to the C.F.R. "Codification of a document is prima facie evidence both of its text and of its continuing legal effect," the court observed. "Publication of the document in the *Federal Register* makes it effective against the world. *But without the retrieval mechanism provided by an adequate index, a person might never be aware of a document containing a regulation affecting him until some Federal bureaucrat produced a copy of the document and attempted to apply it to him. Indeed the affected individual might already have changed his position in complete ignorance of the existence of the regulation. Such ignorance would avail him not, however, since publication in the Federal Register gives him constructive notice of the existence of the regulation.*" (Italics added.) *Cervase* at 1168–1169.

Currently the C.F.R. Index is combined in one unnumbered volume with Finding Aids, (entitled *CFR Index and Finding Aids*) in 651 pages of which the subject index consists of 234 pages. Of course there are other research tools than the subject index which can be referred to in the search for apposite Federal rules and regulations. The many looseleaf services, for one, should not be ignored, although they are privately published and extravagantly priced. There is little doubt, however, but that the C.F.R. subject index, is not analytical, consisting mainly of an arrangement under agencies, with some broad subject headings included. It is intended merely to direct users to the particular titles of the C.F.R. in which they are interested. After that, the researcher must depend on his or her ingenuity or expertise to carry on the search for the rule. The government also provides information and assistance on the use of the Federal Register and C.F.R., by responding to questions for specific information at the following telephone numbers–(202) 523-5266 and 5227.

The present difficulties of access to the C.F.R. arise from the tremendous mass of materials pouring out of the agencies without check and the obvious inadequacies of format and subject indexing methods. Certainly, "we must find a better way" and the legal profession is indebted to attorney John Cervase, for trying to lead us in that direction.

CHAPTER 11

ACCESS TO PUBLIC RECORDS

Responding to a need that a "free society is maintained when the public is aware of governmental actions" and is allowed to "know the process of governmental decision-making and to review the documents and statistics leading to [such] determinations,"[1] the New York State Legislature enacted a Freedom of Information Law in 1974, patterned after the federal Freedom of Information Act.[2] Its purpose was to make available to the public all documents created by and physically controlled by certain governmental entities, subject however, to limitations imposed by the need for "confidentiality." In approving the legislation, Governor Wilson stated: "These bills will provide, for the first time in New York State, a structure through which citizens may gain access to the records of government and thereby gain insight into its workings."[3]

Purpose of Legislation

Effective Jan. 1, 1978 a new "Freedom of Information Law" repealed and replaced the 1974 law. The purpose of the new legislation was to cure certain obvious deficiencies in the 1974 law.[4]

As brought out by Senator Ralph J. Marino, prior to the adoption of the 1974 law, "statutory and case law in New York assured

---

[1] Former Section 85, Public Officers Law, added L. 1974, C. 578, §2; amended L. 1974, C. 579, §1; repealed and amended by L. 1977, C. 933, §1.

[2] L. 1974, Chap. 578; 5 U.S.C. §552 (1970).

[3] N.Y. Session Laws at A-319, A-320 (McKinney 1974).

[4] L. 1977, Chap. 933, Public Officers Law, Article VI, Sections 84–90.

the public's right to review governmental records, but failed clearly to define the records available or to establish procedures for making them available . . . In many situations, however, the public's right to access was denied, because of determinations that the situation did not come within the general 'common law' right to inspect documents."[5]

The effect of the law as amended is to mandate compliance to the law over every public agency of the state. A state "agency" under the law is defined as "any state or municipal department, board, bureau, division, commission, committee, public authority, public corporation, council, office or other governmental entity, performing a governmental or proprietary function for the state of New York or one or more municipalities thereof, except the judiciary or the state legislature."[6]

In essence, the Freedom of Information Law–as originally enacted and as subsequently amended, provides rights of access to records reflective of governmental decisions and policies. The 1974 law, however, only granted rights of access to nine specified categories of records to the exclusion of all others.[7] A rec-

---

[5] Marino, *The N.Y. Freedom of Information Law,* 43 Fordham L. Rev. 83, 84–85 (1974).

[6] Former Section 87, added L, 1974, C. 578, Section 2 and repealed and added by L. 1977, C. 933, Section 1.

[7] The 1974 law enumerated the documents subject to inspection as:

a) final opinions, including concurring and dissenting opinions, as well as orders, made in the adjudication of cases;

b) those statements of policy and interpretations which have been adopted by the agency and any documents, memoranda, data or other materials constituting statistical or factual tabulations which led to the formulation thereof . . . ;

c) minutes of meetings of the governing body, if any, of the agency of government and of public hearings held by the agency. (The phrase "if any" was added to make it clear that the section applied only to agencies which had formal governing bodies. Thus a weekly staff meeting was not considered a governing body. See Marino, supra at 87);

d) internal or external audits and statistical or factual tabulations made by or for the agency;

e) administrative staff manuals and instructions to staff that affect members of the public;

f) police blotters and booking records.

Also available were payroll records for public employees, including their names, addresses, titles, and salaries, but accessible only to "bona fide" members of a news media. Sections 88(1)(g) to (h) of the 1974 law provided as ord[8] which could not be identified as being in one of these categories of accessible records was presumed to be deniable. Thus, as brought out in a speech by Robert J. Freeman, Executive Director of the Committee on Public Access to Records, on Jan. 19, 1978, before the New York State Bar Association:

> "The thrust of the state statute as initially enacted was based upon a presumption that the records were deniable. The responsibility of identifying records fell on the public, and the burden of proof in a judicial proceeding was also borne by the public."

Denial of Requests

Under the 1974 law, unless the information sought could be classed under one of the nine categories, the request could be denied. Furthermore, Sections 88(3)(a) to Sections 88(3)(e) of the 1974 law, denied access to records, which if disclosed would result in an unwarranted invasion of personal privacy.[9] Then again, even if a record was identifiable as being within a category of accessibility, still the agency or municipality could deny access to records which were specifically exempted by

---

well that an agency had to make available final determinations and dissenting opinions of members of the governing body, if any, of the agency and any other files, records, papers or documents required by any other provisions of law to be made available for public inspection and copying.

[8] Section 86(4) of the Public Officers Law defines a "record" as "any information kept, held, filed, produced (added L. 1977, C. 933 § 1) or reproduced by, with or for any agency or the state legislature, in any physical form whatsoever including, but not limited to, reports, statements, examinations, memoranda, opinions, folders, files, books, manuals, pamphlets, forms, papers, designs, drawings, maps, photos, letters, microfilms, computer tapes or discs, rules, regulations or codes."

[9] For example, disclosure of such personal matters as may have been reported in confidence to an agency or municipality and which was not relevant or essential to the ordinary work of the agency, disclosure of employment, medical or credit histories or personal references of applicants for employment, disclosure of items involving the medical or personal records of a client or patient in a hospital or medical facility, the sale or release of lists of names and addresses in the possession of any agency or municipality if such lists would be used for private, commercial or fund-raising purposes, disclosing of items of a personal nature when disclosure would result in economic or personal hardship and such records were not relevant to the ordinary work of the agency or municipality.

statute,[10] confidential information which would result in an unfair advantage to competitors,[11] and part of investigatory files compiled for law enforcement purposes.[12]

Then there were other problems arising from the interpretation of the 1974 Freedom of Information Law. As Freeman noted in his speech:

> "Due to the structure of the original statute, there existed a gray area of records that were neither specifically available under any of the categories of accessible records, nor specifically deniable. As such, the provisions of the original statute simply did not pertain to a multitude of records, and more of those in the gray area were admissible as of right. To compound these problems, although the central provision of the statute was subtitled 'access to records,' the term 'record' was undefined. Items such as factual tabulations stored in a computer that would otherwise be accessible were in some instances denied on the ground that the information stored in a computer did not constitute a 'record.'"

Law's Thrust Changed

The 1977 amendments have changed the thrust of the law so that now the presumption favors accessibility rather than deniability of records or portions thereof. As stated by Freeman:

"The amendments . . . reverse the logic of the original statute. Records are presumed accessible unless they fall within specific categories of deniable records. The public need only 'reasonably describe' the records sought and the burden of proof is on the government in a judicial proceeding by which a denial of access is challenged.

Section 87 of the Public Officers Law now provides that the governing body of each public corporation and agency must promulgate rules and regulations pertaining to accessibility to their records and then make available for public inspection and

---

[10] Section 88(7)(a).

[11] Section 88(7)(b).

[12] Section 88(7)(d). This was based on the federal act which exempts "investigatory files compiled for law enforcement purposes except to the extent available by law to a party other than an agency. . . ." 5 U.S.C. §552(b)(7) (1970).

copying all of its records. The specific categories of deniable records are set forth in Section 87(2)a to (h). An agency may deny access to records because they are:

(a) Specifically exempted from disclosure by state or federal statutes;

(b) If disclosed would constitute an unwarranted invasion of personal privacy under the provisions of Section 89(2) of the Public Officers Law;[13]

(c) If disclosed would impair present or imminent contract awards or collective bargaining negotiations;

(d) Are trade secrets or are maintained for the regulation of commercial enterprise which if disclosed would cause substantial injury to the competitive position of the subject enterprise;

(e) Are compiled for law enforcement purposes and which, if disclosed would–

(1) interfere with law enforcement investigations or judicial proceedings;

(2) deprive a person of a right to a fair trial or impartial ajudication;

(3) identify a confidential source or disclose confidential information relating to a criminal investigation;

(4) reveal criminal investigative techniques or procedures, except routine techniques and procedures;

(f) If disclosed would endanger the life or safety of any person;

(g) Are inter-agency or intra-agency materials which are not:

(1) statistical or factual tabulations or data;

(2) instructions to staff that affect the public; or

---

[13] An unwarranted invasion of personal privacy includes, but is not limited to: disclosure of employment, medical or credit histories or personal references of applicants for employment; medical or personal records of a client or patient in a medical facility; sale or release of lists of names and addresses if such lists would be used for commercial or fund-raising purposes; disclosure of information of a personal nature which would result in economic or personal hardship to the subject party and such information is not relevant to the work of the agency requesting or maintaining it; or disclosure of information of a personal nature reported in confidence to an agency and not relevant to the ordinary work of such agency. An agency, however, may delete identifying details in order to make the record available. It can also reveal such information, when the record concerns person requesting the record, or the person involved consents in writing to disclosure.

(3) final agency policy or determinations; or

(h) Are examination questions or answers which are requested prior to the final administration of such questions.

The Effect

The effect of such specificity has been to eliminate the gray areas of disclosure that characterized the enforcement of the old law. Freeman believes that "the alteration of the structure of the law and the specificity of the grounds for denial of access will result in greater ease of implementation and interpretation by government officials who have the duty to respond to requests and members of the public, who will more readily recognize the logic of the law and the grounds for denial."

It should be noted in this context that although the law generally provides access to existing records, an agency, however, is not required to create a record in response to a request—nor to develop a body of written law or policy.

Then again, the purpose of the Freedom of Information Law is to give the public free access to the documents involved in government decision making, held the Appellate Division in a case in which an agency had failed to index its final opinions, but not to ease the research burden of private litigants, although this may have been the intention of the separate federal sanction, under the federal Freedom of Information Act.[14] Section 87(3) of the Public Officers Law, however, is relevant here for it specifically states that—

> "3. Each agency shall maintain:
>
> "(a) a record of the final vote of each member in every agency proceeding in which the member votes;
>
> "(b) a record setting forth the name, public office address, title and salary of every officer or employee of the agency;
>
> "(c) a reasonably detailed current list by subject matter, of all records in the possession of the agency whether or not available under this article."

---

[14] *D'Alessandro v. Unemployment Insurance Appeal Board,* 56 A.D. 2d 762; 392 N.Y.S. 2d 433 (1977).

Judiciary Law Provision

Although the courts are not subject to the Freedom of Information Law, Section 255 of the Judiciary Law directs the clerk of a court to "diligently search the files, papers, records and dockets in his office" and upon payment of a fee make copies thereof. Agencies which regulate the courts administratively, however, are subject to the act, as they are not considered as a court.

Accessibility to the records of the Legislature is governed by Section 88 of the Public Officers Law. It mandates that the respective houses of the legislature must promulgate rules and regulations pertaining to the availability, location, and nature of records, and, in accordance with such published rules make available for public inspection and copying:

(a) Bills and amendments thereto, fiscal notes, introducers' bill memoranda, resolutions and amendments thereto, and index records;

(b) Messages received from the governor or the other house of the legislature, and home rule measures;

(c) Legislative notification of the proposed adoption of rules by an agency;

(d) Members' code of ethics statements;

(e) Transcripts or minutes, if prepared, and journal records of public sessions, including meetings of committees, subcommittees and public hearings, with the records of attendance of members thereat and records of any votes taken;

(f) Audits and statistical or factual tabulations of, or with respect to, material otherwise available for public inspection and copying pursuant to Section 88 or any other applicable provision of law;

(g) Administrative staff manuals and instructions to staff that affect members of the public;

(h) Final reports and formal opinions submitted to the legislature;

(i) Final reports or recommendations and minority or dissenting reports and opinions of members of committees, subcommittees, or commissions of the legislature;

(j) Any other files, records, papers or documents required by law to be made available for public inspection and copy.

Section 88(3) provides in addition that each house of the legislature must maintain and make available for public inspection and copying:

(a) a record of votes of each member in every session and every committee and subcommittee meeting in which the member votes;

(b) a record setting forth the name, public office address, title and salary of every officer or employee; and

(c) a current list, reasonably detailed, by subject matter of any records required to be made available for public inspection and copying pursuant to Section 88.

Provision for Committee

The Public Information Law provides for a Committee on Public Access to Records (Section 88) whose responsibility it is to oversee the implementation of the freedom of Information Law. Composed of ten members, four from the government and six from the public, the four government members are the Lieutenant Governor, the Secretary of State, whose office acts as secretariat for the Committee, the Commissioner of Government Services and the Director of the Budget. Of the six public members, at least two must represent the news media.

The Committee on Public Access to Records must furnish to any agency or any person advisory guidelines, opinions, or other appropriate information regarding accessibility and deniability to information as provided by Article VI of the Public Officers Law (Freedom of Information Law), promulgate rules and regulations with respect to the implementation of the law, and report on its activities, findings and recommendations to the Governor and the Legislature.

In order to prevent unwarranted invasions of personal privacy, the Committee is required to establish guidelines deleting identifying details or withholding of records otherwise available under the law. In the absence of such guidelines Section 89(2)(a) provides, that an agency may delete identifying details when it makes records available. Section 89(2)(b) provides that an unwarranted invasion of personal privacy includes, but is not limited to:

(1) Disclosure of employment, medical or credit histories or personal references of applicants for employment;

(2) Disclosure of items involving the medical or personal records of a client or patient in a medical facility;

(3) Sale or release of lists of names and addresses if such lists would be used for commercial or fund-raising purposes;

(4) Disclosure of information of a personal nature when disclosure would result in economic or personal hardship to the subject party and such information is not relevant to the work of the agency requesting or maintaining it; or

(5) Disclosure of information of a personal nature reported in confidence to an agency and not relevant to the ordinary work of such agency.

No Invasion of Privacy

When identifying details are deleted, however, or when the person to whom a record pertains consents in writing to disclosure, or when upon presenting reasonable proof of identity, a person seeks access to records pertaining to that person, such disclosure is not deemed to be an unwarranted invasion of personal privacy.

Written requests for a record reasonably described must be answered by the agency involved within a period of five business days; either by providing a record upon payment of a fee or denying access to the record. When access to a record is denied, an appeal can be made within thirty days thereafter to the agency's head who has seven business days to explain in writing the reasons for further denial or provide access to record sought. A copy of such appeal and the determination thereon must be submitted to the Committee on Public Access to Records. An Article 78 (C.P.L.R.) proceeding may be brought for judicial review of the decision denying access to the record. If access to a record is denied pursuant to Section 87(2) of the law, then the agency involved has the burden of proving that such record falls within the provision of Section 87(2).

Access to Records of the State Legislature should be directed to the public information officers of the respective houses of the legislature.

When advise is required pertaining to the Freedom of Information Law write to the Committee on Public Access to Records, Department of State, 162 Washington Avenue, Albany, N.Y. 12231, or call (518) 174-2518.

To date, the Committee has submitted reports annually. They provide considerable information and guidance on the Freedom of Information Law and reflect a professional competence and scholarship which do credit to the Committee and to its executive director, Robert J. Freeman and staff.

Need for Changes

The first annual report notes that there are problems of interpretation and limitations upon the scope of the Freedom of Information Act which require clarification and amendment. It then proceeds to analyze and suggest solutions to the probelms that currently prevail under the Act, of access to Legislative records, inclusion of procedures in the law, fees for copying, privacy, law enforcement records, records of votes, payroll records and reimbursement of attorney's fees.

With reference to access to law enforcement records, for example, the report raises the question whether the state Freedom of Information Act will hamper the efforts of the state law enforcement agencies as the federal Freedom of Information Act has apparently adversely affected the work of the F.B.I. Noting, however, that the federal act permits a federal agency to withhold "investigatory records compiled for law enforcement purposes" which if disclosed would "endanger the life or physical safety of law enforcement personnel . . ."[15] the report suggests that the New York situation is distinguishable, for subsection 87(2)(f) of the New York act, allows an agency to deny access to its records, whether or not compiled for law enforcement purposes, when disclosure "would endanger the life or safety of *any* person." (emphasis added)

Then again, the federal act applies to "confidential information furnished only by the confidential source,"[16] whereas the New

[15] 5 U.S.C. § 552(b)(7)(8).
[16] 5 U.S.C. § 552(b)(7)(D).

York act provides that an agency may withhold records that "identify a confidential source or disclose confidential information relating to a criminal investigation . . ."[17] As a result, the New York law provides a broader base for withholding such information "for it permits an agency to withhold not only the identities of confidential sources or disclose confidential information relating to a criminal investigation. Consequently, an agency need not delete only identifying details relative to a confidential source but rather may in the Committee's view withhold records compiled for law enforcement purposes which if disclosed would 'identify.'"[18] The Committee plans to monitor this situation closely and if the New York Act contains provisions that enable individuals to engage in vindictive acts against others then it will recommend remedial legislation.

Aids to Protect Confidentiality

In an historical comment on privacy, the Committee's first annual report interestingly notes that until the Freedom of Information Law was first enacted in 1974, no other law in New York defined or referred to "invasion of privacy," except for the Civil Rights Law, Sections 50 and 51 which apply only to the unauthorized use of an individual's name or likeness for trade or commercial purpose. There are, however, a number of laws protecting the confidentiality of specific records or categories of records, which the report identifies. Some of them are:

- Coroner's records, autopsy reports (County Law, Sect. 677).
- Inmate and parolee records (Correction Law, Sections 29, 221).
- Mental Health Records (Mental Hygiene Law, Section 33.13).
- Police Records regarding juveniles (Family Court Act, Section 584).
- Unemployment records (Labor Law, Section 537).

---

[17] Subsection 87(2)(e)(iii).

[18] First Annual Report to the Governor and the Legislature on the Freedom of Information Law, 7 (1978).

- Motor vehicles registrations (Vehicles and Traffic Law, Section 202).
- Student records ("Buckley Amendment") 20 USC 1232(g).
- Public assistance (Social Services Law, Section 136).
- Drug abuse (21 USC 1175).
- Police officer's personnel records (Civil Rights Law, Section 50-a).
- Corporate Tax Records (Tax Law, Section 202).
- Personnel income tax records (Tax law, Section 384).
- Rent control records (Unconsolidated Laws, Section 8608).
- Investigation of banks (Banking Law, Section 36).
- Vocational rehabilitation (Education Law, Section 1007).

Other Illegal Procedures

In addition to the above, subsection 89(2)(b) of the Freedom of Information law provides that "an unwarranted invasion of personal privacy includes, but shall not be limited to (1) disclosure of employment, medical or credit histories or personal references of applicants for employment; (2) disclosures of items involving the medical or personal records of a client or patient in a medical care facility; (3) sale or resale of lists of names and addresses if such lists would be used for commercial or fund-raising purposes; (4) disclosure of information of a personal nature when disclosure would result in economic or personal hardship to the subject party and such information is not relevant to the work of the agency requesting or maintaining it; or (5) disclosure of information of a personal nature reported in confidence to an agency and not relevant to the ordinary work of such agency." In this context it should also be noted that the federal act protects against a "clearly unwarranted invasion of privacy."[19]

It is obvious to the Committee that problems of interpretation of subsection 89(2) of the state Act, due in particular to the use of conjunctives, will eventually have to be resolved either by the courts or amending legislation.

---

[19] 5 U.S.C. § 552(a)(2)(c), (b)(6).

Another interesting point the Committee makes in its report is that although an appeal lies under the state Act from a denial of access to a record to the Committee itself, too many appeals are not brought because of the expense involved. Actually, the Committee believes that "agencies have in some instances denied access to records with the knowledge that a member of the public does not have the financial resources to challenge the denial judicially." To remedy this situation, the Committee recommends the enactment of a provision similar to that contained in the federal Freedom of Information Act, which allows a court to assess against the United States reasonable attorney fees and other litigation costs reasonably incurred in any case in which the complainant substantially prevails. In this context, it would not be necessary for the member of the public to prevail against the agency. Rather the fee would be awarded to those representing members of the public who obtain "substantial" access to the record.

Need to Establish Rules

As indicated above, the Committee is directed by the Act to promulgate regulations with respect to its implementation and for furnishing advice to state agencies, the public and the news media regarding it as well.

The Committee staff has prepared thousands of written advisory opinions at the request of the public, representatives of state and local government, the news media and interest groups throughout the state. In an effort to keep interested persons abreast of the nature of the opinions, an index to advisory opinions is compiled and updated approximately four times annually. The index identifies opinions by number and hundreds of "key phrases." A revised index appears in the Second Annual Report. Due to the repetition of the substance of various opinions, reference is made only to opinions that have continuing relevance, precedential value or that are in some manner unique. The opinions rendered under the 1974 Freedom of Information Law are numbered up to 620, the remainder pertain to the amended law, effective Jan. 1, 1978. The quarterly indices are provided free of charge upon request.

By means of the index, copies of opinions on specific subjects can similarly be requested from the Committee. For copies of these indices write to: Committee on Public Access to Records, Department of State, 162 Washington Avenue, Albany, N.Y. 12231. The Committee staff will also respond to telephone inquiries for oral advisory opinions. It now receives more than 100 requests of this type per week. The Committee's telephone number is (518) 474-2518, 2791.

Information regarding the Committee's activity and developments in the Freedom of Information Law is disseminated by means of *Newsvane*, a publication of the Department of State, that is distributed to all units of local government. Each issue contains summaries of advisory opinions or judicial determination that are relevant to the duties of local government.

The Committee also compiles a summary of judicial decisions rendered under the state Act. The summary distinguishes decisions rendered under the 1974 law and the amended law. In addition, statutory citations are provided so that cases dealing with specific areas can be easily identified. The second annual report contains a copy of the then most recent summary (Dec. 15, 1979). It is arranged alphabetically under the title of the case.

The Committee on Public Access to Records and its executive director and staff are to be commended for their excellent work in implementing the effectiveness of the state Freedom of Information Law. The Committee believes that the success and utility of the Freedom of Information Law will depend on its activist role. Certainly the role it has played since 1974, when it was first established, bears this out.

D: PARTICULAR SUBJECTS

CHAPTER 12

A SUMMARY OF SOURCES OF RESEARCH IN ENVIRONMENTAL LAW

"I think that I shall never see
Standing granted to a tree."[1]

Despite this whimsical comment on Christopher Stone's book, *Should Trees Have Standing?*,[2] there is no foreseeable limit to environmental interests–and potential rights–whether currently recognized or not. The purpose of this chapter is to present a summary of the basic primary and secondary sources for environmental research that exist today.

Federal Law

The Basic Statutes

The National Environmental Policy Act of 1969[3] and Reorganization Plan No. 3 (1970)[4] provide the chief Federal authority in this field. The *Act* requires the Federal government to safeguard the environment for future generations[5] and directs its officials to

---

[1] Unsigned book review in 26 Stanford L. Rev., 1488, 1489 (June 1974).

[2] Subtitled Toward Legal Rights for Natural Objects and published by William Kaufman, Inc. in Los Altos, California in 1974, this book urged that natural resources should be empowered to sue and that those who benefit from the endangered resources should speak in their behalf. It is believed that Stone's book prompted Justice Douglas to write his dissent in Sierra Club v. Morton, 405 U.S. 727 (1972).

[3] 42 U.S.C.A. § § 4431 et seq.

[4] 35 Fed. Reg. 15, 263 (1970).

[5] 42 U.S.C.A. § 4431(a).

set out in writing the probable effect of each legislative proposal or major new activity for everyone to see—presumably in the *Federal Register*—before action may be taken. The *Plan* established the Environmental Protection Agency as a co-ordinating body and transferred to it "a variety of research monitoring, standard setting and enforcement activities related to pollution abatement and control..."[6] It took over the work of fifteen agencies: among them the Federal Water Quality Administration, the National Air Pollution Control Administration, the Department of Health, Education and Welfare solid waste control work and the activities of the Federal Radiation Council and the Atomic Energy Commission pertaining to radiation hazards.

The *Act* also established the Council on Environmental Quality as a monitoring agency in the Office of the President. Staffing for the Council was provided in the Environmental Quality Improvement Act of 1970.[7]

In a recent development, Congress enacted on Oct. 11, 1976 the Toxic Substances Control Act[8] which expanded the authority of EPA to collect information on "the effect of chemical substances and mixtures on health and the environment...".[9] to regulate such materials "which present an unreasonable risk of injury to health or the environment and to take action with respect to [those substances] which are imminent hazards,[10] but without creating "unnecessary economic barriers to technological innovation."[11] There are other statutes that empower additional Federal agencies to act. But these are illustrative of the main Federal laws.

Legislative History

The Environmental Protection Agency has published in some thirty-nine volumes a massive collection of Federal statutes, Congressional reports on bills, extracts from floor debates and hearings and related documents divided into the following seven environ-

---

[6] 40 C.F.R. § 1.3.

[7] 42 U.S.C.A. § § 4372 et seq.

[8] 15 U.S.C.A. § § 2601 et seq; P.L. 94–469, 90 Stat. 9003 (1976).

[9] 15 U.S.C.A. § 2601.

[10] Id.

[11] Id.

mental categories: A–General; B–Air; C–Water; D–Solid Waste; E–Pesticides; F–Radiation and G–Noise. Publication of documents in an eighth category—H–International—was planned but the volume has not yet been released.[12] No other branch of Federal legislative activity is so fully documented.

For example, the first of these thirty-nine volumes sets out a detailed legislative history of both the Reorganization Plan No. 3 (1970) that established EPA and the National Environmental Policy Act of 1969. It runs to some 609 pages. The remaining thirty-eight volumes are equally comprehensive. Documents that are not reproduced in full are carefully cited so that their full text can be located without difficulty. It is contemplated that the EPA Office of Legislation will continue to supplement this work.[13]

Regulations

The rules under which the Environmental Protection Agency operates appear in Title 40 of the *Code of Federal Regulations* in four massive volumes that occupy nearly 2,600 pages of complex legal and scientific information. The rules of EPA's Presidential counterpart office—the Council on Environmental Quality—are set out at the end of the fourth volume.[14] They consist almost entirely of instructions for the preparation of environmental impact statements.

Hardly a day goes by without the appearance of new environmental rules, proposed regulations and technical notices issued by EPA and other Federal agencies. They are published in the daily issues of the *Federal Register*. For example, the *Federal Register* for Oct. 3, 1977 contains two special supplements, one proposing new EPA standards for stationary gas turbines,[15] the other proposing changes in the toxic substances control rules.[16]

---

[12] U.S. Environmental Protection Agency, Legal Compilation, Statutes and Legislative History, Executive Orders, Regulations, Guidelines and Reports. Wash., D.D., GPO, 1973.

[13] Id., General volume I, preface at v.

[14] Part 1500.

[15] 42 Fed. Reg. 53,781–53,796.

[16] Id. at 53,803–53,820.

Lest anyone think that EPA is the sole Federal government spokesman on the environment, reference to the next day's issue will dispel the notion. The Department of Labor's Occupational Safety and Health Administration published its 100-page proposal on the "Identification, Classification and Regulation of Toxic Substances Posing a Potential Occupational Carcinogenic Risk" on that day.[17] Similarly, the National Science Foundation announced a series of meetings of concern to lawyers, e.g., one being held by the Subcommittee on Population Biology and Physiological Ecology of the Advisory Committee for Environmental Biology.[18]

Caveat librorum environmentalium emptor!

Case Law

Even users of "Lexis" and "Westlaw" will need some framework of reference on which to build their research. The annotations to the National Environmental Policy Act of 1969 in 42 *USCA* Section 4321 et seq. are exhaustively indexed and analyzed. Section 4322 in that Code, covering impact statements and related subjects, for example, divides the cases into nine major categories and some 518 separate subdivisions. The volume was revised in June 1977. The same section in *United States Code Service* cites numerous law review articles and includes references to *Am Jur 2d* (infra), *ALR Fed.*, *ALR 3d* and other Lawyers–Cooperative Publishing Company publications, but its case notes are limited in number and their presentation does not provide the depth found in the West counterpart.

West has been less successful in its recent revision of the environmental Key Numbers 20 through 43 under "Health and Environment" that are used in *West's Federal Practice Digest 2d*[19] and in its other series of digests. Greater specificity and more subdivisions of the subject would help to pinpoint the cases that a user needs. There are some 4,000 digest paragraphs to cover under these key numbers.

---

[17] Id. at 54,148–54,247.

[18] Id. at 54,033.

[19] Volume 44 at 227–637 (July 1977).

Legal Encyclopedias

The article on "Pollution Control" by Higbee Williams in *Am Jur 2d*[20] makes up for the shortcomings in the same publisher's *USCS*. It lays out the subject concisely. It is studded with references to statutes, various government documents, books and symposium issues of law reviews. Its bibliography follows the organization of the EPA legislative history (supra). Although updated in the 1977 cumulative supplement, this bibliography contains no item published later than 1974. The article itself is a fine introduction to environmental law.

The unsigned article on "Health and Environment" in West's *Corpus Juris Secundum* has the advantage of recency, having been published in September, 1976,[21] four years after the *Am. Jr 2d* article. The *CJS* publication is in two parts, covering first Federal, and then state matters. Its topic analysis at the head of the article is adequate for finding one's particular subtopic. Like most *CJS* articles, however, it is based almost exclusively on case law and includes no bibliography. In a field that cuts across such diverse subjects as biology, physics, economics and the various social sciences, the *Am Jur 2d* approach is superior.

Treatise

Listed here is Frank P. Grad's three-volume work, *"Treatise on Environmental Law."*[22] No other single publication appears to cover the entire field—Federal, state, local, and international—with Professor Grad's authority and with his ability both to analyze and synthesize. Environmental law touches on many values—social, economic, aesthetic. His book is written with sure knowledge and sensitivity. It is also eminently practical.

Law Reviews and Legal Periodicals

The fast-changing field of environmental law has spawned a number of new periodicals. The best-known of these include the

[20] Vol. 61 at 805–1010 (1972) with 1977 Supplement at 35–54.

[21] Vol. 39A at 390–632.

[22] Albany, Bender, 1973–Looseleaf.

Columbia Journal of Environmental Law (Columbia University Law School), *Earth Law Journal* (subtitled *Journal of International and Comparative Environmental Law* and published by A.W. Sijthoff in The Netherlands), *Environmental Affairs* (Boston College Law School), *Environmental Law* (Lewis & Clark Law School and Northwestern School of Law) and *The Natural Resources Lawyer* (ABA Section of Natural Resources Law).

Even more important are the occasional symposium issues and leading articles in the established law reviews. These are indexed in *Index to Legal Periodicals* under the caption "Environmental Law." Three examples:

(1) The Fox in the Chicken Coop: The Regulatory Program of the U.S. Corps of Engineers by Garrett Power.[23]

(2) Symposium on the Fisheries Conservation and Management Act of 1976.[24]

(3) L'Environment, Numere Special (with short English language summaries of the articles, all of which cover either Canadian or Quebec law).[25]

Looseleaf Services

For practitioners the services constitute the most rewarding form of legal publication in this branch of law. A looseleaf service is flexible, it can report changes within days of their happening and it can coordinate and reprint all the kinds of materials from statutes to law review articles discussed above.

The two leading looseleaf services—both multi-volume sets—are BNA, Environmental Law Reporter, and CCH, Pollution Control Guide.

---

[23] 63 Virginia L. Rev. 503–559 (May 1977). The closing sentences of this article sum up, "Once the nemesis of the environmentalists, the Corps is now their hero. In the words of Senator Edward Muskie, "We have put the fox in the chicken coop and it has become a chicken." " (at 559).

[24] 52 Washington L. Rev. 427–745 (July 1977).

[25] 23 McGill Law Journal 163–377 (Summer 1977).

CHAPTER 13

CHECKLIST OF ENVIRONMENTAL STATUTES AND RULES

> "You may not sell any detergent in State A *if* it contains any trace of the substance X which we regard as a contaminant."
> "You may not sell any detergent in State B *unless* it contains substance X which we regard as a counter-contaminant."

What course should a nationwide supermarket chain take in the face of these conflicting regulations? What should the company's lawyers do? How can they keep informed of all the other environmental controls that affect the activities of this single client? This chapter provides a selected checklist of the environmental statutes and regulations of three commercial and industrial states of the United States together with references to a few commentaries on those laws and regulations.

Consumption of Legal Time

For those concerned with the consumption of a lawyer's time, it took just over one hour to gather and another two hours to sift through the environmental regulatory materials for the three states: New York, Pennsylvania and California. Presumably a fifty-state survey could be completed in fifty hours. But it might take ten times longer to understand and apply those rules to the twin problem: (a) In what states may a detergent containing substance "X" be marketed and (b) In what states will the absence of "X" from a detergent bar its sale altogether?

Yet such a survey would be of little value to a client unless it also investigated local regulations in Suffolk County, Schnectady, Santa Barbara, Scranton, Tewksbury Township and every other locality in the United States that might monitor the effect of "X" on its *public* water supply system or on the *privately-owned* wells of its residents.

New York

Statutes. "The quality of environment is fundamental to our concern for the quality of life . . . It is the policy of the State of New York to conserve, improve and protect its natural resources and environment and control water, land and air pollution." These words introduce the New York Environmental Conservation Law (Book 17½ of McKinney's Consolidated Laws, Section 1-0101). The statute is based on a former Environmental Conservation Law (ECL), Chapter 140 of the Laws of 1970 to which has now been transferred certain provisions of the Agriculture and Markets, Conservation, Executive, Public Health and several of the Unconsolidated Laws. A distribution table shows the location of these provisions in the new consolidation.

The wary researcher should not automatically conclude, however, that the legislature has consolidated all the environmental laws in this single title. But it has made a valiant effort to do so.

New York was among the first states to grapple with environmental problems. It even took legislative notice three years ago of the "dangers inherent in the depletion of the world's ozone layer" by restricting the sale of chlorofluorocarbon compounds (Ch. 713, Section 4 of the Laws of 1975). But this is only one of a myriad of topics covered by the "ECL."

Administrative Law. Most of the environmental regulations have been codified in Title 6 of the *Official Compilation of Codes, Rules and Regulations of the State of New York*. Title 6 alone fills some six massive looseleaf volumes. The last five of them are limited to the subject of water resources; the first volume covers all other environmental subjects.

Is this Code easy to use? *Caveat emptor!* There is no separate index to Title 6. The user must therefore rely on the general index to the entire Code or comb through a classified list of topic headings that appears at the beginning of each of the six volumes of Title 6.

The entries under the term "Environmental" in the master index to the entire set of New York regulations occupy only one page. Pennsylvania on the other hand devotes eighty pages of its administrative code index to this one term as an aid to its users.

Reference to other terms, "Radiation" for example, shows that the environmental rules are scattered through other Titles, for example, Title 10 (Sanitary Code) and Title 12 (Industrial Code).

The index shows that "Pollution" rules are chiefly set out in Title 6, but other "Pollution" regulations are distributed throughout Titles 12, 15 and 16. Moreover this is not a true index at all because its "Pollution" entries–thirty-two in number–are not even arranged in alphabetical order. They appear instead in approximate but not exact numerical order of regulatory "Parts."

The New York regulations also contain a catchall Code entitled "Miscellaneous" (Title 21) which consists of some fifty-three short chapters. Some of them embrace environmental matters. One of the most important is Chapter XLII which provides for implementation of the Environmental Quality Review Act (Section 8-0113 of the Environmental Conservation Law). It regulates the drafting and use of environmental impact statements. If this chapter of the regulations is cited anywhere in the index this writer failed to locate it.

All in all the index to the New York regulatory code does much to impede and not enough to assist in locating that State's environmental regulations.

Commentaries. Set forth below are citations to a few articles that may assist the researcher.

(a) *Air:* Koen, R.G. and Ain, S.K. Availability of individual or class actions as a deterrent to air pollution. 16 New York Law Forum 75 (1970).

(b) *Criminal Law:* Criminal responsibility of corporate officials for pollution of the environment. 37 Albany Law Review 61 (1972).

(c) *Pollution Generally:* A Primer on New York's revolutionized environmental laws. 49 New York State Bar Journal 41, 111 (1977).

(d) *Practice and Procedure:* King, J.Y. Procedural approaches and issues in environmental protection in New York. 28 Record 122 (1973).

(e) *Radiation:* Radioactive Waste: a failure in governmental regulation. 37 Albany Law Review 97 (1972); legal setting of nuclear power plant siting decisions: A New York State controversy. 57 Cornell Law Review 80 (1971).

Pennsylvania

Statutes. The powers of the Department of Environmental Resources and most statutory provisions relating to environmental controls are collected in Title 7 (State Government) of the newly designated *Pennsylvania Consolidated Statutes.* This was done pursuant to the state's Reorganization Plan No. 1 of 1972 when the environmental functions of most other state agencies were transferred to the new Department. Citations to the pertinent administrative regulations appear in parentheses after each numbered section of Title 7. Note should be made that the *Consolidated Statutes* is simply the new name for *Purdon's Pennsylvania Statutes Annotated.*

Administrative Law. The Pennsylvania regulations are published in a multi-volume set called the *Pennsylvania Code.* Environmental regulations are collected in Title 25 in two bulky looseleaf volumes. Each provision in this Title directly and specifically implements the statutes that govern matters affecting natural resources, environmental health and safety.

The detailed eighty-page index to this Title, mentioned above, contains references to definitions of some 360 environmental terms and a sufficient number of entries to help a novice find the regulation in point in seconds. This writer's curiosity as to the meaning of "Malodor"—a term cited in the index at Section 121.1—was quickly satisfied. The Pennsylvania meaning is set forth at the place cited in only slightly grander terms than Noah Webster's. But the point is that this index works *for* the user and not *against* him.

The *Pennsylvania Bulletin*—for which New York has no counterpart—is the weekly update service for the *Code.* It is modeled after and in format can easily be confused with the *Federal Register,* which it closely resembles. It contains all new state regulations, notices and other documents required to be filed with the Legislative Reference Bureau pursuant to 45 *Pennsylvania Consolidated Statutes*, Part II. The issue for March 4, 1978, for example, contains a 200-page proposed revision of the Water Quality and Industrial Waste Regulations (at pages 509–708).

For convenience of use and ease of entry the *Code* and *Bulletin* are a cut above those of any other state in which a similar regulatory service exists.

Commentaries. The best local articles are usually published in bar association journals and in the "state" rather than in the "national" law school law reviews. Pennsylvania is no exception, Bruce Ackerman's single article notwithstanding.

(a) *Administrative Law:* Department of environmental resources. (Five articles on various forms of administrative activity by A.N. Farley, E.F. Mannino, A. Sussna, J.N. Kline and F. Speaker collaborating with W.M. Eichbaum. 42 Pennsylvania Bar Association Quarterly 433 (1971).)

(b) *Pollution Generally:* Environmental pollution control laws in Pennsylvania; a survey and analysis. 16 Villanova Law Review 815 (1971).

(c) *Practice and Procedure:* Reath, Henry T. Pollution–the right of private enforcement in the courts. 43 Pennsylvania Bar Association Quarterly 238 (1972); defenses to orders and actions of the Pennsylvania Department of Environmental Resources. 80 Dickinson Law Review 265 (1976); Survey: The Commonwealth court's environmental decisions. 76 Dickinson Law Review 668 (1972).

(d) *Water:* Ackerman, Bruce, and Sawyer, J. Uncertain search for environmental policy: scientific fact-finding and rational decision-making along the Delaware River. 120 University of Pennsylvania Law Review 419 (1972).

California

Statutes. The Public Resources Code, beginning at Section 21,000, contains many of California's environmental statutes.

As in Pennsylvania, the West Publishing Company's edition of the *Code* keys the statutory provisions to the *California Administrative Code* which is the repository of the state's regulations. For example, the first reference in the statutes is to the environmental impact regulations of the Department of Conservation (14 California Administrative Section 800 et seq.). In addition, following Section 21,000 of the statutes, is a list of some twenty law review articles—all written since 1970.

Both New York and Pennsylvania have done a better job of consolidation. California's environmental statutes and regulations are dispersed in many titles through both Codes. Happily the separate title index to the Public Resources Code and the master index to *West's Annotated California Codes* are full and simple to use.

Administrative Law. The California regulations are published in a multivolume looseleaf code called *California Administrative Code*. It is the most expensive state code in the nation and the most voluminous. Title 14, for example, covers numerous environmental topics, including the requirements relating to environmental impact reports mentioned above.

There is a separate, detailed and easy-to-use index to Title 14 and separate indexes to the remaining titles. Their quality is high.

Commentaries. California's novel statutes and regulations have inspired more law review comments than have those of most of the other coastal states combined. A small selection of them follows:

(a) *Administrative Law:* Kane, K.P. From Friends of Mammouth to No Oil, Inc: when does a private construction project in California require an environmental impact report. 52 Los Angeles Bar Journal 142–155 (1976).

(b) *Air:* Passenger vehicle air pollution control in California: enforcement progress and problems. 15 Santa Clara Law 695–724 (Spring 1975).

(c) *Noise:* Mathis, J.P. Urban noise: an insidious but escalating pollutant. 46 Los Angeles Bar Bulletin 438 (Spring 1971). We may yet have a quiet environment: the new California airport noise regulations. 12 Santa Clara Law 79 (1972).

(d) *Pollution Generally:* Fraser, J.E. California Environmental Quality Act of 1970. 7 Journal Beverly Hills Bar Ass'n 25 (1973): Symposium: the environment and the law (some dozen articles ranging over most environmental issues–air, water, pesticides, oil, population, "thermal" and "aesthetic shock." 22 Hastings Law Journal 467 (February 1971).

(e) *Practice and Procedure:* Private action under the public trust: an environmental bill of rights for California. 2 Pacific Law Journal 620 (1971).

(f) *Visual Pollution:* Billboards: Roadside blight in the Golden State. 7 Journal Beverly Hills Bar Association 717 (1973); Yellin, I.E. Visual pollution and aesthetic regulation. 46 Los Angeles Bar Bulletin 425 (1971).

(g) *Water:* Development of the California and Federal water pollution control programs. 5 UCD Law Review 234 (1972); Water quality control in California: citizen participation in the administrative process. 1 Ecology Law Quarterly 400 (1971); Challenge to the California water plan. 22 Hastings Law Journal 732 (1971).

(h) *Water–Oil:* Admiralty law: California sues a vessel *in rem* for oil discharge to its water and marine life. 6 Tulsa Law Journal 257 (1970); Walmsley, D.J. Oil pollution problems arising out of exploitation of the continental shelf: the Santa Barbara disaster. 9 San Diego Law Review 514 (1972).

CHAPTER 14

LEGAL DEFINITIONS

Many a dispute turns on the meaning that courts give to words. Many a legal problem can be resolved chiefly, if not entirely, by reference to a legal definition. What are legal definitions, where are they published and, more important, how do you choose from among conflicting definitions?

Legal Definition

A definition becomes a legal definition when a legislature or a court declares it so. There are two main differences between a legal definition and any other. The first difference is one of result: a legal definition has legal consequences. Based on it a court may, for example, award damages, dissolve a marriage or exclude an alien. The second difference is one of quantity: there are countless numbers of varied legal definitions—of the same word.

Every legislator and every judge, it would seem, is his own Noah Webster. There are, for example, more than 100 different definitions of the word "immediately" in the cases for every one in the dictionaries. The expression "unsolicited goods" discussed below is of special interest to lawyers as buyers of law books. Its use varies widely in the codes of New York,[1] Pennsylvania,[2] California,[3] and Illinois.[4]

[1] New York General Business Law, section 396, subpar. 2.

[2] 73 Purdon's Pa. Stat. Ann., section 2001.

[3] Cal. Civ. Code, section 1584.4.

[4] 12½ Smith-Hurd Ill. Ann. Stat., section 351.

Nor does the language in any of those codes match that used in the United States Code.[5] Even the meaning of so plain a term as "wife" ("a woman joined in marriage to a man"–*Random House Dictionary of the English Language*) has been turned around in order to give to an unmarried woman the proceeds of an insurance policy whose beneficiary clause described her as, "my wife."[6]

The chief repositories of legal definitions are: dictionaries, statutes, regulations and the papers that constitute a legislative history of statutes, court opinions and treatises. An examination of a few of the thousands of definitions in those repositories frequently opens up a fresh avenue of legal research where resort to the digests alone has failed. Some of those repositories like the *New York General Construction Law* and *Sutherland on Statutory Construction,* also provide rules of interpretation for particular words or classes of words. A good illustration is the treatment of the word "immediately" in each of the repositories; beginning with general dictionaries.

General Dictionaries

The American dictionaries that the courts cite most frequently are *Webster's New International Dictionary of the English Language*, 2d edition (1934, with minor changes in its various printings to 1960), the 3d edition (1961) and the *Random House Dictionary of the English Language* (1966). The editors of the later *Webster's* and *Random House* dictionaries collected thousands of recent quotations to show how words were used at the time of publication. Yet for all the claims of currency made by their publishers, both *Webster's 2d* and *Webster's 3d* (more than twenty-five years later) defined the word "immediately" in identical terms: "without interval of time; without delay; straightaway."

The definition in the *Random House Dictionary* is little different, "without lapse of time; without delay; instantly; at once." The general dictionaries then are in substantial agreement.

---

[5] 39 U.S.C. §§ 3001, 3009 and 15 U.S.C. § 45(a)(1).

[6] Doney v. Equitable Life Assur. Society of the U.S., 117 A. 618, 619, 97 N.J. L. 393 (1922).

Law Dictionaries

The law dictionaries are based in part on traditional definitions (such as *Webster's*) and in part on quotations from court opinions. They are, at least up to the year of their publication, usually a more satisfactory source of legal definitions.

However, the test word "immediately" fared little better than it did in the general dictionaries. For example, *Black's Law Dictionary*, 4th edition (1968), citing a 1944 Pennsylvania case,[7] defined the word in virtually the same fashion that *Webster's* used. *Bouvier's Dictionary* quoted an 1878 English case[8] to show that the words "forthwith" and "immediately" have the same meaning. Both dictionaries misstate the views of the two courts. The Pennsylvania court after citing *Webster's* continued, "we have held that "immediately" does not mean instantaneously, but within a reasonable time." The English court also enlarged the usual dictionary definition of this term.

Only the recent *Ballantine's Law Dictionary*, 3d edition (1969) comes close to current usage:

"Promptly, with expedition, with reasonable haste consistent with fair business activity . . . such convenient time as is reasonably requisite for doing the thing."

Words and Phrases

Words and Phrases is a multivolume combination dictionary-digest, with pocket supplements that devotes some thirty-five pages to definitions of the word "immediately." It traces the use of the word from the meaning that courts give it in emergency situations that require the sending up of flares after an accident and that lexicographers always give to it—"forthwith, straightaway"—to situations in which it means as soon as practicable according to the circumstances and therefore defined—"within a reasonable time."

In the course of those thirty-five pages of definitions, *Words and Phrases* covers such a variety of fact patterns and such shadings

---

[7] Drumbar v. Jeddo-Highland Coal Co., 155 Pa. Super. Ct. 57, 60, 37 A. 2d 25, 27 (1944).

[8] The Queen v. The Justices of Berkshire (1878), 4 Q.B.D. 471.

of meanings that it would seem to have exhausted the subject. Moreover, definitions of the word "immediately" in particular jurisdictions appear of course in the separate *Words and Phrases* volume for each of the regional and state digests. But these definitions represent only a fraction of the times that the word occurs in statutes.

Statutes

Legislative draftsmen for the United States Code have used the word "immediately" some 989 times. It is more popular in the Pennsylvania Code, where it occurs 1,470 times. A count of the New York Consolidated Laws shows that the word "immediately" appears 2,143 times.[9] Not all, but many of those 4,602 instances of its use in the statutes are followed by annotations to cases.

Many of the individual state codes and the United States Code contain lists of terms for which statutory definitions have been enacted. They are usually listed in a section of the code's index called "Words and Phrases." For example, the index to *West's Annotated California Code* includes some 131 pages of such defined words. In Illinois under the heading "Definitions" and in Pennsylvania, there are similar lists. New York provides a separate title, the General Construction Law, in its code but has no consolidated list of words defined. Instead, such terms are distributed throughout the code's index.

What about terms that are not defined in the statutes? A recent example is the language used in the "unsolicited goods" laws that have been enacted by the Congress and by the Legislatures of New York, Pennsylvania, California, Illinois and many other states. The language varies from state to state. But the typical statute authorizes the recipient of "unsolicited goods" to keep them as a gift. The shipper or seller then becomes by statutory fiat the "donor" of the goods.

In addition, the federal statute imposes possible liability on the seller ("donor") for violating the United States Postal Laws and for unfair competition under the Federal Trade Commission Act.

---

[9] Aspen Systems Corporation, the legal computer service in Pittsburgh, Pa., supplied these figures in a letter dated Sept. 5, 1972.

The legislative history of a statute and administrative regulations under it often define or explain terms that the statute fails to define. The conference report on the federal "unsolicited goods" law[10] provides some and the Postal Regulations[11] give considerably more help in understanding the term in question.

In New York, two legislative documents[12] discuss the expression "unordered" or "unsolicited merchandise," thus helping to clarify the meaning of the New York statute.

Legal definitions serve as signposts in the solution of legal problems. They help reduce a problem to its basic elements. The advantage of going directly to the great textbook writers for definitions is that those writers have already canvassed their fields. They bring together in one place the key definitions. They are thorough. They are systematic. Most important, theirs are the voices that the courts listen to and cite.

Statutory Construction

The oldest, most heavily documented and one of the best respected of works is *Sutherland on Statutory Construction.*[13] It is unique because nearly half of its text is devoted to definitions or to rules of interpretation of statutes. The balance of the work discusses legislative organization and power.

This is a book that leads the reader by stages from the enacting clause of a statute to the determination of its effective date. It abounds in well known maxims drawn from the cases. One reads: "Words and phrases having a well-defined meaning in the common law are to be interpreted in the same sense under the statute."[14] Or, "A statute clear and unambiguous on its face need not and cannot be interpreted by a court...."[15] Still another, "Effect

[10] H.R. Rep. 91-1363 (1970).

[11] 39 C.F.R. § 123.4(e)–the second of two subparagraph e's in this part. part.

[12] Memoranda of the New York State Attorney General, New York Legislative Annual, 1966 at 29 and 1968 at 78.

[13] 3d ed. Chicago, Callaghan, 1943. Annual supplements.

[14] Section 5303.

[15] Section 4502.

must be given, if possible, to every word, clause and sentence of a statute."[16]

The author proceeds to support and demolish these maxims, to amplify and refine them. He gives the reader such a distillation of the meaning of statutes and such an understanding of their special argot that one may apply his reasoning with confidence to any future statute. If a lawyer ever after misconstrues a statute, he will do so sensibly and elegantly, with the arguments of Ogden and Richards,[17] Gray,[18] Holmes[19] and their successors to give him comfort.

Some specific facts: The heart of the work for purposes of definitions is set forth in its final twenty-seven chapters. It begins with general rules such as Intention of the Legislature (ch. 45), Rules of Statutory Interpretation and Conflict of Laws (ch. 46) and Legislative History of Enactment (ch. 50). The author then proceeds to a discussion of definitions in particular types of statutes, e.g., Penal (ch. 56); Revenue (ch. 67) and General Welfare (ch. 72).

For an understanding of the meaning of statutory terms, Sutherland has no peer.

Unfair Competition

Because of the nature of the subject, there are fewer flat statements of definitions in *Callman on Unfair Competition.*[20]

There is no master list of defined terms in *Callman*. Instead, definitions can be found distributed under various headings in the index and they can also be located after some effort in his very detailed table of contents.

A term like "trademark" is exhaustively analyzed under its various common law and statutory definitions. But the author

[16] Section 4705 (Quoting Kent's Commentaries, 13th ed., 1884, at 462).

[17] The Meaning of Meaning (1936).

[18] The Nature and Sources of the Law (1921).

[19] The Theory of Legal Interpretation (1899).

[20] The Law of Unfair Competition, Trademarks and Monopolies, 3d ed. Chicago, Callaghan, Looseleaf.

very properly refrains from giving precise definitions for such elusive terms as "trade secret," "good will" and "unfair competition." Instead, he offers a penetrating analysis of their use and provides sources of additional aid.

The footnote references are often essential to an understanding of the discussion. For example, the term "public official" is not defined in the text. It merely states that, "There is still much argument concerning the question of who properly qualifies as a public official"[21] and it touches on the broadened meaning given the term by the Supreme Court. However, the footnoted cases and law review articles[22] attempt to answer the question more fully.

In all, the index pinpoints some thirty-five basic terms commonly used in trademark and unfair competition law. In addition, a particularly useful feature is its list, under the heading "False Advertising," of some 200 words and phrases that have been judicially defined or interpreted. They include many advertising stereotypes ("genuine," "gratis," "money-back guarantee," and even "Swiss cheese") that continue to plague consumers and the courts.

Bankruptcy

Webster's and *Black's* dictionaries require only a few words to define such basic terms in bankruptcy law as "bankrupt," "conceal," "insolvency," "stock" and "creditor." Not so with *Collier,*[23] where some sixty-four major bankruptcy terms are listed in the index under the heading "Definitions" and numerous others appear separately throughout the index.

Collier's method is to present first, a statutory definition of each word, if the Bankruptcy Act defines it at all, then an analysis of the legislative history of the defined provision, a review of the leading cases, references to other writings in which the term is discussed and finally his own interpretation of the term. The

[21] Id., section 44, at 314–315.

[22] Note, Who is a "Public Official"? 33 Tenn. L. Rev. 554–559 (1966), among others.

[23] Collier on Bankruptcy, edited by James William Moore, 14th ed. New York, Bender, Looseleaf. A new 15th edition has now appeared.

difference between a dictionary definition and a *Collier* definition is like reading the word "daffodil" in a sentence and seeing the actual flower grow and unfold in one's garden.

A single word illustrates *Collier*'s thoroughness and systematic treatment. "Insolvency is one of the central concepts of bankruptcy,"[24] the author begins. And then he proceeds to expand—brilliantly—on the how and the why of it. Surely, no researcher would go to a digest first if he knew that a *Collier* existed.

Income Taxation

The Internal Revenue Code itself provides a multitude of tax definitions. *Mertens*[25] is probably the most frequently consulted treatise in the field. Some 104 terms that merit extensive discussion are listed under "Definitions" in the index published in 1959. This feature has not been retained in the 1972 supplement to the index, but tax definitions already in the text are regularly updated.

It is interesting to learn about "fair market value" that "the fact that there is no market does not lead to the conclusion that there is no value,"[26] that the term "willful" in connection with tax offenses almost—but not quite—defies definition[27] and that federal law prevails over state law as to what constitutes a corporation.[28] These are simply a few fragments taken from an orderly, comprehensive tax treatise that has succeeded in synthesizing and reducing an astronomical number of statutes, cases and rulings to a bare 20,000 pages.

Securities

Loss on Securities Regulation[29] may be the last of the old-fashioned masterpieces by virtue of the thoroughness of its prepar-

---

[24] Id., par. 1.19 at 97.

[25] Mertens, The Law of Federal Income Taxation. Chicago, Callaghan. Looseleaf.

[26] Id., section 59.01, fn. 6.

[27] Id., section 55A.09.

[28] Id., section 38.03.

[29] 2d ed. Boston, Little Brown, 1961, 1969 Supplement.

ation and the sweep of its scholarship. Definitions may be found by reference to individual words in their alphabetical places in the index and by reference to the subjects in the table of contents. The chapters introducing the principal securities acts discuss statutory definitions and other terms important to those acts. They also provide an analysis of court interpretations and contain numerous references to treatises and law review writings.

Chapter 3 on "Coverage of the Securities Act of 1933" devotes some 105 pages in the basic work to definitions of "security," "person," "issuer," and a few related terms. A supplement to this chapter updates these definitions in an additional 102 pages.

There is a vast difference between a definition in *Webster* or *Black* and one in *Sutherland* or *Loss.* The purpose of this discussion of legal definitions has been to show the variety of publications in which legal definitions appear. It is a mark of exceptional judgment to know in each case whether to go first to a dictionary, a digest, a statute or a treatise. Each has its uses.

CHAPTER 15

LEGAL INDEXES

When a lawyer has exhausted all other remedies and must resort to a book to solve a legal problem, his first stop is usually the index. Every law digest, code, encyclopedia, looseleaf service and treatise has its own index. These legal reference works are virtually impregnable without one and sometimes, lawyers complain, they are unfathomable even with an index.

Who is at fault? The lawyer? The writer? The indexer? The publisher? Probably all of them. Asked if the complaints are justified, the compiler of one of the most highly praised indexes to a legal treatise replied,[1] "Not at all. When you are lucky enough to find what you want, the index is great; otherwise it's rotten." In a more serious vein, he added, "It is simply a question of money. Indexes are time-consuming to prepare. They are costly. Not all publishers are willing to pay for a good one."

Indexes Defined

West Publishing Company's most famous lexicographer defined an index as, "A book containing references, alphabetically arranged, to the contents of a series or collection of volumes. . . ."[2] There is a twelve-page chapter on compiling an index in the same company's instruction book for its authors.[3] Direct quotation from this primer is forbidden. However, it is no trade secret that some legal writers (for West and other publishers) do not always follow its

[1] Collier on Bankruptcy. Albany, N.Y. Bender. Looseleaf.

[2] Black's Law Dictionary, 4th ed., St. Paul, Minn., 1957.

[3] Manual for Manuscript Preparation, Ch. III, St. Paul, Minn. 1972.

simple and sensible precepts. Accordingly, some law book readers do not always find joy and fulfillment in the indexes that result.

Source of Confusion

An index is usually of three types: an alphabetical list of terms, a classified list of terms or a combination of both. The combined form is most frequently used. This is the one that West calls its "Descriptive Word Index." It is found in all West case digests. It is the chief form of entry to these digests. But to many researchers it is a maze to which they have difficulty in finding the key—even when they think they know the appropriate "Key Number."

The reason for confusion is simple. A judge and a digester-headnote writer frequently use different language to describe a situation. A lawyer looking for a case in point may employ still a third set of words to cover the same situation. They think that they are talking about the same thing. They mean to do so. But they fail to get through to one another. Even more important, not all digesters apply the "Key Number" system uniformly.

Such a digesting event occurred when the New York Court of Appeals abandoned its thirty-nine-year-old rule in a landmark case[4] requiring privity of contract between a manufacturer and a remote consumer. It adopted the contrary rule in 1962.[5]

Inadequate Headnotes

Jude Fuld's opening paragraph in the latter case might have given West's digester a hint of what was to follow when he stated in his opinion that we are called upon, "to decide whether, under the facts disclosed, *privity of contract* is essential to maintenance of an action against a manufacturer for *breach of express warranty*."[6] Indeed the crucial words were set before the digester to use. Yet, to that digester the words meant Key Number, "Judgment 185.3 (18)" and no other. The indexer to *Abbott's Digest* added the Key Number, "Torts 15.1." It is not possible to locate

[4] Chysky v. Drake Bros. Co., 325 N.Y. 428 (1922).

[5] Randy Knitwear v. Amer. Cyanamid Co., 11 N.Y. 2d 5, 226 N.Y.S. 2d 363 (1962).

[6] Id., at 8.

this case in the Index to *Abbott*'s under any of these seemingly appropriate words: Privity, privity between parties, contracts, sales, or warranty. A long line of similar cases, however, can be found through these index terms. This case *can* be found through the index under the terms "Judgments," "Torts" and "Products Liability–Manufacturers' Liability."

As a cross-check to what this case stands for, one should check some of the captions used by the official reporter in this case. They include the terms: "Sales–warranties–privity . . . –manufacturer liable to remote purchaser–action for breach of express warranty–privity not necessary."

Most lawyers blame their failure and attribute their success in finding the cases they need on the adequacy of headnotes from which most indexed terms are drawn. For example, the source for each of the thousands of case summaries and index headings that appear in *Abbott's New York Digest* is the original headnote taken from West's *New York Supplement* edition of the New York reports. It is sometimes supplemented by editorial additions. When the headnote writer fails to digest a case adequately, the indexer is likely to follow his lead and the case is thereafter lost to readers.

There are several solutions to indexing difficulties. The publishers can take steps on their side to make indexes more consistent and more useful; the research lawyers can acquaint themselves more thoroughly with the way indexes work.

On the publisher's side, West has already published detailed explanations for users, both at the beginning of most of their digest-indexes and in the law students' handouts. One of the most informative of these presents the West advice in a nutshell when it tells the user of their indexes to ask himself, "What words describe the parties concerned; the places or things involved; the basis of action or issue; the possible defense or defenses and the relief sought."[7] This is sound advice. The first step that publishers should take is to make certain that their own indexes follow that advice. This requires closer editorial supervision of indexers. It may mean even higher costs for digests, but less lawyer time spent in searching cases. It would provide an additional index entry or

---

[7] E.g., sample pages illustrating organization and research techniques in West's Key Number Digests . . . St. Paul, Minn., West, 2d ed 1979 (at 5).

cross-reference in many cases. But that might make the difference between finding and not finding the case in point.

Also on the side of the publisher, the sheer bulk of American court reporting makes indexing a monumental task.

On the lawyer's side it should be emphasized that the privity of contract illustration (supra) is not typical. Most reported cases *can* be found in the digests. These are some basic suggestions for researchers: (1) Learn how each new digest works by spending five or ten minutes examining it before you use it. A veteran of numerous federal court battles recently asked me why his library did not keep West's *Federal Digest* up to date. He did not know that it was updated in the retitled "Modern Federal Practice Digest" and supplemented in *West's Federal Practice Digest 2d.* (2) Use the index in conjunction with a good thesaurus. (3) Note up additions and cross-references in the indexes to one's own library copies of the digest. (4) Let the publishers know when they do a fine digesting job and when they "goof."

In these various ways, lawyers will persuade them that legal indexes are indeed intended for use rather than concealment.

The exellence of a legal index is in inverse ratio to the effort and ingenuity required to use it. If an index to a legal work is constructed so that entry to it must be forced—if it requires the wiliness of a safecracker for entry—then the index is poor indeed. An index should be a key to let you in—not a steel wall to keep you out.

Whether justified or not, such has been the criticism leveled against the *Index to Legal Periodicals*[8] and the indexes to the *Federal Register* and *Code of Federal Regulations*[9] and the *New York City Charter and Administrative Code.*[10]

---

[8]Fratcher, The Decline of the Index to Legal Periodicals, 18 J. Legal Ed. 297 (1966) and rejoinder: Drummond. The Continued Improvement of the Index to Legal Periodicals, 19 J. Legal Ed. 78 (1966).

[9]The Federal Register and the Code of Federal Regulations—a Reappraisal, 80 Harv. L. Rev. 439, 449 (1966) and Futor, Searching the Federal Regulations: Forty-Seven Steps Are Too Many. 45 ABA J. 43 (1959).

[10]Conversations over the past twenty years between a score of New York lawyers with one of the writers complaining of difficulties in finding anything in this index. They reported that the index headings "are too limited" and "many matters do not appear to be indexed at all."

The *Index to Legal Periodicals* is by far the most ambitious of these indexes and the most useful. For the better part of a century, it has continued to index the contents of the leading Anglo-American law reviews. So, despite its limitations, it is important to learn how this index works, what it does and does not attempt to do and how it might be improved.

Evaluation of an Index

An index should pinpoint specific matters within a written work in the fewest possible steps. "Let your fingers do the walking," urge the publishers of the Yellow Pages. An index may be evaluated on three main grounds: (1) its scope and fullness of treatment; (2) the accuracy of its description and (3) its arrangement.

How does the *Index to Legal Periodicals* rate under this test? In scope, it indexes some 425 Anglo-American law reviews and periodicals, but not legal newspapers. For instance, articles in the *New York Law Journal* are omitted. Also omitted are all articles less than five pages long, all book reviews less than two pages in length and some student writings.

Reference to the *Law Library Journal* for February, 1971, and *The Business Lawyer* for January, 1972, illustrates its scope and fullness of its indexing coverage.

Of the seven articles in the February *Law Library Journal*, one is not indexed at all. It is long enough—eight pages in length—but it is student work. Five of the remaining six articles are listed under one subject only. They are also listed under the authors' names.

Two of the articles dealt with information networks and libraries' role in developing them. They were each indexed under the heading "Libraries." One could not find them under the headings, "Information Retrieval," "Information Networks," or even "Legal Research."

The *Index to Legal Periodicals* is arranged in three main sections: First, an alphabetical subject and author list; Second, a table of cases which purports to include every case note published in each of the 425 journals that it indexes; and third, a book review index which probably excludes upwards of 90 percent of the book notes published in those journals. The arrangement itself is excellent. But improvement is needed in the scope of the *Index* and in the refinement of its topics.

Bethany Ochal's interesting article and bibliography on "Microforms on Legal Subjects" is placed under the heading "Bibliography" where it will probably remain hidden forever. Judge John Biggs' eloquent memorial on the late Third Circuit librarian, Jacqueline Fay, is omitted because it did not meet the length test.

Of twenty-six book reviews included in the "Book Appraisals" in this issue of Law Library Journal, only one is listed in the *Index to Legal Periodicals.* In that case, the reviewer combined three books into his eight-page review. The other twenty-five reviews may be lost.

Descriptive Precision

What about both scope and accuracy? The editors promise that "the most specific subject heading is used wherever possible."[11] But it is only in recent years that the editors have begun to sharpen this feature. Some examples from *The Business Lawyer* for January, 1972, show that the *Index* for that year lumped together under the general heading "Securities" two articles on tender offers[12] and one on the problems of SEC enforcement of its rules relating to investment letters.[13] They were easily overlooked among some 125 articles arranged alphabetically by title under this single heading. They were crowded into some five columns of densely-set type. The first of them cannot even be located under the author's name because, though signed, it was a student article.

The second, however, was listed under the additional topic "Consolidation and Merger." A wide-ranging article on intercorpo-

[11] Index to Legal Periodicals. September 1971 to August 1972 cumulation in its Prefatory Note.

[12] Young. Judicial Enforcement of the Williams Amendment at 391 and Aranow and Einhorn. Essential Ingredients of the Cash Tender Invitation at 415.

[13] Samet. The Concept of Fungibility in Securities Laws at 383.

rate conspiracy and foreign antitrust laws[14] and another on trade associations[15] were grouped under the single topic "Restraint of Trade."

Suggested Measures

Some modest suggestions for improvement: Assign more subject headings per article; index all book reviews; and subdivide broad topics.

As a step in this direction, the *Index to Legal Periodicals* has already divided the topic "Corporations" into eight subtopics and has listed cases separately under each of these topics. Moreover, it has returned the formerly separate category "Consolidation and Merger" to "Corporations," where it more properly belongs. It has not only divided income tax articles into subtopics, but it has arranged them geographically as well. It subdivided "Securities" in response to earlier recommendations into "fraud," "insider trading" and "state regulation" and "Discrimination" into three parts.

In addition, the *Index* provides several features that simplify its use.

First, there are numerous cross-references (e.g., "Blue Laws, See Holidays" and "Pension Plans, See also Profit Sharing"). Second, the publisher reprints a list of all the subjects and cross-references used in the entire *Index* in the front of each bound cumulation. Third, it also provides the name, address and subscription price of each periodical indexed. Fourth, if one knows the author of an article, he can find under his name, not only the subject of each of the indexed articles, but also the first letter of each title. Thus, under "Sommer, A.A., Jr." appears the heading "Securities (R)" standing for his article, "Random Thoughts on Disclosure as Consumer Protection." It is the second of twelve articles starting with the letter "R" and cuts down the search from some 125 securities articles to twelve.

---

[14] Werner. The Single Trader Doctrine at 469.

[15] Rozel. Progressive Trade Association Activity and the Antitrust Laws at 479.

Substitute Indexes

Are there substitutes for the *Index*? Several leading law reviews and periodicals publish their own minutely detailed cumulative indexes. Among them are *Harvard Law Review, Yale Law Journal, American Bar Association Journal* and *Law Library Journal.* Good as they are, they each index only one review. The *Index to Legal Periodicals* covers some 425 journals. That is why the recent expansion and its continued improvement are essential to make it a sharper research tool.

The *Current Law Index*, a competitor to *Index to Legal Periodicals*, indexes many legal and law-related journals. It began publication in 1980. It is issued monthly and is cumulated annually. Where the *Index to Legal Periodicals* has been faulted for providing too few entries, this *Index* may overwhelm the user with its detail. In addition, it appears to build its subject heading lists with catch phrases from particular articles rather than from a standard list. For example, the note, "Discovery of Internal Corporate Investigations" (32 Stanford L. Rev. 1163-1181 (1980)), is indexed under "Corporations–Investigations" in the January 1981 issue of *Current Law Index*. Yet that issue of the index fails to include this article under its primary subject "Discovery." Nor is it indexed under its secondary topic, "Attorney–Client Privilege," either.

CHAPTER 16

THE ART OF ADVOCACY—A BIBLIOGRAPHICAL COMMENTARY

Boswell once asked Dr. Johnson what he thought of "supporting a cause which you know to be bad." Johnson replied: "Sir, you do not know it to be good or bad till the judge determines it. I have said that you are to state facts fairly; so that your thinking, or what you call knowing a cause to be bad, must be from reasoning, must be from your supposing your arguments to be weak and inconclusive. But, Sir, that is not enough. An argument which does not convince yourself, may convince the Judge to whom you urge it . . . It is his business to judge; and you are not to be confident in your own opinion that a cause is bad, but to say all you can for your client, and then hear the judge's opinion."

Cicero on Judges

Dr. Johnson's comment brings to mind the distinction Cicero makes that it is the duty of the judge to pursue the truth, but it is permitted to an advocate to urge what has only the semblance of it. It also suggests that the art of advocacy, perhaps, often is best taught by illustration rather than by definition. Otherwise, how can you explain the great success at the Bar of Sir John Holker, who was Solicitor General and afterwards, Attorney General. The late Lord Birkett, who was a famous English Barrister himself, said that Sir John's delivery was so painful, it was a terrible effort to listen to him at all, and yet he had a practice that was worth thousands and thousands of pounds a year. His halting delivery somehow made the jury say, "I feel sorry for that man; we will give him the verdict."

On occasion, we have been requested as a law librarian to suggest what to read on the "art of advocacy." We unhesitatingly recommend first Justice Arthur T. Vanderbilt's lectures on *Forensic Persuasion:* In a mere fifty-eight pages, he gives a wealth of valuable information and advice governing the effective presentation of a case in court from the pleading stage through appellate argument. Justice Vanderbilt agreed with Lord Birkett, that the advocate's role was more than merely to convince, rather it was actually to persuade or "to move the court or the jury to take a desired action."

Vanderbilt and Advocates

Certainly every practicing lawyer should seriously consider how well he or she measures up to the following six factors Justice Vanderbilt believed are involved in the work of an advocate:

(1) The capacity for grasping all of the facts of a case in all of their interrelations and implications quickly and comprehensively.

(2) A thorough understanding of the fundamental principles and rules of the law and the ability to apply them to the facts of a case.

(3) Knowledge of human nature in all of its manifestations and an ability to get along with people generally.

(4) A comprehension of the economic, political, social and intellectual environments of modern litigation, for cases are never tried in a vacuum.

(5) The ability to reason concerning the facts, the law, and penalties involved in litigation, and the environment of a case in such a way as to solve the pending problems in the most satisfactory way possible.

(6) The art of expressing one's self clearly and cogently, orally and in writing.

Other Recommended Books

Then we would recommend Sir Edward Parry's *The Seven Lamps of Advocacy,* another little book reflecting on those different qualities which make an advocate successful–and by success Judge

Parry did not particularly refer to accumulated wealth. Incidentally, Judge Parry's book is worth reading for its anecdotes and wise hints alone. Also to be noted here is Wellman's *The Art of Cross-Examination,* a book which has been a source of instruction and pleasurable reading for a great many lawyers and law students since it first appeared in 1903. Of similar interest is Stryker's *Art of Advocacy,* an "exciting book" which instructs on how to open and close a case, how to cross-examine, and on criminal and appellate advocacy. Note the excellent bibliography as well.

Then there are more practical books such as Judge Edward Re's *Brief Writing and Oral Argument,* Jeans' *Trial Advocacy,* Keeton's *Trial Tactics and Methods,* Levin and Cramer's *Trial Advocacy,* and Bodin's *Civil Litigation and Trial Techniques.*

If we were then pressed for additional readings, we would suggest the biographies, careers and reminiscences of those great advocates at the Bar, such as Lord Birkenhead, Lord Carson, Rufus Choate, Clarence Darrow, John W. Davis, Lord Erskine, Sir Edward Hall, Luther Martin, Jeremiah Mason, George W. Pepper, William Pinkney, Daniel Webster, and Montagu Williams. We would also suggest reading about noted and celebrated trials, such as Coleridge's devastating cross-examination of the claimant, Arthur Orton, in the extraordinary Tichborne Trial, and excerpts from other notable trials as brought out in Wellman's *The Art of Cross-Examination* and Nizer's *The Jury Returns.*

'Pie Powder'

Finally, we would suggest books on Bench and Bar dealing with the court careers of famous advocates for they often set out those qualities which made them great. Unfortunately, some of these books are rather dull, for as one observer has noted, the legal biography is, as a rule, a tedious affair. One lawyer's life is much like another's. There are exceptions, however, such as *Pie Powder.*

Pie Powder is a book of legal reminiscences first published in 1911 by a barrister who wrote it under the name of *Circuit Tramp.* We now know that he was John Alderson Foote, K.C., who was a leader of the Western Circuit in late 19th century and early 20th century England. Biographical in the main, it reflects the author's experiences and memories of the circuit system, as well as its leaders, celebrities and events. Informative, anecdotal, humorous and a delight to read. Fortunately it was reprinted in 1967 by William S. Hein Co., of Buffalo, N.Y.

The enchanting stories he tells us, the sagacity of his thoughts and the sophistication of his reflections on advocacy can be appreciated and advantageously used by the public speaker, the lawyer and even the blasé law student. It deserves the lawyer's attention for the wonderful legal anecdotes alone recounted therein.

Consider for example Lord Bowen, a great lawyer and wit, who later sat on the Court of Appeal. "There was an academic refinement about his humor, a delicacy in his sarcasm, and a kindliness in his wit which made his after-dinner speeches as brilliant as his judgments in the Court of Appeals." His epigrams are known and relished to this day.

Bowen's Wit

A classical example of his wit was the occasion when an address was to be presented to Queen Victoria by the judges of the High Court on the opening of the new law courts in the Strand. Beginning:

> "Conscious as we are of our shortcomings," one of the judges objected to it as hypocritical as it implied that they were really aware *of their* shortcomings."
>
> "That objection can easily be met" said Lord Bowen suavely. "May I suggest that conscious as we are of *each others* shortcomings will read much better."

> "Truth will leak out–even in an affidavit" is also attributed to Lord Bowen.

Edward Bullen, who was also a well-known wit, once read to the Court of Appeals the following paragraph from a pleading in an action of seduction:

"The defendant denies that he is the father of the said twins, *or of either of them*."

Commenting on questions of evidence and hearsay, the author of *Pie Powder* relates what he believes to be a classical example of imperfect recollection by a witness testifying during a trial.

"The prisoner's wife stood at the bottom of the stairs and called out, 'Tom, Tom,' or words to that effect."

Who is the most important person in the court for the lawyer at a specific time? It is "not the witness being examined," he observes, "nor the prisoner in a criminal case, nor the respondent in a divorce case—but rather the stupidest member of the jury."

Certainly, the concise summing up in a civil case attributed to Baron Bramwell should be permanently inscribed in the annals of the Bench and Bar. The author believed it to be the shortest and most intelligible example on record.

The defendant's counsel closed his case without calling a witness whose appearance on the stand had been much anticipated.

"Don't you call Jones, Mr. Blank?" said the judge significantly at the close of counsel's address. "I do not my Lord," replied the lawyer. The judge turned around to the jury and gave vent to a low and prolonged whistle "whe-e-ew," he said, or rather whistled, "Gentlemen, consider your verdict."

'Wrong' Defined

Foote believed that the first and most important quality for an advocate, to enable him to advise on an appeal against the verdict of a jury on a question of fact, is to know the principle upon which the appeal will be decided by the court. In theory, the verdict of a jury ought to be set aside if, and only if, that verdict is wrong. What does "wrong" mean? "The only answer I think that can be given to this question is, that it must be wrong in the opinion of the court which hears the appeal."

Foote considered it fortunate that physicians and lawyers do not always measure sanity by the same standards. In support thereof, he tells the story of what occurred during the trial of 1882 of President Garfield's assasin, Guiteau. One expert gave it as his opinion that a large percentage of mankind were "abnormal" so far as their mental condition went. He put it as high as one in five. "That seems rather a large estimate, doesn't it?" asked the President [sic] of the court. "Might take you in, judge!" exploded Guiteau with a self-approving chuckle.

Origin of Pie Powder

Pie Powder, incidentally, refers to the medieval English Court of Pie Powder (also spelled Pie-poudres," "Pyepowder," "Pide Pulverose" or "Pypowder"). Originally, a county fair court administering immediate justice to merchants, Lord Coke believed its name was derived from the fact that it administered Justice while the powder or dust was still on the feet of the litigants. Others believe the court obtained its name because the merchants who mainly sought justice there had dusty feet from traveling from fair to fair (or *pied poudre*). Historians believe that the law merchant's subsequent development from the middle ages on, was influenced by the decisions on fair trading enforced by the Pied Poudre courts. (For additional information see Gross, the Court of Pie Powder, 20 *Quarterly Journal of Economics* 231–249 (1906).)

Lord Birkett conceded in his Presidential address on *Advocacy* before the Holdsworth Club, that the art of advocacy is "beset with perils of a very special kind, and for that reason the first quality beyond all others in the advocate ... is that he must be a man of character. The Court must be able to rely on the advocate's word. ... The advocate has a duty to his client, a duty to the Court, and a duty to the State; but he has above all a duty to himself that he shall be, as far as lies in his power, a man of integrity." Not all advocates are made to the same pattern. "Some have been endowed with ten talents, some with five and some with one only." These talents he brings out in his book *Six Great Advocates* (Sir Edward Marshall Hall, Sir Patrick Hastings, Sir Edward Clarke, Sir Rufus Isaacs, Sir Charles Russell and Thomas Erskine. Read particularly his final chapter on the art of advocacy.)

Above all, he insisted the advocate had to be not only "a diligent student of law" but also "a diligent student of letters. The virtue of books is somehow communicated to the reader. To live in books with the great and wise spirits of all time is somehow to feel their virtue and mysteriously to share it; and all these things to the advocate in the exercise of his art are beyond rubies. The vocabulary is enriched and enlarged; and stored in the mind for use as the particular occasion demands, are the words the advocate will one day employ, with an effect that he cannot now imagine, at some great moment of his life's work."

CHAPTER 17

THE CHALLENGE OF THE TRANSNATIONAL ENTERPRISE TO LEGAL RESEARCH AND INFORMATION GATHERING

What is the challenge the transnational enterprise raises in legal research and information acquisition? Consider first the role of the lawyer in providing legal advice to a client involved in a transaction affected by rules of international law as well as by the national laws of a number of foreign states. First, there is the problem of orientation—a different understanding of the underlying principles involved as distinguished from resolution of legal problems in a single jurisdiction. Then there is the need to acquire a detailed understanding of the national laws which may affect the international transaction. These can be quite complex when we realize that they can involve foreign laws affecting commercial law, sales, agency, tax and regulatory prohibitions. This process requires, on occasion, such skill in original research in cases, treaties and conventions, statutes and regulations, that American lawyers in the past have not been too eager to assume the responsibility of representing a client who has so many of those diverse and complex legal problems. The comparatively few practitioners who did not specialize in international legal matters, were considered as belonging to a unique class of international practitioners. Since World War II, however, developments such as the formation and operation of the European Economic Community, as well as other regional economic communities, and especially the increasing activities of multinational corporations or enterprises (the United Nations refers to them as "Transnational Enterprises") are forcing the general practitioner to become more aware of their implications in the general business activities of their clients.

How to find relevant research materials and legal principles has become a source of frustration and delay for the uninitiated. To provide constructive instruction on the materials which constitute the basis for research, including general and scholarly literature, as well as the systems of research as they relate to the multi-faceted activities of the transnational enterprise, a Workshop for Law Librarians was held in London on August 21, 22, 1980. Sponsored by New York University School of Law, the British Institute of International and Comparative Law and Oceana Publications, and entitled "The Transnational Enterprise: A Blue-print for Research and Information Acquisition" it stressed as well, the role of international and national organizations which attempt to control the activities of multinational enterprises.

The changing role of international law in the practice of law today, as reflected in the increasing activities of multinational enterprises, is causing lawyers throughout the world to become more sensitive to its implications in both private and government activities.

Unfortunately, for research purposes, the subject content of international economic law and transactions, of relevance to the activities of transnational enterprises is not too well identifiable. As Professor Jackson has noted in his "Legal Problems of International Economic Relations," preparing a book on the subject of international economic regulations is like trying to describe a landscape while looking out of the window of a moving train—events tend to move faster than one can describe them . . . compounded by the lack of definition of the borderlines of the subject."

Although public international law, in its more classic sense, such as it pertains to the use of the sea and of air space, immunity of states, nationality of individuals and corporations, international responsibility of states and international claims and agreements, may on occasion, also be of interest to the lawyer representing a multinational enterprise, public international law in its emerging role in international transactions is dramatically affecting the conduct of multinational corporations. For example, the *United Nations Charter of Economic Rights*, which specifically purports to promulgate principles that should govern international economic relationships, as Professor Simmonds in his "Multinational Corporation Law" has so aptly stated, in areas such as "the peaceful settlement of disputes, the equal sovereignty of states, non-intervention, international co-operation for development, . . . are in accord with traditional principles of international law and novel only in the way they are brought together as instruments in the search for a new international social justice." Chapter II of the *UN Charter of Economic Rights* for example, specifies the economic rights and duties of states, some of which obviously will affect international commerce, especially those on sovereignty over natural resources, on the right of association, on the meaning of juridical equality, on the transfer of technology and on the prohibition of the use of economic, political or other measures as sanctions.

The emerging role of international law in this context, is also manifested in the imminent agreement of representatives of most of the nations of the world on a treaty negotiated by the United Nations Law of the Sea Conference, that will regulate the use of the oceans and their natural resources, considered by the United Nations as "the common heritage of mankind." It is evident to specialists in the field that a whole new body of international maritime law will be reflected in the ensuing treaty, parts of which, will affect the activities of private companies, recovering, for profit, the minerals on the ocean floor. A proposed *International Seabed Authority* will license private deep sea mining outside the 200 mile zones of national coastlines, and in this process, will require the companies applying for mining licenses to sell to it necessary technology to allow the Authority to mine some sites itself. The Authority will also be allowed to tax the private companies for the purpose of aiding poor countries. In essence, therefore, Western mining companies will be forced to "subsidize the competition" by supporting the proposed seabed Authority.

It should also be noted here that the *UN Charter of Economic Rights* considers full economic sovereignty to mean that the "host" state cannot only exercise authority over foreign investments, but can also supervise the activities of transnational corporations and to even nationalize foreign property with, however, an "appropriate" compensation.

European Common Market Law, involving the activities and jurisdiction of the European Economic Community, Council, Commission, Parliament and Court of Justice is reflected in their regulations and case law. Lawyers are particularly concerned on how they affect antitrust, and control of unfair competition, distributorships, licensing, mergers, products liability and consumer protection. The relationships of the United States Government and of American private commercial interests to the European Economic Community, the European Atomic Community and the European Coal and Steel Community, can also be noted here.

Most international business planning cannot avoid the effect of European private commercial transaction law. Lawyers must be aware of the implications of direct investment through branches or subsidiaries in foreign countries, use of commercial agencies or distributorships, patent and trademark licensing, equipment leasing, joint ventures and acquisitions, especially as they are controlled by Common Market Laws. In this context, forms of international contracts, including sales of goods, loans, joint ventures, measures of damages, letters of credit and other security devices, rights of commercial agents, extraterritorial regulation and governmental immunities, as well as the applicability of tax conventions must also be considered.

International economic transactions can also be directly affected by foreign government involvement in the transaction itself. Note that there can be national controls such as tariffs, quotas and export licensing as well as international agreements to control trade and conversely to prevent controls on trade. Highly significant also are the international investment problems of multinational corporations and their relations with local governments in developing countries.

Similarly, international trade arbitration is playing an important role in the settlement of controversies in international trade. Actually, the ever increasing recourse to the international arbitral process by lawyers is a tribute to the superiority of arbitration tribunals over ordinary national courts in the settlement of international commercial disputes. It is also a recognition of the fact that as a rule international commercial and trade disputes are settled by arbitral bodies in a less expensive, more expeditious and equitable way. This development requires lawyers to become familiar with various types of arbitration clauses used in foreign economic arrangements as they pertain among others, to investments, know-how, licensing of technology and rules of procedure in international arbitration.

Recently the United States and the People's Republic of China entered into a trade agreement which calls for private dispute settlement of international contractual disputes. Gerald Aksen has noted in the New York Law Journal in this context, "Governmental encouragement of settling international commercial disputes through prompt and equitable means by private dispute settlement mechanisms is becoming the norm in United States agreements and accords with socialist countries. Previous agreements and accords with Romania, Hungary and Poland also contain provisions whereby the governments recommend arbitration of disputes arising from commercial transaction. In a sense, states are granting recognition to the fact that the customary mode of settling international trade disputes is through the arbitral arena. In the socialist world, most countries have permanent foreign trade arbitration institutions whose principal function is to encourage and resolve multinational trade disputes through conciliation and arbitration."

It is obvious that the tax aspects of international business transactions can never be ignored by a multinational corporation doing business abroad. Similarly, the lawyer must study the effect of doing business in foreign countries integrated into regional economic communities other than the European Economic countries. In South America, alone, for example, there are LAFTA, Andean Pact, River Plate Basin, SELA and others.

Recent developing legal concerns affecting multinational corporations lie in corporate accountability within the framework of evolving multinational codes, export control legislation, new agreements in the area of non-tariff barriers to international trade, such as antidumping duties, customs valuation and government procurement and technical standards, joint ventures under the European Economic Competition laws, particularly joint production and marketing, joint research and development and specialization agreements, the impact of the accounting provisions of the U.S. Foreign Corrupt Practices Act and how they affect

U.S. corporations doing business abroad and finally, the recognition and enforcement of foreign judgments as affected by the Common Market Convention on Jurisdiction and the Enforcement Judgments in Civil and Commercial Matters.

We would like to suggest that for purposes of legal analysis and research, the law pertaining to multinational enterprises is reflected first in the private law of the countries where the multinational transactions take place, (such as commercial law, conflict of laws, business organizations laws, etc.). Then we must review national governmental regulations imposed on the transaction by customs tariffs, tax laws, import controls, products liability, etc. and finally, at the international level, by treaties and conventions.

Basically, our greatest concern in these areas, is that we are dealing with different systems of law affecting the transaction and the uncertainty as to which system will prevail in the event of litigation. The "harmonization" laws of the European Economic Community, based on Article 100 of the Treaty of Rome, for the purpose of unifying the law of its various member nations, has been significant in a limited way in achieving this goal. Internationally, some nations have drafted conventions to unify the laws of signatory nations in such matters as sales transactions, based on reciprocity. Others have developed "model" statutes or laws on a particular subject to be accepted by a number of nations. In this regard there are a number of organizations currently active, among them the Hague Conference on Private International Law, the International Institute for the Unification of Private Law (UNIDROIT) and the United Nations Commission on International Trade Law (UNCITRAL).

E: NON-LEGAL RESEARCH SOURCES

CHAPTER 18

LAW VERSUS SOCIAL SCIENCE: AN INTERDISCIPLINARY CONFLICT

"For the rational study of the law, the black letter man may be the man of the present, but the man of the future is the man of statistics and the master of economics." In essence, this astute conclusion by Justice Holmes delivered in an address more than eighty years ago[1] suggests the context in which legal research must be considered today. It is now recognized that law as one of the social sciences itself is so closely interrelated with the other disciplines of the social sciences that to isolate it would be prejudicial to its validity and viability.

Quite a change has occurred in the concept of law since philosophers such as Hobbes, Bentham and Austin defined it as the command of the sovereign. The influence of Justices Holmes, Brandeis, Cardozo and Stone, as well as the work of the "Warren Court", have shown the relevancy of social, psychological and economic data, especially as they pertain to legislative purpose and history. The courts now recognize the distinction between "legal justice" and "social justice" as a result of Roscoe Pound's writings and the development of sociological jurisprudence. The research of social psychologists is now giving the legal profession a new insight and perception into the administration of justice and the relationship between legal rules and behavior. Heed is now being given to Professor Karl Llewellyn's admonition that law is a means to a social end rather than an end in itself.

With the realization that law and society today are in a state of flux, much research is being applied to Holmes' thought that law

---

[1] "The Path of the Law," 10 Harvard Law Review 457 (1896).

is not a system of abstract rules, nor a state of mind, but rather it is based on behavior—that the law is what the courts will do—that "the life of the law has not been logic; it has been experience. The felt necessities of the time, the prevalent moral and political theories, institutions of public policy, avowed or unconscious, even the prejudices which judges share with their fellow men have had a good deal more to do than the syllogism in determining the rules by which men should be governed."[2]

The recognition of the interdependence of the disciplines of the social sciences raises the question what is the value of each to the other, or more specifically for our purpose, what is the value of the social sciences to the progress of law? Perhaps this can best be understood by identifying the roles, if any, they can play in the comprehension of the milieu in which they operate.

Cairns' Method

The definition of the social sciences has always been a rather imprecise art, reflecting the rapidity with which their scope and purpose have changed in comparatively brief periods of time. As recently as 1935, Huntington Cairns decided to omit social psychology and geography as social sciences in his book on *Law and the Social Sciences* "because apparently they have not reached a stage at which they have many material contributions to offer".[3] Yet, only nineteen years later in *Brown v. Board of Education of Topeka,* 347 U.S. 483 (1954 segregation case), the methodology and findings of social psychologists were used with dramatic effect in the arguments on appeal to the Supreme Court. Actually, Cairns concerned himself only with anthropology, economics, sociology, political science and psychology. He recognized penology as one of the social sciences, but omitted it as having been thoroughly "canvassed" in other works.

Professor Edwin Seligman in his introduction to the scholarly *Encyclopedia of Social Sciences* (15v.) asked the question in 1930

---

[2] Holmes, "The Common Law." (1881) 1.

[3] P. 5.

"What are the social sciences?" After defining the social sciences as "those mental or cultural sciences which deal with the activities of the individual as a member of a group", he distinguished the social sciences (which he listed as politics, economics, law, anthropology, sociology, penology and social work) from the semisocial sciences (which he listed as ethics, education, philosophy and psychology) and from the sciences with social implications among which he includes biology, geography, medicine, linguistics and even art.

Contrast in Definitions

It is interesting to contrast Seligman's definition with that of David L. Sills', editor of the 1968 *International Encyclopedia of the Social Sciences* (17v.). Referring to Seligman's definition of the Social Sciences, he commented that it was apparent from his definition that no final answer could be given to the "What are the social sciences?" since—"like other groupings of scientific and academic fields—the social sciences differ in their scope from one generation to another. There are also within-generation differences: witness the continuing controversies over whether history should be considered as one of the social sciences or as a humanistic discipline . . . whether law is a social science or a body of professional knowledge; whether psychiatry is a social science or a branch of medicine".[4]

Noting that these were controversies not to be resolved in the near future and suggesting that the controversy was perhaps beneficial to scholarship, he wisely concluded that the best answer would be that whoever uses the term "social sciences" should "make clear what he includes under this heading".

Disciplines Listed

Inasmuch as the scope of the *International Encyclopedia of Social Sciences* reflects the thinking of some of the leading con-

[4]P. 21.

temporary specialists in the field, we take the liberty of following its outline in identifying the disciplines of the Social Sciences today. Under each of the following, the editors of the *Encyclopedia* have brought out the concepts, theories, and methods as generally described below in their own words:

Anthropology—includes cultural, economic, physical, political, social and applied anthropology, as well as archeology, ethnography, ethnology, and linguistics.

Economics—includes econometrics, economic history, the history of economic thought, economic development, agricultural economics, industrial organization, international economics, labor economics, money and banking, public finance, and certain aspects of business management.

Geography—includes cultural, economic, political, and social geography, but not physical geography.

History—includes the traditional subject-matter fields embraced in a study of the past and the scope and methods of historiography.

Law—includes jurisprudence, the major legal systems, legal theory, and the relationship of law to the other social sciences.

Political Science—includes public administration, public law, international relations, comparative politics, political theory and the study of policy making and political behavior.

Psychology—includes the clinical, counseling, educational, experimental, personality, physiological, social and practical investigations of human and animal behavior.

Psychiatry—includes theories and descriptions of the principal mental or emotional disorders and methods of diagnosis and treatment.

Sociology—includes economic, organizational, political, rural and urban sociology; the sociology of knowledge, law, religion, and medicine; human ecology; the history of social thought; sociometry and other small-group research; survey research; and such special fields as criminology and demography.

Statistics—includes measurement and averaging theory applied to all branches of human activity, the design of experiments, non-sampling errors, sample surveys, and government numerical reporting.[5]

Contributions to Law

Now—what is the contribution social science research can make to the law? The answer, social scientists respond, lies in the relevancy to the legal profession of the scientific method or research technique as applied in the analysis of social relations. This can only be understood in terms of what the social scientist attempts to accomplish in his research and findings.

Let us, for example, consider the role of the sociologist. Robert Angell describes it well. The sociologist, he explains, studies mutual adaptations of various social entities, personalities, groups, and institutions. As he believes that each of them evolves under the influence of all the others with whom they come in contact, the sociologist seeks to disclose these relationships, to understand their significance and where possible to measure them. Angell adds, that to the sociologist, the law appears as one functional system or institution in our complex life working in interaction with hundreds of others. Whatever happens in the legal order reflects a series of adaptations to a great variety of conditions. By the same token, the other social entities, conversely, are adjusting in many different ways to the legal order. Thus, the social process consists of a system of interstimulation and response evolving out of these mutual influences.[6]

Interestingly, it is not so much the substance of their findings that sociologists can offer to legal researchers as their contribution to a better knowledge of the law, but rather the scientific method they use in empirical research.

Sociologists can offer little information about law to lawyers that lawyers do not know. Lawyers are generally well versed in the

---

[5] Mr. Sills notes that statistics is not generally considered as one of the social sciences. But because of its close origin and relationship to the social sciences, and because the social sciences depend increasingly upon statistical methods for the gathering and interpretation of their data, it was included as a critical auxiliary discipline.

[6] See 31 Mich. L. Rev. 512–525 (1933).

substance of the law they are researching. What they need to learn is how law as one of the social entities comprising the social process adapts to other institutions, such as the family, and the economic system, as well as to groups and personalities. Lawyers can learn from the social scientist (1) how to select a topic and formulate a specific research problem; (2) how to develop a hypothesis; (3) how to collect data relevant for the hypothesis; (4) how to evaluate the hypothesis; and then (5) how to integrate the findings with other knowledge.

The Scientific Method

These "how to" procedures are known collectively as the scientific method. By using this scientific method, legal researchers could learn how to frame investigations in such a manner that they will be able to see legal problems in a more complete light. The use of this scientific method will, as Arnold Brecht has so well stated, supply "a type of knowledge that can be transmitted from any person who has such knowledge to *any* other person who does not have it but who can grasp the meaning of the symbols (words, signs) used in communication and perform the operations, if any, described in these communications. It submits observational testimony, refined as far as feasible by testimony on the conditions under which the observations were made, in order to enable ourselves and others the better to appraise the exactness of the observations made and the plausibility of the conclusions derived therefrom."[7]

We shall not elucidate on the technical features of the scientific method used in social science testing today. Sidney Ulmer's article on *The Scientific Method and the Judicial Process*[8] clearly sets forth how the problem is formulated, how the hypothesis is developed, how the data is collected, how the hypothesis is evaluated and how the facts are integrated. Rather, this chapter contrasts the diverse approach to research taken by the social scientist and the legal researcher.

---

[7] Political Theory 114 (1959).

[8] 7 American Behavioral Scientist 21 (Dec. 1963).

Lawyers are trained and skilled in legal research, but they do not truly understand the methodology involved. Social scientists are trained and skilled in methodology, but lack an appropriate understanding of the technicalities of legal research. In law school, lawyers are exposed to the case or problem method as a device for studying law. When they become practising lawyers, they are mainly concerned with solving specific problems of their clients. When they become judges, they are once again confronted with specific problems to adjudicate—the concrete case rather than the theoretical concept. When they become legislators, they draft laws to solve specific problems once again.

Mechanics and Technique

The problem-oriented research of lawyers has left its mark on legal research. In the main, legal research has become a matter of mechanics and technique, where detailed knowledge of the materials of the law used in research is a necessity.[9] As a result of this approach, lawyers in their research are closely analytical, concisely logical, and dependent on argument by analogy. In essence, they work with facts. First, they ascertain the pertinent facts of their problem by practical mechanical analysis of the data, evidence, and testimony involved. They then determine which legal sources or materials will be used to ascertain apposite law. Then it is merely a question of which position or tactic they will take. If they are drafting a contract or other legal instrument, they will mold or limit the facts to fit the law. If the facts are specific and not subject to change, lawyers will attempt to apply law by analogy to these facts to serve their purpose, such as sustaining a legal position, or overruling or modifying an established precedent. They also ascertain the law in all these situations as a matter of course.

In the search for facts, lawyers often must acquire and depend on knowledge not ordinarily learned by lawyers in law school. At this point, the lawyer starts to take advantage of the materials and data of the social sciences as distinguished from the methodology

---

[9] See Cohen, ed., How to Find the Law. Price and Bitner, Effective Legal Research; Jacobstein and Mersky, Fundamentals of Legal Research—for descriptions of legal materials used in research and the techniques of their use.

of the social sciences. In business and banking, taxation, labor, anti-trust and trade regulation, non-legal materials can be significant for an understanding of the facts. Lawyers are very much aware of the importance of the social sciences in this context, and they are quite alert to taking advantage of them in their research, but only as they provide data, perspectives and understanding to help courts apply or limit the pertinent legal principle or rule or position. Justice Brandeis best exemplified this practice when, as an attorney, he emphasized statistical and economic data to support legal concepts in his argument.[10] The Brandeis brief, however, also exemplifies one branch of work in which lawyers and social scientists fail to agree on the validity of the methodology involved.

Vulnerable Methods

When lawyers depend on the traditional research methods of analysis, logic and argument by analogy, they are on firm ground. They then can apply these methods with some confidence to the primary sources of the law (viz: decisional law and statutory law) in order to arrive at some predictable decision of a court or administrative body. These traditional methods become vulnerable, however, when used to introduce non-legal materials and non-legal values to procure a legal result or establish a legal precedent.

Lawyers now recognize that our predominately urban and industrial society cannot be properly understood in a vacuum. They acknowledge that law cannot be isolated from the social sciences by reason of this development and that therefore the social values of the law must necessarily influence its progress. But how should they assimilate social science data and empirical studies to solve legal problems, when the thrust of these data and studies may perhaps not be too clear, even to social scientists? The "Brandeis brief" is a good example of some of the pitfalls involved.

Brandeis logically deduced that "out of facts grows the law."[11] He used this principle with telling effect in *Muller v. Oregon,* 208 U.S. 412 (1908). An Oregon statute in 1907 established a ten-hour

---

[10] See Muller v. Oregon 208 U.S. 412 (1908).

[11] Brandeis, Business–A Profession, 332 (1914).

working day limitation for women engaged in industrial labor. When the constitutionality of this law was attacked in the courts, Brandeis, who was retained to defend it, submitted a brief of more than 100 pages, in which only two pages consisted of legal argument and the rest drew upon sociological, statistical and economic studies of human experience to establish that long hours of industrial labor would be perilous to the health, safety and morals of women. In this sense, his brief reflected the thinking of a sophisticated sociologist or anthropologist analyzing legal principles and opinions.

Influential Argument

Brandeis' argument had a profound influence on the Supreme Court. Taking judicial notice of these "expressions of opinion from other than judicial sources," the Court acknowledged that they were "significant of a widespread belief that woman's physical structure and the functions she performs in consequence thereof, justify special legislation restricting or qualifying the conditions under which she should be permitted to toil.

"Constitutional questions, it is true, are not settled by even a consensus of present public opinion.... At the same time, when a question of fact is debated or debatable, and the extent to which a special constitutional limitation goes is affected by the truth in respect to that fact, a widespread and long continued belief concerning it is worthy of consideration. We take judicial cognizance of all matters of general knowledge."[12]

The Brandeis brief became an instant success, and since then has been used with telling effect by lawyers to establish the constitutionality of legislation. But the Brandeis brief was used to uphold legislation! How should the courts react when it is used to destroy legislation on the ground of unconstitutionality? It is one thing to uphold legislation by the use of statistics, expert opinions and similar data, for, as Professor Edmond Cahn has so aptly noted, they "are sufficient to establish that the legislature or administrative authorities have acted rationally."

---

[12] Muller v. Oregon 208 U.S. 412, 419–21 (1908).

Lawyers Haunted

If this be so, he continues, "is it ever possible to prove that they have acted otherwise? Shrewd, resourceful lawyers can put a Brandeis brief together in support of almost any conceivable exercise of legislative judgment. . . ."[13] It is in this context that the Brandeis brief has now come back to haunt the legal profession—and it came dramatically to the fore in the famous Segregation Case of 1954.[14]

In the Segregation Case, the testimony of social psychologists was used to establish the adverse psychological effect of school segregation on black children in order to overturn state legislation decreeing it. However, there was also much expert evidence introduced to the contrary, that school segregation was not unreasonable which was supported too by psychological and psychiatric witnesses. By holding such unconstitutional, the Supreme Court demonstrated legislation that despite a Brandeis brief in support of constitutionality, it would hold to the contrary.

Now that "legislation restricting civil liberties is under attack," asks Professor Paul Freund, "would it be right to exclude studies showing the scientific fallacies in miscegenation laws or the psychological damage flowing from segregation in the public schools? Or to require such studies to do more than make a preponderant case—to require at least that they impeach the case for the proponents of the legislation as patently irrational."[15]

Disenchantment

This criticism of the Brandeis brief, reflects some of the disenchantment of lawyers today with the use of sociological data in solving legal problems. As a result, the Brandeis brief is gradually losing its significance in court proceedings. Professor Cahn noted more than twenty years ago that "in the last two decades, many Brandeis briefs have been conspicuously vulnerable in respect of

---

[13] Cahn—Jurisprudence, 1954. Annual Survey of American Law, 812, 813.

[14] Brown v. Board of Education of Topeka, 347 U.S. 483 (1954).

[15] Freund, Review of Facts in Constitutional Cases. Sup. Ct. and Sup. Law. (Cahn, ed.) 47–51.

statistical method, rationality of inferences and assembled data, adequacy of sampling and failure to allow for—or to disclose—negative instances."[16] He then expressed the hope that their quality will improve with a more critical attitude on the judge's part.

What bothers the legal profession is that the courts are giving great weight to the behavioral sciences, even though they still appear to be in their infancy. The legal profession is concerned that they are still imprecise and that their findings have not been established as permanent. Professor Cahn added another important caveat:

> "It is one thing to use current scientific findings, however ephemeral they may be, in order to ascertain whether the legislature has acted reasonably in adopting some scheme of social or economic regulation: deference here is shown not so much to the findings as to the legislature. It would be quite another thing to have our fundamental rights rise, fall, or change along with the latest fashions of psychological literature. Today the leaders of social psychologists are liberal and egalitarian in basic approach . . ." [Suppose later they are to the contrary.] What then would be the state of our constitutional rights?"[17]

Relevancy Questioned

The relevancy of scientific methodology to law has also been questioned from another point of view. In 1935, Felix Cohen suggested that law deals with meaningless concepts and meaningless questions in the context of scientific method, for they cannot be defined in terms of experience. Although they determine empirical decisions of the court, still they cannot be given operational definition.

For example, he cited concepts such as "contract," "title," "due process," "fair value" and "police power."[18] Cohen main-

[16] Cahn, Jurisprudence, 1954. Annual Survey of American Law 813.

[17] Ibid.

[18] Ulmer-Opus cite.

tained that the only meaningful questions in law are: (1) How do courts actually decide cases of a given kind? and (2) How ought they to decide cases of a given kind? Ulmer suggests a third question. Why do courts decide cases of a given kind in a given way?[19]

Another difficulty has arisen in this context—the failure of communication between the social scientists and the lawyer. Very much to this point is a letter written to the editor of *The Law and Society Review*[20] in which the writer bemoans the characteristic obscurity of sociologists' writings.

"As a lawyer," he complains, "I find myself wrinkling my brow over the writings of sociologists. Not that lawyers are guiltless, but I at least feel confident that if I do not understand what a lawyer is saying, it is because he is a poor writer or a muddled thinker. When I cannot understand a sociologist, I think my education is at fault."[21] Some attempt should be made to remove sociologist-lawyer communication difficulties.

Lawyers Need Education

Then again, when a social scientist is called upon to provide legally relevant information for the guidance of a judge so that he could reflect pertinent social values in a specific judicial decision, he is usually asked questions that are not significant to the outcome of the case. Much has to be done to educate lawyers to recognize and skillfully use the competence of professional psychiatrists, sociologists, economics and other social scientists.

The contribution that social scientists can make to legal research is also frustrated today by reason of the limitations lawyers have traditionally placed on their own research. Professor Brown of Yale Law School describes the usual product of legal research as "bite-sized."[22] The end product of the legal scholar too often is reflected only in law review articles which are often repetitive of other articles on the same subject, or case books organized for

---

[19] Ibid.

[20] Vol. 2, p. 341–343 (1968).

[21] Ibid. at 341.

[22] Brown, 7 American Behavioral Scientist 6 (Dec. 1963).

teaching a legal subject. The compilation of a case book he wryly notes is simpler than preparing a textbook, for most of the work has already been done by the judges whose opinions are edited by the case book author. Judge Vanderbilt, however, adds that at least the editing of case books has made accessible the very best cases—"the pure gold of legal principles."[23]

The writing of classic legal treatises unfortunately is now a matter of the past. Today, it is rare to find a new treatise in which the author systematically analyzes and synthesizes into fundamental principles the mass of available materials on a given subject. Today, we rarely come across a *Williston on Contracts*, a *Beale on Conflicts*, a *Wigmore on Evidence*, or a *Pomeroy on Equity Jurisprudence*. Today too, legal scholarship as reflected in the multivolume treatise is corporate and anonymous—the product of a publisher's editorial staff. The use of looseleaf format to keep them current results in the user not even knowing when the author begins and the editorial staff carries on. With this type of legal scholarship, it is understandable why lawyers have not taken full advantage of the research of social scientists.

There are, however, some bright spots in legal research. The American Law Institute, without the aid of the social scientist, has managed to accomplish some law reform by producing uniform and model laws, such as the Uniform Commercial Code and the Model Penal Code. Yet it has accomplished this with little resort to the scientific methods of research.

Similarly, much good work is being done by law revision commissions, judicial councils and similar bodies by dint of sophisticated argumentation, and comprehensive professional analysis of decisional and statutory law. It remains to be seen how much better their work products would be if they reflected empirical studies used by social scientists.

Set out below are some examples of what such collaboration could offer the progress of law if legal researchers were trained in the methods of scientific inquiry.

A new word has recently been coined which suggests the horizons awaiting to be reached by legal researchers—*Jurimetrics*.[24]

---

[23] Vanderbilt, Men & Measures of Law 11.

[24] Loevinger. Jurimetrics: The Next Step, 33 Minn. L. Rev. 455–93 (1949).

Professor Loevinger defines it as the scientific investigation of legal problems using empirical methods. Jurimetrics is a process whereby statistical analysis is made of repetitive quantitative data. Consider the behavior of witnesses.

Professor Loevinger asks, what is the statistical reliability and validity of present scientific methods of detecting deception? What is the comparative reliability and validity of cross-examination as a method of taking testimony? How can the effect of interest or bias upon observation and recollection be measured? Consider the behavior of judges.

What statistical measures will most conveniently summarize the behavior of individual judges in various categories of cases? Consider the behavior of legislators. What practical measures can be instituted for investigating and recording in summary form the patterns of legislature behavior?

Consider legal procedure and recordation. How can ordinary controversies be presented to a tribunal in the simplest and quickest manner? How can the inordinate delays of current procedure, both in presentation and decision, be eliminated or immunized? These are but a few of Professor Loevinger's questions.

Lawyers' Careers

The scientific method can also be used to investigate lawyers' careers, juror's evaluation of expert testimony, behavior patterns of the courts and of judges, the effect of police practices on the administration of justice, the defense of insanity, the homosexual in court, legal aspects of desegregation, the effect of mass media on verdicts of potential jurors, the relationship between legal rules and behavior, the effects of personal, political and economic influence in the decisions of judges, the social effects of legal rules and the ways that the public becomes aware of law.

A law and social science movement in the last two decades has brought closer the possibility of such studies. Programs in law and social science have been founded by the Russell Sage Foundation. The foundation has established formal centers of interdisciplinary cooperation between law and social science at law schools and universities.

Sage established the Center for the Study of Law and Society at the University of California at Berkeley in 1960 that concentrates mainly on sociology research and has published many studies. It also established a center at the University of Wisconsin in 1962 that emphasizes the cross-disciplinary training of scholars in law and the social sciences. It supports faculty members who wish to study in the "opposite" disciplines.

Wisconsin also sponsors a law and society section in the *Wisconsin Law Review* which supports legal scholarship.

Other Programs

Programs were also founded at Northwestern University and the University of Denver in 1964. Northwestern's program is more like Berkeley's, though smaller. It emphasizes the training of graduate students. Berkeley caters to more mature scholars. Northwestern stresses the influence of political sciences and anthropology. A great deal of the work on a leading review in the field, *Law and Society Review* is done at Northwestern.

The University of Denver's program is the first to be located organizationally within a law school. Social scientists are appointed directly to law school faculty and assigned the teaching of substantive law courses such as criminal, as well as more typical interstitial courses, such as sociology of law. Sage has also instituted programs at Pennsylvania, Harvard and Yale. At Pennsylvania, it is known as the Center for Studies on Criminology and Criminal Law. A Center for Interdisciplinary Study of National and International Regulatory Structures was established at the University of Maryland.

Pennsylvania has a variety of joint programs leading to the JD Program and a graduate degree in City Planning, Economics, Business Administration, Public Policy, Analysis and Islamic Studies.

In addition, the Law School and the University Economics Department have established an Institute of Law and Economics as a separate entity that itself administers additional joint degree programs.

Other interdisciplinary programs can also be found at the law schools of Chicago, Columbia, Michigan and New York Universities and in the social science departments at Indiana and Tufts. The Ford Foundation, the Walter E. Meyers Research Institute of Law and the Rockefeller Foundation are also supporting such research.

Law Schools' Role

Interdisciplinary curriculums in specific fields are being created at law schools in recognition of the contribution they can make to an understanding of law and its processes. A new curriculum development at NYU School of Law in the late 1960s is characteristic of this development. Eleven courses in the graduate and undergraduate law curriculum were proposed dealing with urban and poverty law alone. These courses and seminars are taught primarily from new materials developed especially for this program and stress the interdisciplinary approach.

A list of the courses points up its scope. The courses considered are: (1) the law of urban affairs, (2) urban housing and redevelopment, (3) government benefit programs, (4) private law and the poor, (5) social justice, (6) public education, (7) state and local finance, (8) legal services and the poor, (9) urban affairs laboratory, (10) family law and the poor and (11) health services in an urban society. These were to be added to existing courses on poverty, race and employment, workmen's compensation and unemployment insurance, political and civil rights, the law of criminal correction, labor relations and the public employee and non-profit organization.

Professor Karl Llewellyn once urged that the law be constantly evaluated in terms of its effects and that its effects particularly be carefully analyzed.[25] Although this goal can best be accomplished by interdisciplinary research many obstacles still remain in arriving at a compatible and viable research partnership among the disciplines of the Social Sciences. "Law versus Social Science" still appears to be characteristic of this situation.

---

[25] Some Realism about Realism. 44 Harvard Law Review 1222 (1931).

CHAPTER 19

INTERDISCIPLINARY SOURCES FOR LEGAL RESEARCH

The growing dependence of lawyers on the sources, analysis and methodology reflected in interdisciplinary research, especially in the field of administrative law, suggests that the legal profession has much to gain by taking advantage of certain services presently being provided by organizations alert to this situation. The changing nature of legal research has become quite evident during the last two decades. In 1969, for example, an article on "Research Habits of Lawyers," by the Law Librarian of Harvard University, noted that even the opinions of the Supreme Court of the United States referred to research sources rarely cited prior thereto by the court.

- Scholarly material related to legal history.
- Research findings in medicine and social science.
- Documents of administrative law.
- Congressional documents evidencing legislative intent.[1]

Practitioner's Need

Many practitioners are now very much aware of this development and are following closely the efforts of law librarians to provide interdisciplinary sources for legal research. But practitioners need more than access to apposite materials in economics, sociology, political science, science, medicine and government documents. They require skilled and professional assistance in the analysis, application and conclusions reached in order to prepare for a case involving those disciplines. They need the expertise of an organization which can provide technical research in the support of legal concepts which must prevail in a court room before a judge and jury.

For example, consider the following:

1. How would you determine whether from a statistical point of view, it was unreasonable for a defendant, a securities dealer, never to have employed a black person as a sales representative? How would you define the appropriate labor pool of securities sales talent in the geographical area in which the defendant had sales offices? How would you locate the demographic data showing the racial composition of this labor pool for the years covered by the complaint? How would you determine the size of the defendant's work force in those years, compute the expected number of black sales employees from those labor pool and work force figures, apply standard statistical tests to answer the question whether zero blacks in the firm's sales force was unreasonable, and then present those findings in court.

2. Assume that under Internal Revenue Service procedures the method for allocating income between a parent (domestic) corporation and its subsidiary which owned the patent rights and manufactured a product for sale in the United States has been deemed unfair. How would you analyze the formula to reach a more equitable allocation of profits between the two corporations.

3. How would you demonstrate that the foreign exchange rate specified by current law for use in analysis of dumping was not appropriate? Since the adjustment of the dollar-lira exchange rate to change in economic conditions takes about four to six months, use of the proper exchange rate would not support a finding of dumping.

Aid for Lawyers

An organization known as MATHTECH, the Technological Research and Consulting Division of MATHEMATICA, INC., Princeton, N.J., employs a staff of over fifty Ph.D.-level economists, computer scientists, statisticians, engineers, operations researchers, system analysts, public policy analysts and social scientists and is specially constituted to furnish law to support such programs. Over the past few years, MATHTECH has provided the legal profession with assistance involving economic and statistical analysis of the type brought out above. It has also worked with both the government and the private sector in matters dealing with the environment, credit, communications and other regulatory matters. MATHTECH generally provides the following services:

1. Its scientists and legally trained staff critically analyze the legal problem and define its scientific and technical components so that the practitioner can plan the proper strategy for the trial.
2. It translates the scientific findings into easily understood exhibits, testimony and examination questions.

A similar service is also provided by *Lexecon, Inc.*, located in Chicago, Illinois. *Lexecon* has a staff of economists, computer experts, statisticians, research assistants and lawyers. It also retains scholars in economics, statistics, and law in addition to its in-house staff. In litigation support, it provides economic and legal research, statistical computation, computerized document retrieval services and back-up research for economic, accounting, statistical and other expert witnesses. It also prepares, on request, a comprehensive memorandum analyzing the facts and the legal and economic issues in a case. *Lexecon* has analyzed issues of competition and monopoly under a variety of regulatory statutes in industries as diverse as airlines and drugs and has been involved in securities, banking, pollution and tort cases. It also has experience in energy, communication, consumer products, and transportation.

A comparatively new service called The Document Center, in Phoenix, Ariz., provides a means through its fifty WATS lines, to facilitate the filing, search and retrieval of any available data housed within local, state, or Federal agencies or courts on a nationwide basis. By calling the Document Center, toll free, at (800) 528-6077, its president, Lewis Levy, guarantees that "In most instances, the Document Center can locate and retrieve information within a matter of hours from the time a client calls and the data can be on the client's desk, depending on the urgency of the request, within minutes of its retrieval."

Paralegals Used

The Document Center employs a number of paralegals in Washington, D.C., and throughout the country, each of whom has been trained to identify and locate various governmental agency documents. It also claims that it has access to national computer data bases to assist in the research and preparation of in-depth and comprehensive scientific, legal, and technological reports and can expedite locating expert witnesses. Counsel need only name the subject on which testimony is needed, for example, as automotive, railroad, explosion, electric shock, products liability, medical malpractice, environmental sciences and transportation.

In the field of scientific and technical research, great reliance is placed on abstracting services (there are over 1,000 indexing and abstracting services to scientific literature alone) to identify articles on specific subjects in scholarly scientific journals. In the fields of chemistry and biology, for example, *Chemical Abstracts* and *Biological Abstracts* are consulted. Of particular value to the practitioner is H.W. Wilson's *Applied Science and Technology Index* as it refers to articles of a less technical type. To obtain access to reports of various scientific agencies of the government such as NASA, *Government Reports Announcements and Index*, a biweekly publication of the U.S. Dept. of Commerce is quite helpful.

New Service

Once an article is identified, it may be difficult to locate it in a library. A new NTIS service known by the acronym of JACS (Journal article copy service) has recently been announced by the U.S. Department of Commerce (National Technical Information Service, Springfield, Virginia) for all deposit account customers.

JACS will provide rapid access to copies of articles from more than 5,000 scientific and technical journals. It was developed by NTIS to satisfy the need for copies of articles from journals not shelved in a library, or not conveniently available.

JACS publishes a *Directory* for $5 which lists the specific journals from which it can supply articles. It focuses on such scientific and technical fields as agriculture, chemistry, engineering, mathematics, medicine, oceanography, physics, solar energy, and water resources.

Orders can be transmitted by TWX, TELEX or dial-up computer terminal. Orders are also accepted over an "800" JACS telephone number at a small extra charge.

NTIS does not stock journals or articles for filling JACS orders. Rather, acting as a switching power, NTIS relays one's order to other organizations, libraries, information services and publishers. The journal article is then mailed directly from the source within two days of receipt of the order and should be received within six days after the order.

The charge will be modest, usually averaging $6 to $8 for each journal article copy including a standard royalty payment. Where royalty payment is not required, the cost is less. The article price for each journal is indicated in the JACS Directory. Several NTIS customers, such as Bell Labs and the U.S. Department of Labor, have been using JACS during a test period. It is necessary, however, to become a deposit account customer to take advantage of the service.

CHAPTER 20

NON-LEGAL RESEARCH RESOURCES FOR LAWYERS

The interrelation of industry and society is so highly manifest today in the solution of legal problems, that, as the late Chief Justice Arthur T. Vanderbilt of New Jersey expressed it, "An understanding of the social sciences is essential for the lawyer who would perform his full duty to his client. In this period of rapid change an intelligent client will be wise to know not only what the law is today, but what it is likely to be at the time the transaction in question may come up for decision in court."

In a sense, this interrelation of law and the social sciences reflects the addition of a new dimension to legal problems—the public interest. The dominance of this new legal development has become of considerable concern to lawyers seeking "law in the books."

Brandeis and Holmes

"Out of facts grows the law," Justice Louis D. Brandeis, emphasized, for he well knew how to use social facts in litigation. Justice Oliver Wendell Holmes expressed a similar thought when he conjectured: "For the rational study of the law the black letter man may be the man of the present, but the man of the future is the man of statistics and the master of economics."

Lawyers recognize that the law cannot be isolated from the other social sciences. As a result, when seeking law, the practising lawyer realizes, that whereas formerly resort to the traditional sources of the law would have been sufficient for his purpose, today, such research by itself would be found wanting. To be insensitive to social trends, statistics and findings of the social scientists can be critical in the solution of a legal problem.

A New Problem

Current technological and scientific thinking and findings have become important elements in determining whether bureaucratically established criteria and standards for specific industrial and consumer oriented products have been met. Lawyers must now, on occasion, have access to scientific data, sociological statistics and marketing information in arriving at a sophsticated, professional judgment on a specific legal problem.

Obviously, the need to consult such documentation and information is compounding the difficulties of legal research. Aside from learning how these kinds of data affect legal situations, how does the practising lawyer *first* learn of their availability and *second* obtain access to them for research purposes. The average and even the extraordinary law firm library certainly will not be sufficient to meet the thrust of this demand, unless it reflects a very special interest of the firm's clients.

The practicing lawyer engaged in interdisciplinary research outside the traditional structured legal patterns may not realize it, but there are a number of research and information resources maintained by the federal, state and local governments, as well as in the private sector by trade associations and corporations which provide information and research help liberally, on request, and allow the use of their specialized research resources and highly trained staffs for this purpose. Following are some recommended reference tools which can be helpful in identifying these information and research resources.

Business Books

For answering basic business reference questions consult the following:

1. Daniel's *Business Information Sources* (U. of Calif.).
2. Grant's *Directory of Business and Financial Services* (Special Library Associations, 7th ed.).
3. Wasserman's *Encyclopedia of Business Information Sources* (Gale, Vol. 1), Special Subjects, Vol. 2, Geographic Sources).
4. Marke and Bander. Business Sources.

Special Libraries Directories

The *Special Libraries Association,* is a national association of specialized librarians and information specialists, with its home office at 235 Park Avenue South, New York, 10003. Its regional chapters publish local library directories which are helpful in identifying specialized collections of information and resources.

Lawyers in the Greater New York City area can consult: *Special Libraries Directory of Greater New York,* 15th ed. N.Y. Chapter, Special Libraries Association, 1980. Arranged by subject, it lists special libraries, information centers of trade associations, corporations, U.S., N.Y. State and New York City governmental agencies, giving the size and contents of their collections, address, telephone number, staff members and special services offered to the public.

Under *Finance Investment and Securities,* for example, appear:

Federal Reserve Bank of New York, Research Library, 33 Liberty Street, New York (Mailing address: Federal Reserve, P.O. Station, New York, N.Y. 10045) Tel: (212) 791-5670. Featuring as its major subjects, books and information on banking, money and credit, central banking, international monetary affairs, gold and government finance, it also has Special Collections on the Federal Reserve System and U.S. Treasury publications.

American Stock Exchange, Martin J. Keena Memorial Library, 86 Trinity Place, New York, N.Y. 10006. (212) 938-2280. Its major subjects are corporation records (U.S. annual reports, prospectuses, proxies) regulatory agency documents particularly those issued by the Securities and Exchange Commission and stock exchange publications. In its Special Collections it contains Leasco Microfiche Service on all SEC reports for American Stock Exchange listed companies.

Securities and Exchange Commission, Public Reference Room, 26 Federal Plaza, New York, N.Y. 10007. (212) 264-1614. Its major subjects are SEC materials, filings and reports; investments.

Under Industry and Labor:

American Arbitration Association, Lucius Root Eastman Arbitration Library, 140 West Fifty-first Street, New York, N.Y. 10020. (212) 582-6620. Its major subjects are on arbitration (Labor, commercial, international commercial and political, public employees, medical malpractice), community dispute settlement.

New York State Department of Labor Library, 80 Centre Street, New York, N.Y. 10003. (212) 488-6295. Its major subjects are automation, labor economics, unions, industrial relations, health insurance, occupational medicine, pensions, women in industry, radiological health and safety. Its special collections feature releases of state labor departments, state labor laws, publications of Canadian departments of labor.

U.S. Department of Labor, Bureau of Labor Statistics, Branch of Information and Advisory Services, 1515 Broadway, New York, N.Y. 10036. (212) 971-5405. Its major subjects are on manpower, occupational outlook, wages and industrial relations, price and living conditions, productivity, occupational safety and health, foreign labor, economic growth.

Workmen's Compensation Record Library, 2 World Trade Center, New York, N.Y. 10047. (212) 488-3104. Its major subjects are on workmen's compensation (law and court decisions, medicine, statistics, reports and studies). Its special collection is on workmen's compensation laws of all the states.

Under Natural, Environmental Sciences:

Environmental Protection Agency, Region II, Technical Library, Edison, N.J. 08817. (201) 548-3347, Ext. 54. Major subjects: water quality and pollution, environmental quality.

Under Public Administration:

New York Municipal Service Administration, Municipal Reference and Research Center, 2230 Municipal Building, New York, N.Y. 10007. (212) 566-4284. Major subjects are on New York City official documents, history, codes, rules and selected New York State documents. Special collections on civil service, public health, maps (real estate, voting), neighborhood information files, street name collections, legislative reference collection.

U.S. Department of Housing and Urban Development, Region II Library, 26 Federal Plaza, New York, N.Y. 10007. (212) 264-8175. Major Subjects: Legal and technical research on housing and urban development.

A large number of library collections are listed under Social Sciences of which the following are representative examples:

American Civil Liberties Union Library, 22 East Fortieth Street, New York, N.Y. 10016.

American Jewish Committee Blaustein Library, 165 East Fifty-sixth Street, New York, N.Y. 10022.

Brooklyn Public Library, Social Sciences Division, Grand Army Plaza, Brooklyn, N.Y., 11238.

Citizens' Housing and Planning Council of New York, Inc. Library, 20 West Fortieth Street, New York, N.Y. 10018.

Ford Foundation Library, 320 East Forty-third Street, New York, N.Y. 10017.

New York State Division of Human Rights, Reference Library, 270 Broadway, New York, N.Y. 10007.

Research Institute for the Study of Man Library, 162 East Seventy-eighth Street, New York, N.Y. 10021.

The Rockefeller Foundation Library, 111 West Fiftieth Street, New York, N.Y. 10020.

There are several subject directories of Special Libraries on a national scale which also warrant the notice of lawyers.

The Gale Research Company, located in Detroit, Mich., publishes a *Directory of Special Libraries*, edited by Anthony T. Kruzal. It gives information about 13,000 special libraries, information centers and documents centers in the U.S. and Canada, arranged alphabetically by the names of the supporting organizations. It also supplies details on information units operated by business, government agencies, trade associations, professional societies and cultural organizations. This *Directory of Special Libraries* is kept up to date by a volume entitled *New Special Libraries.*

A *Subject Directory of Special Libraries*, edited by N.L. Young, H.C. Young and A.T. Kruzal, also published by Gale Research, classifies by subjects the libraries listed in the *Directory of Special Libraries* in five volumes.

Volume 1–Business and Law Libraries.
Volume 2–Education and Information Science Libraries.
Volume 3–Health Sciences Libraries.
Volume 4–Social Sciences and Humanities Libraries.
Volume 5–Science and Technology Libraries.

PART THREE

Phases of Library Management

A: PUBLICATIONS

CHAPTER 21

GUIDELINES FOR SELECTION OF BOOKS FOR A LAW OFFICE

What constitutes a good book or a bad one can best be shown from actual illustrations. One work regarded as absolutely indispensable to any general practice is *Basic Corporate Practice* by George C. Seward and W. John Nauss, Jr., Philadelphia, American Law Institute–American Bar Association, Committee on Continuing Professional Education, 1977, now in its second edition. The "bad" book: *Toulmin on the Anti-Trust Laws,* Cincinnati, Anderson, 1949–1952 with 1979 pocket parts in seven volumes.

The Test

This is a fundamental test: Find in the foreword or preface the author's or publisher's statement of purpose—what he intends the book to accomplish. Each writer and publisher of a law book gives to the purchaser an "implied warranty of merchantability and fitness." If they fail to live up to that warranty, they should not publish.

After reading *Basic Corporate Practice*, any astute lawyer who has had only limited corporate experience should be able to answer this question affirmatively: Do you now feel competent to form a corporation, advise a client on financing matters with respect to it or to take steps to protect a client in a takeover—whether friendly or hostile? The reader should be able to answer "Yes" with confidence.

After reading *Toulmin on the Antitrust Laws*, on the other hand, the astute lawyer with only a limited antitrust experience must answer "No" to the question: Do you now feel competent to defend a client against Federal monopoly or price-fixing charges or can you now write an antitrust compliance manual for the sales personnel and officers of your corporate clients?

In the case of the corporate work, the warranty stands up. In the case of the antitrust publication, it does not.

Objective Criteria

No practitioner—or librarian for that matter—has time to evaluate in detail each of the publishers' many offerings. It is necessary to use certain objective criteria for screening them. These include:

- The authority of the author.
- The reputation of the publisher.
- The importance of the subject to one's practice.
- Organization and scope of the work.
- Its style and readability.
- Provision for upkeep.
- Format.
- Superiority over any competing works.
- Its initial cost and upkeep expense.

Three of the criteria are discussed below.

The two authors of *Basic Corporate Practice* are themselves veteran corporate lawyers and senior partners in a leading New York firm. They are contributors to *The Business Lawyer* and active members of the ABA Section of Corporation, Banking and Business Law. This Section includes the leaders of the American corporate bar.

By contrast, the late author of the antitrust work was not a nationally known antitrust lawyer.

Reputation of Publishers

The expansion of the legal profession in the past decade has brought an increase in both the number of publications offered and in the number of publishers who offer them. This high volume makes it difficult to give each new title careful evaluation. Lawyers simply do not have time to look at each new environmental or civil rights book that comes off the press. One effective way is to try to look at each new publication in the field of one's specialty and to limit one's examination of other books to the current offerings of those publishers whose books have proved useful in the past.

In general, the ALI-ABA publications have been of a high order. Moreover, the American Law Institute is the sponsor of the *Restatements* and along with the Practising Law Institute the spearhead of continuing legal education in the country.

There are three dominant publishers (Matthew Bender & Company, Lawyer's Co-operative Publishing Company and West Publishing Company) and, in addition, a few smaller houses noted for the high quality of their works. Among these are Callaghan & Company and Little Brown & Company. If a lawyer were to examine their works, those of the local continuing legal education organizations and all books in his specialty, he would probably use up all the time he could allot to book selection matters. Nor would he miss many good books in this way. By employing a professional law librarian, his office would come closer to examining all the best new books issued. It must be remembered that most publishers offer books on approval. Advantage should be taken of this.[1]

Organization of the Work

A quick scan of the table of contents of any book should tell the prospective purchaser if the development of the subject is logical and coherent. A corporate treatise would be well organized if it traced the various corporate acts from inception of the corporation to its dissolution or merger. If in addition the author drafts model forms that may be tailored for use in connection with each of those acts—in various jurisdictions—he is probably a fine organizer. Not only have Seward and Nauss adopted this form of useful organization, but they have drafted at a high level of sophistication some forty forms suitable for use under Delaware law, New York law and the Model Act.

---

[1] See also the article by Diana Vincent-Daviss, "Book Selection at Non-Librarian Firms," New York Law Journal, March 26, 1979, p. 1.

By contrast a reviewer of the antitrust work pointed out

> "...it is going to be difficult to find in this set any comprehensive study of a particular problem in one place. It seems that separating 'Interpretation' from 'Application' has only served to disperse material that should properly be continuous...
> "By treating the various sections of the several acts as separate entities, Toulmin fails to give a comprehensive picture of each particular problem."[2]

Style and Readability

Law textbook writers are not often admired for their style. There are few Gilmores left on the scene. Yet for conciseness and clarity of expression the Seward and Nauss book is a notable one. At the other extreme, a reviewer said of the antitrust work:

> "Any editor might have detected in the author's Foreword the cloudy style, the political bias, the turgid repetitions, and the unselfconscious self-contradictions that characterize the body of this expansive, but not great work."[3]

The first reviewer also pointed out,

> "The extensive use of case quotations makes for a lack of style and the impression is given that this was a paste and scissors job with inadequate editorial synthesis...In Volume 3 a three-page quotation at pages 297–299 is unnecessarily repeated, in toto, at pages 318–320."[4]

Finally, the pleasurable mandate of appraising the new books should be divided among the specialists in each office. No lawyer need devote more than half an hour a week to this work. That time would be repaid in knowledge of what new works have become available and in increased familiarity with one's own office

---

[2] Ratzkin, Jack L., 35 Cornell L. Q. 718–720 (1950).

[3] Schwartz, Louis B., 98 U. Penna. L. Rev. 951 (1950).

[4] See Fn. 2 at p. 719.

resources. This will also give members of a firm or department the opportunity to visit and re-evaluate their own libraries on a continuing basis.

CHAPTER 22

LAW BOOKS FOR THE YOUNG PRACTITIONER *

A successful practitioner, presently in his sixties, when asked which law books helped him most when he first started his practice replied unhesitatingly, "Form books, without them I would have been lost." On another occasion, a New York lawyer responding on how he prepared his briefs on appeal, stated, "First, I check my problem in McKinney's Consolidated Laws of New York—then I select some of the appellate cases annotated under the relevant section or sections—then I read the appellate briefs submitted to the Court in those cases which I obtain at the local bar library, and then I write my own brief," was his startling reply. "What do you do if you can't find a relevant case by this process?" he was asked. "Thank God," he exclaimed "so far I have been lucky."

These two incidents suggest how some lawyers limit their research by depending basically on a limited number of law books, such as annotated codes, selected practitioners' treatises, handy desk references, form books and practitioners' guides.

There is an impression, however, that this situation is changing. Many young lawyers, graduated today from law schools approved by the American Bar Association and the Association of American Law Schools, have been exposed in their law school study to superior law library collections, and are aware of their importance in the practice of law. Moot Court competitions and law review experience have highlighted for them the significance of certain legal finding tools, both traditional ones and those that are depen-

(*This chapter is based on an article published in *Docket Call,* Winter, 1981.)

dent on the new technology. Often it is not the lack of interest--but the scarcity of funds—which causes them not to purchase desirable legal materials.

Growth of On-Line Information Services

By reason of their exposure in Law School to on-line information services, the young practitioner today is more attuned to the on-line informational retrievable systems of LEXIS, WESTLAW, and AUTO-CITE, as well as the many law related data bases available through the Lockheed/DIALOG, SDC/ORBIT, BRS information banks and other systems. Most Law Schools today are training their students in the use of these computer based retrieval systems and they have come to depend on them for legal research more than do older practitioners.

The fees charged by the operators of these systems vary, but generally, the charges are based on computer time plus data communications and off-line print-outs, with discounts granted to high volume users.

The major commercial vendors of computerized law information are LEXIS (Mead Data Central), WESTLAW (West Publishing Co.) and AUTO CITE (Lawyers Cooperative Publishing Co.). LEXIX and WESTLAW contain full text collections of federal and state case law. LEXIS provides specialized libraries on tax law, SEC, copyright, trade regulation and the English system of case reports. LEXIS, at present, appears to be the more popularly used system. WESTLAW is preferred on occasion, because it reflects the West Topic and Key Numbers in its retrieval system. AUTO-CITE is designed for case verification, as well as the current status of Federal and State case citations.

All these systems are, on the whole, too expensive for the beginning practitioner. Although they are not recommended as part of the beginning practitioner's library, still their potential in legal research should be recognized. They are definitely of value in this context, reducing dramatically the time spent in ascertaining relevant authority.

The beginning practitioner should attempt to locate a nearby terminal in a local bar library or through vendors providing these services, or if possible, to arrange for access, with neighboring law firms which subscribe to them.

Microform

The beginning practitioner rarely has sufficient office space. Law books occupy more space on shelves than most other types of books. As a general rule, five law books occupy about one foot of linear space. It does not take too many law books to create space problems in the office. Fortunately, the new technology of microform publication, which makes available on a 4″ x 6″ fiche, or card made of film, approximately 100 pages, is helping this situation. The cost of these fiches is usually less than the hard bound copy of the book. Microform can be of value particularly to the young lawyer specializing in areas of taxation, labor and SEC. Some tax lawyers today, who do not want to be away from their office researching tax problems in a local law library, instead depend on comprehensive tax collections consisting of court reports, statutes, administrative regulations and much that appears in loose leaf services, made available by Commerce Clearing House on microform. The hardware for reading and making facsimile reproductions of the original pages is now acceptable, although the prices average around $1500.00.

So much has been published on microform, it would be worthwhile for the young lawyer to check *Guide to Microforms in Print*. It is arranged by subject and by author/title and gives prices. Many important law publishers are now publishing a great variety of legal publications on microform. Following are some of the more active ones:

- Bureau of National Affairs
- Congressional Information Service
- Wm. S. Hein and Co. (recently merged with Capital Services International)
- Information Handling Services
- Oceana/Transmedia
- Fred B. Rothman Co.

- University Microfilm
- West Publishing Co.

It is important to note how lawyers find law relevant to a legal problem with a specific fact pattern—in order to recommend legal materials to meet the thrust of that exercise. For the materials lawyers use in legal research reflect basically the methodology they use in ferreting out the legal principles they seek. It is therefore instructive to first reveiew how lawyers find law relevant to a legal problem. The books and other materials recommended necessarily will respond to that process. How much a lawyer need purchase for private use in an office depends obviously on the funds available, the space requirements, and the actual special interests the lawyer is pursuing in the practice of law. Some of the materials recommended are obviously rather expensive and occupy much space. They are listed, however, with the thought that they are of value in research for the specific subject or subjects covered and can be referred to in local bar libraries.

In this context, it should also be noted that the proximity of a law library to which the young lawyer has access can be a determining factor in whether a purchase should be made of certain legal publications. In larger cities, there usually is a neighboring law library where apposite new books can be consulted. There are also county and court libraries which serve a similar purpose. In smaller towns and rural areas, it may be necessary to waste valuable office time in order to travel to the library. These are factors which may be significant in whether a new law book should be purchased or not.

It is important to note that there is more than the cost of the book involved, when you purchase law books. Most law book publishers provide up-dated service for their publications, which can eventually become quite costly. This is particularly true with loose-leaf service subscriptions. It is also true of publishers selling multi-volume treatises, such as Matthew Bender, Lawyers Cooperative, Callaghan, Warren, Gorham and Lamont and West Publishing Co. If we add to this listing, annotated codes, court reports, digests, Shepard's, annotated reporters and legal periodicals, the annual up-keep costs alone in the larger research law libraries, amount to approximately 80% of their annual book budgets, allowing only 20% of their annual budget for new materials.

Then again, the materials recommended for use by beginning practitioners, do not reflect the inter-disciplinary approach to law which is presently developing at an augmented pace. Young lawyers have been made very much aware of this inter-relationship at law school and are aware of their implications in the courtroom. Such materials should be ascertained and referred to in the larger, more comprehensive research law libraries to which the lawyer has access.

In this context, it should also be noted that inasmuch as this article is addressed to lawyers throughout the country, rather than to those practising in a specific jurisdiction, it was necessary to eliminate from the recommended listing of law materials, books which are considered as practitioners' works keyed to the law and practice of a local jurisdiction. To have done otherwise, would have made this listing unmanageable.

With reference to the recommended listing of books that follows, there is always the danger that a critical selection of law books will reflect the special interests and background of the author. The authors have attempted to overcome this possible personal bias by drawing on their professional experiences as law librarians.

The prices that are quoted are only to be used as guides to possible cost and do not take into account shipping and handling costs as well as the impact of inflation since the time the price noted was last published.

How Lawyers Find Law Relevant to a Legal Problem

Lawyers, in seeking legal authority, do so to give legal advice to their clients or to draft legal documents for them and also to prepare for litigation as an advocate.

Jurisdictional Analysis

A lawyer involved in legal research first determines the jurisdiction involved—whether the law of a specific state or of the federal jurisdiction, or both govern. Then necessarily, if litigation is anticipated, which court would assume jurisdiction, at the trial or appellate court level. This determination is significant in applicability of rules of law which could be merely persuasive authority or mandatory authority.

Sequential Use of Legal Materials

(1) *Textual Approach.* The orderly presentation of legal principles in a treatise, textbook, article in a legal periodical or in a legal encyclopedia is a good beginning for comprehension of general principles and leading cases, as well as a source for statutes in point pertaining to a specific legal problem.

(2) *Statutes.* When a statute is relevant, lawyers refer to the most current annotated codification of the jurisdiction or jurisdictions involved, e.g. New York and Federal. As part of this research process, lawyers read and analyze those cases which have construed apposite statutory sections. On occasion it is even necessary to ascertain the legislative history of these sections, to determine legislative intent when they were enacted.

(3) *Digests of Case Law.* Digests of Case Law provide references to decided cases arranged by specific subjects. Our case law is reported chronologically by Court system. As the lawyer seeks a case with facts similar to the fact pattern being researched, the Topic and Key No. Digest System of West Publishing Co. is helpful in this context. The West Key No. system organizes the legal points of a case as reflected in the Headnotes of the reported case with other cases with similar facts under a topic and key number, which stands for a specific factual legal point. These cases with related fact patterns are thus brought out together.

Digests can be used most effectively after a case in point has been found. A case reported in a unit of the National Reporter Series refers to topics and key numbers in point. Independently used, Digests refer to topics and key numbers and related cases brought out thereunder.

(4) *Annotated Reporters–(American Law Reports). American Law Reports* refers to case law in depth on a specific subject. ALR annotations to selectively reported cases are helpful for

identifying significance of relevant cases. They also provide textual analysis of the subjects treated.

(5) *Looseleaf Series.* Looseleaf Series are particularly helpful in that they are kept up-to-date as to recent developments in areas subject to governmental regulation and control–such as food, drug and cosmetic law, environmental law, trade regulation, S.E.C., labor and taxation. They bring together in one publication, administrative rules and regulations, statutory text, case annotations, legislative history, related articles, and statutory and judicial developments in these fields. The major publishers of these series are *Commerce Clearing House, Prentice Hall* and *Bureau of National Affairs*.

Making Research Current

Once relevant case law or statutory law has been identified, it is important to determine whether any current statutory development or recent cases have affected their legal import.

(1) Lawyers use "Shepard's" citators for this purpose. Shepardizing a case can reveal sometimes even better and more current cases than the cited case. Then again, citing cases may actually modify, distinguish or overrule the thrust of the cited case. It is also reassuring to learn from Shepard's that subsequent cases generally approve the cited case.

(2) When treatises, encyclopedias, ALR annotations are used, current pocket parts and cumulative supplements should be referred to for subsequent developments. A similar process should be followed for digests and codes. Loose-leaf services, of course, are updated by periodic reports.

Guidelines for Selection of Law Books

The following objective criteria for the selection of law books by a practitioner are suggested:

- the authority of the author
- the reputation of the publisher

- the importance of the subject to one's practice
- organization and scope of the work
- its style and readability
- provision for upkeep
- format
- superiority over any competing works
- its initial cost and upkeep expense

In this context, are you a general practitioner, a tax specialist or labor lawyer? Note whether the book is keyed editorially for the expert or for the generalist. It is always relevant whether a beginning lawyer needs an expensive multi-volume set on a specific subject or simply a well written practitioner's manual. The date of publication is always relevant. Distinguish here between the printing date and the copyright date (usually on the verso side of the title page). Obviously, books written before the revision of a new law, such as those on bankruptcy or copyright, can be significant—but still obsolete.

Then again, to repeat, the availability of a law library where these books are available, and the amount of space in the lawyer's office are factors that affect the purchase of law books.

Many law book publishers send unsolicited flyers, in the form of announcements and advertisements, on their new titles. They are also prepared to send new titles "on approval." Rather than purchase a law book hastily, law firm librarians recommend that these new books not be purchased until there is some real need demonstrated. New titles do not go out of print quickly—in fact some of them can subsequently be purchased at reduced prices. Then again, delaying the purchase provides time to read what the reviewers think about the book and to see if the courts are citing it.

Should a young lawyer purchase the court reports in the jurisdiction in which the lawyer practices, as well as the annotated codes of the state? Here again, space and costs are highly relevant. Publishers and dealers suggest that young lawyers take advantage, instead, of the special deals many law publishers offer them. Unless the lawyer's practice requires it, he or she need purchase only those parts of the code which reflect their special interests. For example, individual volumes of the United States Code Annotated can be purchased from West, and specific volumes of annotated state codes can also be purchased. Thus if the lawyer is interested only in family law or commercial law or property law provisions of a code—why buy the complete statutory set?

Although it is not necessary for a young lawyer to purchase the court reports of the state, still that lawyer has much to gain by keeping informed on local legal developments reflected in current court cases. The West Publishing Co. can provide the young lawyer with the New York Supplement, the New York Digest 3d, McKinney's Consolidated Laws of New York and West McKinney's Forms for these laws pursuant to a special deal for price and payment. Lawyers Cooperative, Bancroft Whitney, Callaghans, Matthew Bender, Warren, Gorham and Lamont, Michie-Bobbs-Merrill are also prepared to make special deals with young lawyers.

It has also been recommended that if a jurisdictional encyclopedia is available, that this be preferred to Corpus Juris Secundum or American Jurisprudence 2d. They give fast answers to questions of law in the jurisdiction involved, whether substantive or procedural, civil or criminal. The references therein to related statutes, cases, forms, annotations and law review articles can serve the purpose of finding tools.

Loose-leaf services are valuable for the practitioner specializing in the subjects covered therein. They bring together in one publication, administrative rules and regulations, statutory text, case annotations, legislative history, related articles, recent statutory and judicial developments in special substantive fields such as taxation and trade regulation.

Law librarians also recommend that the state Shepard's be subscribed to, for even if the citing cases therein are not available in the lawyer's office, still the cases produced by resort to treatises that are in the office can quickly be checked as to their authority. The state Shepard's also refer to law review articles and ALR annotations which can be checked in the local library.

Digests of the case law of the jurisdiction are also helpful for quick reference to local case law, and should be given priority as law materials to be purchased.

A good reference source for finding the occasional citation a lawyer needs to the statutory law of another jurisdiction is Martindale-Hubbell's Law Digest, which is published annually.

Law Book Publishers

The leading publishers of legal publications are:

- West Publishing Co. of St. Paul, Minn.
- Lawyers Cooperative of Rochester, N.Y.
- Matthew Bender of N.Y. and Albany, N.Y.

Then there are Callaghan and Co., Warren Gorham and Lamont, Clark Boardman, Little Brown and Co., Michie-Bobbs-Merrill, Oceana and Law Journal Seminars-Press.

Most of the law books purchased by practitioners are published by these companies.

Note too that some excellent practitioner's books are published by the American Bar Association. The ABA also publishes jointly with the American Law Institute (ALI-ABA) other excellent books of practical value for practitioners. Then there are Continuing Legal Education publishing programs in many states, such as California and Michigan, which offer worthwhile books of practical value to the practitioners of those states.

The law books recommended in the following list are keyed to current subject interests of lawyers. They have been selected with the thought that they would be helpful in providing background, analysis and authority in the fields involved.

RECOMMENDED LAW BOOKS FOR BEGINNING PRACTITIONERS

Accounting

Faris, E. Mc Jr. *Accounting for Lawyers.* 3d edition. Indianapolis, Bobbs-Merrill, 1975.

A standard book.

Hills, G.S. *The Law of Accounting and Financial Statements.* Boston, Little, Brown, 1957.

An authoritative work.

Administrative Law

Davis, K.C. *Administrative Law Treatise.* St. Paul, West, 1958.

Davis, K.C., *Administrative Law Treatise.* 2d ed. San Diego, Ca. U. of San Diego. 1978–1979. 2V.

This is a classic work. The second edition will replace the 1958 edition when it is completed.

Edles, G.J. & Nelson, J. *Federal Regulatory Process: Agency Practices and Procedures.* N.Y., Law and Business, 1981.

Chapters include agency powers, rule-making, hearing process, judicial review and specific procedures of thirteen major regulatory agencies.

Mezines, B., Stein, J.A. & Gruff, J. *Administrative Law.* N.Y., Matthew Bender, 1980.

Purports to treat all aspects of federal procedure administrative law, powers, functions and procedural practices of the regulatory agencies such as FTC, ICC, SEC, HEW, IRS, CAB, etc. and judicial review.

Agency

Reuschlein, H. & Gregory, W.A. *Handbook on the Law of Agency and Partnership.* St. Paul, West. 1978.

A well-received Hornbook.

McCarthy, J. Thomas. *Federal Control of Business, Trademarks and Unfair Competition.* Rochester, N.Y., Lawyers Co-op. 1972.

Well-organized.

Antitrust Law and Trade Regulation

American Bar Association. Section of Anti-Trust Law. *State Antitrust Laws.* Chicago, A.B.A. 1974– IV (looseleaf)

An analytical summary of the statutes and decisional law relating to monopolization, restraint of trade, price discrimination and other forms of trade regulation in each state.

Areeda, P. & Turner, D.F. *Anti-Trust Law; An Analysis of Trust Principles and their Application.* Boston, Little, Brown, 1978.

A systematic analysis of antitrust law in the United States. Well received.

Axinn, S.; Fogg, B.; and Stoll, N. *Acquisitions Under the Hart-Scott-Rodino Antitrust Improvements Act.* New York, Law Journal Seminars-Press. 1979.

A specialized work, updated annually, devoted totally to the law of premerger notification.

Kinter, Earl W. *An Antitrust Primer; A Guide to Antitrust and Trade Regulation Law for Businessmen.* 2d ed. N.Y., MacMillan, 1973.

Although not intended for lawyers—still very useful to those unfamiliar with antitrust law.

Kinter, Earl W. *A Robinson-Patman Primer: A Guide to the Law against Price Discrimination.* 2d ed. N.Y., MacMillan, 1979.

A good introduction to the field.

Sullivan, L.A. *Handbook of the Law of Antitrust Law and Policy.* St. Paul, West, 1977.

Informative and exhaustive, although a Hornbook. Well organized.

Von Kalinowski, Julian O. *Antitrust Laws and Trade Regulation.* N.Y., Matthew Bender, 1969–date.

Comprehensive analysis of the Sherman, Clayton, Robinson-Patman and Federal Trade Commission Acts—section by section.

Advocacy and Trial Technique

Givens, Richard A. *Advocacy: The Art of Pleading a Cause.* Colorado Springs, Col., Shepard's, 1980.

Deals with strategies and tactics of advocacy.

Goldstein, I. & Lane, F. *Goldstein Trial Technique.* 2d ed. Chicago, Callaghan, 1979.

Covers selection of jury, opening statements, direct examination, handling objections, introducing exhibits, expert witnesses cross-examination, closing arguments.

Jordan, Walter E. *Jury Selection.* Colorado Springs, Co., Shepard's, 1980.

See the list of "Do's" and "Dont's." A guide to jury selection—civil and criminal.

Julian, Alfred S. *Opening Statements.* Chicago, Ill., Callaghan & Co., 1980.

Kept current by loose-leaf supplementation. Provides strategy tips, checklist and illustrations in civil and criminal trials.

Agency and Partnership

Crane, J.A. & Bromberg, A.R. *Crane and Bromberg on Partnership.* St. Paul, Minn., West, 1968.
Reviewed as a "more comprehensive text on the subject than a legal encyclopedia."

Reuschlein, H.G. & Gregory, W.A. *The Law of Agency, Partnership and Other Unincorporated Organizations.* St. Paul, West, 1979.
Excellent treatise.

Sell, W. Edward. *Agency.* Mineola, N.Y., Foundation Press, 1975.
Concise explanation of the law of agency.

Steffen, Roscoe T. *Agency–Partnership in a Nutshell.* St. Paul, West, 1977.
Good introductory guide.

Volz, M.M. & Berger, A.L. *The Drafting of Partnership Agreements.* 6th ed. Phil., ALI-ABA, 1976.
Emphasizes drafting of a general or a limited partnership agreement–with forms, comments and tax implications from the practical business point of view.

Arbitration

Domke, M. *The Law and Practice of Commercial Arbitration.* Mundelein, Ill., Callaghan & Co., 1968.
A standard treatise for the practitioner. Provides analysis of state and federal arbitration statutes and of leading court decisions.

Goldberg, George. *A Lawyer's Guide to Commercial Arbitration.* Phila., ALI-ABA, 1977.
Covers the agreement to arbitrate, pleading stages, hearing procedures and enforcement aspects of the

Bankruptcy

Collier Bankruptcy Manual. 3d ed. N.Y., Matthew Bender, 1979.
Handy references to the new Bankruptcy Code.

Collier on Bankruptcy. 15th ed. N.Y., Matthew Bender, 1980.
A recognized authority on bankruptcy since 1898. Comprehensive—in-depth analysis of the bankruptcy law—section by section written by experts in the field. Updated periodically.

Drake, W.H. & Mullins, A.L. *Bankruptcy Practice.* Colorado Springs, Co., Shepard's, 1980.
A "How to" manual for practitioners.

Miller, H.R. & Cook, M.L. *A Practical Guide to the Bankruptcy Reform Act.* N.Y., Law and Business, 1979. (1981 Suppl.)
Really "A Practical Guide."

Weintraub, B. & Resnick, A.N. *Bankruptcy Law Manual.* Boston, Warren, Gorham & Lamoret, 1980.
A practical guide to bankruptcy practice and procedure with forms—current supplementation.

Commercial Law

Anderson, R.A. & Kumpf, W.A. *Business Law.* 9th ed. Cincinnati, Ohio, Southwestern Publg. Co., 1972.
A concise analysis of the law of contracts, agency, commercial paper, corporations, partnerships, property and trusts. References to UCC. Good introductory comments to each chapter.

Anderson, R.A. *Anderson on the Uniform Commercial Code.* 2nd ed. Rochester, Lawyers Coop. 1970–71.
A basic treatise.

Harfield, Henry. *Letters of Credit.* Phila., ALI-ABA, 1979. 167p.
Discusses the basic principles of letter of credit structure and operation in light of article 5 of the UCC.

Hawkland, William D. *Commercial Paper.* 2d ed. Phila., ALI-ABA, 1979.
Discusses the promissory note, certificate of deposit, draft (bill of exchange) and check—which are covered in Article 3 of the Uniform Commercial Code. Also considers the Federal Trade Commission's regulations on the presentation of consumers' claims and defenses and the law of

McGaffey, J.D. *Buying, Selling, and Merging Businesses.* 4th ed. Phila., ALI-ABA, 1979.

Concentrates on areas of business law, such as tax and security law involved in acquisitions—contains documents on acquisitions.

Riegert, R.A. & Brander, R. *Documents of Title.* 3d ed. Phila., ALI-ABA, 1978.

Covers revisions made by Article 7 of the Uniform Commercial Code to the old Uniform Acts dealing with warehouse receipts and bills of lading.

Stone, Bradford. *Uniform Commercial Code in a Nutshell.* St. Paul, Minn., West, 1975.

A good survey. Covers sales process, commercial paper, warehouse receipts, bills of lading and secured transactions.

Community Property

De Funiak, W.Q. & Vaughn, M.J. *Principles of Community Property.* 2d ed. Tucson, Az., U. of Arizona Press, 1971.

One of the few books on the subject of value to a practitioner in ten states.

Conflict of Law

Ehrenzweig, Albert A. *Conflicts in a Nutshell.* 3d ed. St. Paul, West, 1974.

A good, concise explanation of the principles involved.

Leflar, R.A. *American Conflicts of Law.* Indianapolis, Bobbs-Merrill, rev. ed., 1978.

Constitutional Law

The Constitution of The United States of America, Analysis and Interpretation. Wash., D.C., G.P.O., 1973.

A valuable reference source, despite date of publication. Each section of Constitution thoroughly analyzed. Prepared as a reference book on constitutional law for members of Congress. Purports to cite every Supreme decision affecting the Constitution.

Consumer Protection

Epstein, David G. *Consumer Protection in a Nutshell.* St. Paul, Minn., West, 1976.

A rapidly developing field, well set forth in this readable book.

Feldman, L.P. *Consumer Protection: Problems and Prospects.* St. Paul, Minn., West, 1976.

Traces relevant government regulations and describes federal legislation.

Reitz, Curtis R. *Consumer Protection under the Magnuson-Moss Warranty Act.* Phila., ALI-ABA, 1978.

A guide to the intricacies of the law. What is meant by "limited warranty" and "full warranty." Also discusses disclosure of warranty terms.

Contracts

Williston, S. *A Treatise on the Law of Contracts.* 3d ed. Rochester, N.Y., Lawyers' Coop., 1957–80.

Updated and revised by W.H.E. Jaeger. An authoritative treatise.

Corbin, A.I . Corbin on Contracts. St. Paul, West, 1951.

Updated periodically—a standard treatise which has been well received by practitioners.

Corporations

American Bar Association. Section of Corporation, Banking and Business Law. *Model Business Corporatoion Act Annotated.* 2d ed. St. Paul, West, 1971.

Updated with supplement.

Cavitch, L. *Business Organizations, with Tax Planning.* N.Y., Matthew Bender, 1963.

Updated periodically. This is a comprehensive, in-depth, analytical treatise on partnership law and corporation law with federal tax implications treated. Encyclopedic citation of case law.

Fletcher, W.M. *Cyclopedia of the Law of Private Corporations.* Permanent Edition. Chicago, Callaghan, 1959–1979.

Updated periodically, this is a standard treatise in the field with references to decisions, statuses finance law review articles, the Model Business Corporation Act. Publishers claim there are 250,000 citations in the set.

Fletcher, W.M. *Corporation Forms Annotated.* 4th ed. 1958–1979. 10V. $300.00.

The Lawyer's Basic Corporate Practice Manual. Richard E. Deer, Chief Reporter. 2d ed. Phila., ALI-ABA, 1978.

A guide to the closely held corporation. A review of basic corporate practice for the recently admitted lawyer with forms and checklist.

O'Neal, F. Hodge. *Close Corporations (Law and Practice).* 2nd ed. Chicago, Callaghan, 1971.

Updated periodically–standard authority in the field.

Seward, G.C. & Nauss, Jr., W.J. *Basic Corporate Practice.* 2d ed. Phila., ALI-ABA, 1977.

Since the Model Business Corporation Act is the basis for thirty-four state corporation laws, it is used as the basic text for the book. The New York and Delaware statutes are also referred to.

Criminal Law and Procedure

Amsterdam, A.G., Segal, B.L. & Miller, M.K. *Trial Manual for the Defense of Criminal Cases III.* 3d ed. Phila., ALI-ABA, 1974. (revised and updated to 1978)

A classical guide for defense counsel. Provides analysis and guidelines concerning the practical, ethical and tactical aspects of criminal defense, from arrest through post trial proceedings.

Bond, James E. *Plea Bargaining and Guilty Pleas.* N.Y., Clark, Boardman, 1975.

Supplemented periodically. An overview of the guilty plea process and the role of defense counsel, prosecutor and judge.

Cook, J.G. *Constitutional Rights of the Accused.* Rochester, Lawyers' Coop., 1972–1977.

A good treatment of pre-trial, trial and post-trial constitutional rights of the accused.

Federal Rules of Criminal Procedure. 2d ed. Practice comments by Michele Hermann. N.Y., Clark, Boardman, 1980. IV.

A reference guide with full text of rules and advisory committees' notes. Commentary and official forms. Annual Revision.

Prisoners' Rights Sourcebook; Theory, Litigation, Practice. Edited and compiled by M.C. Hermann and M.G. Hajt. N.Y., Clark, Boardman, 1973–1980.

An authoritative sourcebook on prisoners' rights in original articles by lawyers, judges, state attorneys-general, etc.

Ringle, William E. *Searches and Seizures, Arrests and Confessions.* 2d ed. N.Y., Clark, Boardman, 1979–1980.

Annual supplementation—a comprehensive sourcebook.

Dictionaries

Ballentine's Law Dictionary, with Pronunciation. 3d ed. Edited by William S. Anderson. Rochester, N.Y., Lawyers' Coop., 1969.

Citations to ALR and L. Annotations included with definitions. Includes approximately 47,000 legal and law related words and phrases.

Black's Law Dictionary. 5th ed. by the Publisher's Editorial Staff. St. Paul, West, 1979.

Appendix – Table of regnal years
– Time chart of the Supreme Court
– Table of abbreviations

Domestic Relations

Baxter, I.F.G. *Marital Property.* Rochester, Lawyers' Coop., 1973.

Analytic summary of American marital property law, including community property—also covers unmarried cohabitation.

Douthwaite, Graham. *Unmarried Couples and the Law.* Indianapolis, A. Smith Co., 1979.

Includes bibliographical references.

Foster, H.H. & Freed, D.J. *Law and the Family.* Rochester, Lawyers' Coop., 1972.

Updated periodically. Contains many "how-to-do-it" recommendations, as well as practical commentary and analysis of separation, agreements, dissolution, alimony, child custody and support, taxes, estate problems, etc.

Foster, Henry H., Jr., ed. *A Practical Guide to the New York Equitable Distribution Divorce Law.* N.Y., Law & Business, 1980.

A practitioner's guide, with forms, on the new concepts of

maintenance and distribution of property and alimony. Also includes income, gift and estate tax consequences of the equitable distributors choice.

Lindey, Alexander. *Separation Agreements and Ante-Nuptial Contracts.* N.Y., Matthew Bender, 1979–1980.
Contains commentary, forms, cases, practical suggestions, tax considerations and guidance on custody, support and wills. Special solutions for affluent, elderly clients.

Evidence

Binder, D.R. *The Hearsay Handbook: The Hearsay Rule and its 40 Exceptions.* Colorado Springs, Shepard's, 1975.
Although not analytical it does provide a clear summary of the Hearsay rule with references to Am. Jur., C.J.S. and

Federal Rules of Evidence. 2nd ed. Practice Comments by Paul F. Rothstein. N.Y., Clark, Boardman, 1978.
Revised annually—contains official text of the rules governing admission of evidence in federal courts, advisory committee's notes and practice comments.

McCormick, C.T. *McCormick's Handbook of the Law of Evidence.* 2d ed. by E.W. Cleary. St. Paul, West, 1972.
Keyed to Wigmore, CJS and West's American Digest headings, this is an authoritative treatise.

Weinstein, J.B. & Berger, M.A. *Weinstein's Evidence Commentary on Rules of Evidence for the U.S. Courts and Magistrates.* N.Y., Matthew Bender, 1975.
Updated as needed, approximately twice a year. Perceptive and practical answers to Federal Evidence problems.

Wigmore, J.H. *A Treatise on the Anglo-American System of Evidence in Trials at Common Law.* 3d ed., Boston, Little, Brown, 1940.
A classic, authoritative treatise. Updated periodically.

Forms

American Jurisprudence Legal Forms. 2d ed. Rochester, N.Y., Lawyers' Coop., 1971–1974.
Forms, keyed to substantive law, followed by notes and ex-

planatory material–optional clauses for substitute language–drafting checklists–federal tax implications brought out–references to Am. Jur. 2nd and ALR annotation. Updated periodically.

McGaffey, Jere D. *Tax Analysis and Forms, Business Transactions and Estate Planning.* Chicago, Ill., Callaghan, 1977.
Kept current by annual loose-leaf suppls. Provides basic forms followed by specific alternative provisions for corporate structure and compensation, acquisitions, ne and redemption, estate and personal planning, partnerships and real estate.

Rabkin, J. & Johnson, M.H. *Current Legal Forms with Tax Analysis.* N.Y., Matthew Bender, 1948–date.
Updated periodically. In addition to forms, edited and classed by subject, also suggests techniques in the planning of a transaction–tax background discusses the effect of the tax laws on the transactions.

Warren's Forms of Agreements. N.Y., Matthew Bender, 1954–date.
Excellent checklists and commentary on the uses of various agreements.

Immigration and Naturalization

Gordon, C. & Gordon, E.G. *Immigration and Nationality Law.* Desk Edition. N.Y., Matthew Bender, 1980.
Updated regularly–this is an abridgment of the seven volume Immigration Law and Procedure–a convenient handbook which condenses material from the larger treatise–forms.

Gordon, C. & Rosenfield, H.N. *Immigration Law and Procedure.* Rev. ed. N.Y., 1966.
Updated by cumulative supplements–authoritative immigration guide. Forms.

Immigration Law and Defense. 2d ed. by the National Lawyers Guild. N.Y., Clark, Boardman, 1979.
Supplemented annually. Obtaining temporary entry to U.S., lawful permanent residence in U.S., grounds for exclusion and deportation and hearings, administrative appeals, federal judicial reviews, etc.

Wasserman, Jack. *Immigration Law and Practice.* 3d ed. Phila., ALI-ABA. 1979.

A comprehensive overview of visa and admission procedures, exclusion and deportation practices and rights and responsibilities of aliens in the United States.

Labor Law

There are excellent looseleaf services on labor law published by the Bureau of National Affairs, Commerce Clearing House and Prentice Hall.

Bartosic, F. & Hartley, R.C. *Labor Relations in the Private Sector.* Phila., ALI-ABA, 1977.

An analysis and synthesis of labor relations law in the private sector. Covers legality of union-organizing techniques and employer's tactics, procedures and regulations, etc.

Connolly, Walter & Connolly, Michael, *A Practical Guide to Equal Employment Opportunity.* N.Y., Law Journal Seminars-Press, 1979.

Updated periodically. A full analysis of Equal Employment opportunity law with emphasis on affirmative action programs.

Connolly, Walter & Peterson, David. *Use of Statistics in Equal Employment Opportunity Litigation.* N.Y., Law Journal Seminars-Press, 1979.

Exactly what the title says. An annually updated treatise on convincing the trier of fact.

Kheel, Theodore W. *Labor Law.* N.Y., Matthew Bender, 1973–1979.

Covers union representatives, collective bargaining and unfair labor practices as part of a correlated treatise on the law of labor-management practices.

Mamorsky, Jeffrey B. *Employee Benefits Law: ERISA and Beyond.* N.Y., Law Journal Seminars-Press, 1980.

An authoritative treatise on all aspects of ERISA and related subjects. Supplemented annually.

Seidel, A.H. & Panitch, R.L. *What the General Practitioner Should Know about Trade Secrets and Employment Agreements.* Phila., ALI-ABA, 1973.

A handbook, which also emphasizes employer-employee relationship, licensing, know-how, security precautions, anti-trust aspects and law relating to trade secrets.

Law Office Practice

Freund, James C. *Lawyering: A Realistic Approach to Legal Practice.* N.Y., Law Journal Seminars-Press, 1979.
A guide for associates on surviving in a law firm.

Gillers, Stephen. *I'd Rather Do It Myself: How to Set Up Your Own Law Firm.* N.Y. Law Journal Seminars-Press, 1980.
A young lawyer's guide to establishing a law office.

Hildebrant, Bradford. *Financial Management for Law Firms.* N.Y. Law Journal Seminars-Press, 1975.
Running a financially efficient law office.

Singer, Gerald M. *How to Go Directly into Solo Law Practice (without Missing a Meal).* Rochester, N.Y., Lawyers' Coop., 1976.
Covers subjects such as how to trade office space in exchange for legal services, how to bill, etc.

Legal Bibliographies

Recommended Law Books, edited by Richard Sloane. Chicago, ABA, 1969.
Although dated (1969), still this lawyer's guide to the best available books on some seventy-six subjects (1400 titles) is of current value to practising lawyers—especially for its listings of general reference works. Published by the Committee on Business Law, ABA, Section of Corporation, Banking and Business Law.

Legal Research

Price, M.; Bitner, H.; & Bysiewicz, S. *Effective Legal Research.* 4th ed. Boston, Little Brown, 1979.

Jacobstein & Mersky. *Fundamentals of Legal Research.* N.Y., Foundation Press, 1978.

How to Find the Law. Cohen ed., St. Paul, West 1978.

There are also special guides for legal research available in a number of states, as follows:

California

Fink, Myron, *Research in California Law.* 2d ed. Buffalo, N.Y.: Dennis, 1964.

Henke, Dan. *California Law Guide.* 2d ed. Los Angeles, Cal.: Parker & Sons, 1976.

Florida

French, Harriet L. *Research in Florida Law.* 2d rev. ed. Dobbs Ferry, N.Y.: Oceana Publishing Co., 1965.

Illinois

Davies, Bernita. *Research in Illinois Law.* New York: Oceana Publishing Co., 1954.

Illinois Institute for Continuing Legal Education. *Illinois Legal Research Sourcebook.* Springfield, Ill.: Illinois Institute for Continuing Legal Education, 1977. Looseleaf.

Louisiana

Wallach, Kate. *Louisiana Legal Research Manual.* LSU Law School, Baton Rouge, La.: Institute of Continuing Legal Education, 1972.

Michigan

Beer, Richard Lambert. *An Annotated Guide to the Legal Literature of Michigan.* Lake Orion, Mich.: 1973.

New Mexico

Poldervaart, Arie William. *Manual for Effective New Mexico Legal Research.* Albuquerque, N.M.: University of New Mexico Press, 1955.

North Carolina

Kavass, Igor I., and Christensen, Bruce. *Guide to North Carolina Legal Research.* Buffalo, N.Y.: William S. Hein, Co., 1973.

Pennsylvania

Surrency, Erwin C., and Moreland, Carroll C. *Research in Pennsylvania Law.* 2d ed. Dobbs Ferry, N.Y.: Oceana Publishing Co., 1965.

South Carolina
Mills, Robin K., and Schultz, Jon S. *South Carolina Legal Research Handbook.* Buffalo, N.Y.: William S. Hein & Co., 1976.

Tennessee
Laska, Lewis L. *Tennessee Legal Research Handbook.* Buffalo, N.Y.: William S. Hein & Co., 1977.

Texas
Bonner, Marian. *A Reference Guide to Texas Law and Legal History*; Sources and Documentation. Austin, Tex.: University of Texas Press, 1976.

Lebowitz, Leon. *Legal Bibliography and Research: An Outlined Manual on the Use of Law Books in the Texas and Federal Courts,* 2d ed. Austin, Tex., 1957.

Wisconsin
Danner, Richard A. *Legal Research in Wisconsin.* Madison, Wis.: University of Wisconsin Extension Law Department, 1980.

Knudson, William. *Wisconsin Legal Research Guide.* Madison, Wis.: The Board of Regents of the University of Wisconsin, 1972.

Legal Malpractice

Mallen, R.E. & Levit, V.B. *Legal Malpractice.* St. Paul, West, 1977.
Well organized treatise, intended to be national in scope, "and exhaustive in cataloging those reported decisions concerning the basis of a lawyer's professional liability..."

Legal Periodicals

Professional Journals for Specialists

The Index to Legal Periodicals will call to your attention articles by specialists on specific subjects. If you specialize in a certain field, you could consider current subscriptions to journals such as The Food, Drug and Cosmetic Law Journal, and similar journals which are listed in the Index to Legal Periodicals.

Two journals which are of real value to practitioners generally are:

1) *The Business Lawyer* (5 times a year)
Published by the ABA Section of Corporations, Banking and Business Law.

2) *The Practical Lawyer* (8 times a year)
Published by ALI-ABA.

Index to Legal Periodicals, Bronx, N.Y., the H.W. Wilton Co., 1907–to date.
Published monthly except September with a bound cumulation each year. Indexes and 420 leading legal periodicals by author and subject—also has a Table of Cases commented upon and a Book Review Index.

Medical Practice

Louisell, D., Kalisch, J. & Kramer, C. *Medical Malpractice.* N.Y., Matthew Bender, 1960—date.
A practitioner's book on the subject. Covers trial strategies as well.

Pegalis, S.E. & Wachsman, H.F. *American Law of Medical Malpractice.* Rochester, Lawyers' Coop., 1980.
Law, practice and procedure in medical malpractice cases.

Shandell, Richard E., *The Preparation and Trial of Medical Malpractice Cases.* N.Y., Law Journal Seminars-Press, 1981.
A step-by-step guide through medical malpractice cases, from client interview through jury summation.

Patents, Trademarks and Copyright

Campbell, Francis W. *Trademarks: Selection and Protection* (with) Jerry Cohen. Wash., D.C., BNA, 1979 (Corporate Practice Series, No. 18).
Practical information.

Deller's Walker on Patent, 2d ed. by Anthony W. Deller. Rochester, N.Y., 1964–1976.
An authoritative work concentrating on the "how, why and when of conducting a patent from beginning to end." Provides

official forms and Rules of Practice of the Patent Office. Updated periodically.

Gilson, Jerome. *Trademark Protection and Practice.* N.Y., Matthew Bender, 1974.

Kept up-to-date by annual supplements. Comprehensive, detailed and practical.

Latman, Alan. *The Copyright Law: Howell's Copyright Law Revised and the 1976 Act.* 5th ed. Wash., D.C., BNA, 1979.

Succinct and comprehensive standard work on copyright law, including the 1976 Act, international copyright and procedures of the Copyright Office and the Copyright Royalty Tribunal.

Lindey, A. *Entertainment Publishing and the Arts: Agreements and the Law.* 2d ed. N.Y., N.Y., Clark, Boardman, 1980.

First published in 1963, this is a practical guide for the negotiation of contracts in mass communications media with relevant forms. Also provides a survey of state and federal cases and a review of the 1976 Copyright Act.

Nimmer, Melville B. *Nimmer on Copyright.* N.Y., Matthew Bender, 1978.

A recognized authoritative treatise which covers all facets of copyright law affecting literary, musical and artistic property. First published in 1963, kept current with annual cumulative supplements and replacement pages.

Seidel, Arthur H. *What the General Practitioner Should Know about Patent Law and Practice.* 3d ed. Phila., ALI-ABA, 1975.

A handbook for the non-specialist. Also covers protection of design, trade secrets and anti-trust.

Seidel, Arthur H. *What the General Practitioner Should Know about Trademarks and Copyrights.* 4th ed. Phila., ALI-ABA, 1979.

For the non-specialist. Covers new copyright law.

Practice and Procedure

Manual of Federal Practice. 2d ed. Colorado Springs, Colo., Shepard's, 1979.

Guide for lawyers engaged in federal litigation. Covers practice and procedure required by the Federal Rules.

Moore's Federal Practice. 2d ed. N.Y., Matthew Bender, 1948–1980.

Accepted authority in Federal Court and in the 39 states that have adopted or modeled their procedural rules after the Federal Rules. Updated periodically.

Needham, Roger A. *Federal Lawyer's Manual.* Chicago, Ill., Callaghan, 1980.

A summary of the law in major areas of federal practice, such as business transactions, real estate transactions, tax implications, corporations, estate planning, bankruptcy, litigation, federal procedure, law office and practice suggestions.

Wright, C.A. & Miller, A.R. *Federal Practice and Procedure.* St. Paul, West, 1969.

Supplemented annually. Authoritative source, provides full coverage of the field. Criminal law volumes can be purchased separately.

Products Liability

Frumer, Louis R. & Friedman, M.I. *Products Liability.* N.Y., Matthew Bender & Co., 1960–date.

An authoritative treaties. In addition to substantive law coverage, relevant aspects of procedural law are discussed, such as pleading, expert testimony, conflicts of law, class actions and jurisdiction over non-residents.

Hills, Frank S. *Handling the Strict Liability Products Case.* Tiburon, Calif., Law Press, 1980.

Practitioner's manual.

Hursh, R.D. & Bailey, H.J. *American Law of Products Liability.* 2d ed. Rochester, N.Y., Lawyers' Coop., 1974–1976.

Annually revised. Citations to federal and state case law. Draws heavily on annotations in A.L.R.

Kolb, J. & Ross, S.S. *Product Safety and Liability: A Desk Reference.* N.Y., McGraw Hill, 1980.

A well-organized text.

Property

Friedman, Milton R. *Contracts and Conveyances of Real Property.* 3d ed. N.Y., Practising Law Institute, 1975.

A step-by-step guide to a real estate transaction from precontract considerations through closing of title. Practical, yet scholarly, too.

Friedman, Milton R. *On Leases.* N.Y., Practising Law Institute, 1974.

A practitioner's handbook on commercial leases. Step-by-step guidance in drafting a commercial lease.

Halper, Emanuel B. *Shopping Center & Store Leases.* N.Y., Law Journal Seminars-Press, 1979.

An annually updated guide. Forms and explanatory text.

Powell on Real Property, by Richard R. Powell and Patrick J. Rohan. N.Y., Matthew Bender, 1975.

Originally published in 1949, revised and up-dated. An authoritative treatise keyed to the restatement of the Law of Property—local jurisdictional variants are brought out—annually supplemented.

Restatements of the Law

Restatements—Phila., American Law Institute.

Agency. Second (1958).
Conflict of Laws. Second (1971).
Contracts (1932).
Judgments (1942).
Property v.I–II (1936).
Property v.III (1940).
Property v.IV (1944).
Property v.V (1944).
Property Second.
Restitution (1937).
Security (1941).
Torts Second (1965).
Trusts Second (1959).
General Index (1946).

Secured Transactions

Coogan, P.F., Hogan, W.E. & Vaghts, D.F. *Secured Transactions under the Uniform Commercial Code.* N.Y., Matthew Bender, 1968.

For practitioners.

Davenport, W.J. & Murray, D.R. *Secured Transactions.* Phila., ALI-ABA, 1978.
A practitioner's guide to the law of secured transactions as codified in Article 9 of the U.C.C.

Gilmore, G. *Security Interests in Personal Property.* Boston, Little, Brown, 1965.
The standard work on UCC principles, with treatment of pre-UCC law.

Henson, R.D. *Handbook on Secured Transactions under the Uniform Commercial Code.* 2d ed. St. Paul, West, 1979.
Concise and well prepared hornbook on Article 9 of the U.C.C.

Securities Regulation

Loss, Louis. *Securities Regulation.* Boston, Little, Brown. 2d ed. (Vols 1-3) published 1961. Supplement (Vols. 4-6) published 1969.
Kept up-to-date with periodic supplements and revisions, this is a reference tool for the securities and corporation lawyer. A leading treatise in the field.

Thomas, E.B. & Shields, R.E. *Federal Securities Act Handbook.* 4th ed. Phila., ALI-ABA, 1977.
A handbook designed primarily for an issuing company's lawyer.

Social Security

Abraham, A. & Kopelman, D.L. *Federal Social Security.* Phila., ALI-ABA, 1979.
Discusses law governing cash benefits, coverage, eligibility, termination of benefits and Medicare with suggestions for handling claims.

Sweeney, Dennis M. *Practice Manual for Social Security Claims* (with) James J. Lyko. N.Y., Practising Law Institute, 1980.
Helpful manual.

Statutory Construction

Sands, C. Dallas. *Sutherland's Statutes and Statutory Construction.* 4th ed. Chicago, Callaghan, 1973.

The standard American treatise. Thorough, scholarly and comprehensive.

Taxation

Following is merely a small selection of the publications of value on taxation. Note too the section by section analysis of basic tax statutes and tax cases to be found in looseleaf services published and kept up-to-date by Bureau of National Affairs, Commerce Clearing House and Prentice Hall.

Bitker, Boris T. & Stone, L.M. *Federal Income Taxation.* 5th ed. Boston, Little, Brown, 1980.
A standard treatise on Federal income, estate and gift taxation.

Bitker, B.I. & Eustice, J.S. *Federal Income Taxation of Corporations and Shareholders.* 4th ed. Boston, Warren, Gorlean & Lamant, 1979.
A leading tax treatise which integrates in its coverage the 1976 Tax Reform Act and the 1978 Revenue Act and other developments.

Casey, Lawrence F. *Federal Tax Practice.* Chicago, Ill., Callaghan, 1955–1979.
A treatise covering the laws and procedures governing the assessment and litigation of federal tax liabilities. Kept up-to-date by annual pocket parts.

Dubroff, H. & Kahn, D.A. *Federal Taxation of Estates, Gifts and Trusts.* 3d ed. Phila., ALI-ABA, 1980.
Principles of substantive law involved, as well as federal taxation of generation–skipping transfers and federal income taxation with illustrations. Addenda include a completed estate tax return, a gift tax return, and an income tax return for a simple trust.

Prigal, Alan, ed. *Federal Income, Gift and Estate Taxation.* Desk Edition. N.Y., Matthew Bender, 1972.
Kept up-to-date by annual revisions and supplements. Fast answers to practical questions about the tax effects of personal and business finances.

Rabkin, J. & Johnson, M.H. *Federal Income, Gift and Estate Taxation.* N.Y., Matthew Bender, 1942–1980.

Kept up-to-date. Text, practice aids, IRC, monthly and year-end tax planning—annotated analysis.

Torts

Averbach, Albert. *Handling Accident Cases.* 2d ed. Rochester, N.Y., Lawyers' Coop., 1963–1972.

Discusses all types of accident cases. A "how to" guide—in addition to general background, also covers medical, hospital and dental malpractice, products liability and automobile cases. Updated periodically.

Prosser, William L. *Handbook on the Law of Torts.* 4th ed. St. Paul, West, 1971.

A useful one-volume treatise with extensive analysis and citations of cases. Good introductory work. New tort law developments after 1971 should be checked.

Transportation

Dickerson, Thomas A. *Travel Law.* N.Y., Law Journal Seminars-Press, 1981.

A unique treatise on how to litigate travel problems. Updated annually.

Trusts and Estates

Farr, J.F. & Wright, Jr., J.W. *An Estate Planner's Handbook.* 4th ed. Boston, Little, Brown, 1979.

Reflects the implications of the Tax Reform Act of 1976 and the Revenue Act of 1978 on basic estate planning documents such as the will, trusts, testamentory and Currently supplemented.

Manning, Jerome A. *Estate Planning.* N.Y., Practising Law Institute, 1980.

Excellent practitioner's treatise.

Murphy's Will Clauses: Annotations and Forms with Tax Effects. N.Y., Matthew Bender, 1960.

Updated by supplements and revisions. The many will clauses are annotated—checklists—step-by-step for drawing up a will.

Newman, L. & Kalter, A. *Postmortem Estate Planning.* Phila., ALI-ABA, 1976.

A practice text which offers suggestions for minimizing the tax liability of the decedent's estate or the prospective tax liabilities of the estate's beneficiaries. Supplement includes applicable provisions of the Tax Reform Act of 1976.

Page, W.H. *Page on the Law of Wills.* Rev. ed. Cincinnati, W.H. Anderson, 1960.

Current supplementation—a standard treatise.

Robinson, Gerald J. & Schlesinger, Sanford J. *Robinson's Estate Planning.* N.Y., Law Journal Seminars-Press, 1976–1980.

Supplemented annually. Tax planning tips and forms.

Scott on Trusts. 3d ed. Boston, Little, Brown, 1967.

Currently supplemented, this is an authoritative treatise which is highly respected.

Tweed, H. & Parsons, W. *Lifetime and Testamentory Estate Planning.* 8th ed. Phila., ALI-ABA, 1978 with 1979 supplement.

Discusses tax and non-tax factors involved in the *inter vivos* and testamentory disposition of client's estates. Provides forms of wills and trust instruments that, with slight modification, are usable in nearly all states.

Workmen's Compensation

Larson's Workmen's Compensation. Desk Edition by Arthur Larson. N.Y., Matthew Bender, 1972.

Updated with supplements and revisions. An authoritative desk book.

Zoning

Anderson, Robert M. *American Law of Zoning*:Zoning, Planning, Subdivision Control. 2d ed. Rochester, N.Y., Lawyers' Coop., 1976.

Highly authoritative treatise—analytical, comprehensive and well written.

CHAPTER 23

AVAILABILITY OF LEGAL RESOURCES

The fact that one practices in a 150-man Wall Street law firm or in a storefront office in the ghetto has little to do with *how* his legal research should be performed. But it has everything to do with the kind of legal research that he can handle. No matter how large the office, however, no firm can keep—nor should it attempt to buy—all the publications that its practice requires. Where, then, can they be found.

What many lawyers do not know is the extent of research facilities and institutions publicly available in their own cities. There are law libraries, special libraries, government agencies and trade associations in every major city throughout the country. Their resources are waiting to be used.

Legal Wall Map

Nothing can give a research lawyer a greater command of the available facilities than a "wall map" of legal resources in his community. Let him make his own map by starting with a large street map of the city or county. If the city is New York, with its five counties, he can begin with his own borough. Manhattan, for example.

The most important point on that map is the location of one's office. Let's assume that it is in the Woolworth Building at 233 Broadway, near City Hall.

The next most significant points on the map are the buildings that house three heavily used practitioners' law libraries maintained by private associations: (1) The Association of the Bar of the City of New York at 42 West Forty-fourth Street with a book collection that exceeds 410,000 volumes; (2) the New York Law Institute at 120 Broadway with a collection of over 200,000 volumes; and (3) the New York County Lawyers Association at 14 Vesey Street, about 150,000 volumes.

The distance along lines radiating from one's office to any of those institutions determines how much research can be done in an hour or two. It sometimes determines whether or not that research gets done at all. Some lawyers even choose their office locations on the basis of nearness to one of those three law libraries.

The research lawyer should acquaint himself with the book collection and the physical arrangements of each of the three libraries. Their book collections, for example, differ widely in content, scope and size. Since the success of one's work may depend in part on the people who administer those libraries, a lawyer should take steps to learn who knows what at each institution.

Association of the Bar

The Association of the Bar of the City of New York maintains one of the most distinguished practitioners' libraries in the country. The librarian is Anthony P. Grech. Its special features include collections of records and briefs of cases in the United States Supreme Court, the Second Circuit Court of Appeals, the New York Court of Appeals and all four departments of the Appellate Division of the New York Supreme Court.

Although it is not a depository library (one entitled to automatic receipt of all or selected government documents released through the Government Printing Office), its holdings of Congressional documents are extensive. It has transcripts of hearings and copies of reports of the committees whose work affects practicing lawyers and their clients most closely. For example, it keeps the publications of the Senate Finance and Judiciary Committee and the House Judiciary and Ways and Means Committees.

Its foreign collection includes the codes of laws of the principal countries of the world and of many smaller nations.

The main reading room is impressive and stately, with walls of reports reached by circular metal staircases and successively higher balcony catwalks. A good working treatise collection has been placed on open shelves in the main reading room.

One of the most heavily used libraries in New York is the New York Law Institute library. It is unique among the three association libraries in that it is a *lending* library. A lawyer does not have to leave his desk to use most of the books in its collection.

Some of the more notable facts about that collection are these:

1. As a federal depository, it receives on a selective basis most of the congressional reports, hearings and documents that lawyers need in construing federal statutes.
2. It keeps and lends the records and briefs in New York Court of Appeals and Appellate Division cases (except for the Fourth Department) and Second Circuit Court of Appeals cases.
3. It maintains individual digests for most of the states, legal encyclopedias covering the law of all states for which they have been published (e.g., *Texas Jurisprudence* and *California Jurisprudence*) and it contains legal treatises–not merely practice works–for a great many local American jurisdictions.

County Lawyers

The New York County Lawyers Association library serves some 9,600 members. It has a well-rounded Anglo-American law book collection that includes most of the statutes, reports and leading treatises in those jurisdictions. It has a run of Court of Appeals and First and Second Departments records and briefs since 1900 and those of the Third and Fourth Departments since 1935. It is not a depository of government documents, nor does it attempt to acquire current foreign legal materials. But within the scope of its interests–and they are broad–it is a fine library.

Other Boroughs

Each of the other boroughs has its own county or court library. In Brooklyn the largest of these is the Supreme Court Library. Not all lawyers even in Brooklyn are aware that its facilities are open to lawyers who join the library.

Discussion of the law school libraries in New York has been purposely omitted for this reason: The schools have record student attendance and unusual budget strains. The libraries, therefore, have attempted to limit service to practicing lawyers, including their own alumni—politely but firmly.

The 1980 issue of the *Directory of Law Libraries* (American Association of Law Libraries) lists some 120 additional law libraries in the five boroughs of New York. The resources of many of them are open to members of the New York Bar.

Outside New York

Court filing fees provide the principal support for county law libraries in California. As a consequence, California lawyers have access to book collections and research services at a nominal cost. The most extensive of these is the Los Angeles County Law Library (upwards of 650,000 volumes) with branches in Beverly Hills and seven other nearby communities.

Its book collection rivals even the largest law school libraries in the country. Harvard alone surpasses it in size. The Los Angeles County Law Library is especially strong in Latin-American and Asian law. But its European holdings form a respectable part of its collection. It offers both a lending and book delivery service for lawyers that is unmatched by any other library. Two men were principally responsible for this library's remarkable success: Forrest Drummond, the recently retired librarian, and the late Dr. William B. Stern, the foreign law librarian. Their book collection and their level of service set a high standard.

There is no branch of learning that fails to contribute at one time or another, to the information a lawyer needs in his work. The next chapter discusses the questions: Where are non-legal facts found, for example, information about other professions, particular industries, government agencies, people and processes? What special library resources are there in New York and in other American cities?

The research lawyer's map of information sources has numerous gaps to fill.

Value to Lawyers

Where do all these facts lead? Do they increase law office effectiveness? Do they shorten research time and lower the costs of law practice? They do all these things. Their meaning for a practicing lawyer is this: If he knows *what* legal resources the community holds and *where* they are located, he has reached the first objective in his legal research program. He has reduced law office costs by making the most effective use of research time. Fact gathering becomes least expensive when one's local resource map shows the shortest route to the most pertinent collection of facts.

CHAPTER 24

INFORMATION SOURCES

The most valuable trade secret that a research lawyer possesses is his knowledge of information sources: Who knows what? Where is it written down? How can you tell if it exists? What is the fastest way to collect the facts?

As an aid in jogging memory, one of the writers recorded and updated in a small black notebook most of the sources of information that he used in New York and Washington over a period of twenty years. The book was a compendium of specialists, special libraries, quasi-public agencies and associations. Beside each agency name were a few basic facts that told what kinds of information could be supplied and, most important, the name of the person who could be relied on to supply it.

Helpful Publications

Any lawyer responsible for gathering, sifting and interpreting information on any subject will save himself endless hours of work by recording the sources of his *successful* hunts for facts. But until your research lawyer can compile his own guide to local information sources—one tailored to a firm's interests—there are three publications that will serve as excellent substitutes.

The first and best known of them is the "Directory of Special Libraries in Greater New York," now in its fifteenth edition (1980). It was compiled by the New York Chapter of the Special Libraries Association. The directory groups several hundred libraries in some thirty-five major fields: e.g., Engineering, Medicine, Business and Finance. It briefly describes the book collections of each library, tells who may use its facilities and names the librarian. Metropolitan New York has the largest number of diversified special libraries in the country and this directory is the best guide to them. Special library association directories have also been compiled for other major regions of the United States.

Columbia Book

A worthy newcomer that appeared for the first time in 1972 is "Libraries in New York City." It is a product of the Columbia University School of Library Service. Although its purpose was to acquaint Columbia students with the resources of the major metropolitan libraries, this book is packed with information that lawyers will find useful. For example, it describes in some detail the holdings of nearly 100 major libraries: those maintained by the Ford Foundation, International Business Machines Corporation, Newsweek, United Nuclear Corporation and many others. This guide also shows in outline form what New York resources are available in twenty-eight fields of interest from Architecture (eight libraries) to Transportation (four libraries). There are also comments on the specialities of more than fifty Manhattan bookstores, arranged by neighborhood. Despite its age, it remains useful.

The third guide to local information sources is easily overlooked and widely underestimated. It is the New York Telephone Company's "Manhattan Yellow Pages." Among its numerous features are lists of some 1,500 associations, over 300 trade papers and other newspapers, about 1,200 locally published periodicals and both an alphabetical and classified guide to almost all the city's bookstores. Recent examination of "Yellow Page" directories in Phoenix, Chicago, New Orleans, Miami, Dallas and Philadelphia show that they are as informative as the resources in those cities make possible.

Price, Waterhouse Book

Returning to the "Black Notebook" for some highlights, mention should be made of the Price, Waterhouse book collection and its former librarian, Rosemary Demarest—the author of a comprehensive guide to accounting literature (Gale Publishing Company, 1971). The American Institute of Certified Public Accountants is that profession's major association. It has its own 15,000-volume library and is the publisher of numerous accounting guides, rulings and interpretive papers.

The three general business libraries that were consistently useful during the past twenty years are the Chase Manhattan Bank Library (both for the breadth of its book collection and the service of its friendly and knowledgeable staff), the Economic Division of the New York Public Library and the Brooklyn Business Library.

The Economics Division has two major departments, a business library for on-premises research and a depository collection of government documents, together running to over 1,000,000 volumes.

The Brooklyn Business Branch (67,000 volumes and almost an equal number of microforms) is located in Brooklyn Heights, only a few minutes' subway trip from downtown Manhattan. It is both a research center and a lending library.

As an illustration of the kinds of obscure factual questions that come to lawyers, the SEC staff once asked for proof of the claim made in a prospectus that the term "Private Eye" actually originated with the issuer, a nationwide detective agency. Even though the surviving half of the Ellery Queen team, Frederic Danney, told this writer that the question might never be settled, the SEC staff accepted as proof the reference in a crime dictionary that a librarian at Brooklyn Public Library located.

Engineering Library

One of the best special libraries is the Engineering Societies Library, located on East Forty-seventh Street in Manhattan. It is an information center for all the branches of engineering represented by its thirteen constituent societies. Its collection runs to nearly a quarter of a million volumes. For many years it has answered thousands of questions annually both by telephone and mail—even for nonengineers. The library subscribes to some 4,000 engineering journals and other serial publications which the Engineering Index uses in preparing its own abstracting and indexing service in this field.

Getting answers to questions that relate to foreign countries can be a frustrating experience. Few of the local consulates in New York are equipped to answer the kinds of questions that lawyers and businessmen present. Nor do the missions of the various countries to the United Nations ordinarily perform this function.

The best way to get answers is to locate foreign government information centers or their chambers of commerce in New York. Experience shows that the officials who manage the British and Canadian Information Services are expert, knowledgeable and eager to help. They have a good stock of their own government publications and they keep recent issues of their countries' newspapers.

The Chamber of Commerce for Trade with Italy is typical of the best among service-oriented chambers of commerce. The Netherlands is equally well represented in New York by its Trading Society. However, the single word "siesta" among the "Black Book" notes opposite many of the local consulates indicates that there were many afternoons when their telephones were not manned.

The Common Market provides absolutely top-notch service about its activities through the European Communities Press and Information Office.

One fast-changing practice is the manner in which newspapers and magazines furnish information on material that they have published. The *New York Times,* for example, has discontinued its telephone inquiry service. Its bi-weekly index, now computerized, contains the most recent indexing information that *The Times* will provide. The *Wall Street Journal, New York Law Journal, Time, Life, Newsweek* and *New Yorker* still maintain card files on their stories and will locate them on request. Stories that have not yet appeared in the newspapers can be seen on the broad tape. Wire service editors for the Associated Press and United Press will often provide information about those late-breaking stories over the telephone. The Funk & Scott newspaper and periodical index services, published weekly, provides broad *business* coverage. More important, current information in all fields has become available through computer services such as "Lexis," "Nexis" and "Dialog."

In summary, there are usually four major kinds of private information agencies or publications available to lawyers and law librarians who perform nonlegal research: (1) special libraries, (2) trade associations or chambers of commerce, (3) trade newspapers and trade journals, and (4) computer services.

Once it is decided to purchase any publications, it is essential to know where to buy them quickly. New York is the publishing capital of the country. But delays occur because many publishers distribute their books from distant points.

CHAPTER 25

TECHNICAL DATA AVAILABLE WITH ON-LINE SEARCHES

The increasing relevancy of economic, sociological, scientific and technical data in determining whether administratively established criteria and standards for specific industrial and consumer oriented products have been met, is changing the nature of legal research. This interdisciplinary research requirement is imposing new responsibilities on lawyers. Lawyers conditioned to more conventional forms of institutional analysis are uncomforable when faced with legislation, for example, in which Congress directs all federal units to utilize systematically "the natural and social sciences and the environmental design arts in planning and in decision-making which may have an impact on man's environment", as declared in the *National Environmental Policy Act of 1969.* Because of current technological and scientific developments, lawyers engaged in such research must necessarily depend upon the findings of scientists, biologists, sociologists, economists and technicians to develop data to meet the thrust of declared public policy.

Lawyers now are quite sensitive to the implications of this development and when they seek law today, they attempt to consult materials and refer to pertinent and interrelated information in disciplines other than law. Obviously, the need to consult such documentation and information is compounding the difficulties of legal research. How to learn of the availability of these materials alone, is a challenge that is not always successfully met. It should also be recognized in this context, that the "information-explosion" characteristic of the past few decades, provides additional problems of identification and control. The *New York Times* has estimated that "the quantity of information generated in the past ten years alone well exceeds the total from all of mankind's previous history. And the amount of available data continues to expand at a relentless ever-increasing rate".

On-line or interactive searching is the newest and most sophisticated way of locating research, and other kinds of literature-related information sought for a specific subject interest. Recently on-line search services in a wide range of disciplines have been introduced commercially for library and in-house use. Such searches are usually carried out by means of a comparatively inexpensive terminal located in a library, or business office and can just as effectively be installed in a researcher's home.

There are a number of such on-line bibliographic search services which lawyers can profitably utilize when they seek interdisciplinary information. Following are descriptions of those of the better-known ones: *The New York Times Information Bank, (SDC) Systems Development Search Service-Dialog* and *(BRS) Bibliographic Retrieval Service.*

The Information Bank, a subsidiary of the New York Times Co. is a time-shared information storage and retrieval system. It contains a data base of over 1,300,000 abstracts of news stories, articles, essays, surveys and other material published in the *New York Times* newspaper and more than 70 other newspapers and periodicals published in the U.S. and abroad. After completion of on-line practice time, the customer is billed monthly on a standard $110 per hour usage.

There is no minimum usage level nor base monthly charge. Customers are eligible for volume discounts based upon guaranteed annual usage. For an additional charge, the customer is provided with a set of microfiche cards of all the complete material from the *New York Times* newspaper from which abstracts were made for the data base, and currently by week as added to the data base. The customer can also elect to have abstracts printed at the Information Bank data center (deferred print) and shipped to the customer's address.

The equipment needed for an Information Bank installation is one modem and one compatible terminal with keyboard. *Lexis* subscribers can use *Lexis* terminals for access to the Information Bank.

Extent of Coverage

The Information Bank provides detailed informative abstracts of newspaper and magazine articles. Topics to be covered can be specified: broad or narrow, a single name or a combination of subjects. Each abstract retrieved is displayed on the computer terminal along with a complete bibliographic citation for the original article *New York Times* material extends back to January 1, 1969. Normally included are: significant news items, interpretive articles, and articles of opinion or commentary originative, with or exclusive to the source periodicals; biographical material; business and financial news and interpretive articles thereon; editorials; surveys, background or chronological reviews, and similar descriptive material on subjects of general interest; commercial and political advertising when of research value. There is no need to learn a computer language.

The Information Bank provides economic and financial data, trends in finance, industry profiles, regulatory and consumer-affairs material as well as background statistics and data aid in internal reports, stockholder statements, etc.

Uses

The Information Bank suggests that the value of its data base for lawyers is the current information it provides on status of litigation related to companies, products and services in a specific field; liability and damage-claims: suits and settlements; regulatory commission activities; company investments; background on prospective targets; corporate responsibility; role and legal influence of public-interest groups and multinational affairs: currency ratios and banking. It can also be of value to lawyers seeking economic, political and social trend analysis, the impact of government controls and regulations, as well as deregulation, and information about conglomerate activity, subsidiary performance and "take-overs".

Another comprehensive on-line retrieval service is offered by Systems Development Corporation (S.D.C.) Search Service which provides access to AB1/INFORM and over fifty other files. Some of the files of value to lawyers are: CRECORD, comprehensive coverage of the Congressional Record; REDREG, timely monitoring of the Federal Government's regulatory and administrative activities reported in the *Federal Register;* NEWSPAPER INDEX, extensive coverage of issues and events that make news including legal issues and criminal cases; WPI, a comprehensive and authoritative coverage of patents, worldwide and SOCIAL SCIENCE CITATION INDEX, Comprehensive coverage of 100 of the more important law journals with indexing and searching of cited references.

Charges

SDC charges only for what is used. There are no subscription fees and no start up fees. Training is inexpensive and takes a day and a half, at the location of the subscriber. A wide range of terminal types are compatible with the SDC system. Users of the SDC Search Service may either dial directly to its computer in Santa Monica, California, via regular telephone lines, Telex or TWX, or use less expensive Tymet and Telenet communication networks.

SDC uses *ORBIT* search processes, which are easy to learn and quickly responsive. For most of its data bases, SDC charges at three levels: (1) computer time for the period the subscriber is connected with the SDC (2) communication usage, if the subscriber elects to use the cost-saving international network service SDC provides and (3) off-line printing, if the subscriber prefers, in the case of large bibliographies, for example, to order the Orbit system to print the results and airmail to it. SDC Search Service rates vary with each ORBIT data base which will be indicated as they are described below:

Available Data Bases

ACCOUNTANT INDEX. Prepared by the American Institute of Certified Public Accountants and covering the period from 1974 to the present, this service provides access to the literature related to accounting, auditing, taxation, data processing, investments, financial management, financial reporting, and management. The coverage is international in scope, including English-language books, speeches, pamphlets, government documents and journals from the U.S., Canada, England, Australia, South Africa and Japan, among others. Approximately 12,000 citations are added per year. The cost is $65/computer-connect hour, $0.10/citation for off-line printing.

CIS INDEX. Prepared by the Congressional Information Service, Inc. and covering the period from January 1970 to present, this service covers U.S. Congress publications, hearings, committee prints, House and Senate Reports, Documents and special publications, Senate Executive Reports and Documents. Public laws are added on an annual basis. Subject coverage is multidisciplinary and topical, including public service programs, raw materials and consumer products, and legal policies and events. Approximately 12,000 citations are added per year and approximately 1,000 citations are added monthly. The cost is $90/computer-connect hour and $0.25/citation for off-line printing.

CRECORD. Prepared by Capital Services, Inc. and covering the period from 1976 to the present, this service provides comprehensive, current coverage of the *Congressional Record,* including extension of remarks and digest sections. It contains references to bills and resolutions, Committee and subcommittee reports, legislation schedules of committee and floor activities, executive communications and speeches, participation in debates, and inserted materials by members of Congress. References are indexed and cross-referenced in 275 legislative areas. Approximately 40,000 citations are added annually. The cost is $80/computer-connect hour and $0.15/citation for off-line printing.

ENERGYLINE. Prepared by the Environment Information Center, Inc. and covering the period from January, 1971 to date. This service provides comprehensive coverage of over 200 core journals and selected coverage of 2000 other journals as well as reports and surveys, micrographs, conference proceedings and newspaper articles. Subject-area coverage includes energy economics, U.S. planning and policy, international political and economic issues, research and development, environmental impact, electric power transmission and storage, fuel production, fuel transport, nuclear power and industrial, transportation and residential consumption.

Approximately 4,800 citations are added annually. The cost is $90/computer-connect hour and $0.20/citations for off-line printing.

ENVIROLINE. Prepared by the Environment Information Center, this service contains citations on all areas of environmental studies, such as air pollution, chemical and biological contamination, land use, oceans and estuaries, geophysical change and other related subjects. References are gathered primarily from English-language journals, as well as government reports and documents. Corresponds in coverage to *Environment Abstracts.* Approximately 10,000 citations are added annually. The cost is $90/computer-connect hour and $0.20/citation for off-line printing.

FEDREG. Prepared by Capital Services, Inc., this service corresponds in coverage to *Federal Register Abstracts.* It contains citations gathered daily from the *Federal Register.* Subjects covered include, among others, agriculture, business, constitutional rights, consumer affairs, contracts, environment, law enforcement, taxation, technology, trade, transportation and veterans' affairs. Items included are Rules, Proposed Rules, and Public Law Notices. Approximately 18,000 citations are added annually for the period from March, 1977 to the present. Cost is $80/computer-connect hour and $0.25/citation for off-line printing.

FSTA. Prepared by the International Food Information Service, FSTA corresponds to the printed *Food Science and Technology Abstracts.* It covers the literature related to all human food commodities and aspects of food processing, except the production of raw foods. Subject areas included, among others, are basic food science, microbiology, hygiene and toxicology, food economics, food packaging, alcoholic and nonalcoholic beverages, fruits and vegetables, fish and marine products, food additives, food laws, regulations and standards. Source documents gathered worldwide include patents, books, standards and journal articles. Approximately 17,000 citations are added annually, from 1969 to date. The cost is $65/computer-connect hour and $0.12/citation for off-line printing.

INFORM. Prepared by ABI, this service covers business management periodical literature from over 300 journals, in the areas of accounting, advertising, banking, data processing, employee benefits, finance insurance, international trade, labor relations, real estate, statistics, business law, stocks and bonds, taxes, etc. Contains approximately 14,400 citations per year, from August, 1971 to date. The cost is $65/computer hour and $0.10/citation for off-line printing.

MANAGEMENT. Prepared by Management Information Services, this service corresponds to the semi-monthly *Management Contents.* It provides coverage of the business literature gathered from both U.S. and non-U.S. journals, proceedings, and transactions, such as accounting, banking, commodities and goods, economics and finance, government regulations, industrial relations, management, marketing, public administration and government and industry-specific literature. It adds approximately 12,000 citations per year to its data bank (1974 to present) and costs $65/computer-connect hour and $0.10/citation for off-line printing.

NEWSPAPER INDEX. Prepared by Bell and Howell, this service provides broad coverage of international, national, state and local news. The approximately 1,200,000 citations added to the files annually commencing from January, 1976, are drawn from *The San Francisco Chronicle, The Detroit News, The Chicago Tribune, The Los Angeles Times, The Houston Post, The New Orleans Times-Picayune,* and *The Washington Post.* It costs $80/computer-connect hour and $0.15/citation for off-line printing.

NTIS. Prepared by The National Technical Information Service (NTIS) of the U.S. Department of Commerce. This service provides broad and cross-disciplinary information derived from government-sponsored research and development technical reports from over 200 Federal agencies, federally-sponsored translations, and foreign language reports in areas of major technical interest. Multi-disciplinary scope includes aeronautics, agriculture, behavioral/social sciences, biological and medical sciences, chemistry, earth sciences, oceanography, electronics, engineering, energy, mathematical sciences, communications and space technology. This service corresponds to *Weekly Government Abstracts* and semi-monthly *Government Reports Announcements.* Approximately 60,000 citations per year are added to the files which continue to the present from January, 1970. It costs $45/computer-connect hour and $0.08/citation for off-line printing.

OCEANIC. Prepared by Data Courier, Inc., this service provides citations to worldwide technical literature about oceans, including many U.S. and non-U.S. source documents; e.g., associations journals, conference proceedings, government publications and trade journals. Subjects covered include biology/fisheries, geology and meteorology, remote sensing, desalination, pollution, coastal resources, etc., and legal issues. Oceanic covers the period from 1964 to the present and adds approximately 12,000 citations annually. It costs $55/computer-connect hour and $0.10/citation for off-line printing.

RESTDOC. Access to this service, which provides journal literature coverage of agricultural chemicals from 1968 to date (approximately 8,000 citations per year), is controlled by Derwent Publications, Ltd., London, England.

POLLUTION. Prepared by Pollution Abstracts, this service corresponds in coverage to the printed *Pollution Abstracts* publication. Covers non-U.S. and domestic reports, some 2,500 journals, conference proceedings and papers, symposia, contracts and patents, micrograph and government documents in the areas of pollution control and research including air pollution, water pollution, solid wastes, noise, pesticides, radiation and general environmental quality. Beginning with January, 1970, approximately 6,000 citations are added annually. It costs $65/computer-connect hour and $0.15/citation for off-line printing.

RINGDOC. Prepared by Derwent Publications, Ltd., England, this service covers over 400 scientific journals, published worldwide keyed to pharmaceutical subjects. Approximately 50,000 citations are added to the files which extend from July 1964 to the present.

SOCIAL SCIENCE CITATION INDEX. Prepared by the Institute for Scientific Information, this service provides coverage of the journal literature and cited references in the social sciences. Approximately 1,600 journals from around the world are indexed extensively and 2,460 journals in the natural, physical and biomedical sciences selectively, when relevant. In addition to citation retrieval, any document referenced in this service can be ordered on-line. Begun in 1977, approximately 125,000 citations per year are added to its files. The cost is $65/computer-connect hour and $0.10/citation for off-line printing.

TULSA. Prepared by the Informations Services Department of the University of Tulsa, this service covers worldwide literature and patents related to oil and natural gas exploration, development and production in such areas as petroleum geology, well drilling, completion and servicing, oil and gas production, pollution, alternative fuels and storage. It corresponds in coverage to *Petroleum Abstracts.* Begun in 1965, approximately 18,000 citations are added annually. Subscribers are charged $75/computer-connect hour and $0.15/citation for off-line printing, plus a variable license fee.

U.S. POLITICAL SCIENCE DOCUMENTS. Prepared by the University of Pittsburgh, this service provides coverage of 120 U.S. political science journals selected by political scientists for their quality and reference. Strong in foreign affairs and international relations, defense and strategic "area" studies (e.g. Latin America, Africa, Middle East, etc.) urban and governmental affairs. Begun in 1975, approximately 3,000 citations are added annually. It costs $65/computer-connect hour and $0.15/citation for off-line printing.

WPI. Prepared by Derwent Publications of London, England, this service provides citations in depth to documents relating to patent specifications issued by the Patent Office of the major industrial nations. The countries covered since 1963 include Belgium, France, Japan, the Netherlands, South Africa, West Germany, Canada, East Germany, the Soviet Union, Switzerland and the U.S. The U.S., Portugal, Sweden, Austria, Brazil, Czechoslovakia, Hungary, Israel and Rumania were introduced during 1975. It corresponds in coverage to *Central Patents Index* and the *World Patent Index.* Approximately 234,000 new inventions and 264,000 "equivalent" filings are added annually. Cost is provided on request.

Other services provided by SDC SEARCH SERVICE which could be of relevant research value to lawyers, but which space does not permit adequate coverage are: AGRICOLA on agriculture and related subject fields; ASI on statistical publications of the U.S. government; BIOSIS AND BIO6973, correspond to coverage of *Biological Abstracts* and *Bio Research Index,* covering the entire life sciences; CAS 77 and CAS 7276, correspond to coverage of *Chemical Abstracts Condensates* and provides citations to 12,000 journals world-wide, patents from 26 countries, conference proceedings and government research reports; CDI, Comprehensive Dissertation Index to all dissertations accepted for academic doctoral degrees granted in U.S. and in non-U.S. universities. COMPENDEX, corresponds in coverage to *Engineering Index Monthly;* INSPEC and INSP6976, corresponds to coverage of *Physics Abstracts, Electrical and Electronics Abstracts* and *Computer and Control Abstracts;* ISMEC, covering medical engineering, production engineering and engineering management; PSYCH ABSTRACTS, corresponds in coverage to *Physiological Abstracts;* SAE, worldwide coverage of papers concerned with self-propelled vehicles; SAFETY SCIENCE ABSTRACTS, broad, interdisciplinary coverage of literature related to the science of safety; SSIE, covers ongoing and recently completed research in the agricultural sciences, chemistry and chemical engineering, electronics, engineering and mathematics, medical sciences, physics and social sciences; and TITUS, a detailed file of information relating to the textile industry.

Another important on-line bibiographic search service is the *Dialog Information Retrieval Service,* from Lockheed Information Systems, Palo Alto, California. Serving users since 1972, it now has more than 100 data bases available on the system.

The data bases on the *Dialog* system contain in excess of 35,000, 000 records, ranging from a directory type listing of specific manufacturing plants to a citation with bibliographic information and an abstract referencing a journal, conference paper, or other original source.

Some of the data bases available on the *Dialog* system, of value to lawyers, with accompanying costs are:

ABI/INFORM, August 1971–present, 107,000 records, monthly updates (Data Courier, Inc., Louisville, KY)

The *ABI/INFORM* database is designed to meet the information needs of executives and covers all phases of business management and administration. *ABI/INFORM* stresses general decision sciences information which is applicable to many types of businesses and industries. Specific product and industry information is included but does not receive primary emphasis. Approximately 400 primary publications in business and related fields are currently scanned for articles to be abstracted and included in *ABI/INFORM.*

$75 per online connect hour, 20¢ per full record printed offline.

AGRICOLA, 1970–present, 1,340,000 records, monthly updates (National Agricultural Library, Beltsville, MD)

AGRICOLA (former *CAIN*) is the cataloging and indexing database of the National Agricultural Library (NAL). This file provides coverage of worldwide journal and monographic literature on agriculture and related subjects. Since *AGRICOLA* represents the actual holdings of the National Agricultural Library, there is substantial coverage of all subject matter normally contained in a very large library. File 110 contains the citations for the years 1970–1978 in the same format as in the past. File 10 contains citations from 1979 to the present. Both files have similar format and identical coverage and pricing.

$25 per online connect hour, 5¢ per full record printed offline.

APTIC, 1966–September, 1978, 89,000 records (Manpower and Technical Information Branch, U.S. Environmental Protection Agency, Research Triangle Park, NC)

APTIC covers all aspects of air pollution, its effects, prevention, and control from 1966–1976. The records added to the database from 1977 through September, 1978 were taken from periodicals, books and conference proceedings not covered by other major discipline-oriented databases.

APTIC covers the field of air pollution in the broadest sense, including the social, political, legal, and administrative aspects of the field. Subjects treated in this database include: atmospheric interaction, control methods, economic aspects, effects on human health, effects on materials, effects on plants and livestock, emission sources, government participation (legal and administrative), measurement methods, pollution data (air quality and emission inventories), and social aspects and public involvement.

$35 per online connect hour, 10¢ per full record printed offline.

ASI, 1973–present, 55,000 records, monthly updates (Congressional Information Service, Inc., Washington, D.C.)

ASI (AMERICAN STATISTICS INDEX), is a comprehensive index of the statistical publications from more than 400 central or regional issuing agencies of the U.S. Government. *ASI* provides abstracts and indexing of all federal statistical publications, including non-GPO publications, which contain social, economic, demographic or natural resources data; it also covers a selection of their publications with scientific and technical data. All types of publications are covered, whether published as periodicals, as special one-time reports, as items within a larger continuing report series, or as annual or biennial reports. Types of statistical data to be found in *ASI* include population and economic censuses; foreign trade data; Consumer Price Index reports; unemployment statistics; agricultural data on production, yield, prices, etc.; vital statistics; educational data, and much more.

$90 per online connect hour, 15¢ per full record printed offline.

BIOSIS PREVIEWS, 1969–present, 2,600,000 records, monthly updates (Biosciences Information Service, Philadelphia, PA)

BIOSIS PREVIEWS contains citations from both *Biological Abstracts* and *Biological Abstracts/RRM (formerly entitled Bioresearch Index),* the major publications of BioSciences Information Service of *Biological Abstracts.* Together, these publications constitute the major English language service providing comprehensive worldwide coverage of research in the life sciences. Nearly 8,000 primary journals as well as symposia, reviews, preliminary reports, semi-popular journals, selected institutional and government reports, research communications, and other secondary sources provide citations on all aspects of the biosciences and medical research. File 5 contains all the citations from 1972 through the present. The citations for the years from 1969 through 1971 are available in File 55, which is identical in content, format and pricing to File 5.

$45 per online connect hour, 10¢ per full record printed offline.

CAB ABSTRACTS, January 1973–present, 966,000 records, monthly updates (The Commonwealth Agricultural Bureaux, Farnham House, Farnham Royal, Slough, SL2 3BN, England)

CAB ABSTRACTS is a comprehensive file of agricultural and biological information containing all records in the 26 main journals published by Commonwealth Agricultural Bureaus. Over 8,500 journals in 37 languages are scanned, as well as books, reports, and other publications. In some instances less accessible literature is abstracted by scientists working in other countries. About 130,000 items are selected for publication yearly; significant papers are abstracted, while less important works are reported with bibliographic details only.

$35 per online connect hour, 25¢ per full record printed offline or typed online.

CHEMICAL INDUSTRY NOTES (CIN), 1974–present, 294,000 records, biweekly updates (American Chemical Society, Columbus, OH)

CHEMICAL INDUSTRY NOTES (CIN) extracts articles from over 75 worldwide business-oriented periodicals which cover the chemical-processing industries.

$60 per online connect hour, 20¢ per full record printed offline.

CHILD ABUSE AND NEGLECT, 1965–present, 8,800 citations, semi-annual updates (National Center for Child Abuse and Neglect, Children's Bureau, U.S. Department of Health, Education, and Welfare, Washington, DC)

CHILD ABUSE AND NEGLECT will initially contain about 4,500 records of three sorts: ongoing research project descriptions, bibliographic references, and service program listings. Each of the three subfiles deals with material of interest to social workers, family planners, sociologists, educators, criminologists, and legal researchers studying in the field of child abuse and neglect. *CHILD ABUSE AND NEGLECT* includes English-language material only and cites only research projects and service programs in the U.S. Documents covered in the bibliographic file include books, periodical literature, government and research reports, and conference proceedings. Semi-annually, an estimated 400 new bibliographic records will be added. The other two subfiles will be purged and updated on an annual basis.

$35 per online connect hour, 10¢ per full record printed offline.

CIS/INDEX, 1970–present, 110,000 records, monthly updates (Congressional Information Service, Inc., Washington, DC)

The *CIS/INDEX* database is the machine-readable form of the Congressional Information Service's *Index to Publications of the United States Congress. CIS/INDEX* provides current, comprehensive access to the contents of the entire spectrum of Congressional working papers published by the nearly 300 House, Senate and Joint committees and subcommittees each year. These "working papers" in the form of Hearings, Prints, Reports, Documents and other special publications record the vital investigatory, oversight and legislative analysis activities of Congress. Hearings publications contain not only transcripts of testimony from public and Government witnesses, but also a wealth of exhibit reports, statistical data, and articles. Other types of publications contain the reports of specially commissioned studies, analyses of Federal legislation and activities, and compilations of background materials concerning a broad range of issues.

$90 per online connect hour, 15¢ per full record printed offline.

CLAIMS™ /CHEM, 1950–1970, 265,000 citations, (IFI/Plenum Data Company, Arlington, VA)

The *CLAIMS/CHEM* database contains over 265,000 U.S. chemical and chemically related patents issued from 1950–1970. Foreign equivalents from Belgium, France, Great Britain, West Germany, and the Netherlands are included to the extent of approximately 20% of the patents in the file. Over 60% of the records include *Chemical Abstracts* abstract numbers. All patents in the Chemical section of the *Official Gazette* of the U.S. Patent Office together with any patents in the General, Electrical and Mechanical sections of the *Gazette* which are considered to be chemically oriented are included in the file.

$95 per online connect hour, 15¢ per full record printed offline.

CLAIMS™ /CHEM/UNITERM, 1950–present, 452,576 records, quarterly updates (IFI/Plenum Data Company, Arlington, VA)

CLAIMS/CHEM/UNITERM gives access to chemical and chemically related patents. It has the special feature of subject indexing for each chemical patent from a controlled vocabulary designed to facilitate retrieval of chemical structures and polymers. Indexing is prepared from a review of the full text of patent documents; 20 or more uniterm codes are then added to each record. *CLAIMS/CHEM/UNITERM* '50–'70, File 223, parallels coverage of File 23, *CLAIMS/CHEM* '50–'70; *CLAIMS/CHEM/UNITERM* '71–'77, File 224, parallels File 24, *CLAIMS/U.S. PATENTS* '71–'77; and *CLAIMS/CHEM/UNITERM* '78–present.

File 225, parallels File 25, *CLAIMS/U.S. PATENT ABSTRACTS.*

$300 per online connect hour, 15¢ per full record printed offline.

CLAIMS™ /CLASS, 15,000 records (IFI/Plenum Data Co., Arlington, VA)

CLAIMS/CLASS is a classification code and title dictionary for all classes and selected subclasses of the U.S. Patent Classification System. Its use will significantly enhance retrieval of patent data from *CLAIMS/CHEM* and *CLAIMS/U.S. PATENTS.*

$90 per online connect hour, 10¢ per full record printed offline.

CLAIMS™ /U.S. PATENTS, 1971–1977, 485,000 records, quarterly updates (IFI/Plenum Data Company, Arlington, VA)

The *CLAIMS/U.S. PATENTS* database contains all patents listed in the general, chemical, electrical and mechanical sections of the *Official Gazette* of the U.S. Patent Office. Foreign equivalents from Belgium, France, Great Britain, West Germany, and the Netherlands are included for approximately 20% of the U.S. patents in the file.

$95 per online connect hour, 15¢ per full record printed offline.

CLAIMS™ /U.S. PATENT ABSTRACTS, 1978–present, 116,000 records, monthly updates (IFI/Plenum Data Company, Arlington, VA)

CLAIMS/U.S. PATENT ABSTRACTS contains citations and abstracts for all patents classified by the U.S. Patent Office in the areas of aerospace and aeronautical engineering, agricultural engineering, chemical engineering, chemistry, civil engineering, electrical and electronics engineering, electromagnetic technology, mechanical engineering, nuclear science, and general science and technology. It differs from *CLAIMS/U.S. PATENTS* in that it includes abstracts for the patents from 1978 to the present.

$95 per online connect hour, 50¢ per full record printed offline, 25¢ per full record typed online.

CLAIMS™ /U.S. PATENT ABSTRACTS WEEKLY, Current month, 3,000 citations, weekly updates (IFI/Plenum Data Company, Arlington, VA)

CLAIMS/U.S. PATENT ABSTRACTS WEEKLY is a companion to the preceding one. It includes the most current weekly update and records from the current month. Records in the *CLAIMS/U.S. PATENT ABSTRACTS WEEKLY* are transferred to File 25 once a month.

$95 per online connect hour, 50¢ per full record printed offline, 25¢ per full record typed online.

COMPENDEX, January 1970–present, 817,000 records, monthly updates (Engineering Index, Inc., New York, NY)

The *COMPENDEX* database is the machine-readable version of the *Engineering Index (Monthly/Annual),* which provides the engineering and information communities with abstracted information from the world's significant engineering and technological literature. The Ei database provides worldwide coverage of approximately 3,500 journals, publications of engineering societies and organizations, papers from the proceedings of conferences, and selected government reports and books.

$65 per online connect hour, 15¢ per full record printed offline, 10¢ per full record typed online.

COMPREHENSIVE DISSERTATION ABSTRACTS, 1861–present, 648,000 citations, monthly updates (Xerox University Microfilms, Ann Arbor, MI)

COMPREHENSIVE DISSERTATION ABSTRACTS is a definitive subject, title, and author guide to virtually every American dissertation accepted at an accredited institution since 1861, when academic doctoral degrees were first granted in the United States. In addition, CDA serves to disseminate citations for thousands of Canadian dissertations and an increasing number of papers accepted in institutions abroad. Professional (e.g., M.D., L.L.D.) and honorary degrees are not included. All subject areas are covered.

Individual, degree-granting institutions submit copies of dissertations or lists of dissertations completed to University Microfilm International (UMI). Citations for these dissertations are included in the database and in University Microfilms International printed publications: *Dissertation Abstracts International (DAI), American Doctoral Dissertations (ADD),* and *Comprehensive Dissertation Index (CDI).*

DAI lists abstracts of dissertations from American, Canadian, and foreign universities, (copies of most of these dissertations are available from University Microfilms International); ADD supplements DAI by adding citations for other American dissertations written each year; CDI is a comprehensive index for both DAI and ADD. A complete listing of sources consulted in compiling this database can be found in the preface to any volume of *Comprehensive Dissertation Index.*

$55 per online connect hour, 12¢ per full record printed offline.

CONFERENCE PAPERS INDEX, 1973–present, 715,000 records, monthly updates (Data Courier, Inc., Louisville, KY)

CONFERENCE PAPERS INDEX provides access to records of more than 100,000 scientific and technical papers presented at over 1,000 major regional, national, and international meetings each year. *CONFERENCE PAPERS INDEX* provides a centralized source of information on reports of current research and development from papers presented at conferences and meetings; it provides titles of the papers as well as the names and addresses (when available) of the authors of these papers. Also included in this database are announcements of any publications issued or planned for issuance from the meetings; and of available preprints, reprints, abstract booklets, and proceedings volumes as well as dates of availability, costs and ordering information. Primary subject areas covered include the life sciences, chemistry, physical sciences, geosciences, and engineering.

$75 per online connect hour, 15¢ per full record printed offline.

DISCLOSURE, 1977–present, 18,000 records, weekly updates (Disclosure Incorporated, Washington, D.C.)

DISCLOSURE provides extracts of reports filed with the U.S. Securities and Exchange Commission (SEC) by publicly owned companies. These reports, filed by 11,000 companies, provide the most reliable and detailed source of public financial and administrative data on these companies. *DISCLOSURE* includes extracts of the 10-K and 10-Q financial reports, 8-K reports of unscheduled material events or corporate changes, 20-K financial reports, proxy statements, registration reports and prospect uses. *DISCLOSURE* provides an online source of information for marketing intelligence, corporate planning and development, portfolio analysis, legal and accounting research, and corporate finance. Disclosure Incorporated also makes these reports available on microfiche.

$90 per online connect hour, $3.00 per full record printed offline, $1.50 per full record typed online.

ECONOMICS ABSTRACTS INTERNATIONAL, 1974–present, 89,000 citations, monthly updates (Learned Information, Ltd., London, England)

ECONOMICS ABSTRACTS INTERNATIONAL provides coverage of the world's literature on markets, industries, country-specific economic data, and research in the fields of economic science and management. The *ECONOMIC ABSTRACTS INTERNATIONAL* database corresponds to portions of two printed indexes: *Economic Titles/Abstracts* and the *Key to Economic Science and Managerial Science.* Approximately 1,800 journals in addition to books, directories, and reports are abstracted to provide information on all areas of economics. *ECONOMICS ABSTRACTS INTERNATIONAL* also contains information on specific industries and provides data on the investment climate, import regulations, distribution channels and economic structure for markets worldwide.

$65 per online connect hour, 20¢ per full record printed offline.

ENERGYLINE®, 1971–present, 29,000 citations, bimonthly updates (Environment Information Center, Inc., New York, NY)

ENERGYLINE is the machine-readable version of *Energy Information Abstracts* and also includes 8,000 energy/environment records dating back to 1971 from *The Energy Index*. *ENERGYLINE* provides a primary source for information relating specifically to energy. Its data is drawn from many conventional discipline-oriented fields such as chemistry or engineering, but is incorporated into *ENERGYLINE* only as it relates to energy issues and problems. Its coverage includes journals, books, Congressional committee prints, conference proceedings, speeches, and statistics. *ENERGYLINE* provides information on scientific, technical, socio-economic, governmental policy and planning, and current affairs aspects of energy.

$90 per online connect hour, 20¢ per full record printed offline.

ENVIROLINE®, 1971–present, 79,000 citations, monthly updates (Environment Information Center, Inc., New York, NY)

ENVIROLINE, produced by the Environment Information Center, covers the world's environmental information. Its comprehensive, interdisciplinary approach provides indexing and abstracting coverage of more than 5,000 international primary and secondary source publications reporting on all aspects of the environment. Included are such fields as: management, technology, planning, law, political science, economics, geology, biology, and chemistry as they relate to environmental issues. Literature covered includes periodicals, government documents, industry reports, proceedings of meetings, newspaper articles, films and monographs. Also included are rulings from the *Federal Register* and patents from the *Official Gazette*.

$90 per online connect hour, 20¢ per full record printed offline.

ENVIRONMENTAL BIBLIOGRAPHY, 1973–present, 158,000 records, bimonthly updates. (Environmental Studies Institute, Santa Barbara, CA)

The *ENVIRONMENTAL BIBLIOGRAPHY*, covers the fields of general human ecology, atmospheric studies, energy, land resources, water resources, and nutrition and health. Almost 250 periodicals are indexed in *ENVIRONMENTAL BIBLIOGRAPHY*, thereby providing quick-and-easy access to article references for every environment research need.

Librarians, chemists, land-use planners, government officials, and corporate executives, among others, will find this database a functional asset to their work.

$60 per connect hour, 15¢ per full record printed offline.

EXCERPTA MEDICA, June 1974–present, 1,160,000 records, monthly updates (Excerpta Medica, Amsterdam, The Netherlands)

EXCERPTA MEDICA is one of the two principal sources for searching the biomedical literature. It consists of abstracts and citations of articles from over 3,500 biomedical journals published throughout the world. It covers the entire field of human medicine and related disciplines. The online file corresponds to the 43 separate specialty abstract journals and 2 literature indexes which make up the printed *Excerpta Medica* plus an additional 100,000 records annually that do not appear in the printed journals. *EXCERPTA MEDICA* is widely used by physicians, medical researchers, medical libraries, hospitals, medical schools, health organizations, and chemical and pharmaceutical companies. In addition to providing abstracts in all fields of medicine, *EXERPTA MEDICA* provides extensive coverage of the drug and pharmaceutical literature, and of other health related sciences such as environmental health and pollution control, forensic science, health economics and hospital management, and public health.

$55 per online connect hour, 15¢ per full record printed offline.

NATIONAL NEWSPAPER INDEX, 1979–present, 165,000 records, monthly updates (Information Access Corporation, Los Altos, CA)

The *NATIONAL NEWSPAPER INDEX* provides front page to back page indexing of *The Christian Science Monitor, The New York Times,* and *The Wall Street Journal.* All articles, news reports, editorials, letters to the editor, obituaries, product evaluations, biographical pieces, poetry, recipes, columns, cartoons and illustrations, and reviews are included. The only items not included are weather charts, stock market tables, crossword puzzles, and horoscopes. The *NATIONAL NEWSPAPER INDEX,* particularly useful for answering general reference questions, provides a valuable adjunct in such areas as market research, public relations, government relations, journalism, food and nutrition, and the social sciences.

$75 per online connect hour, 10¢ per full record printed offline.

NCCAN (See CHILD ABUSE AND NEGLECT)

NCJRS, 1972–present, 45,000 records, monthly updates (National Criminal Justice Reference Service, Rockville, MD).

The NCJRS (National Criminal Justice Reference Service) database covers all aspects of law enforcement and criminal justice from police; courts; corrections, juvenile justice; community crime prevention; criminal justice system; fraud, waste, and abuse in government programs. Cited documents include both U.S. and international research reports, published papers, books, articles, and audio-visual presentations. Topic coverage ranges from preliminary research to detailed descriptions of successful programs.

$35 per online connect hour, 15¢ per full record printed offline, 10¢ per full record typed online.

NIMH, 1969–present, 375,000 records, monthly updates (National Clearinghouse for Mental Health Information, (NCMHI), National Institute of Mental Health, Rockville, MD).

The NIMH (National Institute of Mental Health) database cites worldwide information relating to the general topic area of mental health. Sources include 12,000 journals (from 41 different countries, in 21 different languages), books, monographs, technical reports, workshop and conference proceedings, and symposia. Also included are Far Eastern literature and non-print media. There is no equivalent print version of the database. There are, however, publications which contain some of the records available online. They are *Psychopharmacology Abstracts* and the one-time publications, *Abstracts of the Standard Edition of Freud, Abstracts of the Psychoanalytic Study of the Child, Woman and Mental Health,* and *Bibliography on Racism.*

$30 per online connect hour, 10¢ per full record printed offline.

NTIS, 1964–present, 765,000 citations, biweekly updates (National Technical Information Service, NTIS, U.S. Department of Commerce, Springfield, VA)

The *NTIS* database consists of government-sponsored research, development and engineering plus analyses prepared by federal agencies, their contractors or grantees. It is the means through which unclassified, publicly available, unlimited distribution reports are made available for sale from such agencies as NASA, DDC, DOE, HEW, HUD, DOT, Department of Commerce, and some 240 other units. State and local government agencies are now beginning to contribute their reports to the file.

The *NTIS* database includes material from both the *hard* and *soft* sciences, including substantial material on technological applications, business procedures, and regulatory matters. Many topics of immediate broad interest are included, such as environmental pollution and control, energy conversion, technology transfer, behavioral/societal problems, urban and regional planning.

$35 per online connect hour, 10¢ per full record printed offline.

POLLUTION ABSTRACTS, 1970–present, 68,500 citations, bimonthly updates (Data Courier, Inc., Louisville, KY)

POLLUTION ABSTRACTS is a leading resource for references to environmentally related literature on pollution, its sources and its control.

The following subjects are covered by the *POLLUTION ABSTRACTS* database: Air Pollution, Environmental Quality, Noise Pollution, Pesticides, Radiation, Solid Wastes, and Water Pollution.

$75 per online connect hour, 15¢ per full record printed offline.

PSYCHOLOGICAL ABSTRACTS, 1967–present, 305,500 citations, monthly updates (American Psychological Association, Washington, DC)

PSYCHOLOGICAL ABSTRACTS covers the world's literature in psychology and related disciplines in the behavioral sciences. Over 900 periodicals and 1,500 books, technical reports, and monographs are scanned each year to provide coverage of original research, reviews, discussions, theory, conference reports, panel discussions, case studies, and descriptions of apparatus.

$65 per online connect hour, 10¢ per full record printed offline.

SOCIAL SCISEARCH®, 1972–present, 765,000 records, monthly updates. (The Institute for Scientific Information, Philadelphia, PA)

The *SSCI* is a multidisciplinary database indexing every significant item from the 1,000 most important social sciences journals throughout the world and social sciences articles selected from 2,200 additional journals in the natural, physical, and biomedical sciences. The *SSCI* includes many important monographs as well. The *SSCI* covers every area of the social and behavioral sciences.

SOCIAL SCISEARCH offers a unique information retrieval technique. In addition to more conventional retrieval by title words of phrases, source authors, journal names, corporate source, etc., it is also possible to search by way of the author's cited references.

$70 per online connect hour, 10¢ per full record printed offline.

SOCIOLOGICAL ABSTRACTS, 1963–present, 99,600 citations, quarterly updates (Sociological Abstracts, Inc., San Diego, CA)

SOCIOLOGICAL ABSTRACTS covers the world's literature in sociology and related disciplines in the social and behavioral sciences. Over 1,200 journals and other serial publications are scanned each year to provide coverage of original research, reviews, discussions, monographic publications theory, conference reports, panel discussions and case studies. The following fields are covered: Methodology and Research Technology, History and Theory of Sociology, Social Psychology and Group Interaction, Culture and Social Structure, Management and Complex Organization, Social Change and Economic Development, Mass Phenomena and Political Interactions, Social Differentiation, Rural and Urban Sociology, Sociology of the Arts, Education, Religion, Science, Health and Knowledge, Demography and Human Biology, The Family and Social Welfare, Community Development, Policy, Planning, Forecasting and Speculation, Radical Sociology, Studies in Violence and Poverty and Feminism, Environmental Interaction.

$55 per online connect hour, 15¢ per full record printed offline.

TRIS (Transportation Research Information Service), 1968–present, 145,000 records, monthly updates (U.S. Department of Transportation and Transportation Research Board, Washington, D.C.)

TRIS provides transportation research information in air, highway, rail, and maritime transport; mass transit; and other transportation modes. Subjects included are regulations and legislation; energy, environmental, and safety concerns; materials, design, construction and maintenance technology; and operations, traffic control and communications. The database records can be either abstracts of documents and data holdings or resumes of research projects. Among the transportation research information services contributing to *TRIS* are the Highway Research Information Service (HRIS), the Maritime Research Information Service (MRIS), the Railroad Information Service (RRIS), the Air Transportation Research Information Service (ATRIS), and the Urban Mass Transportation Research Information Service, (UMTRIS). Use is restricted to U.S. and Canada passwords only.

$40 per online connect hour, 10¢ per full record printed offline.

U.S. EXPORTS, 100,000–200,000 records, annual updates (U.S. Department of Commerce, Washington, D.C.)

U.S. EXPORTS gives export statistics that reflect both government and non-government exports of domestic and foreign merchandise from the U.S. and Territories to foreign countries. The physical movement of merchandise out of the U.S. includes agricultural commodities, U.S. government shipments of all types, intra-company shipments, and purchases made in the U.S. by representatives of foreign governments for foreign governments or firms. The data in *U.S. EXPORTS* is compiled by the U.S. Bureau of the Census primarily from copies of Shipper's Export Declarations which are required to be filed with Customs officials. Use of File 126 is restricted to U.S. passwords only.

$45 per connect hour, 25¢ per full record printed offline, 25¢ per full record typed online.

BRS (Bibliographic Retrieval Services, Inc.), located in Scotia, New York 12302, was established in 1976 to provide libraries and information centers with low cost on-line access to a set of major bibliographic data bases, at costs ranging from $10 per connect hour to $25 per hour (excluding communications and royalty charges). Established primarily for libraries, it provides training and continuing education programs for its users.

BRS offers its users access to more than 10 million bibliographic citations in the subject areas of medicine, biology, chemistry, psychology, education, agriculture, physics, engineering, computer science and business management.

The following set of major databases is available for on-line searching through B.R.S.

- AGRICOLA (1970 to date)
- MEDLARS (1966 to date)
- BIOSIS PREVIEWS (1970 to date)
- CHEMICAL ABSTRACTS CONDENSATES (1970 to date)
- PSYCHOLOGICAL ABSTRACTS (1967 to date)
- DISSERTATION ABSTRACTS (1861 to date)
- ERIC (1966 to date)
- NTIS (1970 to date)
- INSPEC (1969 to date)
- POLLUTION ABSTRACTS (1970 to date)
- PHARMACEUTICAL NEWS INDEX (PNI) (1974 to date)
- INFORM (from ABI) (1971 to date)

MEDLARS. The MEDLARS (Medical Literature Analysis and Retrieval System) data base, produced by the National Library of Medicine, contains citations from over 3,000 English and major foreign language journals in all the basic and clinical biomedical sciences.

BIOSIS PREVIEWS. This data base provides comprehensive coverage of the world's biological and life science literature, including such broad areas as anatomy, bacteriology, biochemistry, cell biology, genetics, immunology, microbiology, nutrition, pathology, physiology, pharmacology, toxicology, taxonomy virology, and zoology.

CHEMICAL ABSTRACTS CONDENSATES. This data base contains citations to the world's literature in chemistry, organic and macromolecular chemistry, analytical and physical chemistry, applied chemistry and chemical engineering.

PSYCHOLOGICAL ABSTRACTS. This data base contains references to the literature of psychology and related disciplines.

AGRICOLA. The CAIN data base, produced by the National Agricultural Library (NAL) contains references to the broad field of agriculture, including agricultural economics and rural sociology, food and human nutrition, agricultural products, animal industry, forestry, engineering, pesticides, plant science, soils and fertilizers and related subjects.

ERIC. This data base, developed by the National Institute of Education contains citations to research reports and journal articles pertaining to the field of education.

NTIS. (See description under S.D.C.)

PHYSICS ABSTRACTS. This data base contains abstracts of journal articles, technical reports, conference proceedings, books and theses in the field of physics.

INFORM. (See description under S.D.C.)

DISSERTATION ABSTRACTS. This data base contains all those citations from the printed Comprehensive Dissertation Index (CDI) published by University Microfilms. It includes references to the dissertations for almost all doctoral degrees granted in the ULSL since 1861 in all areas of the humanities, the social sciences and the physical and life sciences. References are also given to Canadian and foreign dissertations.

POLLUTION ABSTRACTS. This data base contains citations to abstracts from published and unpublished world pollution and environmental information.

New Data Bases currently scheduled by BRS are Social Science Citation Index, Sociological Abstracts, Environmental Impact Statements, Medoc (Government documents in the Health Services) and Conference Papers Index.

The TELENET dial-up communication network provides the major form of access to the BRS computer. Users in cities which do not have a TELENET node may use a special TELENET WATS number, at the cost of $1.00 per hour. Any teletype-compatible on-line communication terminal with a print speed of 10–120 characters per second may be used to access the BRS system. Most terminals (either hard copy or CRT) presently being used to access other on-line services will also be compatible with BRS.

CHAPTER 26

GOVERNMENT SOURCES

Bewildering to lawyers and laymen alike are the layers of federal, state, local and foreign government authority in the City of New York. To illustrate, it takes some fourteen pages of finely printed text in the current classified telephone directory to list the approximately 5,000 telephone numbers of government agencies in the Borough of Manhattan alone.

The research lawyer needs more than a street map to find the way to and through the appropriate government agencies. To help make some sense out of the maze of government services, this column offers a brief guide to the functions and officials of various government agencies as shown in three indispensable directories that government itself has published.

Federal Agencies

The "United States Government Manual" is an annual directory of the agencies in all branches of the federal government. The 1980–1981 edition runs to 957 fact-packed pages and is a Government Printing Office bargain at $8.50.

Its coverage of the Securities and Exchange Commission is typical of the facts it provides for most of the other federal agencies. It names the commissioners, the general counsel and a dozen other policy making or enforcement officials. It cites and summarizes the statutes that the SEC administers. It locates the Washington, D.C., and all the regional offices and points out that registration statements and other public documents filed with the commission in Washington, D.C., may also be consulted in the New York, Chicago and Los Angeles regional offices.

Copying facilities are available at its 26 Federal Plaza office in New York and elsewhere throughout the country. A final note set in bold face type gives the telephone number of the official to contact for further SEC information. This feature is of immense value in obtaining facts from the appropriate office within a division and from the right official within that office.

Comparable information appears in the manual for all other federal agencies.

Additional Features

Three additional features increase the usefulness of this directory in law offices: (1) organization charts of some forty major agencies, (2) an appendix of abolished and transferred agencies and functions, and (3) both a subject and agency index.

By using the "Manual" in conjunction with C.F.R. and the classified telephone directory for New York (or any other major American city), it is possible to identify and locate the appropriate local Federal Government agency.

New York State

The equivalent state publication in New York is the "New York Legislative Manual." It is published in Albany by the state. It names the leading state agencies and their officers, the members of the Senate and Assembly and the committees of the Legislature.

One of its particularly useful features is the summary of the functions of the various Joint Legislative Investigating Committees. These committees publish reports many of which are readily available in law libraries throughout the state. Few Senate or Assembly committees, however, print any reports or make them available to the public. The "New York Red Book," a private directory, contains most of the materials that appear in the state "Manual."

New York City

The little Green Book, formally titled the "City of New York Official Directory," appears each spring. Its publication is one of the city's proudest feats. Not only does it guide its users to all the city agencies, but it offers detailed information about county, New York State and United States Government offices and officials as well. It is a "World Almanac" of government information.

One of its most fascinating chapters is a fifty-page list titled, "Licenses, Permits or Certificates—Where to Apply." It runs from "Able Seamen" (supervised by the United States Coast Guard) to "Yachts, Foreign Flag" (regulated by the Regional Commissioner of Customs). Altogether it covers some 1,300 regulated activities. Its list of officials—federal, state and local—whose names your research lawyers may have to know runs to some 4,500 entries.

Overlapping Services

Earlier the layers of government authority in the City of New York were mentioned. Some examples: In consumer affairs, the city has a main office at 80 Lafayette Street and scattered local offices of its Department of Consumer Affairs. The State of New York has its Consumer Protection Board at 2 World Trade Center. The national body, the Federal Trade Commission, maintains local offices in the new federal office building at 26 Federal Plaza.

On matters affecting environment regulation, the city's agency is the Environmental Protection Administration with headquarters in the Municipal Building. There are numerous branch offices. Its work is divided among the Departments of Air Resources, Sanitation and Water Resources. The State of New York has its Department of Environmental Conservation at 2 World Trade Center that includes a Conservation Department Information Office. The federal counterpart is the Environmental Protection Agency with a regional coordinator and separate agencies in the city for its Air Pollution Control Office, its Pesticides Regulation Division, its Radiation Office, its Solid Wastes Office and its Water Quality Office.

All three branches of government maintain offices in New York and furnish information in the fields of labor law, taxation, commerce and housing. The single subject of federal aid for city housing and other urban projects itself became so complicated that eight years ago *The New York Times* produced a 1,312-page federal aid guide for city officials.

Complex Regulations

Indeed, so complex and varied are the regulations and services of government–at all levels–that no one lawyer can master the operations of more than a few of them. A research lawyer, however, can serve as the clearing house of basic information about them all.

Two useful features in the Manhattan Yellow Pages directory under the headings "Government Agencies–New York State" and "Government Agencies–United States" are the final entries for each. They provide the telephone numbers of officials who will provide more New York State or more United States information than the directory furnishes. But the final entry under "Government Agencies–New York City" may be prophetic. It lists the telephone number for the office of the zoo.

CHAPTER 27

THE BOOKSELLERS

Metropolitan New York is the single largest market for the sale of books at retail in the country. Its booksellers have the largest and most diversified book stocks (both new and used) and there are more of them. Yet when a lawyer needs a particular book, he may have to telephone a dozen or more booksellers before he finds it. Moreover, the varied problems that clients raise and the personal interests of lawyers make it useful for lawyers to get speedy answers to two questions: (1) What books exist on a particular subject? Where can they be purchased? This column will attempt to answer both questions.

Bibliographical Tools

The *Subject Guide to Books in Print* is a catalog that lists nearly a quarter million current titles (including paperbacks) under 63,500 subject headings. It provides the name of the publisher and the price for each item listed. It is published annually in November by Bowker Publishing Company in New York.

This catalog is a one-stop bibliographical search tool for all subjects except law. Since the leading law book publishers do not sell their books through book stores, only a limited number of law books are included in this guide. It is a time saver that is probably worth purchasing once every two or three years. Copies can also be consulted in almost every major book store and public or college library in the country.

For lawyers interested in buying reference books only, Chapters 66 to 76 of *Recommended Law Books* lists and evaluates some eleven classes of reference tools from atlases to quotation books. The first sixty-five chapters cover law books. Like the *Subject Guide*, it too gives the publisher and price for each title. But editions have been revised and prices sharply increased since its publication. It is a non-profit publication of the American Bar Association's Corporation Section (1155 East Sixtieth Street, Chicago) and sells for $5 a copy.

General Booksellers

Booksellers run either general or specialized book stores. Even the largest general bookseller is likely to have a thinner stock of books on a particular subject, diseases of the heart for example, than can be found in the smallest medical book store.

The ten blocks along Fifth Avenue in New York between 47th and 57th Streets include some nine large general book stores. The Scribner Book Store at 597 Fifth Avenue has for many years been one of the city's, if not the nation's, largest and most diversified book store. Across the avenue and a block south at No. 586 is Brentano's which also has a large downtown branch at University Place and Eighth Street. Three of the others, Rizzoli International Book Store, at 712 Fifth Avenue, and two branches of Doubleday Book Shops, at 673 and 721 Fifth Avenue, offer an unusual feature in a city that has been closing its shutters by 6 P.M. These three stores remain open late on weekday evenings providing a bright oasis for late-evening book buyers.

Rizzoli maintains a large stock of American, English and Western European publications, including books on all major subjects, magazines and even current foreign newspapers. Outstanding here are gift books for adults and children. One can probably find handsomely bound editions of Pinnochio in English, Italian, French, Spanish and German, for example. The store is lavishly decorated—not so brightly lighted as the two Doubleday branches—and a joy to visit. Rizzoli is one of Italy's major book publishers and booksellers. They operate a comparable store on Via Venato in Rome.

On Fifth Avenue at Eighteenth Street, Barnes & Noble has its main book store with a stock of 50,000 titles. Many of these are text books. But even after discounting them, its book stock remains one of the largest in the city. Dalton's, a rising new competitor, has opened numerous branches throughout Manhattan.

Lawyers may find it more convenient to deal with a single reliable book dealer in the vicinity of their offices than with any of the major book stores. With over a quarter-million titles in print (not counting fiction), it is unlikely that any general bookseller no matter how large his collection will keep in stock each of the books that lawyers happen to need. The owner of any small book store can obtain books from publishers just as quickly as can his larger competitors.

In the Wall Street area, Stamm's for Books, at 172 Fulton Street, provides downtown lawyers with effective and speedy service (they have their own messengers). The Doubleday branch at 14 Wall Street is another small, but well managed, store that numbers many lawyers among its customers.

University Book Stores

Wherever a great college or university is located, the best local book store is likely to be on campus. It may not even be listed in the Yellow Pages (the City College store appears in the Manhattan Directory, but not Columbia's, Fordham's or New York University's). In Philadelphia, the University of Pennsylvania Book Store keeps a stock of some 28,000 titles, making it easily the largest retailer of books in Southeastern Pennsylvania. In Princeton, the University Book Store is equally well stocked. In Cambridge, Mass., it is the Harvard Co-op that runs the best book store. In Chicago, however, Kroch's & Brentano's (main store at 29th South Wabash Avenue and their nine branches) provide such convenient and good service that Chicago lawyers rarely make the trip to the even larger University of Chicago Book Store.

Specialized Book Stores

New York also supports more specialized book sources than any other city in the country. There are stores stocked only with cookbooks, books about ships, chess and checkers and occult books.

The business and financial community has no single great book store to serve its specialized needs. Downtown, the New York University Graduate School of Business store comes closest. It is at the corner of Church and Thames Streets, one block west of 120 Broadway, and maintains a stock of the leading works in accounting, statistics and related fields. We have even seen copies of the new CCH Tax Regulations and Internal Revenue Codes on its shelves immediately after publication. Uptown, the Taylor Carlisle Book Company, 115 East Twenty-third Street, offers a comparable service.

In medicine, there is at least one good medical book store within a block of most of the major hospitals in New York. Among those stores are General Medical Book Company, 310 East Twenty-sixth Street, New York Hospital-Cornell Medical Center Book Store, 1307 York Avenue, and Julius Levin, Inc., 1391 Madison Avenue (at Ninety-sixth Street).

There is a fascinating collection of shipping, marine and other technical books in the Maritime Book Shop at 24 Beaver Street.

For film, theatre and literary works (both new and used) Gotham Book Mart at 41 West Forty-seventh Street encourages browsing through its shelves that contain several thousand titles in these fields.

One of the best sources for technical books of all kinds is the McGraw Hill Book Store at 1221 Avenue of the Americas. Librairie de France at 610 Fifth Avenue along the south side of the Rockefeller Center promenade and at 115 Fifth Avenue is among the leading importers of books from France. It also deals in Spanish books.

Newspapers and Periodicals

Eastern Newsstand at 2 World Trade Center along the concourse leading to the Path line handles some 1,500 current American and foreign newspapers and periodicals. The same company's Pan Am Building stand has a stock of some 2,000 similar publications. Hotaling's which is located in a booth outside 1 Times Square and in larger quarters within the building provides daily newspapers from major American cities and some 800 foreign publications as well. A fuller account of these and other services appeared in *The New York Times* for October 15, 1980 at C14. "Where to find a copy of *Le Monde* at 3 a.m." is the lead-in line to this story.

Out-of-Print Publications

Most publishers keep their recent trade books in print for a year or two and somewhat longer in the case of expensive technical works. Because the high cost of storage facilities prevents them from storing their unsold books permanently, they sell entire stocks of their older titles to "remainder" dealers. Marboro Book Corporation is an example. Once the "remainder" dealers have disposed of their stock the only way to find any of these older titles is through used book dealers. They are of two types: Those that maintain stocks of used books and those that run search services. Some booksellers do both.

The building boom in Manhattan has displaced many secondhand book dealers, including most of the Fourth Avenue booksellers. Still remaining, however, is the Strand Book Store at 828 Broadway (at Twelfth Street) which has one of the largest used book stocks in the city. Two other first rate used book stores are on East Fifty-ninth Street (Carnegie Book Shop at No. 140 and Argosy Book Store at No. 116). One of the oldest booksellers in New York and still one of its most interesting is Isaac Mendosa Book Company, downtown at 15 Ann Street, just south of City Hall. But after searching through used book stores for several years, it is apparent to us that anyone seeking a particular title in any of them has only a bare chance to find it on the day of his visit.

The out-of-print service is a more sensible way of locating books no longer sold through their publishers. The classified columns of the Sunday *Times* Book Section always list the names of a few such services, as do the Yellow Pages directories in most American cities. One very successful such service that Pegeen Fitzgerald frequently mentions on her WOR radio program is Books-on-File, Box 195, Union City, New Jersey. There is usually no charge for the search and no obligation to buy a book after it is located.

Charity Sale

Finally, a different kind of used book source is the charity sale. One that is worth returning to year after year because of the quality of the books offered and the fairness of the prices is the Summit, N.J., College Club book sale held annually in October for the benefit of scholarship students. It is frequently a fine source for used sets of the *Encyclopedia Britannica* and other reference works.

CHAPTER 28

FTC GUIDES FOR THE LAW BOOK INDUSTRY

What do law book publishers have in common with mail order insurance companies, sellers of wigs and other hairpieces, and packers of dog and cat foods? They are members of the relatively small number of industries that the Federal Trade Commission has decided to regulate through guides to fair practice. The Commission has finally promulgated its "Guides for the Law Book Industry". Law book customers have thus won the opening skirmish in their campaign for equal protection against unfair trade practices.

There are three levels of FTC regulation: trade regulation rules, trade practice rules and sets of guides. Guides represent the mildest form of FTC action. It is incumbent upon lawyers, therefore, to learn how they can ensure maximum protection against the law book sales and publishing practices that the Guides are designed to curb. The four practices most frequently cited by lawyers in their complaints are:

Frequent Complaints

(1) Deceptive advertising.

(2) Failure to disclose the cost, frequency and content of supplemental services.

(3) Unsolicited mailings.

(4) Questionable billing methods.

The Guides became effective on April 8, 1976, eight months after their promulgation. During the period up to their effective date law book publishers and buyers alike had an opportunity to adjust their practices and to ascertain their rights under the new rules. The basic fact publishers and lawyers should know about the application of the Guides is that, "While the Guides are interpretative of laws administered by the Commission, and thus are advisory in nature, proceedings to enforce the requirements of law may be brought under the Federal Trade Commission Act (15 U.S.C. 21-58) which, briefly stated, makes it illegal for one to engage in 'unfair methods of competition in or affecting commerce and unfair or deceptive acts or practices in or affecting commerce, as 'Commerce' is defined therein."

Set forth in summary form below are each of the seventeen Law Book Guides with illustrations of how they may be applied.

Guide One

General Disclosures

Representations by direct mail or by salesmen relating to legal publications must clearly and conspicuously identify the author or editor, the title, publisher, edition (if later than the first), copyright date and date of an earlier version if the book offered is simply a reprint. In addition publishers must disclose whether or not the book will be supplemented, that it is part of a set or series if that be the case, that the subject is or is not more limited than the title implies; and, if a price is given at all, a statement of what the price includes, whether for example, it covers a single volume or all the volumes in a set.

A lawyer who orders *Sweeping on Real Property* is entitled to know if it covers the laws of all the states or only the laws of Pennsylvania, New York or California. If it is merely a reprint of a book that he owns under a different title, that fact must be disclosed. If it is offered for $40, he will have the right to know in advance whether or not it may cost $400 instead, once he pays for the remaining nine volumes that the publisher intends to issue in conjunction with it.

Guide Two

Disclosures Relative to Supplementation

All solicitations for the purchase of law books that provide supplementation should disclose five groups of facts:

(a) The form of supplement, e.g. through looseleaf sheets, pocket parts or replacement volumes or a combination of several forms and their anticipated frequency, e.g. annually or quarterly.

(b) The cost of the latest supplement and the period of time in which future supplements, if any, will be supplied without added cost.

(c) The amount of credit or discount offered in connection with the original purchase.

(d) The fact that supplementation has been or will be abandoned, if in fact that has occurred or will occur within one year after the solicitation.

(e) The minimum cost of supplementing the work for the past two years.

The cost of law book supplementation has accelerated faster than the cost of living generally in the last few years. Upkeep costs are crucial in a lawyer's decision whether or not to purchase a set of law books.

The confusing methods some publishers employ to identify successive treatise supplements for the same work and the erratic fluctuations of time between issues make it difficult for a lawyer to estimate their cost. He may get small comfort from learning the upkeep costs of a work prior to purchasing it. But at least he will no longer be trapped into maintaining a "Daimler" if his practice can be served with a "Datsun."

Guide Three

Disclosures Relative to Texts and Treatises

Solicitations must disclose the estimated number of volumes in a multivolume set and of the anticipated publication schedule. Offers of a set of books should be accompanied by a description of its contents.

Guide Four

New Revisions or Replacement Sets or Series

The offer of a set of books that is to be replaced or revised within one year of sale should be accompanied by notice of that fact. If a publisher fails to give such notice he is expected to offer full refund less reasonable charges for use of the work or, in the alternative, full credit toward the purchase of the new work, less reasonable charges for use of the old work. The publisher is excepted from this requirement if he continues full supplementation of the original set.

Guide Five

Representations, Express or Implied, Describing a Work as "New", "Current" or "Up-to-Date"

This Guide sets a limit of eighteen months from the date of first distribution of a book after which the terms "new", "current", "up-to-date", "announcing", "newly revised" and the like may no longer be used to describe it. If a work is supplemented, however, and legal activity in the fields covered by the work are considerable, then the allowable period of time between the date of the latest supplement and use of an advertisement, heralding the book as "new" will be shortened accordingly. In an exceptional case the period may be lengthened, such as the coverage of legislative activity by a state legislature that meets biennially.

In situations where a publisher fails to clear his stock of a "new" treatise after extended advertising, he sometimes continues to mail to prospective customers copies of the same circular that describes the work as "new" two, three and sometimes even five years after the book's original release. Each mailing induces a few more lawyers to buy the book that some of them already own. These purchases are made in the mistaken belief that the old goods are in fact new. Such advertising is as unfair morally as it is now deemed to be "unfair" legally.

Guide Six

Disclosure Relative to Misleading Titles of Texts and Treatises

A prospective purchaser must be informed that despite the use of an author's name on the title page someone else may be responsible for the edition offered. It also requires disclosure in those cases in which a book was formerly issued under a different title or is based on previously published material.

Guide Seven

Representations Relative to Works Not Yet Published

Solicitations for sales of an unpublished work must not imply that the work is actually printed or published and, if publication of a work is contingent upon receipt of inquiries or orders, that fact must be "clearly and conspicuously disclosed".

Beame on Bankruptcy might or might not become a profitable new legal publication. How can a publisher find out at minimum cost to himself? Some publishers have followed the practice of "market-testing" the publication of its proposed law books with elaborate mail-order brochures. If enough lawyers ordered the book, it was published; otherwise not. This is a waste of lawyers' time and under Guide Seven becomes an "unfair method of competition" unless the lawyer is clearly told that he is being used as an unpaid guinea pig.

Guide Eight

Representations Relative to Jurisdictional Designations

The advertised claims of a work's jurisdictional scope must be neither too broad nor too narrow.

California Divorce Practice should relate primarily to matters of California law and should not cover divorce practice in other states. This Guide is intended to forestall the promotion and sale of three or more additional and identical books, but with different title pages and covers: one called *New York Divorce Practice*, a second, *Divorce in Texas* and a third, *A Practitioner's Guide to Illinois Divorce Practice*. The titles are fictitious. The practice is real.

Guide Nine

Catalogs

This Guide simply requires that law book publishers' catalogs conform to the advertising requirements set forth in Guides 1 to 3 and 5 to 8.

Guide Ten

Subscription Renewal Notices

Subscription renewal notices may be sent only to actual subscribers and notices must be numbered, for example, "Second Renewal Notice".

Publishers of the fictitious looseleaf service, "Space Law Patent Developments", are barred from using a renewal notice as a selling device to new subscribers. This practice is employed to trap unsuspecting law book customers into believing *first*, that they are current subscribers to a periodical or looseleaf service and *second*, that unless they act immediately their subscription will lapse. This practice used to be employed with some regularity by a publisher in Massachusetts and one in New Jersey. But it lost them more face than it gained subscribers.

Sales Problems

Publishers also have problems thrust upon them by their own salesmen. In one instance a well-known New Jersey house employed a moonlighting legal secretary who used his law firm stationery on which to forge the firm librarian's signature to a series of looseleaf service subscriptions. The law firm was mystified at the sudden influx of unordered report bulletins. The publisher was adamant in demanding payment for them. Finally signatures were compared and the firm and the publisher realized that they both employed the same miscreant.

A somewhat smaller publishing house in New York employed a salesman who on his own extended by one year the length of a looseleaf service subscription that a law school librarian told him was being cancelled at the end of its term. The salesman simply entered the extended term above the subscriber's signature on the original order blank that he left with the publishers. The librarian's copy, of course, contained no such extension. The publisher was unconvinced of anyone's wrongdoing and the matter of the altered instrument seemed headed for the district attorney's office. It has since been resolved.

Guide Eleven

Disclosures on Publications

The disclosures required to be made on the publications themselves are chiefly designed to answer two basic questions about each publication: (1) who really wrote the book—a recognized authority in the field or a relatively unknown member of the publisher's staff; and (2) was the book sold earlier in a different format or under a different title, e.g. as part of another set of books, as a series of encyclopedia articles or as a law review contribution?

Guide Twelve

Jurisdictional Designations of Publications

This Guide restates with respect to the titles placed on law books themselves the advertising requirements of Guide Eight, namely that the jurisdictional designation of a law book be accurate. The Commission cites as examples, "Maryland Edition" and "Montana

Real Estate Law". Such titles may be used under this rule only if the contents of works bearing those names justify their use.

Guide Thirteen

Disclosures on Supplements

This Guide requires the same kinds of disclosures on law book supplements that Guide Eleven requires on the title pages of the basic volumes. Buyers of law books are entitled to know who really writes the supplements to purchased books.

They want to know what period of time a supplement covers, when it was issued and whether or not it covers the whole set or only a part. Supplements to law books are almost as costly over a period of a few years as the basic works they cover. Moreover, lawyers often buy law books because of the authority and skill of the authors whose names appear on a title page of a book.

Guide Fourteen

Upkeep Service

The term "upkeep service" includes standing orders, continuations and subscriptions. These purchases represent the greatest portion of a lawyer's investment in legal publications. It is also the source of more subscriber complaints about unfair publishing practices than all the other practices combined. This Guide requires publishers (1) to make advance disclosure of what constitutes "basic upkeep service" and (2) to offer to subscribers the choice of subscribing to "basic upkeep" or complete upkeep service. "Basic upkeep" is defined to include "only those parts of upkeep which are absolutely essential and without which a set cannot remain functional".

Publishers frequently include under upkeep (1) virtually the same case annotations that they published in prior supplements to the same work, (2) reprints of federal or state statutes or regulations that lawyers have already purchased in a different form and

(3) full legislative histories of statutes that either are of interest to a limited number of subscribers or are available at lower cost in a different form.

Choice for Lawyers

Guide Fourteen gives lawyers a choice, based on their individual needs, of subscribing to part, all or none of the upkeep service offered by a publisher. The Federal Trade Commission points out that any merchandise mailed in violation of the "basic upkeep" provisions of this Guide may be treated as a gift as provided by the United States Postal Laws. The Guide prohibits the mailing of either a bill or a dunning communication to a recipient of such merchandise.

Replacement volumes to major sets of law books are being fired off as if propelled from massed artillery pieces. Are all those replacements necessary? The decision to issue replacements will, of course, remain in the hands of the publishers. But Guide Fourteen may lessen the financial incentive to publish *unessential* replacements.

Guide Fifteen

Billing Practices

This Guide attempts to assure to a law book buyer full disclosure of precisely what he purchased, what he owes and which of his payments have been applied to particular items on a publisher's invoice or statement. A note to this Guide points out that, "This section does not relieve an industry member of his responsibilities to comply with the Fair Credit Billing Act, 15 U.S.C. 1601, and law book sellers should note with particularity section 161 of that Act dealing with 'Correction of Billing Errors.'"

Computerized billing in the law publishing industry has been accompanied by numerous abuses. Among these are the failure to credit payments, application of payments to the wrong customers, double billing for the same publication, confusion of approval shipments with actual purchases and the employment of fictitious clerks.

Computer prepared statements of many publishers, are usually a few months behind the facts. Prompt paying firms find it disconcerting to be dunned repeatedly for publications on which they owe nothing. One large firm in New York discovered that a law book publisher had established eighteen separate accounts in the names of various of its partners and associates rather than for the firm library and was applying payments willynilly to one or another of those individuals without regard to the appropriateness of their action or the instructions of their customer.

Publishers sometimes continue to bill for services many months after a service has been cancelled and mailing of supplements cut off; or, in the alternative, publishers neglect to cut off mailings despite instructions to do so and continue to send bills for unordered publications. It is the purpose of Guide Fifteen to eliminate these practices.

Guide Sixteen

Added Materials—Germane Subject Matter

Just because a lawyer once ordered a copy of *Churning on Securities Transactions* is no reason to believe that he has thereby agreed to purchase *Chicanery on the Blue Sky Laws.* Yet a few publishers make it a practice not only to expand sets of books with new volumes that contain material only distantly related to the subjects covered by the basic texts, but they bill and mail the new volumes to all the purchasers of the old set.

These publishers apparently gamble that (1) most copies of the new book will slip through unnoticed and will be paid for, (2) the few recipients of the new book who reject it will conscientiously return it and (3) virtually no one will exercise his rights under the unsolicited mailing provisions of federal and state law.

Guide Sixteen defines the issuance of non-germane publications in conjunction with earlier publications as an "unfair trade practice".

Guide Seventeen

Misrepresentation (General)

This "all other" Guideline sums up the practices relating to misrepresentation that many of the earlier Guides cover in greater or lesser detail. It bars both advertising and publication of legal materials that may mislead or deceive purchasers with respect to the "grade, quality, material, size, contents, authorship, editorship, use, value, price, origin, preparation, manufacture, or date of publication or copyright of any industry product or of any supplementation thereto, or the current or up-to-date character thereof, or concerning any service offered in connection therewith, or in any other material respect."

Conclusion

Taken separately and as a whole the Guides may seem like strong medicine for an old-established industry. But its customers and the Federal Trade Commission believe otherwise as evidenced by the adoption of the Guides after nearly six years of investigation and study.

Will the Guides work? Yes, to a limited extent–limited in part to the degree of attention that law book buyers and an overworked Federal Trade Commission pay to their enforcement and publishers pay to their observance. But it cannot be overlooked that even though Upton Sinclair's *The Jungle* spurred the enactment of the Pure Food and Drug Act of 1906, neither that act nor subsequent legislation and regulation have been able to eliminate consumer abuses from the meat packing industry.

Public scrutiny of industry practices requires great effort on the part of many people. To help ensure fair publishing practices at the lowest cost to the publishers and their customers certain minimum steps should be taken:

(1) Lawyers should familiarize themselves with their basic rights under the Guides;

(2) They should notify the publishers and the Federal Trade Commission of any violations of the Guides by first addressing the publishers and then the Commission's Bureau of Consumer Protection, Washington, D.C., 20580.

(3) They should form local and state bar committees on relations with publishers.

(4) They should cooperate also with similar committees of the Association of American Law Schools and the American Association of Law Libraries.

If all these steps are taken, then *Caveat Emptor*–the old law of the marketplace–may at last be repealed. Since it is naive to expect so complete a result, that grand old law will in any event be heavily amended.

CHAPTER 29

LAW LIBRARIANS QUESTION PRACTICES OF BOOK PUBLISHERS

A recent survey by the Committee on Relations with Publishers and Dealers of the American Association of Law Libraries suggests that law book publishers and dealers need to improve their practices on advertising, selling, billing and related activities. Reflecting the concerns of law librarians administering not only practitioners' libraries, but also those of academic, state, court and bar libraries, the thrust of the analysis and recommendations deserves to be seriously reviewed.

Publishers' Catalogs

Commenting on publishers' catalogs, the librarians generally criticized the failure of publishers to provide full bibliographical information, including author and title as listed on the title page, publisher, publication date and edition. A frequently mentioned complaint referred to the lack in the catalogs of price and maintenance costs and of information indicating that the text of the publication was really, in essence, a reprint from another source.

What do law librarians seek additionally in publishers' catalogs? For one, they would welcome information on how much shelf space a book or multi-volume set requires. Also, they want information on whether the title or author has changed from a previous edition. Librarians also seek an overall publisher's policy statement about standing orders; as well as the form, frequency and cost of updating a specific publication.

Is it a casebook, a treatise, a monograph? are similarly considered of interest to librarians. Tell us also, they suggest, what type of an audience is the publication intended for—students, lawyers, lay persons, etc. Law publishers would help considerably if they were to publish detailed catalogs of their publications. Some were faulted for mailing too many duplicates of their catalogs. On the other hand some should update its catalogs more frequently, especially as to list prices of its publications.

Publishers' Representatives

Telephone solicitation of orders for new publications was objected to as well as unexpected drop-in visits by publishers' representatives. Arrange for an appointment in advance and most librarians would be most hospitable to salesmen. On the other hand, mail brochures, flyers, and other promotional materials on new books in advance, and most librarians would be prepared to discuss the purchase of these new books on the telephone.

Librarians welcome information about new law books and other related publications and thus encourage well-informed publishers' representatives visiting them with such information. However, these are business visits, and should be recognized as such. Keep them short and infrequent. Then again, law librarians objected to such visits when the representative was not knowledgeable about the publications being offered for sale. On occasion, it has been noted that some publishers attempt to sell their publications by circumventing their own salesmen, perhaps to avoid paying them their commissions. Other publishers appear to have difficulties in retaining their representatives for sustained periods of time. Too often, new salesmen appear in rapid succession for the same company. When it is the company's policy to sell its publications only through its own sales people or representative, this can create an irritating situation.

Flyers, Mailed Advertising

Law librarians object to being overwhelmed by duplicate flyers and similar promotional materials issued by publishers about their new law books. The receipt of such multiple copies of advertising creates problems in the identification of a new announcement from follow-up advertising. Check mailing lists, they caution publishers, often they have not been revised in years. After one of the authors was appointed law librarian at New York University, he received much promotional literature addressed to the old librarian for almost twenty years thereafter. Her name was "Miss" Mae Meyers. The stenciled address would invariably read "Mr." Mae Meyers.

If publishers insist on extravagant duplication of flyers, at least, law librarians beseech them, provide the same bibliographic information thereon as requested for publishers' catalogs. Above all, indicate date of availability, as well as date of publication or copyright date. Don't be so discreet about the price of the book. Indicate it boldly and conspicuously on the flyer. Don't bury such information on an enclosed card which quickly becomes separated from the flyer. Usually the price is omitted from the flyer to allow it to be used subsequently with another author, title or number of copies. They would prefer to have charges for separate publications itemized.

As to the format of invoices, they appear to come in different sizes—too large, too small, card size, letter size, etc. Uniformity would be desirable so that they can be easily photocopied and expeditiously processed. In this context, it would be preferable if invoices were stated on white paper to allow for clearer, sharper photocopies. It would also be helpful if the total price would appear in the lower right hand corner.

Matching Problem

Invoices that fail to arrive simultaneously with the receipt of the books purchased create problems of matching. Much too often they arrive either weeks before or after the books, and it takes time to identify them correctly. This situation becomes increasingly irritating when several items are billed on the same invoice and cannot be matched quickly with material purchased. As a result, such invoices cannot be expeditiously processed, have to be rechecked, unnecessary claiming occurs and eventually the entire invoice has to be set aside for review. Law librarians would much prefer separate invoices for each shipment of books.

Additional invoicing problems include incorrect totaling, lack of tax exempt information, failure to provide additional copies of the invoice as required by the library's accounting office, and including only invoice numbers on statements. Invoices which are not identified as "reminders" are similarly considered as problems. Invoices submitted by foreign publishers in their own currency obviously create exchange problems in the fluctuating world of dollar finance. This situation, however, was noted as a problem librarians had to bear.

Some law book publishers and dealers indulge in practices which law library administrators not only resent, but which also raise ethical issues.

Foreign Legal Publications

Law Librarians are prepared to accept the problems of dollar conversion arising from the purchase of legal materials in foreign countries, especially in light of the rapidly fluctuating international financial situation. As long as the foreign dealer seeks only an equitable conversion rate for the dollar in the currency of the foreign country involved, law librarians do not object, although at times their institutions could receive the "short end of the stick". When the representative of the foreign publisher, however, uses this situation to attain an unconscionable "windfall" profit, then it should be brought to account.

This issue was raised with a United States based dealer which sells British government documents in the United States. U.S. purchasers of these government documents are being charged at the rate of $3.00 for the (£) pound Sterling. As the prices are listed in (£) pound Sterling, and as the pound (£) Sterling can be purchased currently at around $2.25, a "windfall" profit of approximately 75 cents was being made on every pound (£) Sterling price listed. When questioned as to "whether this is your policy and what other costs are involved in the purchase of British government documents through your organization." The reply received stated:

"We have been charging $3.00 to the (£) pound Sterling for British Government Documents retailing in Britain for in excess of (£) 10.00. However, because the pound is increasing in value in relation to the dollar we will soon be forced to increase our prices".

No other explanation was given for such an outrageous conversion policy. It should be noted in this context, that this United States based dealer is an agent of Her Majesty's Stationery Office (HMSO) and leading British publishers in the United States. It can be assumed that it receives a substantial dealer's discount from those publishers and make a considerable profit alone on the retail prices it charges for their publications. Other reputable British publishers and dealers conscientiously attempt to convert their prices listed in £ pounds Sterling to the prevailing daily conversion rate for dollars—either by actually listing the price on the invoice in dollars to conform to the (£) Sterling rate—or accepting payment in dollars at the conversion rate on the date of the transaction. Under the circumstances, N.Y.U. will necessarily be required to cancel its subscriptions with this dealer and use another dealer who will be more sensitive to this situation.

Differential Pricing

Differential pricing for institutions and individuals is another publishers' practice of increasing concern to law librarians. A number of publishers are now charging institutional libraries higher prices for subscriptions to their journals than they charge for personal subscriptions. Known as differential subscription rates, the higher institutional price often is equivalent to almost double the price imposed on the individual subscriber. This practice was recently reviewed by the Committee on Relations with Publishers and Dealers of the American Association of Law Libraries and the conclusion reached was that it was "unfair" to libraries. Several respondents urged that differential pricing should be discontinued entirely. Others questioned whether libraries should be included as an institution. University librarians believe that such a practice encourages individual subscriptions at the expense of University subscriptions. Smaller libraries contend that the use of their periodicals was no more excessive than that of individual subscribers. One librarian voiced the belief, which is generally accepted, that the practice actually encourages the library to designate an individual to subscribe and then be reimbursed.

Differential pricing reflects a trend with serious implications not only for libraries, but for researchers and publishers as well. First there has been an inordinate growth of new professional journals with highly selective subject interests. This movement toward proliferation of subject journals results in a dependence on a limited audience attraction. Hence they can only be maintained at high subscription rates which only libraries and similar institutional research centers can afford. In essence, these journals can only be published with assurance of a library market. Librarians faced with decreasing budgets especially in purchase value, note that differential pricing not only adversely affects their ability to purchase new significant professional publications, but actually is contrary to the established custom of offering libraries discounts on new publications. Librarians are now confronted with the choice of purchasing new highly priced publications at the expense of not maintaining subscriptions to more highly priced journals.

Format of Material

The Committee on Relations with Publishers of the American Association of Law Libraries also reviewed the format in which legal materials are published. It concluded that updating has become a significant problem for libraries. The most common problems in this context arise from the lack of adequate instructions or the inconsistency of instructions provided by the publisher. Too often, the publisher fails to provide adequate instructions in withdrawing or discarding superseded material. Uncertainty of supplementation complicates cataloging and reference service as does an unannounced discontinuance of updating. Commerce Clearing House was commended as a good example of a publisher providing consistent and clear instructions. The recent pocket parts of the American Law Institute's *Restatement in the Courts*, on the other hand, was pointed to, as an example of inconsistent updating which will cause problems, since researchers will expect an annual supplement as in past years.

Several other examples were brought out in this context. Newsletter updating for loose leaf services creates unnecessary problems since they are not prominently displayed and instructions on discarding are typically not included. Publishers are urged not to send new editions as updating for old editions, without obtaining permission from the library or better still a purchase order for the new edition.

Infrequent updating also is a problem in libraries. The *California Administrative Code* (Microfiche edition) was listed as a poor example in promising weekly updating, whereas the updating is much less infrequent. State codes in general similarly are poorly updated. A good example of updating is the practice of the Banks and Baldwin Co. to update their materials consistently on a monthly basis.

As to the format in which updating should be made available, most law librarians prefer bound volumes with pocket parts, which permits effective updating and reduction in chance of error. Pocket parts facilitate verification of updating, but pocket parts which become too bulky for the volume should be avoided. Supplementary pamphlets are to be discouraged as they can be lost, overlooked, misshelved or checked out separately from the main volume. The spine stickers provided by the California Continuing Education of the Bar were cited as helpful in coping with the problems of separate supplements.

Looseleaf services are defended and criticized by librarians. Many librarians prefer looseleaf services for their reference ease, especially for information which requires frequent updating. Then again, they are easier to photocopy and occupy less shelf space than bound volumes with pocket parts and replacement volumes. On the other hand, loose leaf services do present filing problems particularly when the instructions are not clear. The loose leaf service is not recommended for state codes in research libraries as replaced pages must be retained to verify older or superseded citations. Other problems related to the loose leaf format are 1) pages multiplying and binders which require splitting before a new binder is provided, and 2) transfer binders and supplementary pamphlets issued with the service which can not independently stand up on the shelf. Matthew Bender's updating system was cited by several librarians as undesirable since the cumulative supplements are frequently larger than the original text and the new information is reintegrated into the volume too infrequently.

The variety of updating formats used for administrative codes also creates problems.

Microforms versus Print

Practically every law library in the United States collects microform editions of legal materials. They are preferred over print for older materials, duplicates and back-up copies. They are also of value for materials not available in print. An additional advantage of microforms is the relative speed with which the material is received, such as the United States Supreme Court briefs.

Generally microfiche is preferred over microfilm in that fiche format permits more than one library user to use the material at a time. Fiche can also be used more expeditiously. For long runs of periodicals, newspapers and similar materials which need to be scanned, microfilm is preferred. Microfiche, however, tends to be disadvantageous because of the time needed to file them and the possibility of their being "lost" by misfiling.

Bibliographic Information

Bibliographic information provided by publishers is considered as generally clear and causing few problems. Occasionally confusion results between the title and series due to the format of the title page. Large multi-volume sets are considered as a potential problem when there are multiple authors, editors and titles.

Loose leaf publications generally create bibliographic problems of identification. Determining the copyright date of a loose leaf service is a problem particularly when title pages are periodically replaced. Loose leaf conferences frequently lack title pages, with resultant lack of information of the title and publisher. Transfer binders for loose leaf publications are also difficult to describe for cataloging purposes.

Reprints often do not sufficiently identify the date of publication of the original publication. The Fred Dennis Company reprints were cited as characteristic of the problems involved in identifying whether a reprint or an original work was involved. State Codes with a variety of types of supplementation and government documents also raise problems of bibliographic description.

A number of respondents referred to the practice of publishers of not adequately distinguishing between replacement volumes and new, revised editions. Obviously this practice not only creates cataloging problems but also problems of whether to retain or discard a volume.

Librarians also are concerned when in the process of updating, the publisher changes the size of the publication or the title page. Publishers are urged to provide adequate information about supplementation along with the updating volume, especially when cumulative supplements are involved.

CHAPTER 30

LAW LIBRARIES' CRISIS: RISING COSTS FOR BOOKS AND JOURNALS

Escalating prices for journals and books are creating a crisis in library service which must inevitably affect availability of research resources in this country. Publishers attribute the accelerating prices to higher costs of production and the "information explosion." Knowledgeable observers of this trend, however, although agreeing with the general explanation not only recognize other contributing factors, but also draw alarming conclusions about its effects on scholarly research in law, as well as other disciplines.

The following figures emphasize the problem library administrators are facing. Based on traditional price indexes which appeared in the July 1977 issue of the *Library Journal* and the February, 1977 issue of the *Law Library Journal*, it is apparent that the average price of a law periodical in the period for 1967–69 was $8.71. In 1976–77, the average price was $17.36, an increase of 99.3 percent. The average price of a law serial service in 1967–69 was $60.87; in 1976–77 it was $126.74, an increase of 108.2 percent. In 1972–73, there were 144 volumes published in the National Reporter System, and the cost to acquire these was $2,071.50. In 1976–77, there were 174 volumes published in the National Reporter System, and the cost to acquire them was $3,287.50; an increase of 58 percent.

In other fields of concern to scholarly researchers in law, the *Library Journal* concludes from an analysis of more than 3,000 titles, from 1967–69 *United States Periodicals* generally increased

[1] I am indebted to Professor Bardie Wolfe, Law Librarian, University of Tennessee for these figures.

from $8.66 a title to $24.59 a title. Thus, with an index of 100 established for the period 1967–69, the index for 1977 was 283.9. *Business and Economics* rose from $7.54 in 1967–69 to $18.62 for 1977 with an index of 246.0. *Chemistry and Physics* from $24.48 in 1967–69, to $93.76 with an index of 383.0 in 1977. *Medicine* rose from $19.38 in 1967–69 to $51.31 in 1977 with an index of 264.8. *Mathematics, Botany, Geology and General Science* from $15.30 in 1967–69 to $47.13 in 1977, for an index of 308.0. *Political Science* from $6.18 in 1967–69 to $14.83 in 1977, for an index of 240. *Psychology* rose from $14.55 in 1967–69 to $31.74 in 1977, or an index of 218.1. *Sociology and Anthropology* rose from $6.11 in 1967–69 to $19.68 in 1977, with an index of 322.1.

United States Serial Services in 1977, based on an analysis of 1,432 titles, had an average price of $142.27 or an increase of 9.9 percent over last year's price of $129.47. The increase was the largest since 1970, when it was 18.9 percent over the 1967–69 base. In 1977, *Science and Technology* services show the greatest percentage of increase over last year—15.1 percent. *Business* services increased by 12.5 percent and *Law Services* by 11.8 percent.

Professor Wolfe projects that continuation costs for *legal periodical titles* amounting to a total cost of $3,975.44 in 1977 should increase to $6.731.88 in 1982 or an increase of 69.33 percent over the 99.3 percent increase from 1967–69 to 1977. *Law Serial Services* will increase from $27,766.06 in 1977 to $56,436.81 in 1982, an increase of 103.3 percent over an increase of 108.2 percent from 1967–69 to 1977. *U.S. Government Document Social Services* will rise from $12,827.52 in 1977 to $23,435.84, in 1982, or 82.69 percent over an increase of 242.3 percent from 1967–69 to 1977.

Scientific journals, particularly, have sharply risen in subscription price. For example, *Inorganica Chemica Acta* (Elsevier Sequoia) cost $26 in 1970. By 1975 the price had gone to $235, an increase of 840 percent. *Biochemica et Biophysica Acta (Springer)* cost $495 in 1970 and $1,551 in 1975, up 213 percent. In the *Humanities and Social Sciences, The Survey of Current Business* (U.S. Office of Business Economics) rose in price from $9 in 1970 to $48 in 1975, an increase of 433 percent. *Historical Abstracts* (ABC Clio) rose from $151 in 1970 to $495 in 1975, a 228 percent increase.

Librarians point to reasons other than inflation for the phenomenal increase in journal and book prices. They particularly are sensitive to a recent practice of some publishers charging institutional libraries higher prices for subscriptions to their journals than they charge for personal subscriptions. Known as differential subscription rates, the higher institutional price invariably approaches almost double the price imposed on the personal subscriber.

For example, the National Lawyers Guild recently published an *Immigration Defense Manual* "designed specifically to assist practitioners in the defense of non-U.S. citizens currently living in the United States, as well as persons attempting to enter the United States." The price for Guild members is $35; for non-Guild members $45 and for libraries, $55. The Haworth Press is charging $18 for individual subscriptions to the *Journal of Divorce* and $35 to libraries. The Plenum Publishing Corporation, publishes *Law and Human Behavior* in collaboration with the American Psychology-Law Society and with the assistance of students at the University of Virginia Law School. The Institutional subscription price is $35; the personal subscription is $20. (Incidentally, personal subscribers must certify that the subscription is being paid personally and not be an institution and that the use of the journal will be limited personally to the subscriber).

Differential pricing of library acquisitions reflects a trend with serious implications not only for libraries, but for researchers and publishers as well. First, there has been an inordinate growth of new professional journals with highly selective subject interests. This movement toward proliferation of subject journals obviously results in a dependence on a limited audience attraction. Hence, they can only be maintained at high subscription rates which only libraries and similar institutional research centers can afford. Hopeful of obtaining some additional income, the publishers of these new journals offer a reduced price to "researchers" and similar "professionals" in the field. In essence, however, these journals can only be published with an assurance of a library market.

In this context, economists William J. Baumol and Junusz A. Ordoner submit an interesting and valid theory—that scientific journals merely serve to promote the professional image of authors of the articles featured therein, and that the articles play a limited role in communicating scholarly knowledge. "The fact is", they maintain, "that a growing proportion of scientific journals have no individual subscribers, but are sold almost exclusively to libraries, and that a very high proportion of those journals are rarely, if ever, requested by readers. This suggests that many journals provide services primarily not to readers but to the authors of the articles for whom publication brings professional certification, career advancement and personal gratification."[2]

Librarians, faced with significantly decreasing budgets, especially in purchase value, resent differential pricing. They particularly note that this policy is contrary to a long established tradition of offering libraries discounts on new publications. For example, the Practising Law Institute announced that effective Sept. 1, 1977, it will offer to federal, state, country, municipal, law school and bar association libraries a 25 percent discount on all its publications. This has always been the accepted practice and, as a result, differential pricing compounded with accelerating prices is exacerbating publisher-librarian relationships to such an extent that it is becoming a matter of public record.

On May 3, 1977, the Conference of Law School Library Directors of Greater New York, consisting of the head library administrators of Brooklyn Law School, Columbia University School of Law, Cardozo School of Law, Fordham University School of Law, Hofstra University School of Law, New York Law School, New York University School of Law, Rutgers University School of Law, Seton Hall University School of Law and St. John's University School of Law, formally resolved:

> "To object strongly to the practice of certain publishers of charging libraries substantially more than individuals for subscriptions to their publications, because this practice adversely affects the development of law school library collections and the quality of legal education."

The law librarian of New York University recently had occasion to express his dissatisfaction with the differential pricing practice

---

[2]Quoted in De Gennaro, Escalating Journal Prices, American Libraries, February 1977, p. 69.

of two publishers. He stressed that they had much to gain by having their publications available in a law library, because reference thereto will stimulate interest in the publication to the point where the publisher will gain much in the way of increased sales. He also indicated that differential pricing can only result in a confrontation with librarians which certainly will not serve the publisher's best interests.

He added the following warning—which reflects the thinking of many law librarians and which suggests the real crisis which must soon arise in library service.

> "I am hereby putting you on notice that it is my policy not to purchase for this law library any of your publications similarly priced (differential pricing) unless there be a compelling demand for them here. I can assure you this goes against the grain. I have always prided myself in anticipating any demand in the library for new publications. Now the situation will be reversed. For the record, I have had no demand as yet for any of your new publications.
>
> I think you are ill-advised in pursuing this policy. Your justification for it that library copies are accessible to more readers than to private subscribers is contrary to a long tradition of publishers seeking such accessibility with the realization that it could stimulate more sales to private subscribers in the future. It certainly also goes against the established policy of many publishers in granting library discounts to libraries."

Articles are appearing in library publications on escalating library prices for books and journals which publishers should seriously review in their own interests. The director of the University of Pennsylvania libraries, Dr. Richard De Gennarro, has issued a clarion call to librarians "to fight back".[3] Reminding librarians that the library market is easy to expand and exploit, he aptly notes:

> "Long ago, publishers discovered that librarians could not resist subscribing to new journals and could only with great difficulty bring themselves to reevaluate and cancel a subscrip-

[3]American Libraries, February 1977.

tion once it was entered. Moreover, publishers know that library serials records and accounting systems are overburdened and inflexible and that librarians are reluctant therefor to tamper unnecessarily with their subscription lists and standing orders. In the old days, before the affluent '60's, the situation remained in equilibrium because libraries were poor and publishers (who were considered to be part of the scholarly enterprise) knew it. Publishers kept both the prices and the number of journals in line with the demand and financial resources of libraries and personal subscribers."

The affluent 60's changed this situation. With expanding library budgets, publishers, especially those in specialized areas, looked to library subscriptions to generate greater profits. But now depression economy has hit library budgets along with the reduction of candidates for advanced degrees at the university level. Librarians are now confronted with the choice of purchasing new highly-priced publications at the expense of not maintaining subscriptions to older, established publications or vice-versa.

Librarians can ill afford to cope with the accelerating increase of periodical subscription prices. Many librarians are having their budgets reduced and the obvious result must be a very severe screening as to the value of a publication before it is purchased. With the increase in prices, the selection process will inevitably result in the discontinuance of subscriptions to many established periodicals. This policy will create a crisis in the sense that the purchase of publications at increased rates will deny the opportunity to maintain other required publications.

Librarians are also taking note of studies, such as the one conducted at the University of Pittsburgh which concludes that academic libraries are spending too much on books and journals rarely used by the academic community. For example, of the materials added to the Pittsburgh Libraries in 1969, only 56 percent actually circulated. Also that many expensively priced journals are not used sufficiently to warrant their purchase. (Engineering students use only 9 percent of journals bought for them; physics students only 37 percent; life sciences and psychology, 22 percent.) Newer publications are used most–80 percent for titles less than five years old. Thus, it is poor library administration to maintain expensive journal subscriptions at the expense of reducing book purchases.

Library studies of particular interest today in light of escalating journal and book prices, are those arguing that approximately 80 percent of library research can be resolved by access to 20 percent of the library collection; that no amount of pooling of resources by library "systems" actually saves money; and that the only real savings in libraries can occur from reduction of staff and services.

CHAPTER 31

LAW OFFICE LIBRARY ECONOMICS

Can any lawyer afford to run a law office and not know where his law book money goes? Is there a workable system for analyzing the costs—and the research value—of law books? The three major problems are (1) the cost of legal treatise supplements, (2) unsolicited mailings and (3) dual reporting of court reports.

Treatise Supplements

The authors of looseleaf treatises ordinarily do not update their own works. Typically this work falls to members of the publishers' editorial staffs whose names do not carry the stamp of authority of a Wigmore or Corbin or Loss. The explanation that "contributing editors" perform this role usually appears on the supplemental title pages of those publications. But it is not the custom for publishers to disclose this fact when the books are purchased.

What does the subscriber receive for his upkeep payments if he does not command the expert attention of the original authors? In most cases he receives packets of case annotations, notices of new regulations and amendments to statutes. They cover matters that a lawyer might expect to verify for himself. Sometimes one finds minor changes in the text of a treatise in these supplements. Another drawback to looseleaf treatise upkeep is that much of the same material is reprinted in supplement after supplement—with law book buyers apparently paying over again for substantially the same material.

The other side of the coin is that supplements do alert lawyers to changes that they might otherwise overlook. Each lawyer must decide for himself whether this "alertness" service performed by relatively unknown researchers is worth $50 or $100 or more a year for each looseleaf treatise in his office.

Proposed Solution

Owners of looseleaf sets might consider dividing them into two categories: (1) those landmark works in rapidly changing fields of law for which almost any fair charge for upkeep would be worth paying and (2) all the other looseleaf treatises in their libraries.

Three works at least belong in the first category: *Collier on Bankruptcy*, *Moore's Federal Practice*, and *Rabkin & Johnson*. Individual practice needs may enlarge or contract the list and these titles are given as examples only. These works should be kept current.

The most sensible step for handling works in the second category is (1) to continue buying the best looseleaf treatises that one's practice requires and (2) to instruct the publishers to furnish no looseleaf supplementation except entire replacement volumes that may be sent on approval.

This will cut upkeep costs and simplify bookkeeping. Indeed, what with delivery of special rulings supplements, pamphlet editions, packets of confusingly numbered looseleaf releases and replacement volumes, it is no simple matter to learn how much one actually pays each year to maintain service on a particular looseleaf legal treatise. With the addition of "piggyback" or add-on volumes that bear little relation to the sets they are intended to complement, it is even harder to keep trace of law book expenses.

Owners of *American Jurisprudence 2d Series* may be surprised to learn that along with the annual pocket supplements the publishers supply two new replacement volumes covering federal income tax law (volumes 33 and 34) each year. The cost of these two books alone is approximately $50 a year. Those lawyers who rely on an encyclopedia for federal tax information may find this a supportable expense. But those who use looseleaf services and the Code probably believe otherwise. A note to the publishers can quickly eliminate this expense.

Law offices do not operate under the accreditation rules of the Association of American Law Schools[1] and are free to renew up-

---

[1] Association of American Law Schools. Executive Committee Rules sec. 8.1(b), as amended through January 5, 1980.

keep services selectively, based on quality and usefulness of the service. These rules appear to require the law schools to subscribe to all upkeep services even when it is apparent that it is wasteful to do so. But, in fact, law school librarians may and should use their own discretion.

Unsolicited Sales

Lawyers receive some five classes of legal publications from the publishers.

(1) Books and services they have ordered;
(2) Those they never ordered;
(3) Supplements to books they own, but on which they have not subscribed to upkeep service;
(4) Books they never ordered but which are similar in format or subject matter to books they do own; and
(5) Additional copies of books or services of which they want one copy only.

There is no requirement of law that any of these books, except those in class 1, be paid for or even returned to the senders. Both under federal statute[2] and New York law[3] unsolicited books are deemed to be gifts. California, New Jersey, Pennsylvania and most other states have enacted similar laws.[4] Whether out of caution or a sense of fairness, most lawyers prefer to return these unwanted unsolicited publications to the publishers. But what happens in practice is that once these books have been stamped as his employer's property, it is the rare clerk who will admit that he has been bamboozled into accepting them. As a result these kinds of

---

[2] 39 U.S.C. § 3009 (mailing of unordered merchandise).

[3] New York General Business Law. sec. 396(2).

[4] California Civil Code. sec. 15.845; New Jersey Statutes Annotated. Title 46. sec. 30A-1. and Purdon's Pennsylvania Statutes Annotated. Title 70, sec. 2001. The American Bar Association Journal published a complete list of these "unsolicited mailing" laws for 45 states in its February, 1975, issue at 196.

mistakes are buried and bills are paid on behalf of lawyers–unnecessarily–year after year. In large offices these mistakes can run to a thousand or several thousand dollars a year.

Distinguishing Books

It is a simple matter to distinguish Class 1 books (those that a lawyer has ordered) from Class 2 books (those he has not ordered). The problems arise in "3," "4" and "5" and a few illustrations are in order.

Class 3. This presents a twofold problem. First, the publishers' form of purchase order for a new looseleaf treatise usually contains a provision for the perpetual flow of upkeep services–until cancelled. But it is easier to induce the flood than to stem it. One lawyer told me, "Cancelling an upkeep service is like playing The Sorcerer's Apprentice." Book buyers who want no upkeep service or who want only selective service must inform the sellers of that fact–explicitly and repeatedly. Second, many publishers do not draw a line between supplements, replacement volumes and new editions. They assume that a lawyer who buys one edition of a book will want to purchase it in all its subsequent editions. The lawyer customer may find himself paying for a great many publications that he never bargained for simply because he bought a book years earlier.

Class 4. Some publishers regularly mail their "piggyback" or add-on works to the owners of basic sets of law books. *McKinney's Procedural Forms* are published in a format so similar to *McKinney's Consolidated Laws* that many experienced researchers mistakenly believe that the *Forms* are the products of the New York State Legislature and therefore purchase them. The publication, *New York Civil Practice, Matrimonial Actions*, Volumes 11A and 11B by Zelt, Edwards and Schwartz is confusingly similar to the basic established set, *New York Civil Practice* by Weinstein, Korn and Miller.

Class 5. The shipment of second and third copies of the same books, when only one copy has been ordered, is an endless source of expense and annoyance to lawyers. When shipments arrive a few days or weeks apart, it is almost inevitable that careless clerks will stamp them and approve the bills.

"It has become a game of wits," one law librarian said recently, "in which the publishers try to trap law book buyers and the librarians try to avoid the snares." Lawyers who busy themselves in the practice of law and don't employ librarians are even fairer game. They can avoid most of the pitfalls discussed in this column by adopting a careful screening system for the acceptance of books and supplements and for the approval of bills.

Dual Reporting Systems

A few years ago it cost only $65 a year to purchase all of New York's court reports, both bound volumes and advance sheets, in the official edition. The state's taxpayers apparently picked up the rest of the cost under a state contract with the publishers. This is a bargain that most New York lawyers wish they could avoid. They give three reasons why they regard the official edition as an albatross.

First, the official edition is less convenient to use than the *New York Supplement, 2d Series*, since it does not employ West Publishing Company's Key Number system. Most lawyers rely exclusively on *"New York Supp."* for their New York research.

Second, since by statute[5] and by court rule[6] the official edition of each case must be cited in court papers, lawyers are forced to spend time locating the volume and page numbers in the official edition that correspond to their *New York Supplement* references. This might be accomplished with *Shepard's* or with the *Blue* and *White* books were it not for the additional requirement to cite the precise pages on which quoted matter appears in the official edition.

Third, its costs upward of $1.50 a volume per year to store books in high rent office buildings. As a result the modest $65 annual tab for the official edition of New York State court reports

---

[5] New York Civil Practice Law and Rules. sec. 5229(e).

[6] E.g., Supreme Court Rules. 1st Dept., sec. 600.10 (11): 2d Dept., sec. 670.17(b), and Appellate Term of the 2d Dept., sec. 731.2.

suddenly jumps to over $1,000 a year in offices that maintain full runs of *Miscellaneous, Appellate Division* and *New York Reports*.

The solution: Repeal both the CPLR requirement to cite the official edition and the court rules that implement it. This step would save the lawyers and the state of New York many thousands of dollars a year.

In reversing an alimony order on grounds other than flaws in citation, a California court suggested the usefulness of a single nationwide court reporting system, "Our labors in the consideration of this appeal would have been immeasurably lightened had counsel, in citing cases from other jurisdictions in their briefs, given us parallel and unofficial citations as well as the official state citations."[7] In short dual reporting is a nationwide nuisance.

An interesting sidelight to this matter is that a former printer of the official New York reports and a well established law book publishing house litigated their respective rights to the State contract for printing the official reports over a period of several years. A judicial history of their dispute is set forth below.[8] Repeal of the dual reporting requirements, of course, would long since have rendered the issues in that controversy moot.

In these various ways, then, lawyers can begin to reduce the cost of legal research in their offices. The most important step—with respect to law book purchasing—is to establish a "failsafe" book-monitoring and bill-paying system tailored to the needs of each law office. It would eliminate expenditures on most unwanted books and supplements.

---

[7] Tomkins v. Tomkins. 89 Cal. App. 2d 243. 200 P. 2d 821, 828 (Dist. Ct. App., 1948).

[8] Matter of Lawyers Co-op v. Flavin, 69 Misc. 2d 493. 331 N.Y. S. 2d 159 (Sup. Ct., Albany Cty., 1971), aff'd 39 A.D. 2d 616. 332 N.Y.S. 2d 616 (3d Dept., 1972), motion for leave to appeal denied. 30 N.Y. 2d 488, 335 N.Y.S. 2d 1027, 287 N.E. 2d 398 (1972); Williams Press, Inc., v. Flavin. 74 Misc. 2d 1082. 346 N.Y.S. 2d 897 (Sup. Ct., Albany Cty., 1973). aff'd 44 A.D. 2d 634. 353 N.Y.S. 2d 970. (3d Dept., 1974).

B: SERVICE TO LAWYERS

CHAPTER 32

LAW-OFFICE LIBRARIANS PAVE WAY FOR LAWYERS

"I would rather lose two of my partners than give up my librarian," remarked a veteran litigation lawyer in a downtown firm the other day.

"My partners cower in the corner when our talking albatross alights," a member of a midtown partnership recently said of his librarian.

Between these points are some 2,000 law-office librarians. Their management and research feats prepare the way for lawyers in several hundred firms and corporate legal departments in New York and in major cities across the country.

Each year a pool of newcomers complete courses in law librarianship and legal research at Columbia University's School of Library Service. They are eager to join the profession. This chapter describes some of the services that lawyers may expect and indeed should demand of librarians. It will also explain to lawyers who have never employed a librarian why they may need one, how much it may cost and where they may find one.

Library Service for Practitioners

The typical law office should demand three kinds of service from its librarian or library staff: (A) Library maintenance, (B) Reference assistance and (C) Future planning.

Library Maintenance. This is how the managing partner of one firm summed up life in his office for a prospective librarian: "We have thousands of books, clients who ask impossible questions and a staff of lawyers who we expect can produce instant answers." We need someone who first of all can keep the books so systematically that we can always find them when we need them, he pointed out. Moreover, the library is a showplace for clients. We want to keep it that way. It is quiet, it is orderly and it is a convenient place for study.

Second, we expect the librarian—and staff—to keep our looseleaf services up-to-date, our advance sheets handy and our periodical subscriptions current. We cannot risk losing a client's trademark because the librarian failed to renew our subscription to the Trademark Section of the *Official Gazette* or a clerk routed it to the wrong lawyer.

Third, our librarian coordinates all our book purchases—on the advice of our own specialists. We don't need three lawyers buying the same book at firm expense. We expect the librarian to control that. He drafts an annual budget and sticks pretty close to it. He keeps track of all bills and approves all payments. So much for housekeeping.

Reference Assistance. The last thing a law office needs is a librarian who tells lawyers how to practice. The first requirement is that the librarian be able to answer factual questions, quickly and accurately. A good librarian is an encyclopedist. He can find a process for making rubber tires as quickly as he can name the public holidays in Massachusetts or Louisiana. Of course, he should be able to find a case, a statute or a regulation, even though the name given is wrong or twisted or ambiguous as so frequently it is.

The librarian compiles legislative histories, prepares bibliographies and alerts interested lawyers to new publications and new developments in their own fields. But his chief virtue is his mastery of branches of learning outside the law.

He knows where to borrow or buy almost any publication, legal or nonlegal. This comes from learning the resources of other libraries, trade associations, book stores and other repositories of publications in his city and state.

Finally, the smart librarian is a teacher. He can explain to new associates the intricacies of the *Code of Federal Regulations* and the *Federal Register*. He can show them how to use the *CCH*

Trade Regulation Reporter, unravel the mysteries of *ALR* indexing and help them find cases in the *New York Law Journal*.

Future Planning. The expansion of the various reporter sets requires constant shifting in crowded quarters. The librarian prepares for library expansion by storing little used sets, by weeding the collection and by alerting his employers well in advance that more space will be needed—and when.

As law office practice grows, its libraries change. No firm in New York had its own library computer eight years ago. Today scores of firms have installed Mead Data's "Lexis" system and a few have also installed "Westlaw". This form of legal research is catching on throughout the country. Whether or not microforms—film and microfiche—are here to stay is an open question. The alert librarian can best evaluate the available readers, the reader-printers and the quality of film and then determine what microforms, if any, to purchase.

Equally important is the range of information data banks that facilitate fact gathering.

When to Hire a Librarian

The law office librarian is the original paralegal assistant. This post has been filled in the large firms for over seventy-five years, long before the term "paralegal" entered the language. Today a firm hires a librarian as soon as the library tasks described above consume more lawyer time than it would cost if a librarian performed them. In addition, and far more important, lawyers hire a librarian simply to avoid the delays and constant frustrations caused by amateur management of their libraries. In either case a competent librarian more than repays a firm for the salary expended.

What to Pay and Where to Find a Librarian

This year's library school graduates can expect upwards of $14,000 a year. Those near the top of the class and those with special talents—or because they offer useful business or library experience—command more to start. Experienced law office librarians earn $20,000, $25,000 a year and higher depending on their ability and experience. In New York the current ceiling is over $50,000. One remarkable attribute to a large number of the older librarians is their stability in their positions. The dean of New York law office librarians was Albert Borner, Sr., who was the librarian at Milbank, Tweed, Hadley & McCloy for almost forty years.

Where They Are

They are probably not making many "Borners" these days. But an excellent source for beginning librarians especially in May and June each year is the Columbia University School of Library Service. Some of their recent graduates have just completed courses in Legal Research and Law Librarianship. Address the Placement Director, or the Assistant Dean, 516 Butler Library Building, New York, N.Y. 10027. Telephone (212) 280-2293.

The classified column "Librarian Openings" in the *New York Times* Book Review section each Sunday is widely read by librarians in the New York area. Finally, the American Association of Law Librarians maintains a vigorous placement service.

CHAPTER 33

LIBRARIAN'S PARTICIPATION IN RESEARCH ACTIVITIES

Along with rent and salaries, a major item of overhead in many law offices often is the cost of maintaining a law library. Although the main purpose of a law office library should be to aid in the solution of legal problems, many firms fail to take advantage of the library's full potential in this respect.

It is the purpose of this chapter to describe the role that a professional law librarian plays in upgrading reference service in a law firm library by applying managerial concepts of librarianship to organization, collection development and research.

"The first thing about our legal system that strikes a European or Latin American lawyer is its sheer bulk." This statement by the late Chief Justice of New Jersey, Arthur T. Vanderbilt, aptly reflects the emerging problems in legal research facing the American lawyer today.

40,000 Appellate Opinions

There was a time around the turn of the Seventeenth Century, when the English lawyer had to contend with a mere 5,000 reported English cases. Today, the American lawyer can consult millions of judicial opinions, increasing at the annual rate of around 40,000 published American appellate opinions alone. There is also a huge mass of federal and state legislation supplemented annually by hundreds of massive volumes of codes aggregating about 500,000 pages by themselves.

In addition, tens of thousands of legal periodicals, government documents, administrative law and regulations (federal and state) foreign law, international law, topical looseleaf services and the literature of the social sciences have not only become indispensable to the legal researcher but have also brought with them attendant problems in their selection and use.

The increasing relevancy of economic, sociological and physiological data in legal research along with the information explosion are of concern to lawyers, especially in connection with the adequacy of their research. As a result, in solving legal problems such as those involving land use, zoning, taxation, labor or antitrust legislation, the American lawyer must now consider the applicability of interdisciplinary research outside the traditional, structured legal patterns he is familiar with.

By reason of this development, law in the books has not only become a formidable problem for lawyers to understand, but the mere process of identifying, locating and referring to these diverse materials has added considerably to the cost of maintaining law offices.

Few Professionals

Although the number of law office libraries is continually increasing in the United States, many of them are not administered by professional librarians. Some of course do maintain professional law librarians and supporting staffs. Many others, however, depend on one of the partners, or a library committee to supervise the work of a "library staff" of clerical employees—others look to their legal secretaries or some clerk to keep "order" in the firm's law library. In the main, however, because office libraries are limited in size, it is not usual to find a professional librarian servicing the firm's lawyers. In a sense, this is a paradox—as lawyers have a tradition of having been helped by professional law librarians while they attended law school.

The reluctance of practitioners to obtain a librarian in their own office is understandable. Being small in number themselves, they believe they can assume the responsibility of selecting and organizing their law collection. Overall direction of the library is usually in the hands of a designated member of the firm. But let us face the logistics of this situation. Every lawyer in the organization is responsible primarily for the contribution he can make to the firm's operations. His importance and position will depend on his ability as a lawyer and not as a librarian. He cannot devote all the time necessary to managing a library properly. As a result, the inexorable growth of reports, statutes and digests alone eventually causes an overflow of shelving into corridors, offices and even in the wash rooms!

Wasted Time

Looseleaf services are not properly filed. Books are kept in the various lawyer's offices in accordance with their special interests. Invariably, unnecessary duplication arises—because books cannot be located and records of their location, if any, become meaningless. The charge-out-system, if any, is so casual, it offers little help in ascertaining who has borrowed a book or pamphlet. The important pamphlets which arrive in the library in profusion from trade associations, federal, state and local government bodies and otherwise—on current legislative developments and other important aspects of the firm's business—are not organized for use because of the time needed to do so—or more so for lack of a plan. Valuable time is wasted just locating materials required for a specific purpose.

Law firms have much to gain by considering their library not as a mere collection of books but rather as an organized information legal center. For example, if the occasion arises for a lawyer to refer to the non-legal materials mentioned before—how does he first identify them, and then how can he locate them? This process, obviously involves more than merely referring to books or other materials which might be in the law firm's library. There is also the need to determine which would be considered the best authority to cite to a court.

In investigating the materials on a subject such as environmental and pollution control, how can the average lawyer obtain bibliographical control over the vast literature of the field, especially apposite non-legal documents, which he could use in developing his legal argument? And if he is fortunate enough or astute enough to learn about this literature, how can he locate them for serious review?

In this context, it is suggested that the law firm's library, if it is to provide the proper back up service to its lawyers, should take on the status of an information center—rather than a mere collection of books. This can only be properly administered and serviced by a professional librarian.

Information Specialist

Too many lawyers fail to recognize that a professional librarian can be of significant assistance to them as an information specialist coordinating the research in the office. This librarian can accomplish much more than merely being a reference assistant and bibliographer. He can organize the library for efficient and economical use. He can suggest sources of information the lawyer can use—even more significantly, he is trained to locate such sources when they are unknown to him.

He can alert the firm's members to legislative developments of special interest to them and prepare legislative histories of statutes the firm considers important in its practice. He can organize the firm's memoranda of law, appellate briefs, opinion letters, and legal forms, so that they can be easily retrieved for reference by the firm's lawyers working on similar subjects. He can do so by analyzing them, and classifying them under subject headings which will reflect the special interests of the firm. At times law librarians have even prepared index-digests of the points of law analyzed in these documents.

The librarian can organize this information center in such a way that every subject of interest to the firm can be retrieved upon demand. The librarian can also analyze special journals, daily newspapers, the Federal Register, special pamphlets, The Congressional Record, federal, state and local government reports and descriptive literature, keep a record of administrative regulations and also circulate newsletters of office bulletins of current developments in specialized fields.

The librarian can in addition maintain proper records of books purchased and circulated as well as catalogue them for reference.

Lawyer's Aide

In the New York State Bar Journal for August 1968 one of the writers summarized the librarian's role in a law firm: He can find a citation or reference, suggest sources of information, verify and translate citations, interpret abbreviations, Shepardize citations, assemble materials for specific projects, prepare bibliographies, explain the use of legal materials in the library, arrange for the borrowing of materials on interlibrary loans from other libraries after identifying these materials as being of value to the lawyer in his research. He will possess judgment in anticipating the research needs of lawyers and resourcefulness in analyzing legal materials and recognizing their relevance to a particular subject or problem.

The librarian can skillfully use indices, conversion tables, tables of cases, citations and other reference tools. He will be of significant help to the lawyer because of his thorough familiarity with legal and non-legal bibliography, as well as of many important non-legal reference sources. He will know where to find the answers to questions involving business, medicine, history, the social sciences, economics, the "new technology."

He will maintain a workable system of recording questions and answers so that there would be no need to later repeat the same research. All that is necessary to enlist the librarian in the service of the inquiring lawyer is a brief session in which the lawyer can outline the problem, establish his goals and limitations and then unleash the librarian in the quest for appropriate materials. In other words, the pattern of research is set by the lawyers in the firm. The librarian can suggest and assist in the research. The final decision as to interpretation of the law is the lawyer's, of course. The librarian and the lawyer make a wonderful team in research.

The late Senator George Wharton Pepper, who was a leading member of the Philadelphia Bar, expressed this well when he spoke on *Lawyers and Law Books* (49 Law Library Journal 438-39 [1965]).

> "The amount of time that is wasted by the active practitioner in doing research which could better have been done by the guide who could steer him to those things which he had to take into consideration to do justice to his case. The amount of time wasted in that way is incomparably more of a waste than would be compensated for by the salary of a law librarian in a big office... who could instruct the man in the firm who was assigned to look up a certain subject, of where he might go with

profit to find what he seeks... the way in which I have spent hours of time in trying to find something which I could have been directed to in a moment by somebody who knew the ground, come before me as a nightmare as I look back and think of the wasted days and weeks and years. A librarian can do his associates in the office far, far more good than it is possible to accomplish when they are left to their own devices."

CHAPTER 34

A GUIDE TO HIRING A LAW FIRM'S FIRST LIBRARIAN

"How can we be sure that we need a librarian?" That is the question most frequently asked by managing partners of medium-sized firms and by the general counsel in corporate legal departments. They are cautious about spending money without the assurance of direct monetary return. This chapter discusses the ways that a librarian relieves a lawyer of work that he would otherwise have to perform for himself and analyzes the financial savings that a librarian effects.

Most of the time that a librarian saves lawyers—and the savings range from ten to twenty hours a week—lawyers can use for billable work. The caveat is (1) that the work is there to be done and (2) that lawyers are efficient enough to devote the time saved to client matters.

The managing partner in one of New York's top firms reported that his firm increased the number of its library employees from one librarian to a staff of twelve over a period of some eight years.[1] The implication is that hardheaded management hires new associates—or new librarians—when it is persuaded that they pay their own way and not before.

---

[1] His was the opening talk at a PLI Seminar on "The Private Law Firm Library" held in New York on July 28 and 29, 1975. The course handbook distributed by PLI bears the same title. Three other publications that give details about the librarian's role in the law office are (a) "The Law Office Library" in The Lawyer's Handbook, Revised edition. Chicago, ABA, 1975; (b) "Law Office Library Needs: Books–Equipment–People", 24 The Business Lawyer 511–518 (1969). It is outdated with respect to costs which have been rising about 10 percent a year; and (c) "Law Office Librarians Pave Way for Lawyers," New York Law Journal, May 13, 1975, page 5.

The chief difference is that a new associate's return to the firm is *direct* and measurable in *hours billed*, while the librarian's contribution is usually *indirect* and measurable in *hours saved*—for others to bill.

A Hiring Formula

A law office can afford to hire a librarian whenever the value of the hours that the librarian saves all lawyers in the office approximates the librarian's salary plus fringe benefits, social security and related costs. That will vary from about six to ten hours a week depending, of course, on the lawyers' average hourly rate.

For example, it will pay a twenty-five-lawyer office to hire a librarian if he saves those lawyers only fourteen minutes each or a total of six and one-quarter hours a week during a forty-six-week year, where the lawyers' average rate is $75 an hour. That totals $20,125. This assumes a librarian's salary of $15,000 plus other costs of about one-third more, or a total of $20,000. Such an arrangement leaves a wide margin for profit since the librarian can actually save lawyers between ten and twenty hours a week rather than a mere six and one-quarter hours.

Discussed below are the three main phases of a librarian's contribution to the law office economy: (1) Library Management, (2) Information Services and (3) Research Services.

Library Management

The chief management components that result in a smooth-running library are these:

(1) Books and services are ordered and paid for with a minimum of fuss and with virtually all steps handled by the librarian. This includes record-keeping, correspondence with publishers, claims for missing issues and the resolution of doublebilling problems—a frequent occurrence in the law book publishing industry. It also involves the sensible routing of publishers' circulars to interested lawyers and discussions with book salesmen. Only the decision to purchase expensive publications need

be left to a library partner. *Estimated Time Saved: Three Hours a Week.*

(2) The book collection is logically arranged and systematically controlled so that the time spent in hunting for missing publications is kept to a minimum. Moreover, it is the librarian or his assistants—not the lawyers—who comb the offices searching for missing books. *Estimated Time Saved: Three Hours a Week.*

(3) The looseleaf services and looseleaf treatises are filed promptly and accurately, errors are quickly corrected, codes and digests are properly supplemented and advance sheets and other serial publications are routed and retrieved by the librarian or his staff with no lawyer effort expended. The library holdings are cataloged and kept to date. *Estimated Time Saved: Two Hours a Week.*

The time saved in library management alone totals eight hours.

Information Services

The trained librarian can save a firm an additional eight hours a week in answering questions about both legal and non-legal matters and in suggesting, locating and borrowing publications on any subject under the sun.

Consider for example the number of cases a lawyer attempts to locate in which he knows the name of only one party—and that is misspelled—or in which he has been told only a few facts about the case or its issues. A trained librarian can often find cases in these circumstances faster than a lawyer can do it.

Consider the statutes and regulations. Ask a librarian to locate the commercial bribery statutes in McKinney's or the Federal Trade Commission rules governing the television repair industry in CFR or in the CCH Trade Regulation Reporter or any provision of law at all in the maze of material published as the New York City Charter and Administrative Code Annotated. The librarian would probably win a speed test on these questions as well. Moreover, the librarian who uses these research tools regularly can instruct lawyers in their use or refresh the memories of lawyers who may last have handled some of these books in law school. *Estimated Time Saved: Three Hours a Week.*

Getting the answers to the myriad of factual questions that arise in a twenty-five-man firm can save at least an additional two hours a week. A librarian's use of *Martindale-Hubbell* to obtain information about lawyers' background, the identity of county seats, the names of court clerks and the various state forms of acknowledgement will save most of that time. Add to that the librarian's ability to obtain information from corporation directories, government manuals and a host of other reference tools that he is trained to use. *Estimated Time Saved: Two Hours a Week.*

The ability to suggest, locate and borrow publications to supplement the firm's collection is one of the librarian's most valuable assets. Each major city in the United States—and particularly New York—has endless research resources that lawyers know little about and librarians are accustomed to exploit. New York remains the country's publishing center. Located there are the major foundations, trade associations and numerous graduate schools—each with its own library. There is a network of librarians—special, business, financial and legal—in all major cities who exchange ideas and lend books. *Estimated Time Saved: Three Hours a Week.*

Estimated time saved through all information services totals an additional eight hours.

Research Services

Librarians vary in research ability no less than do lawyers. By striking a fair average, I estimate that a librarian's research assistance will save a law firm 6 hours a week as follows:

(1) Legislative services that advise a lawyer of the current status of any federal or state bill, alert him to legislative developments on a systematic basis and compile legislative histories of enacted measures for him. This entails organizing and analyzing a large collection of legislative documents—a time-consuming task that lawyers are likely to postpone until shortly before a trial, when many of the papers may be out of print or difficult to obtain. *Estimated Time Saved: Two Hours a Week.*

(2) Litigation services that assist lawyers by collecting background data about the matters in litigation: people, corporations, government agencies, inventions, economic and scientific subjects; sifting through newspapers and magazines; compiling bibliographies; cite-checking briefs and memoranda of law. *Estimated Time Saved: Two Hours a Week.*

(3) The sophisticated indexing of memoranda of law and other office-generated documents will help eliminate duplicative work in any firm. The typical memorandum of law is likely to distil useful information that may have consumed many hours or even weeks in preparation. It is sensible to guard against repeating this work and to make these papers available to all lawyers in the office. *Estimated Time Saved: Two Hours a Week.*

Total time saved through research services: six hours.

Total of all time saved by the Librarian in Management, Information and Research Services Combined: *Twenty-Two Hours a Week.*

The breakeven point for hiring a librarian is his saving of about six hours a week for the firm. This figure aside, the professional law librarian makes a permanent place for himself in the law office in additional ways. He helps keep the library shipshape. He alerts lawyers to new development and new publications and he is immediately responsive to lawyer's needs. He is a member of a profession that practices continuing law library education through graduate library school courses and through the national and local library associations. That "he" embraces both "he" and "she" can be attested to by generations of practitioners who have availed themselves of the services of librarians of both sexes.

CHAPTER 35

LAWYERS AND THEIR LIBRARIANS—IS COEXISTENCE POSSIBLE?

"Our library is a mess and the librarian *can't* seem to do a thing about it."—Managing partner of a major firm, January, 1978.

"Our library is a mess and the managing partner *won't* do a thing about it." —Librarian in a major firm, February, 1978.

Not in the past twenty years have so many lawyers and librarians—without prompting—complained about one another's shortcomings. "I would institute a malpractice suit against our librarian tomorrow," said one practitioner recently, "if the Supreme Court hadn't already dismissed a teacher malpractice action for want of precedent." In that case, the teacher's students could neither tell time nor read traffic signs.

Several librarians have echoed that lawyer's sentiments—but in reverse. What has gone wrong? Is there a solution? This chapter highlights both sides of this strange dilemma.

Space Problems

The proliferation of court reports, the rapid expansion of law offices and the inflated cost of office space have exacerbated space problems. Law books are once again being dispersed along corridors and in storerooms because library shelving has reached its capacity. This has occurred in spanking new and in elegantly remodeled quarters and in firms that had supposedly solved this problem only a few years ago. Library tables are once again piled with yesterday's reserved books, leaving no room for study today.

In many cases the sheer number of lawyers in an office is greater than its management can train, house or cope with. Consequently the appeals of librarians for more space have gone unheeded.

Lawyers need little excuse to stay away from libraries altogether—especially from crowded or noisy ones, or libraries from which books are often missing or in which the users are put down or made to appear stupid.

First result. Work that should be done in the library gets done in lawyers' offices—if it is done at all.

Second result. Librarians' space requests are met with the response, "Nobody uses our library. We don't need more space." A telephone booth would soon be large enough to house the few library users if that attitude prevailed.

Third result. Librarians whose advice is ignored stop giving any. They eventually lose touch with law office needs altogether.

Fourth result. Managing or library partners and their librarians view the firm as if from separate planets. They no longer talk to each other.

'Book' Collections

What is a "book"? In the law office any publication useful in the firm's practice should be treated as a book and placed in the library. Traditional "volumes" aside, this includes any scrap of paper—preliminary memorandum, brief, summary of a telephone conversation, inventory of lawyer skills or computer blip. Some privately drafted forms might be excepted.

Librarians who have been accustomed to handling mere "books," periodicals and newspapers are either intrigued or perturbed by the new forms in which printed and nonprint legal matter appear.

There is hope for those who are (1) intrigued or (2) perturbed. For those who reject the new technology out of hand there is a problem. Management has accepted it. Coordination of legal resources goes on apace. If law librarians do not participate in this work members of some other profession will.

First result. The realm of librarians begins to shrink.

Second result. The problems librarians are called on to handle are reduced in number and scope.

Third result. Librarian complacency, indifference and boredom grow.

Fourth result. Again, managing partners or library partners and their librarians no longer talk to each other.

Library Service

"I would like to sentence our librarian to a year of Sundays listening to Dr. Norman Vincent Peale preach his sermon on 'Enthusiasm.'" So spoke a member of the New York Bar a few weeks ago. He added quickly, "I get all the books I need. But there is less than evenhanded service to associates. Reminds me a little of Uriah Heep."

Responded a librarian, "He needs the sermon more than I do." Then the librarian really got wound up. "Some of the associates treat me and my staff like Colson's grandmother—doormats," he said. "Half the time they fail to sign for the books they take and then they complain when we can't find them. They rifle sheets from the looseleaf services. They grind out cigarettes in the carpet, spill coffee on the tables and steal the ashtrays and bookends. Uriah Heeps they are with the partners though."

Thus have members of two noble professions fallen prey to their own frustrations. The firms have grown too fast—without systematic planning or co-ordination. **The results**: inadequate library quarters, lessened demand for service and perfect missing of the minds.

Some Remedies

Law librarians were the original "paralegal" assistants before that term was coined. For many years a band of dedicated librarians performed unique services for lawyers. Earlier chapters of this book detail some of those lawyer-supporting feats. Suddenly a few of those dedicated librarians are in disfavor. Some have failed to grow with their jobs. Others have been ignored or bypassed. In a few cases the firms have simply failed to utilize one of their most valuable resources right at hand—their own librarians.

First remedy. Let each managing or library partner set down his library expectations—as though the world were perfect and his librarian a genius—and then double those expectations. Work gives the greatest satisfaction when one's intellectual capacity is stretched to the limit. A car simply runs better on all cylinders than on one or two.

Second remedy. Let each librarian describe his own role—as it is and as it might be if Dr. Pangloss were running the world.

Third remedy. Exchange the statements. Read, meet and discuss them.

Fourth remedy. Begin to narrow the distance between one another's expectations. If continuing library education is needed it should be encouraged. If further education is pointless that fact should be recognized and dealt with. After all a librarian—no less than a managing partner or administrator—who is a success in a fifty-lawyer firm may become a disaster when the firm reaches 150 lawyers.

Fifth remedy. Begin to recognize and reward superior library performance. It may be useful in some offices to bill library research on client matters in the same way that paralegal services are billed.

Libraries are in ferment because the offices they serve are in ferment. The discussions between management and librarians will crystalize the issues and help restore the law office library to a key position in support of law practice.

CHAPTER 36

LAW LIBRARIAN PLACEMENT SERVICES

"...like she's some hired girl we keep around the house but that we don't like very much."—From Act One of "Our Town."

With those words Dr. Gibbs chides his teenage baseball-playing son for letting his mother chop the fire wood. If they also apply to any firm and its librarian then that firm has reached one of three impasses. Under "Impasse A" the firm's practice may have outdistanced the librarian's intellectual development. Under "Impasse B" the firm and its administrators are simply out of touch with law office librarian skills and attainments. Under "C" the firm has probably failed to explain in what ways it expects the library to support the practice of the office. None is fatal. All are unnecessary.

The purpose of this chapter is to make certain that the words Dr. Gibbs spoke do not apply in any office. The chapter lists some of the placement services that help find suitable librarians for lawyers. It details the functions that law office librarians perform. Finally, it discusses some of the steps that lawyers can take to integrate the work of librarians with office practice and help maintain employment stability on library staffs.

Placement Services

To overcome "Impasse A" a checklist of three kinds of librarian placement services is set forth below: (1) professional associations, (2) newspaper advertising and (3) library schools.

Professional Associations

The American Association of Law Libraries has a placement committee which maintains a job placement center at the headquarters hotel during the association's annual convention. Other associations are:

Law Library Association of Greater New York (LLAGNY): Helene A. Weatherhill, c/o Sullivan & Cromwell, 125 Broad Street, New York, N.Y. 10004. Telephone: 212-558-3778.

Greater Philadelphia Law Library Association: Teresa N. Clarkson, c/o Duane, Morris & Heckscher, 16th floor, 100 South Broad Street, Philadelphia, Pa., 19110. Telephone: 215-854-6248.

Southern California Law Library Association: Laura M. Strain, c/o Latham & Watkins, 55 South Flower Street, Los Angeles, Calif. 90071. Telephone: 213-485-1234.

The New York group has the largest number of members and its placement chairman regularly discusses openings with prospective employers and job-seekers. Like her counterparts in the other cities she is a one-person clearing agency for law office library jobs in New York. There are similar regional associations in Boston, Chicago, San Francisco and several other cities. The local bar librarians can put people in touch with the placement chairmen.

Newspaper Advertising

The New York Times publishes librarian openings in the classified columns of its Sunday Book Section. These columns are read by librarians all over the country—whether law trained or law library-employed or not.

The Association of American Law Libraries publishes its quarterly *President's Newsletter* that circulates among and is read by almost every law librarian in the country. Contact Larry Wenger, Placement Chairman, University of Virginia Law Library, Charlottesville, Va 22901. Telephone: (804) 924-3694.

This free service lists professional librarian openings throughout the country.

Library Schools

The following three library schools maintain placement services of varying degrees of effectiveness. The best of them are Columbia's in New York and Drexel's in Philadelphia.

(1) Columbia University School of Library Service Placement Office, Butler Library Building, New York, N.Y. 10027. Richard Troiano is Placement Director. Telephone: 212-280-2291 or 2293. Columbia offers two courses that for the past eight or ten years have concentrated on law office library needs. The School's graduates continue to hold a large number of law office librarian posts in the New York metropolitan area.

(2) Drexel University School of Library and Information Science, Thirty-third and Market Streets, Philadelphia, Pa., 15104. Contact Jane Spivak, Placement Director or Assistant Dean Catherine Ohler. Telephone: 215-895-2478. The single Drexel law library course is modeled after the Columbia courses and provides many of the Philadelphia law offices with library personnel.

(3) Pratt Institute Graduate School of Library and Information Sciences, Brooklyn, N.Y. 11205. Theresa Maylone is in charge. In her absence contact Assistant Dean Rhoda Garoogian. Telephone: 212-636-3710 or 3802.

II. Librarian Functions

To eliminate "Impasse B"—under which lawyers are unaware of their librarians' capabilities—job descriptions of three law office library positions are set out below: those of head librarian, assistant librarian and library clerk.

Librarian—Job Description

(1) Supervises the library and its staff in carrying out the firm's or company's directions as to management of the library; this includes its physical arrangement and appearance, reference services, distribution of tasks, and the selection, training and evaluation of the library assistants.

(2) Responds to reference questions at various levels of difficulty, e.g.

(a) Find the text of Section 7 of the Clayton Act (1) when the bill was introduced; (2) when the law was enacted in 1914 and (3) just prior to the 1950 amendments.

(b) What are the various components of the West *Federal Digest* system? Does the green set replace, partially replace or merely supplement the red set? What if anything does the blue set replace? In which set or sets are current pocket parts filled?

(c) Find all the statements Mayor Beam made about New York City's debt securities during 1976.

(3) Instructs lawyers in techniques of legal research, e.g. in the use and the finding, indexing and updating features of the various looseleaf services and of the *Federal Register* and *Code of Federal Regulations*.

(4) Compiles legislative histories of Federal and New York statutes (to the extent that any documents are published).

(5) Selects new books with the assistance and approval of appropriate lawyers of the firm or corporate legal department; reads all pertinent book announcements and reviews, e.g. all reviews published in the ABA Section journals, viz., *The Business Lawyer, The Antitrust Lawyer* and *The Tax Lawyer*.

(6) Alerts lawyers to new developments in their own fields, through a library bulletin, reprinting and circulating tables of contents of current law reviews and by personal contacts.

(7) Keeps abreast of new information and retrieval systems of interest to the firm and of changes in the "Lexis" libraries.

(8) Drafts and implements the library budget.

(9) Participates in professional library association activities.

(10) When needed performs the duties of the assistant librarian or library clerk.

Assistant Librarian—Job Description

(1) Answers telephone requests.

(2) Responds to simple reference questions, e.g.

(a) Find the Clayton Act in *USCA*.

(b) What is the county seat of Kent County, Michigan?

(c) What was the exchange rate for the West German mark yesterday?

(d) When did the United States Supreme Court grant certiorari in *U.S. v. K*? Has a date been set for argument?

(e) Who is Chairman of the Federal Trade Commission? When did he assume office?

(3) Untangles and corrects filing errors in the various looseleaf services and also files the more difficult services;

(4) Handles library bills and resolves problems with the publishers.

(5) Catalogs the new treatises and monographs.

(6) When needed performs the duties of the library clerk and of the librarian in his or her absence.

Library Clerk—Job Description

(1) Delivers and shelves books.

(2) Maintains circulation records; searches for missing books and retrieves routed advance sheets.

(3) "Reads" the book shelves to correct errors or inconsistencies in shelving books.

(4) Opens and sorts the mail as follows:

(a) Books, law reviews, advance sheets and the like;

(b) Invoices and correspondence relating to them;

(c) Book and periodical advertisements;

(d) All other mail.

(5) Records receipt of items in "4a" above and routes appropriate publications in accordance with firm instructions.

(6) Claims, that is, writes or calls for missing issues of report letters or journals from the publishers.

(7) Answers the telephone in the absence of the librarian or assistant.

(8) Picks up books and other publications outside the office in the absence of available firm or company messengers.

Employment Stability

The first step in overcoming "Impasse C"—the failure of librarian and lawyer to appreciate what the other is doing and why—is to establish a direct line of authority between an interested library partner or senior counsel and the librarian. A library committee can never substitute for a boss. But by its inaction or indifference it can persuade the library that the "office" does not care how the library is run.

Second, a monthly or bi-monthly meeting between that partner or counsel and the librarian will help resolve problems and explain what important new matters the librarian can become involved in and why. The librarian in turn can explain how the library can contribute to the effective completion of that work.

Finally, librarians are professional employees and like lawyers—a number of law office librarians belong to both professions—they should be encouraged to participate in professional association activities.

CHAPTER 37

BILLING CLIENTS FOR LIBRARY SERVICE

"I have five briefs to cite-check today," the librarian in a litigation-centered midtown firm told me recently. The firm's managing partner defended the practice of assigning this work to the library when I questioned him about it later in the day and added, "He doesn't know it yet, but a sixth brief is on the way." Down the street the managing partner of another firm had just reported, "Our library is a source of heavy expense to us–unreimbursed overhead–and we intend to keep that expense to a minimum."

The truth is that a private law firm library has a potential earning power that few firms think to tap. One's librarian may be the source not only of information and service but of income too.

The issue of whether to tap that earning power by billing clients for library services was debated at the annual meeting of the American Association of Law Libraries held in June 1978 in Rochester, New York. Los Angeles law librarian Laura Strain urged the affirmative before an audience of some 200 law office librarians and easily carried the day. One of the writers chaired the session and took the negative because no one else could be found to speak publicly against it.

Billing Advantages

Billing can produce unanticipated income for a firm as shown in the ten kinds of library activities set out in the schedule below. This is its prime advantage according to economy-minded managers.

But library billing may earn subtler and more valuable dividends as well. It will draw the librarian and the staff into the mainstream of the firm's practice. It will give the librarians a sense of participating in the court battles and the corporate transactions from which they have traditionally been insulated. This sense of belonging is of immense morale value. It may even tip the scales when votes are counted in any forthcoming union organization drive.

Higher income to the firm and higher employee morale sum up the advantages.

Billing Disadvantages

The added income from library billing may seem of minor importance to a firm whose annual billing reaches several million dollars a year. Yet no firm would voluntarily reject $25,000 or $30,000 a year in additional income. That sum may be only a fraction of the librarian's potential billings.

However, some clients may view this practice as a plain nuisance—particularly if they are already concerned over the high legal fees they are currently paying. Moreover, they can point out that, "Library services were always free in the past. What has changed to force this surcharge on us? It is as if we registered at our accustomed hotel and were suddenly told to pay for the soap, the towels and the fresh sheets. We would resent that."

This is partly a spurious argument if the billing is for *new* kinds of service not previously performed by librarians and if it is done expressly for a single client. Clients would actually pay two or three times as much if lawyers were to perform any of the ten kinds of functions recommended below for librarians. Indeed lawyers do perform many of them but frequently do not bill in full for time spent on such routine work as checking citations or consulting *Shepard's Citations*.

Another disadvantage is that it will be a nuisance to those librarians who are unaccustomed to accounting for their time—even though they would be expected to account only for the billable portions of it.

It has been urged also that librarians will neglect the routine work of running the library in favor of requests to work on income-producing projects.

Income-Producing Schedule

The ten illustrations below typify the kinds of income-producing matters in which trained law office librarians are equipped to engage. A firm whose librarian and staff participate in half of these matters can recover a fair share of its annual library investment. Readers may want to compute their own firm scores by answering "Yes" or "No" to the statement—Our librarian:

(1) Cite-checks briefs and memoranda of law.
Yes__ No__

(2) Checks the foregoing documents against the appropriate *Shepard's Citations.*
Yes__ No__

(3) Alerts lawyers to published comments about lawsuits in progress or about merger negotiations and other corporate events that affect clients by searching newspapers, periodicals and government documents, e.g., congressional hearings—with or without the aid of a computer.
Yes__ No__

(4) Compiles security prices for use in SEC filings or in estate valuation.
Yes__ No__

(5) Analyzes prospectuses, proxy statements and stock exchange listing applications for language used in connection with particular kinds of corporate proposals or announcements, e.g. cumulative voting, finders' fees, insider advantages and executive or director compensation or indemnity plans.
Yes__ No__

(6) Compiles bibliographies of books, articles or documents on subjects directly related to particular client matters.
Yes__ No__

(7) On any problem new to the office, e.g., interpreting covenants not to compete in connection with a lawsuit or the drafting of a model employment agreement, the librarian collects the basic publications that a lawyer needs to solve the problem. These might include the appropriate looseleaf services (antitrust and labor), national and state legal encyclopedia articles, law review writings, chapters in treatises (viz., *Callman*

on Unfair Competition and Trademarks), the pertinent West digest volumes with Key Numbers indicated, and any memoranda of law already produced in the office. With this background—or some part of it—a lawyer is equipped to solve the problem or to employ "Lexis" or "Westlaw" more profitably in trying to resolve it.

Yes__ No__

(8) Identifies and locates corporate forms and precedents in connection with particular client matters.

Yes__ No__

(9) Reviews for their factual accuracy proposed Congressional testimony or other statements that clients may make or that partners may make on their behalf.

Yes__ No__

(10) If law trained, handles occasional legal problems for clients, e.g., on immigration, trademark and divorce matters, in fields of law to which no associate is regularly assigned; and if not law trained, responds directly to simple factual inquiries of clients, e.g., by providing the publishers of a magazine with background data for its feature stories.

Yes__ No__

Summary

The issue of billing clients for library services has not been prejudiced. There are pitfalls to overcome whether a firm does or does not follow the practice. In some situations the practice may boomerang and it will have to be abandoned. In others it may accomplish all that has been urged for it. Firms and clients differ in outlook. Librarians differ among themselves in skills and motivation. What will work in one firm may fail in another. The experience gained from billing for paralegal services may be of some value when applied to librarians. But the two kinds of work are vastly different. This column only raises questions on the subject. Each firm will want to answer them for itself.

CHAPTER 38

PITFALLS AND PROBLEMS OF CONSTRUCTING A LAW LIBRARY

"What is the Legal Department afraid of—that a book may fall on someone?", the insurance vice-president of a national transportation company asked.

"No, but a floor might, or at least your lawyers believe that it might," was the reply.

This conversation took place during arrangements for a $2 million indemnity insurance policy that the company required before library planning might start.

The floor load is the greatest peril—the *grand mal*—in law library planning. But inattention or indifference to any detail will determine whether lesser perils—the *petits maux*—may also lay the library low. A successful library is the combined effort of informed lawyers, the office manager, librarian and library consultant on one hand and the architect and contractor on the other. The failure of even one of these people to listen may defeat the efforts of all the others.

This chapter highlights the construction problems that typically confront law office library planners. In addition to (1) location and floor area, it covers (2) the floor load; (3) shelving specifications; (4) furniture; and (5) lighting, carpeting and window treatment.

Location, Floor Area

Ideally, the library should abut the offices of its heaviest and most frequent users. These are usually litigation lawyers. But every department in the office deserves attention when the location is set. Otherwise it will be difficult to overcome the pressure to maintain separate satellite libraries.

Tax and labor libraries are the most common branches. But force of personality as often as usefulness to the firm will determine if there are to be others. Many firms maintain thriving corporate or business libraries. A Seattle firm has an admiralty branch. A Boston firm probably holds the national record for the number of its branch libraries—five in all: tax, labor, municipal, real estate and a combined probate and trust satellite.

The advantages of a single central library are exemplified in a large New York firm that has recently merged its tax branch into the main library. All groups in that firm have easy access to the entire collection. That firm's library occupies less space today than a main library and various branches would require. Moreover, it has a solid record of exemplary service to lawyers. Indeed no strong department will give up the advantage of quick library access outside or across the hall from its offices without at least the promise of superior service.

Satellite libraries have serious drawbacks. The chief ones are that (1) satellites are expensive to maintain and difficult to control; (2) they usually offer poor service if they offer any and (3) they further split the firm into independent compartments making it harder, for example, for corporate, pension, tax and litigation lawyers to consult or have any familiarity with one another's book collections.

Even though there is no optimum-size area for a law office library, experience shows at least that lawyers will use a spacious, well-arranged library and they will stay away from a cramped one. The number of lawyers, library assistants and number of volumes in the collection—projected into some future year—will provide a fair gauge of space needs. But the nature of individual firm practice and lawyers' styles cannot be overlooked.

Floor Load

Next to file departments the library has the greatest concentration of "dead weight" in the office. Older buildings such as the

Fidelity Building in Philadelphia and 15 Broad Street and 120 Broadway in New York can usually support the heaviest loads. They are built like fortresses. Floors in buildings erected after World War II may require reinforcement. In such buildings aisles may have to be widened between ranges of book shelves and concentration of files of documents sharply limited. Advice on this subject is the joint responsibility of architects and building engineers.

Engineering standards for libraries call for a weight-bearing capacity of 175 pounds per square foot for floors containing book stacks; 250 pounds per square foot for compact shelving.

Rental agents for the newer buildings have justified higher rents in part on grounds that the floors are hung from outside piers and therefore they have fewer inside columns and more unimpeded usable space. Yet at the same time they fail to advise prospective law firm tenants that their files and book collections may present a floor load peril.

Solution: Learn the load limit first; sign the lease later.

Shelving Specifications

The use to which book shelving is to be put should determine its dimensions. The typical volume of court reports measures about 10½ inches in height by less than 7½ inches in depth. Oversize volumes constitute a minor proportion of law firm book collections.

Yet in recent months architects and contractors have ignored these facts and attempted to install book shelving in several law office libraries that simply did not meet the needs of those libraries. In one office more than 10,000 volumes had to be removed from shelves while the contractor cut down the bases of each unit so that the promised book capacity could be reached. This occurred directly after moving day—to the firm's inconvenience, reshelving expense and annoyance.

In another firm the shelves are so much deeper than the books are wide that the books give the raggedy appearance of raw recruits in a badly disciplined regiment. The amount of steel wasted might be used to build one fifth again as many shelving units.

To accommodate the requisite number of volumes in one of these firms the contractor virtually eliminated the base of each unit altogether. Lawyers must get down on hands and knees to reach the bottom shelf.

The same architect and contractor recently submitted a shelving proposal for approval by a different firm that combined all the foregoing errors—previously pointed out to them—and added some new ones as well.

Solution: (1) Determine shelving requirements precisely; (2) insist on detailed shop drawings before approving any shelving proposal; (3) inspect two or three installations that the proposed architect designed and the contractor completed; and (4) question the office manager and librarian about the performance of that work and their satisfaction with it.

Furniture

In order to meet the seating requirements for lawyers in a Boston firm, the architect proposed that four lawyers be placed at a table six feet long and three feet wide. It must be recognized that even though lawyers are neither larger nor smaller than people in other occupations, they tend to spread their books and papers as far as they can reach. A table that is eight or nine feet long and four or five feet wide will seat four lawyer-readers. A smaller table will drive them back to their rooms. Similarly, a single study carrel should be at least four feet wide.

In another firm the consultant recommended a commodious study table but failed to realize that its scale would overpower the small room in which it would be placed.

Chairs are more than a matter of comfort and taste. The high-slung swivel chairs are a peril to lawyers who study with their feet higher than their heads. Upholstered library chairs wear out quickly. The old wooden "bank of England" chairs are reasonably comfortable and will last 40 or 50 years.

In any situation, tall lawyers will bump their knees while short lawyers cannot reach the floor and must let their feet dangle in the air.

Solution: Supply a few seat cushions—as is done at Penn—and offer a few adjustable chairs for the out-size or under-size lawyers.

Lighting, Carpeting and Window Treatment

Lighting fixtures are satisfactory if they cast an even light of sufficient intensity on all book shelves and table surfaces—without shadows. In one newly installed library in New York, one can read the volume numbers of books on the top two or three shelves and on the second shelf from the bottom. But the middle and bottom shelves are unevenly lit and it is hard to distinguish volume 358 from 385, for example. In the library whose bottom shelves sit at or below carpet level one cannot pick out the right volume without stooping to near ground level.

Similar problems exist unless lighting fixtures above study tables, carrels and file cabinets are correctly placed. The problem is further compounded by the use of book racks—an essential feature in most libraries—that may themselves, but need not, cast a shadow on the table surfaces.

It is no economy to install carpeting in only part of the library. Carpeting will help muffle the noise of footsteps, conversations, typewriters and telephones. Other measures may have to be taken to eliminate noise altogether.

The best carpeting for office library use is a mixture of tough wool fibres and the perfect coloring has been discussed before. It combines most of the following shades: coffee, mustard, bread crumbs, butter, catsup, pickle juice, Kleenex and tobacco ashes.

Solution: Keep food and drink out of the library and establish snack areas in your office at a distance from the library.

Finally, in a windowed library draperies are an advantage over venetian blinds. The latter are invariably raised or lowered to uneven levels and look unsightly. Draperies can be adjusted to keep out the sun's direct rays without disturbing the library appearance. Moreover, like carpeting draperies muffle sound.

CHAPTER 39

FACTORS FOR PLANNING A LIBRARY: COST, SPACE, CONTENTS, USER COMFORT

"Good grief, it's my butcher," gasped the librarian as she fainted beneath a shelf full of Federal Reporters. Enroute to Beekman Downtown Hospital in New York, the ambulance attendant heard her mutter, "When I ask for a three-inch steak, he gives me four; when I ask for an eight-pound roast, I get a ten."

What brought on this delusion? The librarian had just met the firm's new architect, shelving contractor and decorator. This trio works the law firms by day, but one of them the butcher shop at night. Because the librarian's condition is "grave", and her doctors forbid visitors, she was unable to report which is which. But this column sets out all the clues needed for full identification.

Planning a law office library involves four practical matters; where, what, who and how much. That is (A) where should it be located; (B) what publications, furnishings and equipment will be placed in it; (C) who will use it and work in it; and (D) how much will it cost?

Given the good will, wisdom, professional experience and selflessness of the planners, the resulting library can become the pride of the office. Without these qualities it may become the office scourge. This chapter is a tale chiefly of two cities, Boston and New York, and of joint library planning by insiders (librarians, lawyers and office administrators) and outsiders (architects, contractors, decorators and consultants).

Library Location

To achieve maximum use the library should be located adjacent to the offices of its heaviest users in one compact rectangle. This is easy to accomplish in a six-man firm. In a 60-lawyer office and in firms or departments with 100 or more attorneys it becomes increasingly difficult to achieve.

Noise created by foot traffic, telephones, typewriters and staff conversations forced one New York firm to gerrymander its library, separating the study tables and main book collection from the library staff by a long corridor. This slows service to lawyers. But it restores the quiet atmosphere of a professional library.

Lawyers gravitate towards a windowed library and tend to avoid an inside one. They prefer a single level, without steps. Considerations of space persuaded one New York firm to install a three-tier library in the inner core of a building's two storeys several years ago. Recently, that firm was forced to establish an overflow basement library—some 40 floors and two elevator trips from its main library.

A Boston firm rejected the proposed optimum library location last year to avoid relocation of that firm's file department at a cost of about $35,000. An alternative location was chosen—also a desirable one—and that sum was saved.

As to satellite libraries—discussed below under "Political Considerations"—the fewer the better. They tend to fragment large firms into private compartments creating serious divisions, both social and professional.

Contents of Libraries

A library's contents reflect the interests of the clients and usually include five elements: (1) intellectual resources, that is, the books, serials and documents; (2) its storage facilities—the book stacks and file cabinets; (3) lawyers study facilities; (4) machines and other fixtures; and (5) a staff work area, including a librarian's office.

(1) Space is a prime concern. In general, the intellectual resources, book shelves and aisles between occupy about half a

library's total area; the study tables and carrels about three-eighths; and the staff work area when combined with the micro-form, "Lexis" and other equipment the remaining eighth.

(2) The more compactly the books are stored, the more room may be left for study—or for further expansion. This is partly a function of good planning and partly one imposed by floor load limits.

(3) The choice between enclosed study carrels or tables at windows is less important than the provisions for adequate study space in the first place. It is adequate if each space is no smaller than four feet wide. In a Boston firm provisions have been made for group consultation in a "Battle Room" at one end of the library—invaluable both in research done in preparation for trial and in daily postmortems after court recesses.

(4) Individually the new machines occupy only a few square feet each. But as microforms become more popular—and more books are replaced with film—offices will require additional reader-printers. A single "Lexis" terminal requires a private carrel and should be so placed that two lawyers may use it together. With the advent of "Lockheed", "Dialog" and other outside computer information services comes the need for more machine space in the library.

(5) The staff work area should be contiguous and not split. The librarian should have visual control over the staff and most of the library.

A large Boston firm that complained of the inadequate size of its 1,000 square foot library decided to double the library size. The firm based its decision on a benchmark whose own inadequacies had been apparent for many years. The result: after some discussion it was agreed to triple, rather than double, the size of the library and to continue to rely on some corridor shelving, while retaining three separate branch libraries as well.

Resistance to providing adequate staff work space could be overcome if office planners realized that library assistants need as much work space as any other group of employees—and probably more. If this space is not provided the library staff tends to encroach on lawyers' study facilities and in effect to drive lawyers back to their room.

It is easy to forget that a private library is a vital organ in the practice of law. Lawyers use it. Staff members work in it. Paralegal assistants frequently spend many hours in it. Law firms tend to rely on it for "offices" for summer associates. Messengers and clerks sometimes spend their lunch hours in it and others use it as a convenient passageway between two ends of the floor. The best planned libraries include study space for one-fifth of the lawyers in the office (including paralegal users) and a suitable work space for each staff member. The other uses mentioned are best discouraged.

The cost of library space is the same as for file rooms, lunchrooms and lawyers' offices. It runs from eight up to as much as $60 a square foot. Taking $20 a foot as a low average, the 1,000 square foot library costs $20,000 a year in rent; the 5,000 square foot library, $100,000 annually. With 100 lawyers, that comes to a charge of $1,000 each.

Proposals that librarians bill clients for their own research services are gradually being accepted. This practice may help lessen the objections to providing adequate law office study facilities for lawyers and sufficient work space for librarians.

Tell a man that he has made an arithmetical, or even a legal mistake, and he will usually accept your proof without rancor. But tell him that he has no taste and he is likely to resent it. Such differences are at the bottom of many disputes among architects, decorators and their lawyer clients.

One solution is for everybody concerned to visit several law office libraries, both new and old, in order to test their own reactions to various styles in library design. What architects, contractors and decorators fail to accept is that once they finish their work, their lawyer clients must live with it. What lawyers overlook is that the architects, contractors and decorators regard each piece of work as their own artistic property. They resist tampering with its architectural integrity.

When our librarian fainted at the sight of one member of this trio and gasped, "Good grief it's my butcher," she was referring both to aesthetic and practical matters in which they (or one of them) had failed other clients: the ugly and uneven distribution of book shelves, the disastrous newspaper cabinet (see below), the narrow aisles between file cabinets, the failure to follow simple directions as to depth of shelves and height of shelving units.

After all, is there a real difference between a butcher who supplies a 10-pound roast and an architect who specifies a 10-inch shelf—when they were directed to furnish eight pounds in one instance and an eight-inch-deep shelf in the other? The librarian saw none.

Political Considerations

Office politics enter the library picture in two ways: (1) the location of the library and the maintenance of branch or satellite libraries and (2) the choice of architects and decorators.

Library Installations. The librarian can give the best advice about location by keeping records of the volume of library use by departments, for example, among litigation, corporate, commercial and tax lawyers. But it requires the power and tact of a presiding partner or corporate general counsel to overcome the demands for separate branch libraries—whenever those demands are ill conceived—of tax, labor or other specialist groups within the office.

Choice of Architects and Decorators. The best way to make a choice among architects or decorators is to examine their past work. Equally important are interviews with lawyers, office managers and particularly with librarians who have worked with them. It is one thing to get a job done right after a dozen blunders. It is another to get it right the first time. Looking without talking cannot determine which happened in a particular case.

"Bank of England Chair." The Bank of England Chair is the most comfortable chair ever designed for long term library study. It supports the back, it relaxes the arms and fits one's legs and the contour of the rest of the body. And it lasts a lifetime.

Those in the University of Pennsylvania Law School library were purchased in the early 1920's. They have no upholstery to wear out though cushions may be placed on them. They come with and without a swivel platform.

Decorators usually object to them because they are oldfashioned looking. A New York decorator recently selected some 30 upholstered chairs at a cost of about $450 each or a total of $13,500 to be placed in an office library. Lawyers in that firm preferred the "Bank of England" chairs at about $100 each. The librarian and library consultant urged that the cheaper chairs be purchased and for once the decorator was overruled—at a saving to the firm of about $7,500 every few years since the upholstered chairs have a short life and the "Bank" chairs a long one. These chairs appear in the current Jasper Seating Company catalog and, in response to requests for them the *New York Law Journal's* art director provided an illustration of one in that paper's issue of December 19, 1978.

Recently, however, lawyers in a conservative Boston firm rejected the "Bank" chair as too conservative and announced that they would probably choose a more expensive, but contemporary, rival chair—despite the rival's predictably short life span.

Newspaper Cabinets

The immediate availability of hard copies of current runs of half a dozen or more newspapers is essential to the practice of law in large city offices. Equally essential is an adequate place in which to store those papers.

Despite the existence of microforms, it is not uncommon to find a year's run of *The New York Times, Wall Street Journal, Washington Post, New York Law Journal, City Records* and *National Law Journal* on library shelves in New York offices. In other cities local newspapers are substituted for some of the New York papers.

Newspapers are bulky and difficult to store neatly. They are best kept on deep shelves behind closed doors. An issue of *The New York Times* measures 12 inches by 15 inches when folded and it is stored two stacks to the month or 24 per year. A year's run of the *Wall Street Journal* with the same dimensions will fit in 12 monthly stacks.

A recent experience in New York points up the need for preliminary shop drawings for this cabinet and for every other piece of library furniture and equipment as well. In this case, the architect discussed the required dimensions of this cabinet with representatives of his law firm client on four separate occasions. Yet his finished product is a disaster. There is room for only two stacks of the *Times* per shelf when each paper is folded and placed lengthwise on the shelf—with wasted space on all sides. When placed "widthwise", the shelves will hold three stacks. But the papers stick out over the forward edge of each shelf by some two or more inches—like limp fish. Meanwhile the doors are hung so far away from the forward edge of the shelves that they open out 21 inches across a three-foot aisle—effectively blocking the aisle.

The architect's response to this kind of complaint—after four discussions on the subject: "You say we talked about this. Maybe we did and maybe we didn't."

Moral: Get the dimensions in writing—with a shop drawing—before you permit work to start.

Conclusion

Ada Louise Huxtable's eloquent editorial (*The New York Times* for January 31, 1979) contains a stern warning for office planners. In it she makes these points.

> (1) "Almost half of the offices in America are being done over today... and half of American office workers are miserable."
>
> (2) "The bosses... believe that worker satisfaction increases with the latest fashions in office interiors. Few workers agree. They resent the slick, inflexible, impersonal arrangements... New office systems simply regiment discontent. The workers want more, not less, privacy; better workspace and easier access to essential equipment. They rate these things higher than raises or fringe benefits."
>
> (3) "Their call is not for more stylish design but for more considerate and comfortable design."
>
> (4) "Those who spend more time in offices than at home find the psyche continually assaulted. Gild not the lily, perfume not the air; when the designer comes in, let the worker beware."

CHAPTER 40

MOVING THE LIBRARY OF A LAW FIRM

"The shelving was not in place in time." That is the chief obstacle Arthur Morgan Jr. has encountered in a career of large firm moves at Morgan and Brother, where he is a senior officer. Care in preparation is the key to a successful transfer of a library—whether the move is to a point several miles away or merely to another floor in the same building. The move entails precise measurements both in the old and in the new quarters and demands skills that can only be acquired with experience. A handful of lawyers and librarians possess them.

What to Move

A law library consists of more than books and documents. It includes furniture, file cabinets, microform equipment, copiers, often a computer terminal and ranges of book shelving. Whether or not the old shelving is salvaged will affect the move directly. The use of old shelving in the new location will require additional lead time since the shelves must be cleared of books, dismantled, moved and reassembled in a designated location at the new site by moving day. By the time all this is done, much of the saving effected by the salvage operation may have evaporated.

Weeding the Collection

The best time to shed unused and superseded law books is *before* the move. A list of the library's holdings should be circulated to all lawyers with a request to grade the books on a scale running from "indispensable" to "useless." This survey will tell the firm or corporate legal department what it needs to know about the collection as well as about the judgment of the attorneys. Since it costs upwards of $1.50 per volume a year to store books in high-rent districts, it is sensible to retain in the library all books that are needed—but no others.

Adding to the Collection

Systematic additions to the collection should be decided on at moving time. These will include works that the office has always needed but somehow failed to purchase. Records of repeated borrowing of the same works or of research that required the repeated use of the same works in other libraries are good indicators of the need to expand the library. Guides such as the ABA *Recommended Law Books* (Chicago, ABA, 1969) and its forthcoming supplement should be used. The *youngest* lawyers in the office—those who do most of the research—can often give the best advice. It may be that a second run of court reports (New York or Federal) is needed. If the office has a librarian it should, of course, be his responsibility to make recommendations.

Preparing for the Move

The first step is to measure the linear feet of shelf space occupied by the current book collection and all proposed additions to it. This includes all publications, whether kept in pamphlet boxes, file cabinets or on book shelves. The second step is to project the growth of that collection over a period of about ten years. There should be a line-by-line record showing the space needs for every set of books in the office, for example, from *Abbott's Digest* to *Words and Phrases*.

Assign a fixed location in the new library for each set, leaving adequate space for expansion. Law book collections expand at the rate of about 5½ to 6 percent a year. Enter that fixed location on an inventory list—one page for each section of shelving in the new library. Simple errors in arithmetic can throw the entire move out of kilter. The figures should therefore be checked and rechecked in advance of moving. Copies of the inventory sheets should be affixed to the appropriate sections of shelving at the new location for the guidance of the movers.

Books should be packed about one shelf per carton and the cartons numbered consecutively. Both the contents and the shelf locations in the new library should appear on an outside label. Provision should be made for oversize books and for shelves wider than the standard three-foot width. Information about them should appear on the inventory sheets.

The Mobile Book Range

It is also possible to move several hundred books at once on a mobile book range. Morgan and Brother first used one of them successfully in a law firm library move fifteen years ago. Other moving companies have imitated their design and also use them. Arthur Morgan prefers to use the mobile ranges in combination with book cartons. The reason: The "mobiles" are limited in number and cannot fit in all corners of a library.

File cabinets should be transported full if the movers can manage to do so. Otherwise, the same inventory and labelling procedure should be followed for their contents.

During the short period when the book collection cannot be used, arrangements for the use of other libraries should be made. When five major New York firms moved to the Chase Manhattan Building over the course of about twelve months several years ago, they shared library facilities during one another's moves.

Moving Day

Conferences between the movers and the office personnel assigned to oversee the work should be held well in advance of the move to assure complete understanding of their respective duties. By moving day all packing should be completed, all shelves in place at the new location and all employees at their assigned posts.

Old Location. Care should be taken that cartons do not break open or file cabinets spill. Most important, someone should remain behind to see that every carton, cabinet and piece of furniture or equipment has actually left the premises and been loaded onto *your* movers' trucks.

New Location. The movers wil unpack the cartons and reshelve the books according to the directions given them. If each section of shelving has been carefully labelled—with an accurate inventory sheet affixed to the top—books will be shelved properly. It is wise to employ one's own staff members to help direct traffic and to make minor adjustments in the placement of books *after* the movers have completed shelving books in each section of shelving. They should "read" the shelves, volume by volume, to ensure that books are in numerical order and that space is left for missing volumes. Should volume 334 *Federal Reporter Second Series* follow directly after volume 332, the shelf reader can quickly make room for the missing book. If he overlooks it, someone else will have to replace a few hundred volumes later on.

Pitfalls to Avoid

Faulty planning by two of the five firms that originally moved into the Chase Manhattan Building required complete rearrangement of their libraries and reshelving of over 25,000 volumes in those firms shortly after the move was completed. In one case, so much space was left between sets of books that the library looked like an empty warehouse. Just the reverse occurred in the other firm. Within a year the library had to be expanded and all the books reshelved a second time. Careful measurements and accurate projections of growth could have obviated the extra work, expense and inconvenience.

Moving Expenses

A word about costs. Only recently it cost about $4 a square foot to move a law office in New York, but closer to $6 to move a law office library. A 2,000 square-foot library could be moved for about $12,000 or a little less. But planning errors delay the movers and increase their charges. Inflation is sharply increasing those costs.

It is possible to keep almost the entire book collection on shelves in the old location until about one week before the move. Packing can be done in a week's time and the move completed over a weekend–in both cases with extra help. By Monday morning one can enter the new office and see the entire book collection back on shelves ready for use in the new location. Skillful preparation and the experience of *professional* movers make it possible.

CHAPTER 41

FIRE, WATER AND SMOKE PROTECTION

"First came the fire, then the smoke, next the firefighters with their water hoses, the sodden pages, the broken spines. Then came the forty thieves; then only stench and dust and choking throats and charred remains."–Old Welsh legend.

Get the people out first! Or, at least, insulate them from danger whenever a high-rise office building catches fire. That was the unanimous opinion of tenants and their employees, the Fire and Buildings Commissioners and of everyone else concerned with both the fire that started at 299 Park Avenue during the evening of June 23, 1980 and earlier fires in similar buildings that were constructed before the enactment of New York's skycraper fire-protection law in 1973. All but a handful of the major New York law firms maintain their principal offices in those pre-1973 buildings.

Four of those firms are tenants at 299 Park Avenue. Each maintains its own private library and extensive client files. One library runs to 30,000 volumes, another to 12,000, a third to 8,000 and the fourth contains a smaller, but specialized, book collection.

Once the people are insulated from danger, what else should be saved and how can it be done? This chapter discusses four aspects of fire protection: (1) The 299 Park Avenue Experience; (2) Tangible possessions of a law firm; (3) Preventive measures including insurance; and (4) The New York Fire Protection Law,[1] its provisions, legislative history and adequacy.

[1]New York Local Law No. 5, 1973, amended by Local Law 28, 1975 (codified in the Administrative Code of the City of New York Sections C19-161; C19-170 and C28-504).

The 299 Park Avenue Experience

More than 125 persons were injured in the fire that started in the Bank of America offices on the twentieth floor of this model forty-two-story glass-front building.

Shards of glass fell to the surrounding sidewalks as the sealed-in windows blew out or were smashed under heat that exceeded 1,200 degrees fahrenheit. This time most of the injuries were caused by smoke inhalation and most of the victims were firemen. The fact that it occurred in the evening kept injuries and damages far lower than a daytime fire would have inflicted.

Water and Smoke. Water coursed down the sides of the building and through the windows drenching books and papers that were left on window sills in the offices of Olwine, Connelly & Chase on the seventeenth and eighteenth floors of the building, according to Charles M. Waygood, a member of the firm. Their library was untouched, however, because it is located across the floor from the fire source and three floors below it.

Six floors above the Bank of America offices where the fire started is the 8,000-volume library at Baer, Marx & Upham. Smoke billowed through its library, impregnating books with soot. Every book had to be removed from the shelves, wiped clean and replaced. Even so, the smell of smoke remained heavy for several weeks, the firm's librarian, Brooke Zimring, reported.

Twelve floors above the fire, the 30,000-volume collection at Debevoise, Plimpton, Lyons & Gates suffered similar smoke impregnation. Again, the books were removed, wiped clean and reshelved.

Fire Damage. No library books were burned in this fire. However, intense heat can melt microfilm before it ignites a printed page. Nor is microfilm damage from melting or from obliteration of its "printed" text immediately detectable. Each reel or fiche must be examined in its entirety. Undetermined after this fire, but a matter of concern in the future, is the condition of the microfilm collections in the law libraries at 299 Park Avenue. How much heat is needed to destroy film? Some metal cabinets can serve as virtual incinerators rather than as protective vaults. Molten film can even seal the drawers it occupies if, on cooling, it forms a hard lava-like mass. Whether or not film is the best solution for a law firm's space problems, its fire resistant qualities should be reexamined.

Theft. Charles G. Moerdler, former Buildings Commissioner in New York and now counsel to the building's owners, acknowledged that fire and theft go hand in hand. He pointed out that the building hired special guards shortly after the fire. Earlier, Mr. Waygood had praised the efforts of members of the New York Fire Patrol who covered desks and files with tarpaulin. Their organization is an arm of the New York City Board of Fire Underwriters. They follow firemen in an effort to minimize fire insurance claims. When asked about thefts, Mr. Waygood acknowledged the loss of typewriters and of other personal articles after the fire. Did this loss shake his confidence in the Fire Patrol? he was asked. "Not at all," he replied, "Anyone could have removed his firm's property."

The 299 Park Avenue fire provided a painful lesson for the firemen who fought it. It may have brought home to lawyers how vulnerable they are to personal injury and property damage in the very place where they spend most of their working hours.

Tangible Possessions of a Law Firm

The Library. The library is a firm's most visible single investment. Its collection of books, periodicals and documents aside, there is often a valuable card catalog and a record of subscriptions and of routed materials. These records alone represent many hundreds of hours of work. They cannot be recreated overnight.

Specially designed tables, chairs and library counters are expensive to replace, particularly if they were custom-made by architectural woodworking companies. The book stacks, files, other office furniture and equipment (computer and word processing equipment), carpeting, lighting fixtures and works of art are major investments.

Work Products. Whether incorporated within the library or not, the tangible work that lawyers have reduced to writing over a period of five or ten years may be just as valuable as the book collection. These are the memoranda of law, briefs, opinion letters and office forms and precedents. The index to these collections of documents is their most valuable feature.

Work in Progress. Lawyers' notes on pending matters are often irreplaceable. So, too, are records of unbilled time. A firm that regularly bills clients for 15,000 or 20,000 hours of time a month for its services can no more stand the loss of that billing information than can a one-man practitioner who works a modest 150 or 200 hours in the same period and suffers the loss of his own billing records.

On any day before a fire starts each lawyer's office may contain a staggering accumulation of clients' papers and firm property. This may include tax returns, trust instruments, wills (usually returned to a vault each evening), agreements in progress, confidential correspondence, even complete office files and library books. Multiply this accumulation of papers and books by 100 attorneys and the lawyer pack rat becomes the firm's greatest liability. Ordinary prudence should make each managing partner or office administrator adopt a fire alertness plan that works for his own firm.

Preventive Measures

There are three main ways through which a law firm can protect itself against the consequences of fire: (1) Insurance; (2) Duplication of records; and (3) Orderly practices.

Insurance. It is rare to recover all fire losses through insurance. The practice of law is an intellectual exercise and many of its most valuable tangible records, lawyers' work products, for example, defy traditional valuation procedures. But whatever can be valued should be covered by insurance. Lloyd's of London have always prided themselves on their willingness to cover exotic kinds of losses. A law firm's legal opinions and unbilled time may be no more exotic than other kinds of property that are currently insured.

It is axiomatic that insurance works best for those who maintain meticulous cost records that can be duplicated and kept in a safe place off the premises. Those records should include all tangible property: book collection, furniture, equipment and works of art.

Coverage should include losses through fire, theft and vandalism. As an interesting sidelight, the Harvard Club in New York no longer buys original works of art because in the words of its president, "We can't keep them on the walls. They simply disappear." Law firms might take heed.

Additional coverage for personal injury to members of the firm and its employees should be considered even though the building owners have basic responsibility. The reason is that the firm may incur liability if the existence of two facts can be proved: (1) knowledge or even imputed knowledge or dangers to the health and safety of its employees and (2) continued inaction in the face of that knowledge. Smoke inhalation is the chief cause of injury in office building fires. Smoke from burning wood or paper is serious enough. But smoke from burning plastic furniture or paint or from insulation containing asbestos is more insidious. It may serve as a time bomb that triggers diseases years later. Hence the need for coverage.

Duplication of Records. In many libraries it costs almost as much to catalog a book as to purchase it. The expenditures made to index documents and to catalog books justify the additional costs of duplicating those records on microfilm or by computer. As a minimum a duplicate copy of the library's shelf list should be maintained. This is a record of the book collection in the order in which it is arranged on the shelves. Especially useful are computer records of the subscription and routing lists. They will help speed the restoration of library routines to normal within hours after the firemen leave the scene. Office files, unique client papers and lawyer work products justify similar duplication.

Years of work go into the creation of memoranda of law, legal opinions, briefs, forms and precedents. They should not be exposed to the risk of destruction when they can be duplicated at a reasonable cost. Such a program must include the creation and maintenance of suitable indexes in order to reach this material after it has been copied or stored.

Orderly Procedures. The most important step a firm can take is to require orderly methods of work. At the end of each working day all except the most essential books should be returned to the library and office files to the files department. As soon as possible, but certainly before the end of each day, unique client papers should be placed in fireproof vaults or cabinets.

Desktops should be cleared of all papers daily. This includes desks used by lawyers, supervisors, library and files personnel—everyone without exception. Waste paper, including food wrappings, should be disposed of promptly. Even better, smoking should be discouraged in the library and file rooms and food and drink should be restricted to specific locations—preferably outside the library and files.

The Olwine experience at 299 Park Avenue was an inexpensive lesson for everyone: keep looseleaf services and other library books and papers off the window sills where they may become waterlogged.

Compliance with the fire drill and sign posting requirements of Local Law 5 and its implementing Fire Department regulations will help keep the firms alert to fire dangers and to the most advanced means of self and property protection.

Since water damage from sprinklers is a potential hazard to library books, it makes sense to consider installing sprinklers that spray fine white powders instead of water. This is a suggestion made by Mr. Moerdler. He pointed out that these sprinklers are more expensive than water sprinklers. We did not discuss the effects of inhaling these powders. If they are relatively harmless, this step would eliminate water damage without increasing the number of personal injuries.

Finally, managing partners can use potential fire damages to curb disorderly and wasteful work practices.

The Fire-Protection Law

The Provisions of Local Law 5 and Its Amendment. This law[1] was enacted after extensive studies appeared to establish the following basic facts:

(1) In any serious fire it is not possible to evacuate everyone who is present in a high-rise office building. Hasty evacuation of several thousand people down fire stairs may result in panic, causing injuries or deaths;

(2) Firemen cannot scale the walls since ladders now in existence are not tall enough to reach beyond 100 feet;

(3) Fire hoses cannot extinguish fires more than 10 floors up or those deep in the interior of office buildings;

(4) Elevators set aside for use by firemen have failed to work properly—trapping firemen inside; and

(5) The large open spaces in post-World War II buildings help speed the course of fires and the flow of smoke from one end of a floor to another.

With these facts in mind, Local Law 5 came into being. It provides:

(1) A fire safety plan to organize and effect evacuation from perilous areas without panic;

(2) An alarm-communications system, including elevator recall, to alert occupants to danger and to direct safe evacuation and effective internal fire fighting; and

(3) In centrally air-conditioned buildings, either complete sprinklerizing, or both subdivision of open-floor areas with fire-resistant partitions (known as compartmentation and a system of smoke control to provide for safe evacuation."[2]

Members of the building industry challenged the constitutionality of this law and at Trial Term of the New York Supreme Court they succeeded in obtaining a judgment invalidating most of its provisions on June 29, 1977.[3] They complained (1) that the law was confiscatory; (2) that its provisions at the least were too expensive to implement; (3) that its requirement of compelling tenants or their employees to risk their own lives in fighting fires

---

[2]McCallin v. Walsh, 64 AD 2d 46 at 53, 407 NYS 2d 882 (1st Dept. 1978).

[3]McCallin v. Walsh, NYLJ, Feb. 1, 1977 at 7, col. 1M (Sup. Ct. Trial Term 1977).

was unconstitutional, and finally (4) that the technical engineering changes required by the law simply would not work or, in the alternative, that there were not enough competent contractors to make the required installations. Trial Term was reversed and all provisions of Local Law 5 were held valid and enforceable on July 20, 1978.[4]

The history of the law unfolded during this litigation.

Legislative History. Immediately after a devastating fire, everyone seems to favor the imposition of stringent protection for people and property.

> "Local Law 5, as well as its amendment was, in part, a legislative response to two major fires which took place in New York City within a four-month period in 1970. The first occurred at 1 New York Plaza and involved a 50-story office building. The second involved a 46-story office building at 919 Third Avenue. The property damage was in excess of $12,500,000. Five persons lost their lives. Over 100 people were injured. Investigation of these fires 'raised serious questions regarding the adequacy of the city's fire safety requirements.'"[5]

The court referred to a City Council Building Committee Report.[6] In the previous year an Advisory Committee appointed by the Mayor to review New York's fire safety laws produced its report[7] that recommended the enactment of provisions similar to those ultimately adopted after extensive public hearings as Local Law 5.

But as the memory of fire's terror recedes, the cost of protection begins to overshadow its benefits. That was the inevitable response to Local Law 5 of those who pay the bills.

---

[4] McCallin v. Walsh, 64 AD 2d 46, 407 NYS 2d 882 (1st Dept. 1978); aff'd 48 NY 2d 807, 413 NYS 2d 922, 386 NE 2d 833 (1978).

[5] Id. at 51.

[6] This report dated Dec. 13, 1972 is part of the trial record in McCallin (supra fn. 4).

[7] Report of the Mayor's Advisory Committee on Fire Safety in High-Rise Buildings, December 1971. Also included in the same trial record.

The plaintiffs' proposed findings of fact[8] and their various affidavits filed in the *McCallin* case (supra) throw further light on the building industry's view of that law. Some extracts are set out below.

> *Finding No. 35:* That the construction costs involved in allegedly making these buildings more safe is completely disproportionate to the results to be achieved.
>
> *Finding No. 38:* The deaths which occurred at 919 Third Avenue and 1 New York Plaza would occur again given the changes as promulgated by Local Law 5.
>
> *Finding No. 39:* That the five deaths which occurred in those two buildings resulted from building employees and non-professional people going to the fire floor to either fight the fire or going to warn other tenants in the building of the fire.
>
> *Finding No. 58:* At the current rate of operation the building at 444 Madison Avenue would need 44½ years to recoup its investment (in fire prevention alterations).
>
> *Finding No. 60:* 78 percent of New York City Group E high-rise office buildings (those governed by Local Law 5) operate at a loss.
>
> *Finding No. 82:* That the duties involuntarily imposed on private citizens under threat of criminal prosecution entail risks and dangers to them.

Extracts from a Representative Affidavit[9] follow:

> *Par. 4:* "One fact relevant to all our contentions about the disastrous impact of this law and the related rules is that 140 Broadway is mortgaged, as I am confident are most of the buildings whose owners we represent in this action. Violation of their provisions may constitute an event of default precipitating foreclosure, resulting in loss of this property which has an assessed valuation of $42,100,000. Yet, in evaluating various Building Code requirements of Local Law 5 we have determined

---

[8] A part of the trial record in McCallin (supra fn. 4).

[9] Id., Affidavit of William Zimmerman, a partner of 140 Broadway Company.

that they are in significant instances dangerous as well as exorbitant in cost when compared with other safe and available alternatives not permitted to be employed under this law..."

Par. 8: "The effort to install sprinklers throughout our building in accordance with the schedule set forth in Local Law 26 of 1975 necessarily would entail installation work during ordinary business hours, which in turn would seriously disrupt the numerous businesses of our tenants, heighten the risk of fire in the building and render the evacuation of occupants in the event of fire extremely hazardous..."

Another Affidavit[10]

"My affidavit relates specifically to the costs imposed under the Smoke Control System provisions, the Compartmentation provisions, the Communication-Alarm System provisions and the elevators modifications provisions of this law. I know the magnitude of the costs of compliance with those provisions. Such capital costs normally are financed by mortgage loans... But in the foreseeable future, mortgage money in adequate amounts will be available only for a comparative few of the Class E office buildings 100 feet or more in height in New York City..."

"The business of commercial real estate in New York City is in deep trouble. While estimates may vary, it is safe to say that some 25,000,000 to 30,000,000 square feet of rentable office space in this City is vacant. Whole buildings stand unoccupied."

"The prospects for the future are not encouraging..."

This news may astonish those who dodge multi-story building cranes and construction crews as they shoehorn their way through the side streets of New York in the Fifties east of Fifth Avenue. Similarly, it may puzzle managing partners of law firms who cannot expand their office occupancy because the competition for space is so keen.

---

[10] Id., Affidavit of Leone J. Peters, Chairman of the Board of Cushman & Wakefield.

The City's Fire Commissioner[11] and Building Commissioner[12] each submitted opposing affidavits which stressed the perils of high rise office building fires and the role played by air conditioning systems in fanning fires and forcing smoke through its ducts, the necessity for the law and the reasonableness of its provisions. An *amicus* brief[13] related the facts about several recent office building fires. It also detailed the legislative history of Local Law 5 and emphasized its eminent practicability.

The law has been upheld. Are tenants of office buildings now perfectly safe? Returning to the 299 Park Avenue experience, it is apparent that perfection is some way off. Is Local Law 5 adequate? That remains an open question.

Adequacy of the Law. The 299 Park Avenue building "was in complete compliance with the law," *The New York Times* reported.[14] Yet this serious fire occurred and many people were injured.

Ned Steele, writing a follow-up story in the *New York Post,*[15] pointed out that exemptions from the law are regularly granted, "More than 100 waivers from requirements in the code have been approved by a city task force since the law was enacted in 1973. Another 400 to 500 buildings—half the city's skyscrapers—are expected to apply for similar breaks in the near future, according to industry sources."

The waivers granted in those cases, he reported, excused building owners from requirements such as installing "advanced alarm systems, sprinkler systems and fireproof partitions" and from rewiring elevator controls so that they "automatically return to the lobby during a fire."

---

[11] Id., Affidavit of John T. O'Hagan, Fire Commissioner of the City of New York.

[12] Id., Affidavit of Jeremiah T. Walsh, Buildings Commissioner of the City of New York.

[13] Id., Brief of Amicue Curiae. The New York Sprinkler Contractors' Association.

[14] June 25, 1980, p. B3, Cols. 1–4, attributing this opinion to Charles G. Moerdier, former Buildings Commissioner and now counsel to the owners of the building.

[15] June 27, 1980, p. 8.

The law is apparently applied selectively and generous grants of waivers, exemptions and variances from its provisions have become commonplace.

Accordingly, prudence would make managing partners of law firms take the following protective steps:

(1) Ascertain from their landlords whether applications for waivers or exemptions from any provision of Local Law 5 have been filed or granted,

(2) Obtain notice of any proposed hearings on those applications so that they may send representatives or record their written comments with the task force empowered to grant the applications; and

(3) Seek to require as a condition to the grant of any waiver or exemption the guaranty of the payment of liquidated damages that might be incurred in any subsequent fire. In order to eliminate litigation, proof of a relationship between the exemption and those damages should not be required.

In the last analysis, self-help is probably the best though not the only course to take: It should be basic to require orderly work habits of lawyers and of all firm employees. The library and files should serve as models for the rest of the office. Those who prepare for fires may succeed in avoiding them.[16]

---

[16] A detailed study of library fires and methods of fire protection for libraries appears in Morris, J., Managing the Library Fire Risk, 2d ed., Berkeley, Univ. of Calif., 1979.

CHAPTER 42

THE GRAND RAPIDS EXPERIENCE: "TO MOVE OR NOT TO MOVE"

To move or not to move; that is the question;
Whether 'tis wiser for a firm to suffer
The slurs and barbs of outraged partners
Or to push out the narrow walls of troubles
And by moving end them? To stay, to go?
To dream of noble corridors and rows
Of books all neatly placed, and quiet study halls?
To wake again to this calamity of so long lease
What more to suffer before we leave
The cramp-ed quarters and cruel frustrations
Our firm is heir to?

But that the dread of higher rents,
The unknown landlord before whose terms
We all must bow and sometimes quail, drugs the will
And makes us rather bear our squalid quarters
Than fly to others that we all prefer.
Thus prudence does make sluggards of us all.

–Hamlet Outraged,
Act III, Scene 1

Introduction

What can the rest of the country learn about law libraries from Grand Rapids? Nearly everything. This thriving midwest city supports a 30,000 volume bar library. Or rather, 98 per cent of the city's 900 lawyers support it through their dues.

The library exhibits in microcosm all the problems that beset practitioners' libraries everywhere. It is overcrowded. The treatise collection cannot keep up with the needs of its members. This is a problem of finance, not of book selection. The fuller the service to members, the more that the librarians—barely two full-time persons—are called on to do. The library is both understaffed and underfunded. A familiar story so far.

The City's Advantages

Yet the Grand Rapids Bar Association has four distinct advantages. It has an outstanding Executive Director—Mrs. Marjorie C. Wilcox—who enjoys the enthusiastic support of the members. Its governing body—the Library Committee and Board of Trustees, chaired by Grant C. Gruel—recognizes the gravity of the problems and is facing them squarely. The loyalty of its members is evidenced by their numbers. Moreover, most of them are 35 years of age or younger. Their careers are closely affected by the services of the Association. Finally, Grand Rapids is located in western Michigan at some distance from any large, metropolitan research center. This Association is all they have. Meanwhile, its members must compete with lawyers who have immediate access to larger research facilities in other cities.

Space

The Association occupies some 3,313 square feet of space on the 10th floor of the Old Kent Bank Building. Some nine other law firms maintain their offices on the six floors just below the Bar headquarters. They number nearly 200 lawyers. The presence of the Bar in this building has always been a great magnet in attracting and keeping lawyer-tenants.

The Bar Association uses all but about 300 square feet of its space for the library. To function adequately it needs an additional 2,500 square feet of adjacent space almost at once. The book collection, study facilities for its members, staff work areas and the new library machines together will absorb that much space.

The Association is now at a crossroads. It is growing and its needs are growing. Like any large firm it is casting about for a solution. Set out below are four alternative choices. The right decision will help sharpen the research support it gives the members. The wrong decision will reduce their ability to compete and will cause some falloff in memberships. It may even cause a few of the strong firms to form their own competing building library. That would be a disaster for the Bar Association.

> (1) *First alternative.* It might stay in its present quarters if some 2,500 square feet of adjoining 10th floor space were made available. This would require extensive building renovations to meet the library needs summarized above.
>
> (2) *Second Alternative.* An unappealing choice is to stay where it is without gaining more 10th floor space. The collection would be sharply weeded of all its lesser used works that would then be stored on shelves in some nearby building in *dry space* and a few publications would be converted to microforms. This choice does nothing to alleviate the lawyer study or staff space problems and should be rejected.
>
> (3) *Third Alternative.* A popular solution with some associations and large firms is the ownership of a building designed to its specifications. This step would give the Association leverage to take as much space as its expanding activities required. The remaining space would immediately attract lawyer tenants, the most stable kind of tenancy, and assure to the Association a permanent solution to the space problem and a steady source of additional income.
>
> (4) *Fourth Alternative.* Rented quarters afford another attractive choice. The handsome Pantland Hotel, now being restored, has suitable space. It may be difficult for the hotel to find a tenant for that space. The Association would be a great catch for the Hotel.

A block closer to the courts than the Pantland is the new Grand Rapids Civic Center, now nearing completion. Mrs. Wilcox, the Executive Director of the Association who has been on the scene for many years, regards the new Civic Center as the better choice of the two.

The owners of two other downtown buildings, one not yet completed, may find it profitable to give the Association some inducement to move in. Landlords do not overlook the magnet effect of the Bar library on potential lawyer-tenants, publishing plants, letter shops, restaurants and other allied professions and services.

The considerations that impel a large firm to choose one site over another are similar to those used by the Bar Association. Among them are cost, convenience, appearance and flexibility for adjacent expansion.

Financing

The Grand Rapids Bar must also consider one special financial factor. It occupies its space rent free and has a lease for ten more years. This occupancy represents nearly $20,000 a year and is a strong inducement to stay. (The estimate is based on other available space in Grand Rapids at six to seven dollars a square foot.)

However, one lawyer called it "the albatross around our neck."

That this is at least partly an illusory gain can be proved in two ways. First, the inadequacy of the present space will become more critical in each passing year. The Library will suffer a loss of its efficiency. Lawyers will begin to avoid it and memberships might fall off. Moreover, the Bar cannot afford the risk that strong groups of lawyers will band together to form a competing building library. That would place the remaining members of the Bar in severe jeopardy.

Second, if any one of the other alternatives is chosen, then the members of the Bar will continue to prosper and the Association will have earned its fair share of that prosperity. The members will enjoy the use of the expanded book collection, the time-saving study facilities and superior staff services. The savings that the members effect must be attributed in part to the Bar.

It does not require a cost accountant to reach this conclusion. Lawyers are trained to weigh tangible and intangible values such as these every day.

"In their hearts they know I am right." See once more the passage from *Hamlet Outraged*. Then the Bar will rise to make the bold decision.

CHAPTER 43

THE NON-BOOK AND THE LAW

Roberts, in his biography of F.E. Smith, later Lord Birkenhead, relates that when he once rose in court to open a case before Mr. Justice Ridley and a jury, the judge observed: Mr. Smith, I have read the pleadings, and I do not think much of your case." "Indeed, m'Lud, I'm sorry to hear that," was the immediate reply, "but your Lordship will find that the more you hear it, the more it will grow on you." It is pleasant to note that not only did the judge burst into laughter, but that Smith continued with his case—and won it!

This story brings to mind that many attorneys, in a similar manner, have arbitrarily prejudged the use of microfilm and other non-book materials in their work to the extent that they are depriving themselves of an opportunity not only to facilitate their research, but also to economize in the conduct of their practice.

Dynamic Developments

The legal profession is on the threshold of two dynamic developments that must eventually so affect the practice of law that not too many years from now the average attorney will wonder how lawyers of our day managed to cope with the overwhelming bulk of legal authority presently to be found in books. One of these developments is computer retrieval of legal information and the other the availability of legal materials in miniaturized form. Much as the legal profession anticipates the time when the on-line terminal in every practitioner's office—with instantaneous access to all statutes, cases, administrative rules and regulations, law review articles and treatises—will be a reality, still it is not exactly feasible to plan on it for some time to come.

Then again, computer retrieval is costly and involves tremendous input of source materials. The miniaturized version of legal source materials, however, is a resource that lawyers can presently use advantageously and even later with the advent of the computer retrieval era. The lawyer seeking to retrieve legal materials on a "one-to-one basis," that is, being directly involved in the research process vis-a-vis the materials to be analyzed, should now look to this "non-book" development as a matter of course.

The ability to miniaturize the printed word on film or paper has been with us for more than a century. As early as 1839, an English scientist named Benjamin Dancer reduced a document twenty inches long to one-eighth inch in length and by the use of a 100-power microscope was able to read it. During the Franco-Prussian War, secret messages were photographed on microfilm rolls which were attached to the legs of carrier pigeons to be delivered between Paris and Bordeaux. In the 1930's, microfilm began to be used commercially, especially by banks, for the preservation of records of cancelled checks. Today microfilm is used by business and public agencies for many purposes—primarily to preserve records and as a means of conveniently storing tremendous numbers of records referred to frequently.

By the 1950's, libraries began to adopt this microform technology and as microform viewers and viewer/printers became less costly in the 1960's, publishers began to edit and publish software and manufacturers began to produce hardware to meet the requirements of library readers and users.

General Availability

Today under the generic name of microform or microform materials, there is available to the legal profession many published sources of the law. The term microform actually is descriptive of any form of printing either on film or paper which contains micro-images. Some micromaterials are on a 35-mm roll film, some on 16-mm roll film, some on 24 x fiche, some on 42 x or 48 x COM fiche and some on 75 ultrafiche. Microfilm in 35-mm is the most popular form used. It is recommended by experts in the field for storage of large numbers of pages which run continuously in sequence and are updated infrequently, such as court reports, session laws, etc.

Microfiche is a sheet of microfilm in the form of a card 3" x 5" or 4" x 6" containing multiple micro-images in a grid pattern. It usually contains identification information of the micro-images on the fiche which can be read by the naked eye. Depending on the reduction, microfiche contains from sixty-four to ninety-six pages on each 4" x 6" card. Ultrafiche, presently being used by the West Publishing Company, can contain as many as 1,600 microimage pages of a National Reporter System volume on a 4" x 6" fiche. Fiche is generally used for single volumes and when updating is necessary.

Microform serves many purposes today. It reduces space used in libraries, especially in practitioner's office libraries, for the storage of books which are relatively used infrequently, such as early state court reports, session laws, Attorney-General opinions, bar association materials and state administrative documents. It allows for the preservation of deteriorating material due to the destructive force of our polluted air. It also permits the preservation of complete collections of excessively bulky to bind and shelve materials because of limitation of space or budget, as legal newspapers (e.g., *New York Law Journal*) and official gazettes of foreign countries. Finally, it allows access to materials which are unavailable otherwise, such as out-of-print books, and Records and Briefs of the Supreme Court of the U.S., the U.S. Circuit Courts and appellate state courts.

Other Purposes

Law librarians today are purchasing legal micromaterials for other reasons as well. When more than one set of a serial publications is required for reference, such as additional copies of the National Reporter System or the *Harvard Law Review,* in order to save space, they maintain one or two copies of these materials in original bound volume form and add the other copies in microfilm or microfiche.

The development of reader/printers and reader hardware has reached the stage today where it is comparatively easy for the user to read the microform on a screen and to make facsimile copies of pages he wished to carry away with him.

Resistance to the use of microform, however, still is prevalent in the field of law. Unfortunately, despite expert opinion to the effect that for some purposes microform may in fact be used more advantageously by the practitioner than the traditional book, the problems of standards for microform publication and hardware still present major obstacles to large-scale practitioner acceptance of non-book forms. As a result, there appear to be serious reservations about practitioners becoming a market for these micromaterials. Then again, most attorneys want to work with the published volume, turning pages, scanning them and even making notes in the margins.

It is our thought that the problem of standards will always be with us and that practitioners will eventually adjust to the facts of life. True, standardization is preferred. It would be great if all forms of micromaterials with different reductions could eventually be read in hardware compatible for all. There is little doubt, however, that microform technology will eventually develop hardware to accomplish this purpose and uniformity in hardware and software in this field will become prime criteria for acceptance. But until then, we can manage. Actually, practitioners have so much to gain by adopting micromaterials for their office libraries, that the present and temporary inconvenience resulting from lack of uniformity in size, arrangement of images, reductions and format of micromaterials are far outweighed by their advantages in legal research.

To explain: First, on reading habits. Of course, lawyers prefer to hold books in their hands rather than read them on the screens of microform viewers. Yet, psychologically, those who hold books when they read because they enjoy the feel and satisfaction of doing so, react differently to the bound volume. For example, some prefer different sizes of books for their convenience. The size of the bound volume as we now know it was not always the preferred one. Reading habits change along with the thrust of the times.

Dr. Samuel Johnson fancied books small enough in size to be held in the hand and carried to a comfortable place to read. Walpole, on the other hand, preferred larger bound volumes. In one of his letters, he lamented, "What a pity it is I was not born in the golden age of Louis the Fourteenth, when it was not only the fashion to write folios, but to read them, too." Trevelyan records that Macaulay read Plato in an oversized folio, sixteen inches long by ten broad, and weighing almost twelve pounds. Thus, we have preferences expressed for extremes of big and little books. There was a time when giant books, in Elephant Folio Size, were in demand, especially for maps. Now that there are more ingenious ways of dealing with such material, the necessity for the Elephant Folio is gone.

The manner in which lawyers maintain libraries can change with their reading habits and requirements. The accepted norm can become an anachronism of the past. During the late Victorian period, when the common law courts closed in London and the assise judges toured the circuits from town to town, it was an ordinary spectacle for fifty to sixty barristers to accompany the assise judges. No barrister with any business on the circuit thought it safe to travel with at least a hundred weight of legal literature of his own to fall back upon. The Western Circuit had a "Circuit Van," which was an enormous vehicle like those used for the removal of furniture and was always conveyed at very considerable expense by rail or road wherever the assises were being held. Its primary and nominal use was to convey the "book boxes" of those barristers and there were many such. After a while, and due to the effect of the Judicature Acts, the Circuit Van disappeared. The author of "Pie Powder," published in 1911, recalled, "I know of one man who cherishes his 'book-box' still, but it rests in well-earned retirement in his country house, and few of the present generation can ever have seen one."

Lawyers, too, will eventually change their reading habits because of the felt necessities of the times. The use of microform is just the next logical step. Actually, a user of microform can find the citation he seeks in microfilm, or microfiche, as quickly or even more so than in a set of books on shelves. Lawyers who are used to working with bound volumes should have little difficulty in adjusting to microform. True, there may be a period of awkwardness, when they first start to use microform. The way to do anything easily, however, is to do it often. Lawyers are used to books because they have handled thousands of them in their research. A similar use of microform should bring added confidence and comfort in their applicability to legal research.

Actually, lawyers today have become accustomed to research methods, rarely followed thirty years ago. When they read an opinion or analyzed a statute then, they copied copiously in longhand the relevant parts thereof they wished to quote or use otherwise in their briefs. Today, they make photocopies of the originals and work with these copies rather than with the original pages. As long as the lawyer has access to the materials required in his research, it makes little difference where they came from—the bound volume or the microform edition. The end product is the same—a photocopy of a page. Rather than resist the introduction of microform into his private law library, the lawyer should change the emphasis of his library purchasing to guaranteed access to legal sources he can then reproduce, rather than depending on the vicissitudes of access to law collections in bar libraries, etc. In this context, practitioners' libraries would be well served with microform editions of standard materials.

It should also be noticed that the practitioner is given more mobility by microform than possible with hard copy. The roll of microfilm or the few microfiche representing bound volumes can be easily brought into his office or the library area of his office or even to his home and be read there. All that would be required thereafter would be for the practitioner to insert the fiche or the microfilm in the reader/printer, read the page on the screen and make a hard-copy photograph when necessary. Actually, once the citation to the volume and page of the reporter or law review article is known, the end result can be the same.

Ingenious Promotions

Manufacturers of microform hardware are ingeniously promoting these developments. The Bell and Howell Company is now advertising: "Take a microfiche reader to bed with you" in selling its "Brief Case Microfiche Reader." Weighing only five pounds, it is compact enough to fit in a briefcase and sells for $99. It projects, too, so that if you tire of reading your microfiche in the conventional manner, you can project the full image on a wall. "DASA

Microfiche Readers" are small and light enough to use on your lap and sell for 250 Swiss francs. The "Princeton Microshelf" can house microform reels with the most recent volumes of hard copy. Hence, it is now possible to store conveniently both hard copy and microfilm collections together by converting existing shelf space with little physical change to floor space and location.

A number of major publishers have entered the microform publishing field and are significantly developing microform collections of legal materials. Special committees of law librarians working closely with the innovative Trans-Media Publishing Company of Dobbs Ferry, N.Y., have jointly contributed to a growing understanding of the role of microform in law libraries and an increased receptivity to non-book publication. They have also helped activate the American Association of Law Libraries to view microform as an area demanding organizational attention, at least as far as standards for technical, editorial, bibliographical control and hardware are concerned.

Not Complete Answer

Now, microform is not the complete answer to the problems of library space and preservation. It is merely a new form of library material which can be used to improve library collections and services. Many publications in hard copy will remain with us. Every legal research library will continue to maintain thousands and thousands of them. But as library material, microform deserves to be treated as such. Thus, if enterprising publishers are prepared to invest in legal micromaterials, the legal profession should take advantage of their productivity.

Consider, for example the following: Transmedia has published on 35-mm roll microfilm all the American State Reports prior to the National Reporter System, and the West Publishing Company has published on ultrafiche all the volumes of the National Reporter System, 1st Series. Combined, these two microform publications allow a law office to maintain about 6,300 volumes or approximately 5.5 million pages of case reports of all the stages and the federal jurisdiction from around 1800 to approximately 1940 in infinitesimal amount of space in comparison with what would be required to shelve the bound volumes.

Transmedia has also published on microfilm the Lawyers Reports Annotated from 1888 to 1918, the Trinity Series (American Decisions, American Reports and American State Reports), the Code of Federal Regulations, 1939 to 1971, Federal Cases (1789–1879), the Irish Reports, Scottish Law Reports, the United Nations Treaty Series and the Statutes of the Realm. Commerce Clearing House has published in ultrafiche its tax services and the Congressional Information Service the Library of the Working Papers of the U.S. Congress. Similarly, other publishers have produced U.S. Congressional Hearings 1869–1969, U.S. Federal Register, U.S. Administrative Regulatory agencies rules and regulations.

Fred B. Rothman & Co., has made available on microfilm complete collections of the *Harvard Law Review, Yale Law Review, UCLA Law Review, Columbia Law Review, Cornell Law Review, Virginia Law Review* and other leading law reviews. Information Handling Service, recently merged with Capital Services International, and Bureau of National Affairs now have available for sale a microfiche collection of all American States and Territory Session Laws and similarly the Records and Briefs of the U.S. Supreme Court Reports, and even the *New York Law Journal* is available on microfilm. In fact, the holdings of law libraries of micromaterials have become so significant a part of their law collection, that in recognition thereof the Association of American Law Schools in its Executive Committee Regulations for accreditation purposes allows a law library to meet its 60,000 volume minimum requirement by counting up to 20 per cent thereof in microform. Each volume reproduced in micromaterials can count as a volume on the same basis as if reproduced in book form.

Cost to Lawyers

One final thought: Have lawyers ever considered how much it costs merely to maintain on a library shelf one law book already paid for in full? Are they aware that book storage costs reflect a significant element in office overhead? Law Librarians have noted that the rate of library collection growth is of a geometrical, rather than an arithmetical order. Fremont Rider in his classic, "The Scholar and the Future of the Research Library," dramatically concluded in 1944—and incidentally his findings have been borne out—that research libraries double in size nearly every sixteen years. Imagine what this is doing to the space problems of these libraries. As the British statesman Gladstone noted in 1890 while commenting on the increase in books in geometrical progression "... a vast, and even bewildering prospect is before us...."

Law books are shelved approximately 10 to 15 per square foot. This figure includes aisle space and shelves 7 feet 6 inches high. Hence, if you are paying rent at $10 to $15 per square foot and you are maintaining a collection of 1,500 books on your shelves, you are using for this purpose approximately 100 square feet costing you in rent approximately $1,000. Some experts have actually concluded that it costs the average lawyer renting law office space in the Wall Street area approximately one dollar per volume just to keep it on a shelf. Study and staff space increase the cost about fifty percent.

On the other hand, very few institutions maintaining law libraries, given the economic conditions that prevail today, can afford to build new facilities to store the vast inflow of law books they are presently being subjected to and still retain the older and less frequently used materials they have acquired in the past.

Reporter System

Note, for example, that there are 2,300 volumes comprising the First Series of the National Reporter System. They not only weigh about three or four tons but also occupy 269 linear feet or the equivalent to seventeen of the interior-free standing sections of shelves in the library from floor to ceiling. The Second Series of the National Reporter System grew in 1972 in terms of space at the rate of 24.5 feet. The West Publishing Company has determined that the first series of Ultra Fiche occupies only three feet and that only a small amount of additional floor space is necessary for its reader/printers and viewers. Actually, no more than table space for one library researcher.

In a different context, the Librarian of the New York County Law Library at a conference held at New York University in 1973 brought out that the cases decided and published in only volume

36 of the official New York Appellate Division Reports, Second Series, were supported by briefs submitted by interested parties, as well as the records therein, bound in over 300 volumes of Records on Appeal: In that library, of the 165,000 volumes housed there, almost 50,000 of them consist of these Cases and Points. Unless this growth can be stopped by microfilming the alternative was clear—they had to be selectively discarded.

Under the circumstances, both practitioners and law librarians should realize that to buy micromaterials either in replacement of bound volumes they now own, or as new acquisitions is in reality a capital investment, rather than a mere purchase of library materials. The alternative is extremely high overhead or extremely high maintenance costs, or a limited collection of materials.

Judge Leonard P. Moore, in *Syracuse Broadcasting Corp. v. Newhouse* (295 F. 2d 269, 2d Cir. 1961), in holding in error a trial court's refusal to allow plaintiff to exhibit, through a microfilm reader, microfilms of newspaper items, said at 273–274: ". . . . in this machine age when civilization itself is on the verge of being buried under a mass of records, documents and files, courts . . . will have to adapt themselves to the use of such mechanical devices as are being created to avoid this peril."

Lawyers will similarly have to adapt themselves to the use of these "mechanical devices." Perhaps the French have the answer when they say: "L'apetit vient en mangeant."

CHAPTER 44

THE EMERGING FORM OF MICROFILM IN LAW LIBRARIES

The late Senator Dirksen told a story about the man who fell from the fortieth story of an office building and as he passed a horrified man looking out of a window at the tenth floor, that man tried to encourage him by shouting, "Don't worry, so far you are all right."

Two of the main concerns disturbing law librarians today are shortage of stack space for ever expanding collections of law books and the rapid deterioration of valuable research materials on poor quality paper. There are other concerns, of course, such as unavailability of desirable research materials.

Costly Storage

Librarians are involved with interrelated problems of book selection, cataloging and classification, binding, readers' service and book storage. By far the costliest of them is book storage, a fact which many of them either ignore or are unaware of—and the reason is that in our accounting practices, book storage costs are almost entirely concealed costs.

An explanation of why so little has been done about book storage until recently, could be that it was the result of the development, along in 1890's of a new form of book storage, the so-called all metal "book stack." This was so great an improvement over all other forms of book storage that had preceded it, that the library profession accepted it as not only a better book storage, but as almost a perfect one—the ultimate in book storage.

As a matter of fact, however, the use of book stacks is not really efficient at all. Books are housed on ranges of shelves, set up, back to back in parallel immovable rows. To give access to the books on these rows of shelves "aisles" are provided between each facing pair of rows. These parallel rows of shelves and aisles are multiplied in successive, vertical superimposed "decks" or floors and constitute what we term a "bookstack".

Now note the following: the ratio of cubic feet of space occupied by aisles is greater than that for shelves on which books are stored; 36 inches for the aisles and about 16 inches for the shelves. Actually the ratio is somewhere between aisles and shelving of around 65 percent to 35 percent, considering the walk ways required between walls and the end of the row of shelves. In this context we should also note, that it is good library practice not to use more than two-thirds of each shelf for book storage, to allow for necessary expansion.

Unused Space

The end result is that about 85 percent of the stack space area, is not used and actually is empty space. If you have 10,000 square feet of stack areas, you are only using about 1500 square feet for the storage of your book collection.

When Professor Plucknet, the legal historian, was doing research on his "Concise History of the Common Law" at the Harvard Law School Library in the 1930's, he was asked what he thought about its collection. "Harvard Law Library," he replied, "greatest law library in the world, half a million books and all of them lost." At that time, he was referring to the problem of missing books, and books in use, which we are all familiar with, and which is characteristic even today of many law liraries. Today, however, a more important dimension has been added to the availability and access to legal materials. Our books are disappearing, because they are actually turning into dust. Self-destruct, so to speak! An article in the *New York Times* (July 16, 1978), reporting on the conclusions of experts in the field, notes that "for all its look of permanence, a new book these days has a life-expectancy of only thirty to fifty years." A book purchased today, around the year 2,000 will be yellow, brittle and crumbling. So overwhelming is the number of books turning to dust, that of the 18 million books presently in the Library of Congress, 6 million (one third of the collection) are presently too brittle to read.

Until the middle 1800's, paper was made from linen rags coated with gelatin. Thereafter, paper was made from wood pulp coated with aluminum compounds. The alum-rosin impregnated in the wood pulp paper gives off sulfuric acid that eats away at the paper. "This process, combined with rough handling, humidity, heat, mold and cockroaches, means that most books won't survive." Also significant in this destructive process is our polluted air, which contains substantial amounts of sulpher dioxide and other noxious chemicals. One way of solving this problem would be to print books on durable paper. This would be too costly, and as book prices are already too high, publishers are reluctant to do so, especially as libraries purchase only about 10 percent of their books.

Considering these factors, in essence, along with the information and publication explosion, library administrators are rapidly being placed in the role of the man hurtling down from the fortieth floor of the office building. "So far we are all right." But what do we do in the time left before they hit the sidewalk?

Little Time Left

Law librarians who have given any thought to the future development and organization of law libraries, now believe that there is little time left to face the challenge of an increasing lack of book storage in libraries, and the accelerating rate at which books are decaying on our shelves.

The growth of law-library collections in the last thirty years has taken on such proportions that Fremont Rider's prediction in 1944 that research libraries will eventually double in size almost every sixteen years is becoming more and more significant in our calculations.

Law in the books has become such a formidable storage problem and economic factor for law libraries that any administrator concerned with their maintenance and use must now take stock not only of how to cope with the increasing cost of book storage and the increasing lack of shelf space, but also with the obvious deterioration of older books and their replacement in more permanent form.

Today, under the generic name of microform (micrographics) or micromaterials, there is available to the legal profession many published sources of the law. The term, microform, actually is descriptive of any form of printing either on film or paper which contains micro-images. Some micromaterials are on 35mm roll film, some on 16mm roll film, some on 24 x fiche, some on 42 x or 48 x COM fiche and some on 75 ultrafiche. *Microfilm* in 35mm is the most popular form used. It is recommended by experts in the field for storage of large numbers of pages which run continuously in sequence and are updated infrequently, such as court reports, session laws, etc. *Microfiche* is a sheet of microfilm in the form of a card, 3 inches by 5 inches or four-by-six inches, containing multiple micro-images in a grid pattern. It usually contains identification information of the micro-images on the fiche which can be read by the naked eye. Dependong on the reduction, microfiche contains from sixty to ninety-eight pages on each four-by-six-inch card. *Ultrafiche,* presently being used by the West Publishing Company and CCH can contain as many as 1600 micro-image pages of a National Reporter System volume on a four-by-six-inch fiche. Fiche is generally used for single volumes and when updating is necessary.

Multi-Purpose Product

Microform serves many purposes today. It reduces space used in libraries, especially in practitioners' office libraries, for the storage of books which are relatively used infrequently, such as early state court reports, session laws, Attorney-General opinions, Bar Association materials and state administrative documents.

It allows for the preservation of deteriorating material due to the destructive force of our polluted air. It also permits the preservation of complete collections of excessively bulky to bind and to shelve materials because of limitation of space or of budget, as legal newspapers (e.g., *New York Law Journal*) and official gazettes of foreign countries. Finally, it allows access to materials which are unavailable otherwise, such as out-of-print books, and records and briefs of the Supreme Court of the U.S., the U.S. Circuit Courts, and state appellate courts.

Law librarians today are purchasing legal micromaterials for other reasons as well. When more than one set of a serial publication is required for reference, such as additional copies of the *National Reporter System* or the *Harvard Law Review,* in order to save space, they maintain one or two copies of these materials in original bound volume form and add the other copies in microfilm or microfiche.

The development of reader/printers and reader hardware has reached the stage today where it is comparatively easy for the user to read the microform on a screen and to make facsimile copies of pages he wishes to carry away with him.

Actually, lawyers have become accustomed to research methods rarely followed thirty years ago. When they read an opinion or analyzed a statute, they copied copiously in longhand the relevant parts thereof they wished to quote or use otherwise in their briefs. Now, they make photocopies of the originals and work with these copies rather than with the original pages. As long as the lawyer has access to the materials required in his research, it makes little difference where they came from—the bound volume or the microform edition. The end product is the same—a photocopy of a page. Rather than resist the introduction of microform into his private law library, the lawyer should change the emphasis of his library purchasing to guaranteed access to legal sources he can then reproduce, rather than depending on the vicissitudes of access to law collections in bar libraries, etc. In this context, practitioners' libraries would be well served with microform editions of standard materials.

A number of major publishers have entered the microform publishing field and are significantly developing microform collections of legal materials. Special committees of law librarians, for example, working closely with the innovative Oceana/Trans-Media Publishing Company of Dobbs Ferry, N.Y., have jointly contributed to a growing understanding of the role of microform in law libraries and an increased receptivity to nonbook publication. They have also helped activate the American Association of Law Libraries to view microform as an area demanding organizational attention, at least as far as standards for technical, editorial, bibliographical control and hardware are concerned.

Microform is not the complete answer to the problem of library space and preservation. It is merely a new form of library material which can be used to improve library collections and services. Many publications in hard copy will remain with us. Every legal research library will continue to maintain thousands and thousands of them. But as library material, microform deserves to be treated as such. Thus, if enterprising publishers are prepared to invest in legal micromaterials, the legal profession should take advantage of their productivity.

Bibliographical Notes

The lawyer and law librarian interested in acquiring a more sophisticated understanding of microform should consult the materials listed in the following annotated bibliography: Schwark, Sabine and Breakstone, Barbara R. Microform Update: Current Trends for Law Libraries (In 71 *Law Library Journal,* 149–155, Feb. 1978).

This useful bibliography attempts to list major publications and other sources available in 1978 for microform information arranged under 1) general information about microforms, 2) bibliographic sources for microforms available, 3) sources for information about equipment, 4) available journals, 5) associations relating to microforms and 6) miscellaneous works such as Guidelines for Handling Library Orders for Microforms, Microfilm Source Book, Micrographic Index to journals, books, reports and pamphlets covering micrographics and related fields housed at National Micrographic Association (NMA).

Note particularly the following: Diaz, Albert J. *Microforms in Libraries: A Reader.* Westpoint, Conn., Microform Review, 1975.

Consisting of reprints primarily, it still is an excellent introduction to the use of microforms. It explains how to organize the collection and obtain bibliographic control and provides a basic understanding as well of standards and specifications and user reactions. It has no index.

For comprehensive lists of microforms currently available on the market check the following: *Guide to Microforms in Print,* 1961–. Westpoint, Conn., Microform Review. It provides an annual cumulative list in alphabetical order, and in 1976 incorporated *Interna-*

tional Microforms in Print. Thus, it covers U.S. and World thereafter. It is in two parts: *Author/Title* and *Subject,* with prices.

As the *Guide to Microforms in Print* does not list dissertations, consult the following for this purpose:

Dissertation Abstracts, 1938–. Ann Arbor, Mich., University Microfilms International. Abstracts and indexes university dissertations available on microfilm from the publisher, University Microfilm—Includes law items along with humanities and social science.

For bibliographical sources see also *Legal Materials in Microform: A bibliography.* 2d ed. published by Brigham Young University Law Library (1976), *Legal Series in Microform,* 1977–1978, published by University Microfilms and Tseng, Henry P. *Complete Guide to Legal Materials in Microform,* published by University Publications of America, (Wash., D.C. in 1976).

For a comprehensive listing of microform masters from which copies can be made at a reasonable price, refer to: *National Register of Microform Masters,* 1965–. Published annually by the Library of Congress, it is arranged by main entry. Entries for 1965–75 have been cumulated in six volume set.

There are many publishers of law related micro-publications such as Commerce Clearing House, Congressional Information Service, William S. Hein, Information Handling Service, Law Reports, Inc., Microform Review, Oceana/Transmedia Inc., Fred B. Rothman & Co., Transmedia Publishing Co., United States Government Printing Office, University Microfilm, West Publishing Co. Some issue their own catalogues, others individual pamphlets, etc. Rothman's "Green Slips" lists a number of them as released.

For microfiche reproduction of micropublishers' catalogs, see *Micropublishers' Trade List Annual,* 1975—published by Microform Review.

The best source for a critical analysis of the worth of a microform publication is *Microform Review,* published since 1972 by Microform Review, Inc. of Westport, Conn. Contains excellent articles on the technology and use of microforms in libraries. Its evaluations of new microforms are highly reliable. Note for example its review of the various editions of the U.S. Supreme Court Records and Briefs (3 Microform Rev. 132–133 (1974), 4 Microform Review 224–28, 312–20 (1975)). Other worthwhile journals are: *Law Library Journal* (features articles on microform) and the

Publications Clearing House Bulletin published by the AALL Committee on Relations with Publishers (see v. 1, p. 2–3 June 1978).

For information on Microform Hardware, the National Micrographics Association *1979 Buyer's Guide to Micrographic Equipment, Products and Services* is "designed to be a concise introduction and a continuing reference to many valuable sources of currently available products and service." For more detailed equipment information, NMA publishes the *Guide to Micrographic Equipment,* a directory that provides specifications for cameras, readers, reader-printers, processors, duplicators, enlargers, COM recorders and special items. The 1978–79 editions (7th) is available in two volumes: Production Equipment and User Equipment. See also the N.M.A. publication *How to Select a Reader-Printer* (1974) which describes general types of readers and reader-printers available as well as what to look for, such as illumination control. The American Library Association provides a critical evaluation of library equipment in its *Library Technology Reports* (1965–). Its reports on microform equipment are informative and evaluated from a librarian's viewpoint. This has been called the "Consumers Report of library materials." Note, too, *Micrographics Equipment Review,* published since 1976 by Microform Review of Westpoint, Conn., which is especially helpful for its nontechnical appraisal of user equipment for libraries.

CHAPTER 45

AUDIO CASSETTES: A NEW SYSTEM FOR TRAINING LAWYERS TO DO BASIC LEGAL RESEARCH

For twenty-five years, this writer has watched newly admitted lawyers, law students, and even their professors, struggle to find a case in point or stumble about as they search for the applicable statute or regulation and for the proof that it is currently in force. Their methods are uncertain, their time consumption extravagant. Betty W. Taylor, editor of *Audio Research in the Law* (Condyne/Trans-Media Distributing Corp., Dobbs Ferry, N.Y. Five cassettes (two sides each) and accompanying treatise (280 pp.) and Director of the University of Florida Law School Library, maintains that lawyers are unlikely to master legal research methods unless they pursue a series of skillfully drafted, practical exercises. This recorded and written work—to which five other law school librarians contributed—provides those exercises together with a comprehensive legal research program.

Audio cassettes are peculiarly fit for legal research training because they permit the listener (1) to hear the instructions about the use of a particular legal reference tool, (2) turn over the device at any point in order to examine particular features of that tool and (3) resume listening to instructions about the next or any other reference work.

The Taylor "publication" in the form of cassettes runs for about three hours, and includes a treatise that complements, but does not repeat, the recorded guides.

Each component in the work is built around one or more problems dealing with a central subject: the loss or unauthorized use of a credit card. It opens with dictionary definitions of terms used in the credit card industry and then leads lawyers through each phase of legal research, ending with one of its finest chapters: "Shepard's Citations."

The method is fourfold–(1) to state the bare facts about the use, scope and updating features of a particular reference tool, *American Law Reports Annotated,* for example; (2) to propound a credit card problem that involves its use; (3) to instruct the user to turn off the tape and consult (a) a volume of *ALR* that it cites and (b) the accompanying text in order to solve the problem; and (4) to sum up what has been taught, and presumably learned, about that reference tool.

This work is a model of clarity and conciseness and a tribute to Betty Taylor and her contributing editors, all of whom are experienced law school librarians.

Following are the contents of *Audio Research in the Law,* the editors and their law schools:

(1) Introduction to the American Legal System–Frederick S. Baum (Cardozo).

(2) Dictionaries, Encyclopedias, Periodicals–Roy M. Mersky (Texas).

(3) Treatises, Practice Books, Looseleaf Services, Dictionaries –Betty W. Taylor (Florida).

(4) Case Law and Digests–Dan Henke (Hastings).

(5) Annotated Reports–Betty W. Taylor.

(6) Statutory Law–Julius J. Marke (New York University).

(7) Administrative Law–Robert C. Berring (Harvard).

(8) Citators–Christine Anderson-Brock (DePaul).

A final cassette and chapter on government documents have recently been released.

Highlights and a Drawback

Some of its highlights discussed below demonstrate how effective *Audio Research* is as a learning instrument. But they also point up a minor drawback; the speed with which specific references to

CFR or *Shepard's Citations* supplements, for example, become obsolete. A sophisticated lawyer can take two or three outdated references in stride, but not more. He will realize that the publication referred to on the tape must have been revised after the tape was released. But a law publisher should plan to update his publications regardless of whether they appear in spoken or in printed form. This may of course already be in work.

Administrative Law

On the Administrative Law tape, and in its related chapter in the treatise, the editor makes clear through references to the *United States Government Manual* the framework of the federal government and the relationships between the federal agencies and Congress on one hand and the federal agencies and the courts on the other.

Using the credit-card theme, he analyzes the contents of a typical issue of the *Federal Register* and he explains how rules and regulations come into being and how they are eventually codified in the *Code of Federal Regulations.* Next he explains with great skill the use of the various finding tools for both the *Federal Register* and *CFR*.

But even as he spoke and wrote, the government altered and improved the makeup of those tools–making obsolete a portion of his remarks. This tape is too good and too important to stand as published. Its publisher has promised to revise and update it. At that time its state administrative law section could be expanded to cover credit-card regulation as shown in periodic bulletins and administrative codes of two or three major commercial states.

Shepard's Citations

It is a mark of the high quality of the final chapter–on *Shepard's Citations*–that this listener's interest was actually heightened, even after listening to all the other tapes–some of them twice–during more than four solid hours.

This chapter contains as lucid an introduction to the major *Shepard's Citations* as can be found anywhere. Its varied credit-card problems force the listener to learn the system.

But its greater virtue is in pinpointing the less obvious features in *Shepard's* publications—those that most lawyers never knew or quickly forgot. Some examples: The precise order in which the different kinds of citations appear in each of the publications: the publications that cover law review articles on the law of particular states, those that contain attorney general opinions both federal and state, the location of *Lawyer's Edition* annotations and the relative advantages of regional and state *Shepard's* for various purposes.

Remaining Chapters

There are impressive sections on the use of treatises and practice books, on the interrelationships of the components of *American Jurisprudence, ALR* and other general research works, a detailed guide to both "Lexis" and "Westlaw" and extensive information on non-legal research indexes and guides.

These and the remaining chapters on case and statute law—drafted with thoroughness and skill—together with the practice exercises give the practitioner or student a combined listening and reading guide to American legal research.

CHAPTER 46

AUDIO CASSETTE TAPES AND CONTINUING LEGAL EDUCATION

A convenient, time-saving and inexpensive method of keeping abreast of changes in the law and of learning techniques and "know-how" from acknowledged experts in the field, is available today to practitioners in media format known as audio cassettes. Audio cassette tapes have been used extensively throughout the country in the last decade for Continuing Legal Education (CLE) programs and are steadily growing in use. Their value lies in the recognition that practising lawyers have little time to devote to post graduate law courses, or even to the more abbreviated CLE programs offered by bar associations, law schools and commercial CLE organizations. When properly edited and condensed into one-hour segments on tape, busy lawyers are provided the opportunity to squeeze the information taped into their discretionary time. Many of them take advantage of commutation hours to catch up on their legal homework.

Acceptability to Lawyers

It has been established that audio cassettes are more acceptable to lawyers than the "talking face" or "talking head" on videotape when it is desirable to have a straight lecture-type format. The straight lecture type format is prepared when there is a need to disseminate information quickly, which occurs when a new law or a comprehensive revision of a code goes into force. In those situations all that is sought by the attorney is the substance of the lecture rather than the appearance of the speaker. Actually, it could be quite boring to watch a person speak for an hour or two at a time.

Combined with the low costs involved, audio cassette listening for straight lectures appears to be more attractive and user acceptable, than videotapes. There are occasions when a live Institute program is videotaped on a subject of significant current interest to lawyers, such as the Tax Reform Act of 1976, and then made available to lawyers for purchase or rental almost immediately after they were produced. In those situations the urgency of the material can compensate for the lack of visual appeal. However, the producers of audio cassettes are similarly aware of the urgency of informative and instructive tapes on these new developments and release them expeditiously such as Condyne/Transmedia did for the Tax Reform Act of 1976.

Use by Law Libraries

Audio cassette tapes are easy to use and relatively inexpensive. As a result they have become so popular that law libraries are now using them extensively as part of their multimedia activity. They have become sufficiently inexpensive and the tapes and tape players are small enough and light enough in weight to allow them to be circulated to the library's users. As they can be heard with headphones, this permits their use in libraries, offices and even at home, without interfering with the concentration of others in the room. Furthermore, special installations of wiring and soundproofing are not necessary—a feature which makes them highly attractive in libraries. Actually, compatible tape players have been so extensively purchased for private use, even in automobiles, that the ordinary library user need only request the tape itself to be borrowed for a short period of time.

Magnetic audio tapes are used in audio cassettes information recording. Experts in the field believe they are superior to disc recording, for they can be heard without the use of a phonograph needle or stylus which prevents the physical wearing out of the tape through use. Magnetic tapes are also compact and hence can not only store an hour's lecture on a comparatively small cartridge, but also can be played on light weight, physically small, portable tape recorders. Added mobility also results from the fact that they operate efficiently on battery-operated models as well as those supplied by electric current. As most audiotapes today are recorded on cassettes and cartridges, which operate automatically, they save the unusual wear and tear of manual threading. All that need be done to use them is to insert them in the cassette player.

Anatomy of Product

Audio tapes are made of plastic and coated with a layer of iron oxide or chromium oxide. The thickness of these tapes is measured by a MIL. One mil equals one-thousandth of an inch. The standard thickness of tapes are 1.5 mil, 1 mil, and .5 mil. Tape reels are available in the popular sizes of three, four, five and seven inches in diameter. A three-inch reel will hold 150 feet of 1.5 mil tape; a four-inch reel 300 feet, a five-inch reel 600 feet and a seven-inch reel, 1,200 feet. All reels accommodate a tape that is one-quarter inch wide.

Cassettes are labelled with a capital C followed by a number which reflects the playing time. Thus C15 indicates a total playing time of fifteen minutes; C20, thirty minutes; C45, forty-five minutes; C60, sixty minutes, C90, ninety minutes and C120, 120 minutes. No matter which of the length of playing times indicated above, they can be housed in the same size cassette. This is achieved by using a thinner tape on the longer playing cassette. The thinner the tape, the greater the possibility of jamming in the cassette, an occurrence which usually prevents it from being used again. It would appear that the sixty-minute playing time tape would thus be preferable to the ninety-minute and 120-minute format.

In this context, it should also be noted that a full-track tape recorder records and plays back the recorded presentation only on the full width of the tape. A half-track tape recorded uses only one-half the width of the tape. This permits the half track tape to be played on both sides, for when completed on one side, it can be turned over, and after being threaded through the recorder, the other half can be heard. There is also a greater track tape recorded which can record on four separate tracks.

Mostly Half-Track

Obviously, for commercial purposes, the tracking format of the tape must be compatible with tape recorders and tape players generally in use. Otherwise a full-track recording played on a half-track recorder would be of poor fidelity. The reverse situation will cause both tracks to be heard simultaneously. Most cassette recorders and tapes used today commercially are in half-track format.

There are a number of national commercial producers of audio cassette programs for lawyers. Probably the largest CLE leader in the field is Condyne/Transmedia of Dobbs Ferry, N.Y., founded in 1969 as Condyne, Inc. It is a member of the Oceana Group of publishing companies in Dobbs Ferry since 1974. Condyne has produced more than 250 titles since its beginning, 120 of which are currently in circulation. New law tapes are released approximately every six weeks by Condyne.

The Condyne CLE Service, known as Condyne Law Tapes, covers many fields of law. A quick check of the Condyne catalogue reveals subjects such as real estate, estate planning, corporate and SEC, business and banking, criminal, constitutional, personal injury and litigation, taxation, international and multinational and legal research. The programs feature lectures by practitioners and legal scholars who have achieved recognition in their fields of expertise. They create substantive materials for Condyne, either by directly recording their own remarks or submitting written manuscripts which are later recorded in Condyne's studios by professional narrators. Seminars of national CLE groups, such as Southwestern Legal Foundation, California Attorneys for Criminal Justice, the American Branch of the International Law Association and similar organizations also are purchased by Condyne and sold individually or as sets.

ALI-ABA, a Big Producer

Another well-known national producer of audio cassette tapes for lawyers is the American Law Institute–American Bar Association Committee on Continuing Legal Education known popularly as ALI-ABA. Located in Philadelphia, it reproduces live recordings of its seminars in various fields of law such as Federal, Civil and Criminal Litigation, Anti-Trust, Arbitration, Bankruptcy, Corporations, Environmental Law, Evidence, Franchising, Housing, Investments, Legal Ethics, Nuclear Energy, Professional Corporations, Real Estate, Shopping Centers, Taxation, Uniform Commercial Code and Zoning.

Other companies in the field nationally are ATLA (American Trial Lawyers Association) of Washington, D.C., which prepares counseling cassettes for its membership on a subscription basis, and on a limited basis, and Commerce Clearing House of New York and Chicago, which offers some prepared programs in tax law. Some recent ATLA audio cassettes have been on products liability litigation, persuasion in advocacy, proof of damages, contemporary criminal defense techniques and psychology, preparation and settlement in the civil case. ALI-ABA, ATLA and CCH also use experienced and leading members of the bar and professors of law to lecture on the subjects involved.

An audio cassette program in which lawyers may be peripherally interested is run by the Center for the Study of Democratic Institutions of Santa Barbara, California. The Center is a non-profit, educational institution whose purpose is to identify and explore the basic issues underlying a democratic society and to widen the works of discussion about them. Center meetings and conferences are recorded and edited into audiotape/cassette programs on education, political science, international relations, law and justice, economics, sociology, psychology, communications and other subjects in the social science and political science fields. Most of their programs run thirty to sixty minutes. A recently announced program of Cassette recordings on the Future of the Criminal Justice System covers "Toward a New Jurisprudence;" "International Law," "The Police Role in the Year 2000:" "Pre-Trial Arbitrators:" "Proposal for a New Model, and New Kinds of Crime," "New Methods of Control: The System Grows."

Many state bar associations also produce live seminars in various fields of law, or prepared texts recorded in a professional studio. They vary in price generally from approximately $20 to $150 a packaged program.

To suggest the broad scope of legal subjects available in audiocassettes, reference should be made to the October 1978 issue of

The Record of the Association of the Bar of the City of New York, pages 440–449. Under the heading "The Library," the staff lists by subject the audio-cassettes in the library's collection. Many of these are lectures delivered at the association under the sponsorship of LACE, and issued by ALI-ABA. This list will be kept up-to-date by including new cassettes in the library's periodic publication of "recipient acquisition."

CHAPTER 47

COPYRIGHT LAW AND PHOTOCOPYING IN LIBRARIES*

Consumers of intellectual property (educators, researchers, scholars and librarians) and copyright owners (publishers and authors) are presently joined in a battle over library photocopying of copyrighted publications, the outcome of which could have serious consequences for research and the free flow of information.

Two developments brought this confrontation to a head before the enactment of the new copyright law. One was the case of *Williams and Wilkins v. U.S.* (decided by the U.S. Court of Claims on Nov. 27, 1973, 487 F. 2d 1345), which was scheduled for review by the U.S. Supreme Court. The other, the approval by the U.S. Senate on Sept. 9, 1974 of S. 1361, a bill for the general revision of the copyright law. The *Williams and Wilkins* case raised the issue whether libraries may photocopy, without profit, copyrighted publications in their collections, at the request of, and for the sole use of, their readers and other libraries. S. 1361, perhaps in anticipation of the Supreme Court decision, imposed in its section 108(g) such restrictive limitations on library photocopying amounting to "systematic reproduction" of "multiple" copying, that if approved by the House in that form, would sound the death-knell for network planning among libraries and destroy the possibility of an adequate national library and information system.

Clear Issue

At stake was whether libraries could improve the flow of information by taking advantage of the many technological develop-

*This was written before the enactment of the new copyright law. It should be read with chapter 48, following.

ments in photocopying and telecommunications techniques available today, without infringing on the rights and privileges of the copyright owner. In essence, the issue was clear. In light of the new technology in replication and communication, how do librarians and information specialists promote scholarship and research and preserve the public's right of accessibility to information and at the same time allow for the incentive necessary for creators of intellectual property to continue to create, and for their publishers to remain in business.

Over the years, much thought has been given to this problem. Copyright authorities, educators and scholars reflecting the felt needs of both owners and users of intellectual properly have spoken endlessly at conferences and written voluminously on the subject. As far back as 1785, Lord Mansfield stated the problem well in *Sayre v. Moore* (102 Eng. Rep. 139).

> "We must take care against two extremes equally prejudicial; the one that men of ability who have employed their time for the service of the community, may not be deprived of their just merits and the reward of their ingenuity and labor, the other that the world may not be deprived of improvements, nor the progress of the arts be retarded."

Marshall McLuhan, with his customary insight, aptly suggested the stark realities of the problem when he wrote: "In the age of Xerox, the reader becomes a publisher and so does the school room."

Purpose of Protection

Generally, the purpose of copyright protection is to encourage and reward authors of intellectual works and other creative artists to produce such works for the benefit of society, by granting them the exclusive right during a specific period of time to copy, or otherwise multiply, publish, sell or distribute them, as well as to prepare derivative works based upon the copyrighted work. They are also given the exclusive privilege to perform and record these works and to license their production or sale by others during the term of the copyright protection. Basically, the purpose of copyright, as is stated in Article I, Section 8, Clause 8, of the U.S. Constitution is "to promote the progress of science and the useful arts." This implies that the copyright holder's rights are not necessarily absolute, for the monopoly granted serves the added purpose of stimulating the development of scientific and other types of knowledge and to encourage the dissemination of this knowledge to the public.

To avoid frustrating this purpose, most countries have adopted the concept of a "fair use" or a "fair-dealing" doctrine, which permits individuals and institutions other than the copyright owner to use the copyrighted material in a reasonable manner without the owner's consent. In essence, the "fair use" doctrine attempts to balance the rights of the owners of copyrighted works to their just economic rewards against the rights of scholars and researchers to use these works conveniently in their scholarly endeavors.

As the "fair use" doctrine is an equitable rule, each case is determined by its own facts. The courts in the U.S. generally apply guidelines laid down initially by Justice Story in *Folsom v. March* (9 Fed. Case 342, CCD Mass., 1841) in deciding whether an infringement of fair use has occurred. S. 1371, the new copyright revision bill, reflects these decisional guidelines in its Section 107, when for the first time statutorily it recognizes the principle of "fair use" and lists the following factors to be considered in determining whether a particular use falls within this catalog:

> "(1) The purpose and character of the use;
>
> "(2) The nature of the copyrighted work;
>
> "(3) The amount and substantiality of the portion used in relation to the copyrighted work as a whole; and
>
> "(4) The effect of the use upon the potential market for or value of the copyrighted work."

However, as brought out in the Senate Report of the Judiciary Committee to accompany S. 1361, "The endless variety of situations and combinations of circumstances that can arise in particular cases precludes the formulation of exact rules in the statute.... Beyond a very broad statutory explanation of what fair use is and some of the criteria applicable to it, the courts must be free to adapt the doctrine to particular situations on a case-by-case basis."

No Commercial Advantage

S. 1361, Section 108, provided that under certain conditions, it is not an infringement of copyright for a library or archives to reproduce not more than one copy of a work, if made without any purpose of commercial advantage for purposes of preservation and security of unpublished works in the library's collection, to replace damaged copies, out-of-print works and of one article or other contribution to a copyrighted collection or of a periodical or of a small part of any other copyrighted work at the request of a user or by another library pursuant to an inter-library loan provided the copy becomes the property of the user for private study or scholarship. It also permits unsupervised photocopying on the library premises by the user provided there is no violation of copyright.

These provisions appear to be generous to a certain extent but in subsection (g) of section 108, the blow falls! Subsection (g) provides that the rights granted by this section extend only to the "isolated and unrelated reproduction of a single copy" and therefore does not authorize the related or concerted reproduction of multiple copies of the same material whether made on one occasion or over a period of time, and whether intended for aggregate use by one individual or for separate use by the individual members of a group.

Subsection (g) also provides that section 108 does not authorize the "systematic reproduction" of copies of copyrighted works whether or not multiple copies are reproduced. The Senate Report states "Systematic reproduction . . . occurs when a library makes copies of such materials available to other libraries or to groups of users under formal or informal arrangements whose purpose or effect is to have the reproducing library serve as their source of such materials."

Objections Raised

Library administrators and scholars vehemently object to section 108 and particularly its subsection (g) believing that it affects the viability and feasibility of our national library and information system in that its effect is to make it impossible to plan network planning among groups of libraries and also makes it improper for a public library system to use photocopy as a means of supplying the needs of its branch libraries for little used works.

Replication of copyright works is daily taking place in libraries as part of the educational process. At present, it is primarily reflected in reprographic reproduction (reproduction by photographic methods or processes analogous to photography), and is an established and recognized practice in library administration, teaching and research.

Reprography in libraries and for educational purposes should not be confused, however, with computerized retrieval of data and information, which in its present state of development is still not a serious threat to owner of intellectual property, but which could eventually become so. Researchers, librarians and educators in the future will then become involved with new techniques of electronic document storage and computerized information-retrieval systems just as they are presently learning about the tremendous potential of miniaturization and remote transmission of data.

Pressing Problems

Currently, however, the most pressing problems facing owners and users of copyrighted publications lie in the reprography area as distinguished from electronic information systems.

Scholars, researchers and librarians, relying on the doctrine of fair use, have always felt free to copy by hand the works of others for their own research and study needs. When copying machines became available, it was a simple transition for them to extend their note-taking to photocopying. Publishers maintain that the new machine-copiers have made replication of their copyrighted works so easy and inexpensive that their sales are being detrimentally affected to the point that if allowed to continue, they will eventually be forced out of business. As a result, the creator of information would lack the income from his ideas to maintain a degree of independence.

Educators particularly object to any limitation of their right to make machine-copies on the grounds that they, like librarians, are not doing so for profit, nor for any direct or indirect commercial advantage, but rather to promote the educational process.

Natural Extension

The traditional library position on reprography in libraries is to the effect that not only under the Fair Use doctrine, but also as a natural extension of customary library service, a library may make a single copy of copyrighted material it has purchased, for the scholarly use of any of its readers or another library, requesting such service, if done without commercial advantage. Librarians maintain, that such service, employing modern copying methods has become essential. They also assert that the present demand can be satisfied without inflicting measureable damage on publishers and copyright owners. Librarians also argue, no matter who is involved, whether it be the librarian, the publisher, or the creator of information, the main concern should be the public interest in access to information. Copyright protection should not be an impediment to transferring information.

This confrontation between owners and users of copyrighted works raises the question, why is there so much photocopying being done at present in libraries? The information explosion has created an overwhelming amount of printed information available today to the extent that it appears to be doubling every ten years. This phenomenon has been accompanied by an increasing demand for quick information. Thus, the time spent in reducing information to a usable, convenient form is time wasted for the researcher. Furthermore, the scientist or engineer needs ideas from others to form his own.

Thus, as Charles P. Yerkes has pointed out: "The researcher, student, scientist, or engineer does not really want the copy he has. . . . He is fundamentally looking for ideas. The fact that it is on a piece of paper in this particular form could not matter less to him. He is looking for ideas within the paper: 'Hattery and Bush (eds.), *Reprography and Copyright Law* (71–72, 1964)'.

It should also be noted that a considerable portion of copying activities involves duplications of non-copyrighted materials, such as government publications or copying under conditions the "fair use" doctrine would allow.

Publishers' Position

Publishers allege that although libraries are not in the business of photocopying for profit, still by doing so, they are depriving publishers of the opportunity to sell additional copies and even to maintain their current subscriptions in the *Williams and Wilkins Case* involving a U.S. Government library's unauthorized photocopying of copyrighted medical periodicals for and at the request of medical researchers and practitioners, the U.S. Court of Claims not only held this practice constituted "fair use," but that "there is inadequate reason to believe, that it (the publisher) is being or will be harmed substantially by these specific practices" 487 F. 2d at 1354 (a contrary conclusion was reached in the minority opinion).

Actually, it is the opinion of a considerable number of observers that if most of the users in libraries who photocopy copyrighted materials would be deprived of this opportunity, or be required to pay an extra fee to do so, they would not pay the extra fee or would not purchase the original material. Then again, researchers, scholars and academicians rarely purchase all or even a few of the books and journals they refer to in their research. They receive complimentary copies and reprints of articles or they borrow library copies. Only if these sources fail to provide the materials sought, do they resort to photocopying. The publishers' complaint that photocopying is depriving them of profits because of lost sales may therefore not be a completely valid conclusion. Many of the potential sales the publishers envision are not of the type that ordinarily occur.

While libraries and large industrial organizations are principally involved in photocopying of copyrighted works (also there is much private and casual copying by students, faculty and others in university libraries), still they continue to purchase many new titles and journal subscriptions, as well as maintaining the older subscriptions.

Economics of Publishing

In this context, we should also review the economics of publishing. It is an established fact that publishers of scientific and technical journals, publish limited editions of their issues so that they often are unable to sell additional copies on demand as early as two months after publication. They do not invest in maintaining stock of back issues of their publications, and hardly ever reprint them, thus depriving themselves of the opportunity to sell their back issues on demand. Still they are insisting on the payment of fees additional to the subscription price of the publications, for photocopying rights of these back issues.

Then again, publishers, specially in the areas of scientific and technical reference works, do market research before publishing new titles and publish them only when assured that libraries will purchase them in addition to specialists in the field. When they determine that the sale of a particular work will be limited, the list price established is increased to reflect this in order to insure a profit.

Surveys have also established that as many as 80 per cent of authors of scientific articles are more interested in dissemination of their articles than in receiving royalties. In the scientific field, it should also be noted, authors not only do not receive remuneration for their articles, but often are required to pay for the cost of having them published or absorb the cost by purchasing a stated number of reprints. It has also been noted that subjects dealt with in scientific literature and some of the other disciplines such as law have become so specialized that most researchers in those fields are interested sometimes only in one out of the many published in a particular journal. Reprography in libraries and documentation centers appears to be the only obvious way today for researchers to have access to the many scholarly resources of their field.

Publishers' Complaint

Publishers complain, however, that they are bearing the economic brunt of this development. The hardware and paper used for reprography are bought and paid for by libraries. Why shouldn't publishers be given additional income for the right to make copies of their copyrighted works? They also add that even though scientists, etc., pay for publication of their research papers, they should be concerned with the survival of the scientific journals which give them an opportunity to disseminate their findings and research reports.

Librarians and educators respond that their institutions have nothing to gain by photocopying for others as they receive no commercial benefit from it. Their purpose is only to promote research in the sciences and humanities in the public interest. They are involved with access to acknowledge and its bibliographical control so that scholars, educators, scientists and others involved in research can use such data in their research and in the process create new information and materials. Why should librarians, under these circumstances, be caught in the middle of the conflict between owners and users of copyrighted works, and be required to take sides? When librarians become concerned with the economics of the new technology in this context, they are side-tracking their ulterior purpose of dissemination of information in the public interest.

Library institutions do have an interest in the reproduction of copyrighted works for their own internal, non-profit purposes. They have a vital concern in conserving copies of periodicals and of works in their collection which are out of print. They also have an interest in reproducing mutilated or missing pages of works in their collection. Then again, in order to concerve their collection, they recognize the need to photocopy materials in their collection for other libraries requesting them on inter-library loan. Ground rules should be negotiated for these purposes but not at the expense of limiting the free flow of information, and certainly not with the added cost to libraries for administering a system involving payment of fees, licensing, etc., for the benefit of owners of copyrighted works.

Restraints Not Sought

Publishers insist that they are just as interested in the free flow of information as the users of their works. They do not wish to impose prior restraints on access to copyrighted works rather they wish to encourage such use, but by the same token their economic concerns should be met. Therefore they support the imposition of a fee or licensing system, either mandatory or voluntary, for photocopying privileges in which the librarian and educator become accountable to the publishers on behalf of their users. The Senate

Committee Report to accompany S. 1361 appears to reflect the Committee's approval of some sort of licensing plan. For not only does it recommend that "representatives of authors, book and periodical publishers and other owners of copyrighted material meet with the library community to formulate photocopying guidelines to assist library patrons and employees," but it adds, "concerning library photocopying practices not authorized by this legislation, the Committee recommends that workable clearance and licensing procedures be developed" (p. 122).

Librarians are concerned that the administrative costs of accounting for photocopying can eventually become prohibitive and will erode library budgets for book purchases, etc. It should be noted in this context that most library institutions, even large government libraries and private libraries with substantial resources, face economic problems which could force them to discontinue photocopying or continue it at the expense of cutting down on their book budgets.

It is questionable, too, how profitable such a system would be for the owners of copyrighted works and how the fees thus collected would be equitably distributed. A knowledgeable publisher. Curtis Benjamin, has stated, that such systems are not "cheap" and "easy" and he doubts whether "nominal" fees could provide the financial support required for charging, accounting, paying and receiving fees and for dividing them with authors. The publishers would be paying nickles and dimes to collect pennies. The answer, he believes, may lie in the payment of substantial rather than nominal fees, substantial enough to absorb the cost of the system, or in a government subsidy of a million dollars or more annually.

Administrative Cost

It has also been pointed out that more than $300 million a year would have to be spent to maintain an administrative system of royalty payments to authors, whereas the total royalty payments to authors in 1967 was between $250 to $300 million (Breyer, *The Uneasy Case of Copyright,* 84 Harv. L. Rev. 281, 1970). This estimate was based upon the Committee to Investigate Copyright problems (Office of Education, U.S. Dept. of H.E.W. Project No.

7093, 1967), which concluded that 1.8 billion pages of copyrighted material would be copied in 1969.

It is also obvious, in this context, that the exemptions granted for photocopying under the doctrine of "fair use" would not be applicable, nor for that matter would publications in the public domain be excused from imposition of a copying fee.

Then again, individual researching scholars, who would have to pay the copying fee of five or six cents a page, and who could not afford to do so, would either forsake the use of such materials or hand-copy them at a great sacrifice of time and effort as they would with a straight library loan. Either way, the publisher will not gain any additional fee payments and only those privileged scholars who could afford the payment of a flat fee for photocopying and the additional cost of library administration could take advantage of it. As one copyright observer has noted, "The situation of scholarly photocopying is essentially unlike the artistic copyright situations where ASCAP and BMI operate. Most of those involve performance which create income. Library copying is service-oriented rather than fee-generating. Indeed, many libraries operate at break-even point or at a loss and cannot afford to subsidize scholars. Society would lose the benefit obtained from the dissemination of useful information to other scholars (Yanow, Copying, The Reconciliation of Conflicting Interest, 3 Rutgers J. Comm. 328, 343, 1974).

Elimination Seen

Thus, as many experts have concluded a photocopying licensing system could result in the complete elimination of photocopying by libraries. This would not only have the effect of making it impossible to proceed with network planning among groups of libraries but would compel researchers and scholars to make their own photocopies independently on unsupervised self-operating photocopies located in the library, thus bypassing the library and avoiding the fee completely. On the other hand, the cost to copyright owners of recovering damages for copyright infringement through the courts would be so onerous that only large government or corporate libraries could be sued.

Recent developments suggest that the solution to the photocopying problem lies elsewhere. Librarians and the educational community would prefer to cooperate with the publishing industry. Publishers complain that photocopy costs are so cheap that libraries, etc., are encouraged to make these copies at the expense of purchasing extra copies. But this trend is being reversed. Photocopying used to cost about 25 cents a page, then was reduced to 15 cents to 10 cents and now to 5 cents. But photocopying costs are rising. Ten cents is now required to make a photocopy in many libraries and with paper, chemicals, labor, etc., dramatically rising in cost, we probably will be facing 25 cents charges not too far in the future. At the same time the computer costs are being reduced at an astonishing rate.

Technological advances such as miniaturization of computer circuiting have made possible vast increases in computation speed from about 2,000 multiplications a second on an IBM computer in 1952 to more than two million a second today. Thus, although in 1952, it cost $1.26 to do 100,000 multiplications on an IBM computer, today they can be done for one cent. These lowered computer costs make it practical to use computers in an ever-widening range of applications.

Availability

With the available modern technology, publishers should be able to provide, on a competitive basis, copies of their publications required by educators and researchers without imposing a licensing or fee system on library institutions. The film strips, charts, chapters, or pages of books and the reprints of articles could all be supplied by the publishers on a cost-plus-royalty basis, low enough to encourage or entice libraries and school districts to purchase multiple copies from them rather than photocopy them. Publishers could cooperatively become involved in "demand" publishing. They could establish cooperative regional offices to service these requests or develop alternate systems on university campuses. Eventually, these systems could be linked up with computer storage and retrieval units that would provide practically instantaneous transmission, remote, ephemeral, or hard copy. Once the dissemination of copy is centralized within the control of the publishers, a logical solution to the photocopying problem is possible.

Publishers claim that the user of copyrighted materials is becoming a publisher by the use of photocopying machines. One way to remedy this is for the publishers to establish an improved publishing service that will provide photocopies and service at a competitive rate.

Some publishers are preparing for this future by establishing prototype systems on an experimental basis. McGraw-Hill and the Institute for Scientific Information are now offering rapid retrieval of great quantities of published information by establishing information centers and computer-based index and abstract files to provice "on-demand" publishing at competitive prices. An article by Paul Doebber entitled "New Computerized Services Provide Speedy (But Not Free) Copies On Demand," published in the Nov. 18, 1974, issue of *Publishers Weekly,* should be read by all publishers and members of Congress. Rather than run to the Wailing Wall, publishers should take heed, gird their loins, change their mode of operation radically and join the age of the Non-Book.

CHAPTER 48

NEW COPYRIGHT LAW: THE "FAIR USE" DEBATE

Since the new copyright law (Pub. L. No. 94-553, 90 Stat. 2541 (1976), 17 U.S.C. sec. 1 et seq.) went into force on Jan. 1, 1978 a highly disturbing confrontation appears to be brewing on the very same issue that contributed to the delay in its passage for almost twenty years—namely library and educational photocopying of copyrighted works.

Not surprisingly the same contending parties are in the forefront of the fray and the rhetoric and commentary, revolve, once again, around the doctrine of *fair use.* At stake is how to accommodate photocopying of copyrighted materials by teachers, librarians, scholars and researchers (who do so without seeking any commercial advantage) and still preserve the legal interests of the copyright owner of the materials so replicated. As in the past, the same issue is once again being raised—how to keep knowledge and the economy free especially in light of the information explosion and the new technology.

Evolution of Copying

Scholars, researchers and librarians, relying on the doctrine of *fair use,* always felt free to copy by hand the works of others for their own research and study needs. When more and more sophisticated copying machines became available, it was a simple transition for them to extend their note-taking to photocopying from copyrighted material. Publishers contend, however, that these new machine copies make replication of their copyrighted materials so easy and inexpensive that their sales are being detrimentally affected to the point that if allowed to continue they would be forced out of business.

Traditionally, the library position, as well as that of the educational community, has been to the effect that under the Fair Use Doctrine, a single photocopy may be made by a library of copyrighted materials it has purchased, for the scholarly use of any of its readers, or another library requesting such service, if done without profit. Librarians claim that such service employing modern copying methods has become essential and that the demand for such copies can be satisfied without inflicting measurable damage on publishers and copyright owners.

Librarians also assert that copying by librarians primarily is for the benefit of their library users. Library users often want their own copy of a journal article or part of another published work. This is so because even if they would be willing to purchase these materials in most instances (specially with reference to scientific, technical and medical publications), they are not in print, or not available for other reasons.

The modern library today offers service more in the nature of an information resource. Hence, it cannot serve the interests of its users by purchasing additional copies of works. Not only would this be a financial strain on its resources, but basically it is impossible in advance user demand for particular works except for occasional publications of significant interest. Thus, if additional copies could not satisfy the needs of its users, then the only alternative would be to permit photocopying by librarians and justify it as being analogous to unsupervised copying by individual users under the *fair use* doctrine.

The Publishers' Argument

Publishers, however, maintain that although libraries are not in the business of photocopying for profit, still by doing so they are depriving them of the opportunity to sell additional copies and even to maintain their current subscriptions. Furthermore, they insist, even if photocopies are not available for sale, still they can impose fees for photocopying of their copyrighted works under certain conditions and even the *Fair Use* Doctrine does not justify unauthorized photocopying by libraries. The publishers too have a similar interest as librarians in allowing access to their publication but argue that if such access can only be accomplished by photocopying, then a small license fee paid for such a privilege would certainly not be a barrier to it.

Congress attempted to meet the thrust of both these positions by providing a compromise solution in section 108 of the new law and accepting as minimum standards a compromise position on permissive library photocopying in the form of guidelines negotiated by CONTU (Commission on New Technological Uses of Copyrighted Works) between representatives of the publishers and authors on one side and researchers, scholars and librarians on the other.

And here is the rub in the pending new copyright conflict! Librarians contend that the new law is fairly explicit about the rights granted to library researchers, etc., as they relate to the photocopying of copyrighted works and similarly to librarians making such photocopies for library purposes.

The Librarians' Interpretation

For example, they point to the provisions of section 108 and note that as they interpret them, librarians can easily accommodate their own interests (e.g., preservation or replacement of library materials) to the photocopying by libraries as allowed thereunder.

As long as a library's collection is open to the public or available to outside researchers (even on a limited scale and under prescribed conditions) and the copying is not done for commercial advantage and copies made include a notice of copyright, then such a library may legally reproduce an unpublished work in its collection for purposes of preservation and security; it may also reproduce for purposes of replacement a published work that is damaged, lost or stolen after a reasonable effort has determined that an unused replacement cannot be obtained at a fair price; and it also allows the reproduction of an entire work or a substantial part of it, by the library, if it is determined, after a reasonable investigation, that a copy cannot be obtained at a fair price.

Librarians also note that under section 107 pertaining to *Fair Use,* libraries are permitted to make photocopies of copyrighted works when appropriate under the four criteria set forth therein. *Fair use* has been defined as the right to use copyrighted materials in a reasonable manner without the copyright owner's consent. The doctrine is obviously a limitation on the copyright owners' exclusive rights (section 106) to the work and, as developed by the courts over the last 100 years, is looked to by librarians, teachers, researchers, scholars, and others as permitting the use of such copyrighted works without authorization from the copyright owner for purposes of criticism, comment, news reporting, teaching (including multiple copies for classroom use), scholarship or research.

The purpose and character of the "fair" use—including whether such use is of a commercial nature or is for non-profit educational purposes, the nature of the copyrighted work, the amount and substantiality of the portion used in relation to the copyrighted work as a whole and the effect of the use upon the potential market for or value of the copyrighted work—are the factors courts refer to in determining whether the use made was fair.

The real battle that is coming to a head, however, relates to multiple photocopying as distinguished from single photocopying. It is in this context that, subsection 108(g)(1) and subsection 108(g)(2) and the *Fair Use* Doctrine (section 107) and the CONTU "Guidelines for the Proviso of Subsection 108(8)(2)" are differently interpreted by the copyright owners and publishers on the one side and the researchers, librarians, scholars, etc., on the other.

As indicated above, libraries may make single photocopies of copyrighted works for the preservation and replacement under conditions specified. Under subsection 108(f) researchers may make single copies of copyrighted works on unsupervised photocopying machines on the library's premises provided the criteria of the *Fair Use* Doctrine are met and a notice to that effect is placed on the machine. But, under subsection 108(g), the critical problems arise, for they pertain to multiple copies and systematic reproduction made by libraries.

Subsection 108(g)(1) provides that the photocopying rights granted by section 108 extend only to the "isolated and unrelated reproduction of a simple copy" and therefore do not authorize the "related or concerted reproduction of multiple copies of the same material whether made on one occasion or over a period of time and whether intended for aggregate use by one individual or for separate use by the individual members of a group."

This language must be read with subsection 108(d) which permits a library to make a single copy for a user requesting a copy of all or part of one article from a periodical or small part of another copyrighted work taken from the library's own collection or from that of another library (interlibrary transaction), provided the copy becomes the property of the user, and is made for private study, scholarship or research. The library also has to display a warning notice of possible copyright infringement by the user and place such notice on the order blank.

Legislative Construction

Subsection 108(d) on the other hand must be read with subsection 108(g)(2) which provides that the rights granted in subsection 108(d) do not extend to cases where the library "engages in the systematic reproduction or distribution of a single or multiple copies in material described in subsection (d)." At the insistence of the library community a proviso was added to 108(g)(2) which allows a library to participate in interlibrary arrangements when the receiving library limits the receipt of such copies from supplying library so that in the "aggregate," they do not "substitute for a subscription to or purchase of such work."

What is meant by "systematic" is not too clear, if at all, under the legislative history of the section, although a Senate Report which predated the proviso gave several examples of "systematic" which aroused the library community to the point where Congress responded by accepting as a minimum the guidelines heretofore mentioned, describing what libraries can do under subsection 108 (g)(2).

The guidelines as set forth in a Congressional Conference Report states that they "are not intended as, and cannot be considered, explicit rules or direction governing any and all cases, now or in the future. It is recognized that their purpose is to provide guidance in the commonly-encountered interlibrary photocopying situations, that they are not intended to be limiting or determinative in themselves or with respect to other situations. . . ."

In essence, section 108 provisions and the CONTU guidelines for the proviso of subsection 108(g)(2) permit library copying that exceeds *fair use.* Section 107 *(fair use),* it is to be remembered, allows the making of single copies provided the four factors indicated can be construed favorably to the user. Once *fair use* is involved, librarians contend, each photocopy transaction stands on its own, and subsections 108(g)(1)(2) do not apply even if more than one copy is made. Publishers take a different view and disagree.

The CONTU Guidelines

The CONTU guidelines allow a "requesting" library to obtain on interlibrary loan at least five copies during a calendar year of an article published in a copyrighted periodical within five years prior to the date of the request. The sixth copy thus obtained will be considered a violation of systematic photocopying of copyrighted materials to the extent that the library receiving such sixth copy "does so in such aggregate quantities as to substitute for a subscription or the purpose of such work." The "receiving" library must indicate in its request for a copy that it still had not received more than five copies and keep records of these requests for three years.

It should be noted, that there is no clarification of what, if any, are the penalties involved for a violator other than the obvious implication that a copyright owner may institute an action for infringement of copyright. Note too that the guidelines pertain to interlibrary loans only and not to any other situation, as, for example, on premises photocopying in private controlled and organized research institutions.

The guidelines also apply only to periodicals which have been published within the last five years, and do not apply to periodicals over five years old. Then again, if the requesting library has a subscription to the periodical, the guidelines do not limit the number of requests for photocopies obtained on interlibrary loan.

Non-Profit Institutions

Congress also established classroom guidelines for copying in not-for-profit educational institutions with respect to works and periodicals as the minimum and not the maximum standards of educational *fair use* under section 107. These permit multiple copies equivalent to one copy for each student in a class to be made for classroom use or discussion provided the copying meets tests of brevity and spontaneity. Brevity for poetry is a complete poem if less than 250 words, and 250 words of a longer poem, and a complete article, story or essay of less than 2,500 words or an excerpt from any prose work of not more than 1,000 words or 10 percent of the work, which ever is less, but in any event, a minimum of 500 words.

To meet the test of spontaneity, the copying must be made at the instance and inspiration of the teacher and the decision to use the work and the moment of its use must be so close in time that it would be unreasonable to expect a timely reply to a request for permission. Such copying incidentally may not be used to create or substitute for an anthology; "consumable" works for teaching may not be copied; and the copying can be for only one course in the school, nor more than nine instances of such copying for one course during one class term, nor may more than one short poem, article, story, essay, or two excerpts be copied from the same author, nor more than three from the same collective work or periodical volume during one class term.

Guidelines for educational use of music have also been established.

Librarians and teachers are concerned about the implications of section 108. The guidelines for classroom teaching and interlibrary loan sections 108(g)(1) and (2) particularly are seen as preventing the implementation of many vital library functions (including network planning) made possible through advances in modern photocopying and telecommunication techniques.

The Major Concern

The major concern of librarians is that subsection 108(g)(2) could be interpreted to negate the grant to libraries in section 108 to make single photocopies of copyrighted works and the applicability of the *fair use* doctrine. They are also concerned that "systematic" can be used to whipsaw them. Subsection 108(g)(1) departs from "single" and "multiple." If "systematic" swallows up "single" and the applicability of the *fair use* doctrine, librarians refuse to accept it. Then again, the concept of library single photocopying as *fair use* could be limited under subsections 108(g)(2) to "isolated" and "unrelated" single copying.

The Association of American Law Schools voiced its concern about the guidelines for teaching, as "restricting the doctrine of *fair use* so substantially as to make it almost useless for class room teaching purposes. Requiring a law school teacher to meet all three tests of brevity, spontaneity and cumulative effect stifles the use of copyrighted material for classroom purposes."

It is in these areas, as well as in others, that the publishers allied with authors seek to force the educators, librarians, researchers, etc., to accept interpretations of the law which it appears, by reason of their refusal to do so, can eventually only be resolved in the courts.

Copyright Clearance

The publishers and authors have established a Copyright Clearance Center (C.C.C.), a not-for-profit corporation, to facilitate the collection of royalty payments for photocopying of copyrighted publications which exceeds *fair use* under the new copyright law. They are seeking to arrange for all publishers, especially of scientific, technical and medical periodicals, to participate in this system.

The publishers claim that the library associations refuse to cooperate with them in arranging for such taxing of library photocopying, and as a result, they must proceed independently. They also seek to obtain acceptance of additional guidelines pertaining to corporate library photocopying, intralibrary photocopying, and publications more than five years old. They cannot understand why the librarians refuse to negotiate to establish these additional guidelines, especially with reference to intralibrary guidelines (that copying which the library does for its own use).

Above all, the publishers and authors consider most uncooperative the refusal of librarians to participate in the development of a workable payment mechanism to facilitate permission and payment for large scale copying. This they assert reflects the librarians' basic political strategy "not to facilitate implementation of the new copyright law and to make implementation as difficult as possible and then after a year or two, to persuade Congress that section 108(g)(2) has proved unworkable and should be reviewed."

"We believe the strategy of the library associations is, in fact, determined resistance to the new law, although they are seeking to disguise this blatant truth in various circumstances," the publishers have written.

Purpose of Center

The purpose of the CCC, according to the publishers, is to provide libraries and others the opportunity to make legitimate photocopies of copyrighted materials for a "reasonable" fee, beyond that which is permitted as "fair use" or beyond the additional copying privileges provided in section 108 and the CONTU guidelines.

In addition, the publishers have independently developed their own "guidelines" for photocopying by for-profit corporate libraries under the new copyright law. If, according to their guidelines, a photocopy cannot be made without the copyright owners permission, then that is the time to obtain an automatic clearance through the CCC by paying a fee per page, establishing by each participating publisher in the CCC.

The library profession is concerned about these tactics which "tend to misrepresent the library position on copyright and question the integrity of the leadership of the library community." Robert Wedgeworth, executive director of the American Library Association, recently advised all Association of American Publishers (AAP) members that "the major copyright issues on which publishers and librarians differed were resolved with the enactment of the Copyright Revision Act of 1976. This view appeared to be confirmed when representatives of publishers, authors, and librarians, under direct interrogation in October, 1977, by CONTU Commissioner Perle, replied in turn that they had no recommendations for changes in the law regarding photocopying in libraries at the time. Mr. Wedgeworth continued:

> Statements by the AAP and the Authors League, Inc., have attacked the library community for our willingness to negotiate matters which we believe were settled in the new law. Representatives of the library community have never refused to negotiate legitimate issues concerning copyright. However, we believe that pending the report of the Register of Copyrights on library photocopying mandated by section 108(i) of the new law, we have negotiated all issues necessary for the implementation of the law.
>
> "According to testimony presented before the National Commission on New Technological Uses of Copyrighted Works (CONTU) by several witnesses, the factors affecting the financial viability of journal publishing, for example, are far more complex than library photocopying and the pursuit of further decline of journal revenues. According to research efforts sponsored by CONTU, statistics of library photocopying activities and descriptions of publisher practices have tended to support the library community's position on copyright. . . . It may be that with some experience in working with the new law and having had an opportunity to review the final report of CONTU, problems may be identified which can be resolved through further discussion between copyright proprietors and user groups. . . ."

In the meantime, librarians are being advised by the constituent member associations of the Council of National Library Associations that they exercise fully the rights granted them by the new copyright law before entering into a fee-paying copyright clearance agreement. If there are subsequent decisions, judicial or Congressional, the acceptance of such agreements can be cited as an established criterion. For most library photocopying, it is simply not necessary to request permission or pay any fee to the copyright holder.

It is important that librarians understand and exercise fully these rights. For example, some journals are not copyrighted. Others allow photocopying. Sections 107 and 108 permit other types of photocopying as indicated above. On those occasions on which a library may wish to make multiple copies not permitted by the law, they are advised that copyright clearance should be obtained. The library has three courses it could take: (1) decide that the excess copying can be avoided, (2) request permission from the copyright owner, (3) obtain permission and pay the fee through a centralized service for copyright payments, such as the Copyright Clearance Center.

In this context, it should be noted that librarians can eventually develop their own clearance centers with publishers and NTIS is working on another. It is premature to make a reasoned comparison of services now being established because all details are not known. The Council of National Library Associations has said: "In approaching the law and guidelines, relentless liberalism is no substitute for good judgment and a basic understanding of the law's intent to balance the rights of creators on the one hand and the public's right to access to information on the other."

CHAPTER 49

LAW LIBRARY CONSULTANTS

"Advice is seldom welcome and those who want it the most always like it the least."—The Earl of Chesterfield.

Lawyers want to practice law. They don't earn a living managing their office libraries. Consultants earn a living by offering advice to lawyers and librarians. In the process, consultants may create the illusion that their advice will free lawyers from all management responsibility.

Nothing is further from the truth. Not even a good librarian can accomplish that. However, the consultant does perform a service and usually earns his fee. Since we have traveled that broad street for many years—as lawyer, librarian and consultant—we offer some advice about our three professions together with a few recollections about libraries that were helped—and those that seem untouched—by our professional efforts.

Long before the unshelved books block the aisles, the unfiled looseleaf service bulletins spill down the window sills like confetti and the California volume of *Martindale* disappears for the third time in a week, long before those things happen, the law office needs H-E-L-P. Whether that help comes in the form of a consultant, an enlarged office—or simply a new broom—depends on factors discussed in this chapter. Assume that a consultant is the best starting place or that everything else has already failed.

The Use of Space

Problems of library size and location, satellite book collections and interior arrangement are of primary concern. After a brief study the consultant usually "knows" how to resolve those problems. Curiously enough, other people in the office also "know." They include the lawyers, the librarian, the architect and almost without exception, the interior decorator. Just as curiously, they seem to "know" different things.

Lawyers agree that the best location for a library is just outside each lawyer's door. Some of them attempt to prove it by keeping a major portion of the firm's collection in their own offices–forever, if possible.

Other lawyers would discontinue the hoarding of books so long as a satellite library contained the requirements in their specialty. Tax and labor branches are typical. But we have worked in offices with separate branches covering admiralty law, pension matters, trusts and estates and municipal bond law–both state and local.

Librarians and most consultants prefer a consolidated library where the librarians can concentrate their services to lawyers and keep an eye on their readers and the books at the same time.

'The Heavies'

The beginning architect may try to make a splash with a three-tiered wall of books that requires a crane to reach, while the decorator is content to set aside a corner in which to nurture a pine or palm tree–depending on the climate–and to reserve one wall to simulate a gondola gliding along the Grand Canal in Venice (This is for the windowless library). Meantime, the consultant and librarian play the "heavies." "First, let's find room for the books, the lawyers, the staff and the new machines," they urge.

In all seriousness, the consultant is a watchdog. He makes certain that tables and carrels are people-size, not pygmy-size, that aisles are navigable and shelving adequate for reporter-height books. In one San Francisco company the marbled office corridors are nearly fifteen feet wide. But the aisles between stacks of books in its law library measure only twenty-nine inches.

The consultant is a moderating and moderate influence in all respects save one. That is in his projection of future needs. For example, it is the rare managing partner who believed that the book collection ten years hence will occupy the space estimated for it.

The unfairest feature of consulting work is that it is needed at all. On many occasions the consultant's recommendations are the very ones voiced earlier by the librarian. But they went unheeded.

The Book Collection

There are two patterns that one finds in office libraries along the entire Eastern seaboard and across the country. The first reflects either the remarkable usefulness of certain publications, such as *Rabkin and Johnson,* the BNA *Tax Management* service and *Bittker and Eustice* or the uncanny success of publishers' sales campaigns. In the case of my examples there is no question but that these are superior works.

The other pattern results from the unwillingness of many lawyers to part with any books at all—even those that have remained untouched for a quarter of a century or longer. This pattern the consultant should be able to alter simply by reciting the annual cost of storing even a single book in high rent office buildings.

As for the usefulness of any office collection, that comes with a knowledge of law books on one hand and a discussion of the nature of each individual practice on the other. A successful New Jersey real estate lawyer used to keep only two books in his library, but he kept six secretaries occupied. Other office libraries need 25,000 or more volumes.

The best way to ensure a library's continued usefulness is to try to maintain a balance between the breadth of practice in any branch of law and the extent of coverage of the book collection. The consultant can set standards and draft a collection development plan. But it is the imaginative librarian who can make the plan work.

Library Management

Office practices are too different—and the talents of administrators and librarians too varied—for any single method of library management to work everywhere. In this writer's experience the best run libraries have been those run by expert librarians who assumed maximum responsibility and in whom the firm or department placed utmost confidence. In those libraries the librarian reported to a managing or library partner or to a senior attorney.

The worst run libraries have usually been those in which an uninformed librarian reported to an equally uninformed office manager.

D: LAWYER WORK PRODUCTS

CHAPTER 50

COORDINATED LAW RESEARCH

I

"The large law firm behaves like a hundred separate windmills," a member of an old-line Wall Street firm pointed out recently. "We save about 5 percent of the power we generate—and dissipate the rest," he explained. The small firm fares little better. Can legal research ever be coordinated and its results reused? Three factors are already imposing order on a prodigal profession and causing lawyers to curtail their wasteful research practices:

(1) The merger of some firms hundreds of miles apart and the consequent need to integrate their combined practices;

(2) The increasing cost of law firm legal talent[1] and the parallel growth of corporate legal departments. Those departments are themselves subject to audit by budget-minded company officers who exercise more stringent financial controls than do the members of law firm management committees; and

(3) The prospect of broadened lawyer advertising and its effects on competition between lawyers.

---

[1] A New York Times story on Feb. 4, 1977 pointed out that the private defense of "Government officials in civil suits stemming from Government surveillance activities" will require some $4.8 million next year and that lawyers were hired by those officials last year at some $50 to $75 an hour—at government expense. Federal budget officers, apparently unfamiliar with going rates, were reported to have "passed out" when they heard of it. Is this a sign that much higher rates cannot be endured?

Conservation of Talent

There are signs that the spirit of conservation of talent has begun to sweep across the legal fraternity.

Item: A sixty-man firm in the Midwest persuaded the dean of a respectable law school to join that firm as its research partner.

Item: A comparable Florida firm has begun recruiting to fill such a position. Coordination of research is their primary goal.

Item: Computerized legal research has become commonplace in law offices in the metropolitan centers in the United States.[2] Many American law schools are currently giving their students instruction in the "Lexis" system of legal research.[3]

Item: A large New York firm is conducting an experiment on the computer storage of a major portion of its research results: opinion letters, briefs, memoranda of law.

Item: The "Big Case"—particularly the large antitrust case—has become virtually impossible to prosecute or defend without an individually tailored computer program.[4]

Item: A firm in Richmond, one in Philadelphia and another in Washington, D.C. have each hired a supervisor to co-ordinate the work of their growing battery of paralegal assistants.

The Immediate Future

Can a law office survive any longer—and not co-ordinate, preserve and control its research efforts? Lawyers ask this question with increasing frequency.

During the 1980's, research coordinators will direct the research programs of the offices that are *still expanding.* By 1990, certainly

---

[2] "Lexis" is reported to have some 100 subscribers in New York City alone and over 20 in Philadelphia.

[3] These include among others Harvard, Yale, Penn, Virginia and Michigan.

[4] The largest private antitrust suit—up to the end of World War II—was successfully defended by a battery of lawyers who stored digests of the pertinent documents in a few hundred shoe boxes, after categorizing them in ingenious fashion. What was praised as inventive then would be unworkable for today's "Big Cases", each involving several millions of documents.

by the year 2000, private "Rand Institutes" in each of the great *surviving* law offices will filter, probe, evaluate and solve their legal problems.

The less effective firms will not wither away. But the problems left for them to handle are likely to be less rewarding—both intellectually and financially.

The Research Lawyer

The research coordinator performs two essential functions that in most offices are poorly executed or are not performed at all. First, he explains to his partners and associates the best lines of attack for any new problem that enters the office and he marshals the legal and factual resources needed for solving it. But he does not himself solve the problem. Other lawyers do that. Second, he maintains control over all the research "paper" in every branch of law that his own firm or office generates. He becomes familiar with the intellectual resources—legal and non-legal—available to lawyers everywhere. He is the office encyclopedist.

The research lawyer sits in at the discussions of each new problem that enters the office. He keeps abreast of all research being conducted there and he makes himself available to all lawyers at every stage of their work. With experience he can help apply solutions found in one branch of law to problems in another. At the same time, he reads and criticizes the research output of the office. He makes it his business to know (1) current legal literature, (2) the intellectual resources of his community—libraries, universities, trade associations and government agencies—and (3) the people in other professions, business and government who can facilitate the research side of the office work.

Meanwhile, he organizes the research output so that past office experience on any subject can be retrieved instantly. This entails either careful indexing and analysis or computer storage of the memoranda of law, opinion letters, briefs and corporate, commercial and personal "precedents" in the office. It also requires a system that alerts all lawyers to the existence of any document in this storehouse of knowledge that may be pertinent to their work—a system moreover that performs in timely fashion and not six months after the event.

Inconsistent Advice

Two lawyers who shared a single office in an uptown New York firm several years ago—the senior at the window, the junior at the door—were assigned to work for different partners. By coincidence they were each asked to resolve a series of "doing business" problems for different clients that involved similar kinds of activities in the same states. They began work on these projects the same Monday morning, each spending about two weeks in research. They read the same statutes, cases, law review articles and memoranda of law. At the end of the research, each produced his independent solution to the problems in the form of a heavily annotated memorandum and presented it to the partner who had initiated the work.

The two partners failed to discuss these matters with each other. Nor during this two-week period did the two associates converse about anything more important than the firm's impending choice of new partners—a decision likely to prove as disastrous, they agreed, as all previous choices had been. The result: two weeks of wasted legal effort and two clients who received not altogether consistent advice.

Bridging the distance between basic research coordination—most firms are prepared for that step—and the formation of an in-house "Rand Institute" is a matter of many months or years of careful planning. It may require special preparation in the law schools and will demand greater recognition of research talents in the offices. A few forward-looking firms and corporate legal departments have taken the first steps in that direction. That a coordinator reduces waste in legal effort is alone reason to hire one. His is a new kind of legal career that will soon be open throughout the profession and not merely in the exceptional offices.

II

Dinosaur, mastodon, pterodactyl—lawyer. Must we share the tomb of our predecessors in some future Museum of Natural History? Can we survive the accelerated upheavals in government, business, technology and society, upheavals that form the very springboard of law practice?

The managing partner who could boast only ten years ago, "Ours is the least managed of all the major firms," was praising its freedom from tyranny. Yet he was also exposing the cause of its potential extinction.

The Problems

Today's law office has more to fear from waste and paralysis within than it does from depredation and raiding without. Twenty years of law office observation has helped put the chief problems in focus. They include:

(1) The increasing difficulty and cost of providing sophisticated legal advice;
(2) The accelerating complexity of statute, regulatory and case law, federal state and local;
(3) The rising perils of mistakes through malpractice insurance costs;
(4) The proliferation of law office-created research papers; and
(5) The continued expansion of both law firms and corporate legal departments.

The Solution

The solution, in a word, is coordination. A few lawyers are beginning to control the flow of work through their offices. Some even take time to evaluate and preserve it, in most cases with computer assistance. It is no longer utopian to designate one partner as a full-time research co-ordinator whose job is to pull together all the threads of completed research, and to create an "investment bank" of legal experience within the office. The components of this "bank" include memoranda of law and their drafts, opinion letters, briefs, office files, private files, diary records, forms and precedents, and library collections.

Those phases of law practice that have already been successfully coordinated or automated are discussed below.

Federal Legislative History

It has become commonplace in the major law offices to compile legislative histories. A typical history includes variants of all bills, extracts from the daily edition of the "Congressional Record," committee prints and reports, transcripts of hearings and presidential statements. One firm's collection of legislative histories has become so celebrated over the past forty years that some federal agencies prefer to rely on this private resource instead of on their own histories. This is true even of legislation in their own fields of activity.

In order to ensure completeness, this work begins as soon as bills are introduced. Some essential elements of these histories, particularly the committee prints, are issued in limited quantities. An invaluable guide to their compilation is a commercial serial publication, "Congressional Information Service" known as "CIS."

The West publication, "United States Code, Congressional and Administrative News," which is keyed to that publisher's "United States Code Annotated", reproduces the full text of at least one committee report on every major piece of federal legislation. It cites the remaining reports. But it is no substitute for a full legislative history.

State Legislation

Because it has broad mercantile and real estate interests in every state in the Union, one company is compelled to monitor the progress of virtually all bills introduced in each state legislature. For example, some of the detergent products that it markets may contain a substance that environmentalists seek to *ban* in one state, but which are *required* to be used in others. This company has devised an automated legislative monitoring system that alerts company officials to impending changes.

Many of the law firms also have in-house alertness services that at least cover the activities of their home state legislatures. The commercial services that provide the basic facts for this work in New York are the "Legislative Index" and the "New York Legislative Service".

Survey of Corporate Laws

It has been the practice of a firm whose clients include several companies on the "Fortune 500 List" to summarize the annual changes in the corporation laws of each of the fifty states and the District of Columbia. This summary does not purport to supplant the landmark ABA work, "Model Business Corporation Act Annotated", but rather to be used in conjunction with it.

The firm's annual memorandum would be more useful if it also attempted to show the probable effect of statutory amendments, and if it extended its coverage to (1) the Canadian and provincial company laws, and (2) the company laws of the other nations in which its multinational corporate clients do business.

Memoranda of Law

"Our memorandum of law file is a mess," is a complaint voiced repeatedly in law offices on both coasts. Yet, there are a few firms and corporate legal departments that have had considerable success in collecting, pruning, analyzing and indexing their memoranda of law.

Two related problems remain to be overcome. The first involves duplicate efforts. Firm members or corporate counsel often assign the same or substantially similar problems to different lawyers at various times. Frequently no record of this work is kept, or one partner fails to inform his other partners of work in progress. The result: double or triple efforts, and unreasonably high costs to answer legal questions previously answered.

The second and corollary problem is that most legal work in an office is complete *before* a formal memorandum of law can be cast in final and literate form. By that time new problems must be solved. It is only human nature, and sound professional practice, for those new questions to take precedence over ancient history. But the results again are lost efforts and increased expenses.

Corporate Forms and Precedents

Many lawyers take justifiable pride in the quality of their draftsmanship. But few of them are able to locate examples of particular provisions in agreements or trust instruments that they have drafted in the past. One major firm has developed a special aptitude for analyzing, indexing and preserving its corporate forms and precedents. Its superiority stems from the intellectual gifts, the ingenuity and persistence, of a single employee. The system is deficient only to the extent that it has had to rely on the hurried, and sometimes reluctant, cooperation of a few hundred very busy lawyers.

Research with "Lexis"

Mead Data's "Lexis" libraries or data base now provides full text access by computer to federal and leading state statute and case law. In addition, it includes a full federal tax library that contains among other documents all items published in the "Cumulative Bulletin" and in the weekly "Internal Revenue Bulletin". Its SEC coverage is notable for its direct access to "No Action" letters. There is no counterpart indexing system to this broad pasture of SEC correspondence to match the "Lexis" service.

West Publishing Company offers a competing system that is limited to the cases reported in its National Reporter system.

Numerous law schools have installed "Lexis" equipment during the current school year, and approximately 100 law firms in New York City subscribe to "Lexis". Cooperative arrangements have still to be worked out to bring this service within the means of single practitioners and small firms.

Library Catalogs

On two successive days recently the general counsel of a large corporate legal department and the managing partner of a 150-man law firm complained of the inadequacies of their law library book catalogs. One said, "I know we have this antitrust work, but for the life of me I cannot find it in the catalog". The other reminded me that their former librarian, now retired, had carried most of this information in his head over a period of nearly fifty years. Since that librarian was gifted with both an inquisitive mind and a photographic memory, his was a formidable "catalog" indeed.

That firm is beginning to create an automated catalog by analyzing the contents of each current treatise in its collection. It expects to provide not merely one or two subject headings for each work, but a large number of "descriptors" depending on the complexity and usefulness of the work. The New York University "Annual Institute on Federal Taxation" is an example of a work that merits fuller subject analysis than can be expected from Library of Congress printed catalog cards.

Another office includes in its multiple library catalogs (1) a detailed index to its memoranda of law, and (2) a careful analysis of the contents of all prospectuses filed with the SEC. For example, a search under the topic, "Finders Fees", will disclose the details of all such payments in public offerings over a period of some twenty-five years.

Most firms are unwilling to spend the money that sophisticated cataloging costs. One New York law librarian with a strong background in business and finance has created outstanding catalogs for the two firms in which he has worked. But he remains virtually alone in this respect.

Computer Link

The time is ripe for lawyers to face and resolve the problems created by the accelerated complexity and growth of law practice. Not until recently has any law office made a serious effort to orchestrate, and automate, all its research work.

Lawyers who fail to do so are not going to lose their clients—not right away. But it is inevitable that clients will seek out lawyers who consistently answer their questions with wisdom, accuracy and dispatch.

"We moved our work from two old-line Philadelphia firms to a young, aggressive firm", counsel to one corporation told me recently. His reason: the older firms got careless. "Our work was being performed by second-team associates, inadequately, and at their convenience, not ours."

Law, lawyers and computers are now irrevocably linked. Those lawyers who were already choking on the "paper" their research efforts have created know this to be fact. Lawyers who were bright enough to create this situation are also bright enough to extricate themselves from it.

III

"You must hack through much deposit
Ere you know for sure what was it
Came to burial with such honor in the files
Only seven seasons back—beneath the files."

Rudyard Kipling

The profession of law is the second oldest and, until recently, it remained the most conservative of all professions. "Save everything, find little, tell your partners no more than they have to know and do each job over again from the beginning," has long been the lawyer's credo. Five years ago, my first *Law Journal* column (March 24, 1972) suggested that such a credo was outmoded. The very survival of lawyers depending on their ability to coordinate—not bury—their research efforts. Hire a research coordinator, it urged. To this writer's knowledge no firm did so—then.

Times Are Changing

But today all this is changing. Almost weekly, a new law firm or corporate legal department has begun to coordinate its research. Today, the question most frequently asked is how to coordinate, not why.

No lawyer who has ever lost a file can forget the Circumlocation Office (Dickens' *Little Dorrit*) where "all the business of the country went through" and none ever came out. If no one else in your office can locate the file or even remember that it existed, then your office is ripe for coordination.

In numerical terms, a ten-lawyer office is large enough. A fifty-man office will soon be outstripped by competitors if it fails to coordinate. In terms of variety of practice, corporate lawyers must consult with tax lawyers, both groups work with the environmentalists and the litigators. Their separate and combined research papers, together with their discussions, form the office investment bank of legal knowledge. Unless that knowledge can be "withdrawn" the instant it is called for, your bank is insolvent. You need a coordinator.

Importance of Quality

Just as important is the quality of that research. The American philosopher, Morris Raphael Cohen, used to remind his logic students of the weekly discussions between two ignorant and misinformed "thinkers". After exchanging all the misinformation they had acquired during the previous seven days, they would part more ignorant than when they had met—each looking forward to the next week's "exchange of ideas". If meetings in any office ever resemble these, that office is ready for a coordinator. Even if they do not, the *direction* that a research coordinator brings to preliminary discussions of new matters make his presence invaluable.

What Coordination Achieves

The effective research coordinator achieves three advantages for his firm or corporate legal department: (a) He helps clarify the issues in any legal problem; (b) He is best equipped to anticipate what facts will be needed and to marshal the kinds of information on which sound legal decisions are based. The reason: his experience cuts across all fields of law and many other branches of learning as well; and (c) He brings to his post the ability to organize, index and retrieve that information at will. Since he has no further responsibility in the solution of legal problems—other lawyers do that—he experiences few of the pressures under which negotiators and trial lawyers work.

The House of Rothschild grew powerful nearly 200 years ago in part because it employed fast sailboats and carrier pigeons to transmit information ahead of its competitors. Today's law research coordinator uses the computer and many other sophisticated tools—both mechanical and intellectual—to accomplish a similar purpose.

Who Should Become A Coordinator?

The first prerequisite for the research coordinator is a broad rather than a specialized legal education. A grounding in economics, statistics and accounting is essential. Knowledge of computer technology is useful. The successful coordinator must have the innate ability to analyze complex problems and to write effectively about them.

Second, he must have developed systematic research skills before he tries to coordinate anyone else's work; and

Third, he must have an understanding of—even a passion for—the basic principles and facts of the major branches of learning from aeronautics to zoology and anthropology through history to semantics.

This above all is lawyers' work. A law librarian or paralegal assistant can help implement the work of the law research coordinator. But legal training is indispensable if the coordinator is to advise and to participate at each stage in the solution of legal problems.

How a Coordinator is Recruited and Trained

The rapid growth in size of law offices and the complexity of problems lawyers handle have created new legal opportunities. Many of these are in the management of research in firms, corporate legal departments and government agencies. They will soon be recruiting with this new legal profession in mind.

The law schools educate potential research coordinators each year—consciously or not. These are the men and women who by temperament and ability prefer research to argument, management and organization to negotiation. Their contribution is just as essential to law office success: it is simply different. Their rewards should match their contribution. At the outset, they should be assigned for six months or a year to work successively in each major legal department in the office: for example, corporate, taxation, litigation and antitrust. After two or three years a decision can be made whether or not research coordination is for them.

There is a psychological constraint on entering this work which the law office can help overcome. Will the research lawyer be placed on the partnership track or be sidelined to a role as "permanent associate"? If the keenest law graduates are to enter this profession they will expect reassurance on this point. These generalists will participate in every major matter that the office handles. With experience, their advice on *how* to solve legal problems can only become more sophisticated and more valuable. They will serve as the human link between the lawyers currently practicing in the office and the total recorded and unrecorded office experience.